THE
DARK
SIDE
OF
KNOWLEDGE

EXPLORING THE OCCULT

There are more things in heaven and earth,
Horatio, than are dreamt of in your philosophy.
—SHAKESPEARE

 ADDISON-WESLEY PUBLISHING COMPANY
READING, MASSACHUSETTS
MENLO PARK, CALIFORNIA
LONDON • AMSTERDAM
DON MILLS, ONTARIO • SYDNEY

THE DARK SIDE OF KNOWLEDGE

EXPLORING THE OCCULT

ALBERT SHADOWITZ

PETER WALSH

ISBN 0-201-07331-5-H
ISBN 0-201-07332-3-P
ABCDEFGHIJ-MA-79876

To
Naomi, Sarah, and Rebecca
and to
Rosemarie

PREFACE

We have been asked why two working physicists should waste their time writing a book about the occult. Our answer is based on the traditions of science itself:

Within the mysteries of the universe there are truths which are knowable—Who knows where they are?

It takes patient, open-minded investigation of the mysteries in all fields, unlikely as they may seem, to uncover the really important truths.

Our book concerns itself with the knowledge that lies in the darkness, beyond the present edge of science; with the obscure and occult knowledge, veiled from general view, whose hidden nature lends mystery and enchantment to its study. We term this "The Dark Side of Knowledge."

While much that is accepted in the popular occult is not trustworthy, there is a fine thread of truth woven into its lore. Where this thread comes to general view and is verified, lore passes into science. Alchemy laid the basis for chemistry, astrology became astronomy. It appears now that a science of general extrasensory perception phenomena is slowly evolving from the mysteries of the psychic. Our purpose here is to outline portions of the unknown, to investigate the factual basis of its lore, and to determine, as best we can, the truth it holds.

Though we suspect that popular lore, as a whole, does not contain a large fraction of truth, we also suspect that any widespread, long-lived belief about the world must somehow reflect nature. Belief, like any other human faculty, evolves continuously under the impact of our confrontation with nature. A long-surviving popular lore, then, probably contains some truth. For a scientist, the fascination of the dark side of knowledge is this: the truth it may contain must lie beyond, perhaps well beyond, the frontier of scientific knowledge. Science has not yet been able to recognize this truth and transform it into knowledge. But this small content of truth in the lore can point the way for science to evolve into completely new directions.

This book seeks an understanding of the seemingly irrational through rational means. The changing of the unknown, even the absurd, into the obvious constantly illuminates the fabric of human history. Our work is directed along that path. We have no desire to indoctrinate. We wish only to examine, to scrutinize, while exploring the dim paths that take us beyond the edge of certain knowledge.

This book grew out of a course we introduced in the physics department at Fairleigh Dickinson University. We hoped that the rigorous discipline of physics would help us analyze and weigh the occult in a reasonably objective way for our students. The years of teaching these students has infected us with their enthusiasm, and we now hope to share some of that enthusiasm with the reader.

We owe a great debt to Dr. George E. Courville who, as the acting Dean of the College of Science and Engineering at FDU, made our course in Nature and the Occult possible. And we are appreciative, indeed, for the painstaking contribution made by Phyllis Rind in typing many drafts of this material. We thank the staff of Addison-Wesley for their cooperation, hard work, and confidence in us and in the book. Finally, we are grateful to the many students in this course, for they treated us neither as prophets of a New Truth nor as purveyors of pseudoscience; simply as investigators examining the texture of a strange, intriguing material.

Nutley, New Jersey   A. S.
Stirling, New Jersey   P. W.
September 1976

CONTENTS

THE INTERNAL WORLD

PART ONE

CHAPTER ONE THREE TALL TALES

- *The Witch Doctor's Spell*
- *D. D. Home* ■ *The Flying Monk*
- *A Preview*

THE WITCH DOCTOR'S SPELL

Dr. Colin Turnbull, a well-known and respected English anthropologist, recently worked in the Ituri Forest of Africa, where he lived with a small, friendly pygmy tribe. A nearby tribe, the reserved Ndaka, expected Turnbull to take up the work of a dedicated missionary, Patrick Putnam, who had worked among them until his recent death. But Turnbull could not do Putnam's work; he was completely unfamiliar with missionary work; it just was not his calling. The Ndaka, who considered Turnbull a sort of son of the deceased Putnam, became very angry when Turnbull refused, and they then resorted to witchcraft. The following is Turnbull's account of his experiences.

The witchcraft business started off simply enough and at first I was secretly amused. Not for long. They do things to upset you. Unexpected things. If you walk through the village and greet someone by name, he will just walk past as though you didn't exist. A few of these encounters and I said to myself, "The hell with you, friends. So I won't talk either." So I walked by and didn't say a thing; and they would act surprised and hurt and ask me what was the matter, what had they done to alienate me.

No matter what I did, it was wrong. If I approached a group, they would stop talking except for a word or two they wanted me to hear. The words usually indicated that Sabani, the local ritual doctor, had made witchcraft against me and that my fate was sealed.

Then I began to feel sick. Food wouldn't stay down, and I began to vomit. Here I was, an Oxford graduate, sitting in the midst of a little African village succumbing to psychological warfare. There might have been humor in it, but I couldn't see it. Sometimes, the witch doctor helps matters with poison. I was well aware of this and I asked my friends, the pygmies, whom I could trust to bring me my food.

But the food wouldn't stay down. I was becoming very weak—and I recognized the danger. I couldn't leave my house because I could scarcely move. Finally, one of the pygmies said the only way I could save myself was to make magic back. Things were serious and I was so desperate that I didn't even think of the absurdity of a veteran anthropologist making magic against a native witch doctor.

I felt foolish but I made a fire and I put some of my personal belongings into it—which is considered very powerful medicine. To make sure that the entire village knew what was going on, I had one of the local boys get me the wood and stand by while I made some Turnbull magic. In this way the village and the elders and Sabani would hear of what was going on.

For whatever reason—and I don't even pretend to know the answer—the next day I was feeling a little better. Within three days I was back to normal.

A year later, when I had gotten to know Sabani better and we were on fairly good terms, I asked him if he had made magic against me. He admitted he had. I asked him why I had recovered and he told me that he heard I was making magic back and that since he didn't know how powerful mine was the villagers agreed to call off the curse.*

How does a rational person assess such a story? To one reared in the Western traditions of science and technology the psychological overtones are obvious: the witch doctor is a specialist in human psychology and uses it here. His magic is not hidden. And Turnbull played the witch doctor's game. Yet, Turnbull's words hardly portray a psychological basis for the effect of the witchcraft. He certainly didn't believe in the witchcraft at first; nor, perhaps, does he even now. The fascinating thing is that the sickness stopped when the witch doctor stopped making magic, *not* when Turnbull actually learned about it a year later. Unknown to Turnbull, his calculating reaction had caused the witch doctor to remove his

---

* From *New York Sunday News*, Pictorial Section, 28 May 1972, p. 21. Copyright 1972 New York News Inc. Reprinted by permission.

magic. But was the method by which the illness started, and stopped, a rational phenomenon? Or was it really magic?

We are left with a bit of a puzzle. Perhaps Turnbull was exaggerating; his story, however, seems quite honest and factual. Maybe the explanation lies in the realm of the psychological—a fantasy world, even hysteria. Unfortunately, terms like *psychological* and *hysterical* can rarely be tested scientifically in the context of such stories. Although an explanation such as *psychological in origin* sounds scientific, it may have as little scientific basis as, for instance, a supernatural explanation. There is a lack of sufficient information by which to judge the story. So, usually, we just forget about such a story. It is an oddball; but we feel sure if we knew all the facts the explanation would be ordinary.

D. D. HOME

Let us consider a case that achieved some notoriety a century or so ago. Daniel Dunglas Home was born in Currie, Scotland in 1833. His mother was said to be a seer who could foretell the deaths of friends and relatives. Home was sickly throughout his life; he contracted tuberculosis as a child and never fully overcame the disease. Visions came to him early in life. Upon the death of his mother he moved to America to live with an aunt and, once there, many unsettling occurrences took place. Tables moved, noises and raps were sounded, furniture flew about. Home now found himself the possessor of many magic-like powers.

Spiritualism was rampant at this time, and people were fascinated by unnatural phenomena. But Home required no dark or dimly lit rooms to perform. Reports have him moving tables, raising them, floating up himself, producing voices, reading people's thoughts—all in broad daylight, in impromptu display, often before large numbers of people. He knew no secret to his powers: he had only to get in the right mood and relax. He said he communicated with spirits; and, common to the times, voices attended his demonstrations.

• In Springfield, Massachusetts, a William Bryant (perhaps the famous poet), and David Wells (a scientist from nearby Cambridge), attested to Home's ability. While being held by his arms and legs, Home caused a table to rise several inches in the air.

• In Italy at a gathering for Home, tables again moved, the great chandeliers rocked, and warm spirit hands shook hands with guests.

• Nathaniel Hawthorne wrote, "They are absolutely proved to be sober facts."

• Lord Adare spent several months observing Home closely and in 1870 privately published a factual account of his findings: fireballs passed through solid objects, spirits appeared; Home floated out a third-floor window and into another window in a separate room and then back; Home played with fire, carrying a burning coal without injury, which when set down on paper, instantly ignited the paper; as always, furniture moved about.

• In 1871 the scientist William Crookes, young and not yet world renowned, investigated Home thoroughly and published a paper attesting to Home's ability to alter his own weight at will, to cause objects to move, and to handle fire. This paper earned him the scorn of the scientific community. Twenty-two years later, Crookes, now a famous physicist but still courageous in withstanding the opinions of his colleagues, recalled factually:

> On one occasion he called me to him when he went to the fire and told me to watch carefully. He actually put his hand in the grate and handled the red-hot coals in a manner which would have been impossible for me to have initiated without being severely burnt. I once saw him go to bright wood-fire, and, taking a large piece of red-hot charcoal, put it in the hollow of one hand, and covering it with the other hand, blow into the extempore furnace till the coal was white hot and the flames licked around his fingers. No sign of burning could be seen then or afterwards on his hands . . . .
>
> The best case of Home's levitation I witnessed was in my own house; on one occasion he went to a clear part of the room, and after standing quietly for a minute, told us he was rising. I saw him slowly rise up with a gliding movement and remain about six inches off the ground for several seconds, when he slowly descended; on another occasion I was invited to come to him, when he rose 18 inches off the ground, and I passed my hands under his feet, round him, and over his head when he was in the air . . . .
>
> During the whole of my knowledge of D. D. Home, extending over several years, I never once saw the slightest occurrence that would make me suspicious that he was attempting to play tricks.[1]

The displays of magical feats by Home were, indeed, so common that the observers became sated. Hawthorne stated, "I cannot force my mind to take any interest in them." Adare eventually lost interest too, not seeing where the phenomena could lead.

As with any outstanding success, detraction was inevitable. Dickens attended no seances, but called Home a scoundrel. Robert Browning referred to Home as "that dungball"; though his wife, Elizabeth Barrett Browning, was quite convinced by Home. Harry Houdini, the famous escape artist, magician, and foe of magical frauds, stated: "His active career, his various escapades, all indicate that he lived the life of a hypocrite of the deepest dye."[2] No one, however, has actually produced any evidence, whatever, of fraud on Home's part although his closely scrutinized and active career stretched over 20 years. Home retired from public life in 1872. His powers apparently remained with him until his death in 1886. Houdini was then only 12 years of age.

How do we explain the magic powers of a man like D. D. Home? Was he the classic example of a successful charlatan? Then the famous scientist, Crookes, was a fool. Or were there perhaps some unusual magical powers he possessed. Then the famous magician, Houdini, was a fool. Well, it was a long time ago, over a century now—Who knows?

THE FLYING MONK

As another case, even further back in time, let us consider the Flying Monk, Father Joseph of Copertino, born Guiseppe Desa in 1603 in Apulia, Italy. He was a strange, sickly lad, poor in his studies but aflame with a desire to attain holiness. He led an ascetic life from an early age, punishing his body with starvation and flagellation, thereby further undermining his health. Rejected by the Capuchin Order, he became a Franciscan priest at the age of 22. Then began an amazing career of miraculous behavior which culminated in his canonization as a saint within the Catholic Church.

Sainthood has changed its significance throughout the history of the Church. Technically, a saint is someone believed to be in heaven, either because of martyrdom or as a reward for having led an outstanding and holy life. In the early Church there existed no formal canonization procedures for determining sainthood—popular belief and tradition were sufficient. In 933 A.D. Pope John formally canonized the first saint, and an official procedure for canonization gradually evolved, culminating in the legislation of Pope Urban VIII in 1634 and of Pope Benedict XIV somewhat later. This legislation provided that a candidate's holiness, and any writings and miracles cited as evidence of holiness, were to be investigated and brought before an ecclesiastic tribunal for judgment. A "Devil's Advocate" would handle the case against sainthood, guarding against evidence that was not genuine. Thus the judicial process of canonization was a means of examining the evidence of behavior that was supposed to be miraculous and was assumed to be evidence of holiness.

Now then, according to the canonization reports, Fr. Joseph *flew*. Isaac Newton to the contrary, Fr. Joseph was said to be able to defy the universal law of gravitation. His ascetic practices brought on a trance state apparently akin to the Hindu state of meditation, *samadhi*. When in this state, it was reported, Fr. Joseph floated in the air—sometimes a few inches, sometimes several feet, sometimes as high as a church. And he might sail 30 to 40 feet away. He seemed to have some control over the flights, and it was said he could lift heavy objects. One story had him raising a cross that ten men could not handle. His flights were witnessed by common people, by dukes, by kings, by philosophers, and even by one pope. He converted the Duke of Brunswick to Christianity by his flights. Leibnitz, the philosopher and coinventor with Newton of the integral calculus, witnessed one such flight. On the Flying Monk's deathbed his attending physician noticed that Fr. Joseph was floating six inches in the air.

Father Joseph died at the age of 60. Hundreds of depositions poured in to the canonization tribunal, all attesting to his miraculous life. He was proclaimed a saint in 1667, only four years after his death.

What are we to say of the story of the Flying Monk? Humbug? Leibnitz was an idiot? Perhaps. It was over 300 years ago. There are no witnesses left, no photographs or other evidence—just tales which one may either believe or disbelieve, depending on one's bias.

A PREVIEW

Stories like these abound in all the places on Earth and at all times. In our "scientific age of reason and enlightenment," being unable to find a plausible explanation, we tend to let these isolated, unexplainable episodes fall to the bottom of our minds—we forget them. Much as the dust from the skies settles continually through the seas to form a rich layer of sediment on the ocean floor, there have now been formed many thick layers of incredible stories underlying much of our folklore, our literature, our thinking. There they lie, hidden from view—occult.

In these chapters we are going to examine some of this rich, dark occult sediment on the floor of the unknown. Does it hold anything of value? Or is it all just fool's gold? Our own approach is an open but cautious one. We are motivated chiefly by curiosity, the *sine qua non* for scientists. We have no particular wish to press the correctness of the various points of view we have developed as a result of our study. Readers may form their own conclusions.

CHAPTER TWO
THE MAGIC WITHIN

Beyond the Natural ▪ *Acupuncture*

▪ *Photographing the Aura?* ▪ *The Seat of Magic*

▪ *The Dutch Fakir* ▪ *Biofeedback*

▪ *One Brain, Two Minds?*

▪ *Automatic Writing* ▪ *Nervous Plants*

▪ *Fact or Fiction?*

BEYOND THE NATURAL

In treating the occult—knowledge that is hidden from us—the topics divide naturally into two broad categories. Some phenomena concern the internal workings of the human mind, while others are concerned with various external influences. In keeping with this natural, twofold classification, in the first half of our book we will deal with occult phenomena within the individual, and in the second half with phenomena external to us and the world we inhabit. This chapter deals with a number of phenomena which undoubtedly belong in the first category. It explores verified mysteries, arising within humans, which reveal the magic of our natural being. These vaguely glimpsed workings suggest paradoxical and extraordinary feats. We will later discuss in greater detail several of these mysteries; here we briefly visit a number of them, seeking the hidden magic within humanity.

Before we begin the pleasant task of running our hands through the rich sediment of some magical facts, it seems worthwhile spending a few moments on Fig. 2–1. Here we have taken the category of all unknown phenomena, within and outside of the human and divided it into three classes: *natural, paranatural,* and *supernatural.* All unknown phenomena belong in one of these classes, and the diagram provides an indication of their distribution.

Natural explanations of occult happenings (or *reported* happenings) include, on the one hand, hidden physical causes, poor observation, and just plain mistakes, as well as, on the other hand, hysteria, exaggeration, fraud, and deception. Happenings of this type—the ghost at a faked seance, a weather balloon mistaken for a UFO, the loser at gambling forgetting all those times that lucky 7 did him in—undoubtedly comprise the main body of occult reports.

Our book is not particularly concerned with occult manifestations of this type, and we have not included many examples. The reader must keep in mind, however, the fact that the *overwhelming* percentage of occult reports will end up in this category.

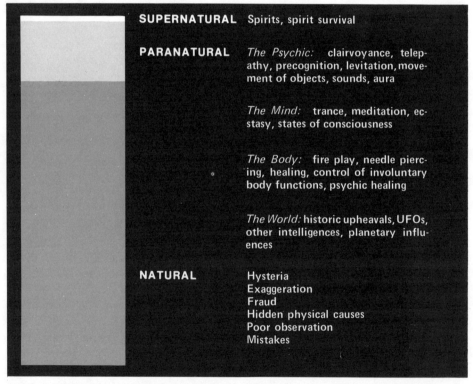

Fig. 2–1. Unknown phenomena. This figure, which divides these events into three classes, suggests that *natural* causes constitute the major portion, by far, of our occult knowledge. This book, however, is chiefly concerned with the fascinating remainder, the *paranatural* and, to some extent, with the extremely small and hypothetical portion, the *supernatural.*

In the derivation of the word "paranatural," the root "para" commonly means "besides," "other than." So a paranatural phenomenon is some kind of event other than a natural, normal one. For some paranatural phenomena there is no natural explanation within the presently known laws of nature, yet there is more than adequate scientific evidence to assure the reality of the phenomena. Extrasensory perception and psychokinesis are examples: they promise a more fundamental understanding of nature, eventually, than we presently have. For other paranatural phenomena there seemingly does exist an explanation within the known laws of nature, but it has so far eluded us. Acupuncture and the existence of trance states or voluntary control of normally involuntary bodily functions are examples. Such phenomena are not outside our present understanding of the laws of nature, but are simply somewhat outside our present capability of applying these laws. These phenomena would be close to the boundary between natural and paranatural phenomena; but this boundary is a fuzzy one. The paranatural phenomena are the basic material of this book.

The term "supernatural" is reserved here for those phenomena which may conceivably be genuine but which are too "far out." These phenomena lie so far beyond the bounds of our present knowledge and experimental capabilities that a convincing explanation for them still eludes us.

Theodore Roszak, a widely read critic of established science, has strongly challenged the tendency of science to "reduce all things to terms that objective consciousness might master." According to him, science assumes the character of a "campaign against the legitimate mysteries of man and nature." Roszak seeks to subordinate science to society and "to ground it in a sensibility drawing on the occult, mysticism, the Romantic movement."[1] These views apparently express a feeling among many Western people against the dogmatic disregard of personal experience taken by science in the name of objectivity.

Our aim in this book is neither to attack nor to overemphasize science. Our purpose is simply this: by employing a rational approach toward topics which are generally regarded as irrational, trusting to enhance our knowledge of man and the universe, to confront the mysteries that walk silently with us as we explore the paths of the universe.

We will first look into the obscure and hidden universe *within* us. What we seek are those few nuggets of golden truth hidden in the vast mass of debris and sediment that has accumulated for millenia at the bottom of the ocean of our beliefs about our place in the universe.

ACUPUNCTURE

A young woman lies, clad in white, on a table in a Chinese hospital. Technicians busily worry needles that protrude inches into the air, sticking into her arms, face, and shoulders. Without anesthesia, the young woman carries on a smooth conversation, in a soft voice, with the attendants as well as the doctor. The doctor is removing a thyroid cyst from her neck. Her heart rate, blood pressure, and respiration remain rock steady throughout the entire operation.

The Western world has shown a growing interest in such now commonplace examples of the ancient Chinese art of acupuncture, used both for therapy and for anesthesia. Claims have been made that it can cure ailments ranging from acne, through hernia and psoriasis, to ulcers; but we are just beginning to obtain sufficient evidence to test these assertions scientifically. When it comes to anesthesia, however, there is ample evidence that appendectomies, tonsillectomies, gastrectomies, or even open-heart surgery may be painlessly performed on patients who remain fully conscious. In fact, the patients can talk, drink chicken soup, or listen to the doctors—all this without any of the usual aftereffects of ordinary anesthetics. No lowering of the blood pressure or pulse rate, no postoperative nausea or vomiting, no respiratory difficulties or lung congestion. Even though anesthetics are not used, however, acupuncture patients are often sedated before an operation.

Acupuncture has been practised in China for nearly 5,000 years and perhaps longer. In 2600 B.C., Huang Ti, the Emperor, instructed his court physician to write a text on acupuncture. The resulting "Yellow Emperor's Classic of Internal Medicine" is the earliest summary of the practice. But, although acupuncture has been practised for so long, there is little real understanding of how this ancient art works. The Chinese explanation of acupuncture rests on the ancient Tao philosophy that the human being, like the rest of the universe, is a mixture of two opposites—yin and yang. These encompass bad and good, earth and heaven, negative and positive, death and life, valley and mountain, grief and joy, body and spirit, feminine and masculine, the mental and the physical. All is well when the two components are present in the proper proportions. But when the proportions of the two are unbalanced a person is ill. The needles of acupuncture probe certain sharply defined spots in the human body. Here, with skill, the proper balance of yin and yang may be restored.

According to the Taoist philosophy there is a flow of vital energy, *Ch'i*, along various lines in the human body. These lines, called meridians, have been carefully mapped. Their general direction is along the length of the body and its limbs; a map of the meridians would not be too dissimilar from a map of the blood vessels. The meridians, however, do *not* coincide with the blood vessels, or the nerve fibers, or with any other organic bodies we presently know. They have a seemingly intangible existence. At any one of various points on these meridians—many hundreds of points which have been precisely located—the insertion of a needle can greatly affect the circulation of this presumed vital energy. By physical measurements, these acupuncture points on the meridians seem to be points of lowered skin resistance and higher electrical potentials and they are points which seem to avoid the arterial blood system.

There are 14 major meridians; 12 main meridians are each associated with a particular vital organ in the human body, while one runs along the front of the body and another goes along the back. An illness of one of the organs of the body is connected with a malfunctioning of the meridian associated with that organ. The proper spot for an acupuncturist to insert a needle in order to correct, say, a specific ulcer condition, is liver 1, *ta-tun*, on the big toe of the left foot. Pericardium 4, *hsi-men*, midway up the arm, controls nosebleed; *ho-ku*, liver 4, between thumb and forefinger, controls toothache.

How do students of acupuncture learn which organ is malfunctioning? This is a subtle art which utilizes the beats in the two radial pulses, one at each of the patient's wrists. These pulse rates vary in response to minute pressures which are applied to the wrists with the fingers. By detecting small, subjective differences in the responses to this pressure the acupuncturist can locate the difficulty—first distinguishing between a left or right meridian, then between an upper or lower meridian, and finally tracking the malfunction down to one of the meridians in a given quadrant. Knowing the meridian, the next step is to determine the various spots along it in which to insert the needles. This must be done very precisely—to within about 1/16 of an inch. There are some 500 to 800 such points, although only about 100 are now in regular use.

Presently, the needles are metal, sharp pointed, and thin, varying in length from half of an inch to a foot. While they are sometimes inserted to a depth of only 1/32 of an inch below the surface of the skin, there are cases where as much as an inch or two of the needle may be forced in—without pain. Sometimes the needles are rotated continually after insertion, and sometimes an electrical potential of six or eight volts may be applied to the metal needles, resulting in currents of the order of several milliamperes. Figure 2–2 shows acupuncture needles in the face of a young girl. She gives no indication of pain.

The beginning of a scientific theory to account for the action of acupuncture is now under way. According to the proposals of Melzack and Wall, the needles stimulate large A-beta fibers in the peripheral nerves. These fibers produce impulses which jam the response of the spinal cord, the *substantia gelatinosa*. This jamming, in effect, closes a nerve signal gate in the spinal cord; pain signals, which are transmitted over the small C fibers, are thus blocked by the jam and do not reach the brain. Recently Wall, one of the two physiologists mentioned above, emphasized that Chinese hospital practice tends both to relieve anxiety and to instill confidence in the patients. Wall believes that these factors, combined with the distracting local (but not painful) sensation of the needles, may explain the main anesthetic effects.[2] Some doctors have claimed that the effect is a form of hypnosis, but others explain it as a placebo effect.

The experiences of a number of Western practitioners attest to its effectiveness, as well as to its limitations. Acupuncture works on animals, but not on children under about ten; the children scare too easily. Dr. Felix Mann, whose work is now a standard reference in the field, has practised acupuncture extensively in England. He finds it valuable for reversible diseases, but of no value for irreversible ones such as broken bones and cancer. A Russian, Dr. Victor Adamenko, has found that the skin resistance at the acupuncture points is lower than that at normal skin regions—as little as a tenth or even less. On the basis

Fig. 2–2. Acupuncture. A vivid illustration of one application of this ancient art. This young girl is being treated at the Tsung I. I. Yen Hospital in Peking. Amazingly, the needles produce only a very slight sensation. (© Paolo Koch, 1974, Photo Researchers, Inc.)

of this fact he devised an instrument, the tobioscope, which is essentially an ohmmeter. This measures the skin resistance at specific locations in order to detect the acupuncture points accurately.

Since acupuncture does not provide muscle relaxation, additional anesthesia may be required in abdominal surgery in order to relax the muscles of patients with well-muscled abdomens. Curious sensations are felt by patients in their deep viscera during such operations when acupuncture is the anesthetic. As with any system of pain relief, acupuncture may not cure the source of the pain. Its use, for example, in cancer of the chest can relieve the suffering but does not cure the cancer.

Acupuncture can also be misused. Often the correct acupuncture points are very close to each other. The practitioner must be careful to needle the precisely correct point. Otherwise, the patient's problems may only be compounded.

Probably the one cause which did more than any other to revive interest in the United States in the efficacy of acupuncture as an anesthetic was the newspaper story written by James Reston on the front page of the *New York Times*. Reston, now Vice-President of the *Times* and for many years its star Washington reporter, was one of the first Americans permitted to visit China. While there he suffered an attack of acute appendicitis and had an operation. The usual anesthetics were given, but Reston subsequently encountered considerable discomfort in his stomach. While still in the People's Anti-Imperialist Hospital he was treated by acupuncture with three needles, one inserted into his right elbow and the other two below his knees. The pain disappeared after an hour or so, and his story of the details became worldwide news. Later visits by American physicians who witnessed actual acupuncture operations while touring China produced even more impressive reports. A prominent ear surgeon, Dr. Samuel Rosen, spoke after his visit to a Chinese hospital—"I have seen the past, and it works."

PHOTOGRAPHING THE AURA?

There are many systems in the body—the skeleton, the nervous system, the blood vessels, and the muscles. Is this physical body, this collection of objects, all there is? Clairvoyants have long claimed the ability to see a second body, a human double, that interpenetrates the physical body we have been discussing. A number of names have been given this phantom body; the etheric body, the astral body, the subtle body, are a few. This phantom body, extending beyond the physical body in beautiful colors—blue, yellow, red—is called the aura.

Can the aura be pinned down scientifically? Can it be photographed? In the early 1900s Dr. Walter Kilner, of St. Thomas' Hospital in London, declared that he could see the aura by looking through glasses stained with dicyanine dye. In his book he claimed that the aura extends six to eight inches from a person.[3] But, much more recently, a fascinating technique has been reported by many, capable of photographing an aura about living things. This technique has been highly developed in the Soviet Union over the past three decades and is named, after its main developer, Kirlian photography.

Semyon Davidovich Kirlian was an electrical technician in the Soviet Union. In 1939 he became intrigued with the photographic patterns produced when living objects were placed in a high-frequency field. The first living object he tried was his own hand, directly connected to a high-frequency electrode. He received an electrical burn for his efforts. But he also obtained a photograph that so captured his imagination that he carried on three more decades of research, improving his techniques continually.

What Kirlian found—actually, rediscovered—was that a beautiful, colored pattern formed around any object placed in the high-frequency electrical field. With living objects, fingers and plant leaves are good subjects. Such patterns are particularly complex and impressive.

The basic phenomenon in Kirlian photography is not really new. The great Yugoslav-American experimenter, Nikola Tesla (1856–1943), had taken photographs of giant electrical sparks which leapt from various parts of his body when he was connected to one of his inventions, the Tesla coil. This is an inexpensive laboratory device that delivers a high-frequency, high-voltage electrical field at a very low current to any object in its immediate vicinity.

The "electrography" started by Tesla was investigated later by a Czech, Navratil; by an American, Nipher; and, in 1939, by two other Czech scientists, Prat and Schlemmer. This was the same year that Semyon Kirlian began his exploration, apparently unaware of the previous work. With his wife, Valentina, he pushed the technique into many unexplored areas, including its use under a microscope and in the production of Kirlian pictures of moving objects.

The typical Kirlian apparatus consists of a pulsed high-frequency source operating at some frequency between 75 kilohertz and several megahertz. An object on a photographic plate is set between two metal plates covered with insulators. The plates act as electrodes when connected to an electrical source. Human contact with any high-frequency source can be dangerous, and the insulators act as protective devices.

The pattern that is seen is often referred to as a radiation, since it appears to come from the object being tested; but the pattern and its vivid colors are actually due to a very common physical effect, the breakdown of the air surrounding any object in a high-voltage electrical field. Nonliving objects, such as coins, will produce such breakdown patterns quite as efficiently as living objects do. Indeed, patterns will also be produced when there is nothing but air between the plates. The pattern is just the outline of numerous miniature lightning strokes.

Although the pattern appears to radiate from the living object it actually comes from the electrical field which is applied by the metal plates, a field which surrounds and penetrates the object. We know that any living object is a veritable complex of electrical circuitry, embedded in the cells of the living tissues. These cells distort the applied electrical field. The characteristic, startling aura produced by the miniature lightning pattern is, really, to be expected of any physical body being photographed in a Kirlian apparatus.

Because the condition of the body tissues affects their electrical properties, and therefore their Kirlian patterns, Kirlian photography offers promise as a medical diagnostic tool. An infected leaf will produce a different pattern than will a healthy leaf, even though there is no visible difference between them. Kirlian noted that his own finger pattern became noticeably fuzzy just before the onset of certain vascular attacks from which he suffered. Emotions, fatigue, illness, a drink of vodka, even thoughts, have been reported to affect the Kirlian patterns.

We have already noted that the acupuncture points on a person's body are regions of low electrical resistance. These points on the body may be expected to alter the field in a Kirlian apparatus, so the Kirlian pattern might be employed to pick out the acupuncture points on the body. Indeed, Dr. Mikhail Kuzmich Gaikin, a surgeon in Leningrad, found that the brilliant flares in certain Kirlian photographs coincided exactly with the acupuncture points mapped out by the Chinese in the distant past.

Whether the actual Kirlian photographs can be interpreted on a wholly physical basis is unknown at present. Some initial work suggested that more than the physical body was involved. The first reports from Russia stated that when a Kirlian photograph was taken of a leaf with a section cut out, the pattern of the whole leaf still resulted, as if the phantom astral body of the leaf were still whole. There have been few replications of the "phantom-leaf effect" among the numerous attempts in this country to duplicate it, and the point is still an open one.

At present the most reasonable premise is that the Kirlian patterns are purely physical. Tests should certainly continue, to ascertain whether there are any nonphysical contributions to the patterns produced in Kirlian photography.

THE SEAT OF MAGIC

The entire organization of the individual nerve cells, considered as a single unit, is called the nervous system. In humans this consists of a vast network of nerve fibers in all parts of the body. This network feeds a central nerve cord, running through the hollow cartilage and bone of the spine, which acts as a flexible coat of armor to provide mechanical protection. The spinal cord, in turn, feeds the brain, which is also encased in a protective coating—the skull. The brain, together with the spinal cord, is called the central nervous system. It is all very similar to the way we humans have designed our telephone systems, with lines to the individual subscribers coming from the main trunk line, emanating from the central exchange, with the latter guiding the routing of messages.

The central nervous system controls two main actions. Conscious, voluntary actions are produced in the sensory-somatic system. Here things are sensed consciously, and voluntary action results: a man stoops to pick up his baby son. On the other hand, the autonomic nervous system controls unconscious, involuntary actions: the man's heart rate accelerates as he picks up his giggling child. The autonomic nervous system is split into two units: the *sympathetic nervous system* and the *parasympathetic nervous system*.

The sympathetic nervous system prepares the body for action. For example, it dilates the pupils, accelerates the heartbeat, and expands the bronchi in the lungs. On the other hand, the parasympathetic nervous system restores the body to a more restful and normal state by constricting the pupils, slowing the heartbeat, and contracting the bronchi.

Although the involuntary part of the central nervous system is generally outside a person's conscious control, manipulation of this involuntary nervous system seems to be at the very core of many psychic practices.

The trance state induced by Voodoo rituals or ecstatic *cabala* practices stimulates the sympathetic nervous system. The meditative state produced by transcendental meditation, *samadhi,* or yoga acts upon the parasympathetic nervous system. By practices which assist both the imagination and the will, control of these systems produces distinct *physical* changes. These place the magus, the shaman, or the witch doctor into the altered states of consciousness we commonly associate with psychic phenomena. Spirit communication is often claimed when, in such a state, the medium's hand writes, involuntarily, a strange message, or when the mouth speaks in a strange voice. Distinct physiological effects encountered in these states have, indeed, been measured.

The magic-like feats of firewalking, sleeping on nails, or bloodless skewering of the flesh also apparently involve a control of involuntary actions. Astonishing feats of control of the normally involuntary functions have been demonstrated in the laboratory. Control of skin temperature, blood flow, heart rate, complete muscle relaxation—all have been demonstrated in research laboratories. Such demonstrations tend to verify, to some extent, tales told from the ageless lore of witchcraft and magic.

In a broad sense, then, we see that at the control of the autonomic nervous system lies the very seat of personal magic. One extraordinary individual who shows this magic-like control was born in the Netherlands.

THE DUTCH FAKIR

As a young boy, Jack Schwarz had an avid interest in occult abilities. Born in 1924, at the age of 9 he was already practicing hypnotism, and he even showed modest powers as a healer. Later he read Reich and Steiner, studied the Rosicrucians, and learned of theosophy, meditation, and the Hindu fakirs. A natural mystic, he devised his own system of meditation, putting his learning into self-practice. At 16 an odd incident triggered a new lifelong career.

The lad worked in the town of Dordrecht, in a clothing store. Clothiers, who always need pins, find that a convenient place to store them is in the lapel, and Jack followed this tradition. One day a friend in the store jokingly slapped him across the chest. Jack immediately tried to shut out all pain, mentally—and he succeeded. When he pulled out the pins, he noticed the little holes left by them—but he also noticed that there was practically no blood. No pain. His curiosity with his feat led him, hurriedly, to test himself on a bed of nails, emulating the Indian fakirs he had learned about.

A bed of nails is a terrible looking test of a fakir's powers. But it can look more frightening than it actually is. If the nails are not too sharp, and if they are spaced close together—say three inches—practiced fakirs can straddle the bed without having the nails significantly penetrate their tissues. Relaxation is essential, so that the tissues yield to the nails, spreading the body weight over the widest possible area of the nail point. And a skin purposely toughened helps immensely against penetration. There may still be considerable pain, however, which it is necessary for fakirs to block from their minds.

Jack Schwarz enlisted a carpenter to build him a bed of nails and meanwhile posted notices about the town of his upcoming pain-defying feat. The bed had very sharp nails spaced some seven to eight inches apart, to really test his fragile skin. In full view of the townsfolk, the 16-year-old boy laid himself down upon the mattress of nails, thereby inaugurating his career.

This feat did not leave him without wounds, for the nails penetrated his flesh to a depth of half an inch. But, almost miraculously, there was little bleeding and no infection, and within 15 minutes the wounds were almost invisible, with no permanent scarring.

Jack's talents have been tested extensively in this country. He moved to the United States in 1957, lecturing and demonstrating. Recently he displayed his abilities at a number of research laboratories, including the Menninger Foundation, the Veterans' Administration Hospital in Topeka, Washington University in St. Louis, and a hospital in Vancouver, B.C. "One of the main reasons I'm subjecting myself to study at places like the Menninger Foundation," he stated, "is to try to dispel some of the occult, mystic nonsense people become hung up on. There are so many fantastic things that are real."[4]

Figure 2–3 shows Jack Schwarz at the Menninger Foundation, thrusting a dirty knitting needle through his left bicep muscle while he is hooked up to the laboratory's recorders. Although he bleeds, just as anyone will, he can control the

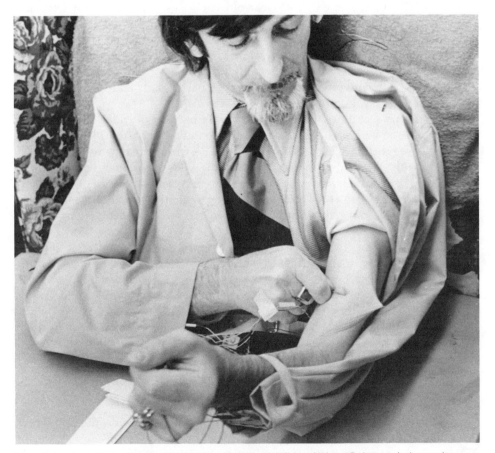

Fig. 2–3. Jack Schwarz. In tests at the Menninger Foundation, Schwarz is here shown mentally controlling his bleeding as he pierces the biceps of his left arm with a long piece of steel. (Photography by Don Richards, Menninger Foundation, Topeka, Kansas.)

bleeding mentally. After the needle is withdrawn there is no black or blue mark and no permanent scar is left. No infection occurred in the two-week period during which he was observed after the test itself.

The apparatus recorded heart rate, brain-wave voltage, brain-wave frequency, skin resistance, and skin temperature. Nothing abnormal showed up in the recordings. The main indication of his mental preparation was a gradual slowing of his brain pattern, until the pattern consisted of, roughly, 80 percent alpha waves. These waves are associated with deep relaxation.

Jack's feats have been matched in many ways. At the Menninger Foundation, the Indian mystic, Swami Rama, displayed amazing control over his body temperature, brain-wave pattern, and heart rate. He could change the temperature of two nearby points on the palm of his hand by nine degrees; and he could, almost completely, stop his heart function at will. Again, on April 26, 1956, Shri S. R. Khrishna Iyengar, a 48-year-old yogi, was buried alive for over nine hours without harm while his heartbeat, respiration, and other life signs were monitored by professionals of the World Health Organization. Finally, as yet another example, at the annual festival of *Thaipusam* in Singapore, hundreds of worshippers test their faith by hastening, in loping strides, across a fiery, hot bed of coals. A Hindu physician examines the participants and, as in years past, once again finds few injuries.

Jack Schwarz's abilities extend beyond sleeping on nails. Like the fakirs and D. D. Home, he seems to handle fire with impunity. He claims, like many other mystics, to see the auras surrounding people. These consist of many colors, which fluctuate with the body rhythm and health. Like the noted English witch, Sybil Leek, by reading the aura he can not only tell much about a person's health but he can also recall various important moments of that person's past. His informal readings have greatly impressed the technical people who investigated him.

Interestingly, Jack Schwarz gets by with only two hours sleep a night, a leftover from his days in the Dutch underground. He seems to overcome the physical necessity each of us has to dream. He does so by meditating for a half hour, a period during which the day's events parade forth as vividly as in a dream. The secret of his power lies in his mental imagery. When resting physically on the nails, he protects himself from any harm by a vision: he is mentally standing next to the nails rather than on them. He does not *allow* this vision of himself to lie on the nails. His powers lie in the mind.

BIOFEEDBACK

Substantial headway has recently been made in laboratories on the problem of training people to command their unconscious minds to perform conscious tasks. This control extends over subtle, involuntary functions of the autonomic nervous system—including extreme muscle relaxation, blood-flow control, and brain-wave control. The technique that has heralded this progress is called biofeedback.

Biofeedback training is the latest in a sequence of Western techniques that control the normally involuntary functions of the body. An earlier technique, discovered by Johannes Schultz in 1910, is called autogenic training. Common in Europe, this technique achieves relaxation and inner calm by using phrases such as "I feel very calm," or "My legs, arms, shoulders are heavy and relaxed." Hypnotism, self-hypnosis, autogenic training, and biofeedback form a hierarchy of methods, not necessarily clearly distinct, for acquiring inner control of oneself. Hypnosis places the least self-control in the individual, biofeedback the greatest. These methods complement the Eastern methods, such as yoga and Zen, which are philosophically based.

Biofeedback training is illustrated by the following technique, employed for combating migraine headaches. Sufferers of migraine headache have cold hands. A migraine headache apparently results from a circulation difficulty that inhibits blood circulation in the extremities, thereby leaving the hands cold. Increasing this circulation combats the migraine.

Temperature detectors, placed on the patient's forehead and right index finger, are wired to a meter which records the amount by which the temperature of the forehead is higher than that of the finger. The patient is given the mental task of moving the meter needle toward zero, indicating a smaller temperature difference. The patient has to warm his or her hands by increasing the circulation of the blood. The technique earns its name from the fact that information on how well this task is being accomplished is *fed back* to the patient, so the patient always knows how well he or she is doing.

By picking up subtle cues the patient learns how to control movement of the needle, thereby controlling the involuntary function being measured. With the migraine sufferer, relaxation of the muscle extremities increases the blood flow. Usually, to get the patient moving along in the right direction, some autogenic training is injected by having him or her repeat such phrases as "I feel very relaxed," or "My hand feels relaxed and warm." Eventually the patient can disregard the meter, "knowing" the hand-warming technique. At that stage of the patient's training, migraine headaches can be aborted before they set in by using the new technique to alter the circulation in the desirable direction.

In some cases, upward of 80 percent of migraine patients tested have been aided by this technique after several sessions. Biofeedback training has also been successfully used in the control of hypertension, insomnia, and muscle tics.[5]

Biofeedback is not limited to the use of a meter and its needle. One common method for aiding the attainment of a relaxed attitude uses a tone generator. The relaxation is achieved by enhancing the occurrence of alpha waves in the brain. These have a frequency range from 8–10 cycles per second. So an electrical filter selects this range of waves from all those picked up by electrodes applied to the head. The greater the alpha waves, the larger the output from the filter. This electrical output is then used to control the intensity of a sound wave emitted by a loud speaker. The users attempt to make this tone as loud as they can by altering their thinking patterns.

ONE BRAIN, TWO MINDS?

"One brain, two minds?" This intriguing question was raised by Professor Michael Cazzaniga of New York University on the basis of the medical histories and tests of certain brain-damaged patients and epileptics and of some laboratory experiments with monkeys and chimpanzees.[6] In Professor Cazzaniga's question, the "mind" is specifically restricted to the *functions* of consciousness: sensing, learning, eating, loving. We are familiar with the extreme cases of double personality met in a few individuals troubled with psychological problems. Professor Cazzaniga brings up the question of a "double mind" in considering the bisected brain of both animal and human.

The human brain is split into two hemispheres, left and right. These two hemispheres are connected by the great cerebral commissure, the *corpus collosum*, consisting of 1.2 million nerve fibers which span the midline of the brain. There is, also, a smaller, anterior commissure. The left hemisphere of the brain deals with the optic nerves viewing the right side of an image; and the right hemisphere, similarly, handles only the left side of the image. When we look straight ahead the objects to the right are processed through the optic nerves of the eyes to the left hemisphere of the brain.

In addition to this right-left reversal of the stimuli from the external world, the two hemispheres have several other, separate, functions. In the normal person, for example, the left hemisphere controls speech while the right hemisphere is literally mute—without speech. But each side of the brain can read, learn, remember, initiate actions, show emotions. Separate memories are stored in the right and left hemispheres. The connecting *corpus collosum* assures that the left side knows what the right side is doing.

Epilepsy results when there are an excessive number of electrical impulses in the nerve cells of the cortex's gray matter. These originate in one area of a hemisphere of the cortex, then spread throughout both hemispheres. Epileptic seizures can be alleviated if the connection between the hemispheres is severed. This inhibits the spread of the electrical impulses between the hemispheres. Operations of this type, which sever the *corpus collosum* and anterior commissure, have recently been performed on epileptics and have proven to be largely successful. Figure 2–4 shows how the optic nerve transmits signals to the two halves and also how the *corpus collosum* connects the two halves.

Epileptics on whom this operation has been performed appear to be entirely normal. Although the hemispheres are physically separated, there are numerous ways in which they naturally communicate in normal living. When such an epileptic talks, the left hemisphere speaks. Both ears will hear the words, however, and the left ear allows the right hemisphere to listen to the left one. When looking at objects, both eyes scan left and right and both hemispheres see the same scene. While the left hemisphere guides the writing of the right hand, the eyes supply the right hemisphere with the knowledge of what the writing is all about.

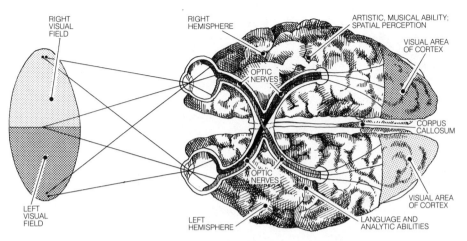

Fig. 2–4. The brain's split personality. Because of the left-right reversal of the eyes' lenses, one side of the cerebrum receives signals only from the opposite visual field. Ordinarily the two sides are connected by the *corpus collosum;* if this is cut, strange effects appear. (The *New York Times Magazine*, September 9, 1973, p. 33. © 1973 by The New York Times Company. Reprinted by permission.)

In laboratory tests, however, this communication between the left and right hemispheres can be suppressed, and some strange features of a "double mind" then arise. An epileptic whose *corpus collosum* has been cut so that this hemispheric communication is suppressed is set down in such a way that instructions, flashed only to the left visual field, command the subject to pick up one of a number of objects with the left hand. A spoon, a pencil, a prism, and a screwdriver are hidden from the epileptic's view below a screen, but they can be handled freely with the left hand.

The command "Pick up the spoon" is flashed to the left visual field. The subject, looking straight ahead, sees the command; but the information is fed to the mute right hemisphere. Asked what he or she saw, the patient says "Nothing." The only side connected with speech, the left hemisphere, is forming that answer. It is responding only to objects lying at the right end of the field of vision, and it has not seen the command. Meanwhile, however, the right hemisphere is responding to the message flashed at the left side of the field of vision. It has guided the left hand in feeling among the objects.

And while the left hemisphere honestly says "Nothing," the right one correctly guides the hand to pick out the spoon. One brain. Two minds?

AUTOMATIC WRITING

In the split brain, one half of the brain does not know what the other half is doing. In automatic writing, the conscious brain does not know what the unconscious brain is doing. Thus, automatic writing falls within a general class of phenomena known as automatism that results from unconscious muscular activity. A medium, speaking in a trance state with a new voice, is displaying automatism. The Ouija board also illustrates this type of activity: motion of the planchette along the Ouija board toward the different letters or words on the board results from unconscious muscular motion of the people whose hands rest upon the planchette. A number of people have cultivated the similar automatism where, also, the hand is guided by a power beyond the conscious: the technique of automatic writing.

The message obtained by automatic writing is sometimes looked upon as a communication from the dead. If asked to do so, the writing will supply a name— and often, a well-known one. William Shakespeare is kept quite busy, on the other side, guiding many a hand on this side.

In legitimate cases, it is quite certain that the person whose hand is being guided is not consciously producing either the physical writing or its contents. It is also certain that the automatic writing is *not* all-knowing. Sometimes, it is true, the writings are inexplicably accurate about things beyond the normal knowledge of the person whose hand is being guided; but quite often the writings are incorrect. They certainly do not hold the future in hand, and they cannot be counted on to predict coming events; nor can they tell, accurately, of events that occurred in the past.

Most people appear capable of developing the power of automatic writing. Competent guidance, however, is essential. The techniques can become a dangerous refuge from reality, and for those with any emotional instability the experience can bring on deep psychological problems. The automatism may then spread, and the whole body may become convulsed in an uncontrolled muscular spasm. The writings themselves should never be uncritically believed.

One famous case of automatic writing cropped up with Judge John Worth Edmond, a famous exponent of spiritualism. Through the hand of Dr. George T. Dexter, this worthy judge carried on an extensive communication with, ostensibly, both Sir Francis Bacon and the famous Swedish seer Emanuel Swedenborg. These communications were published in 1853 by Judge Edmond, and they formed part of the basis of Judge Edmond's espousal of a real spirit world.

The communications to Judge Edmond show little similarity to the actual writings of either Bacon or Swedenborg. This elementary fact eluded the usually keen-witted and critical Judge Edmond. He had first encountered these spirit manifestations in a time of stress, after the death of his beloved wife. However, the dissimilarity did not elude Dr. Dexter, whose hand was being guided. He was particularly skeptical, and continued to voice his skepticism during a test— while his own hand defended Bacon's identity!

A second notable example of automatic writing took place with Mrs. John H. Curran, nearly half a century after Judge Edmond's experiences. Mrs. Curran, who never finished high school, became interested in the Ouija board with a neighbor. After a couple of weeks play each night, Mrs. Curran began to get intelligible results. As the messages unfolded, Mrs. Curran found she had "contacted" a person named Patience Worth. That patient claimed to have lived in

England in the seventeenth century, to have come to America, and to have been slain by Indians. As time progressed and Mrs. Curran became more proficient in these contacts, she eliminated the Ouija board and resorted only to automatic writing.

Patience Worth, who was rather reticent about her life, proved very facile with language. Asked to write poetry, she swamped Mrs. Curran with poems. One night she dictated a poem of 25 lines, starting the first line with *A* and marching, in succession, through all the letters to *Z*, leaving out only *X*. Patience then turned to fiction. She guided the writing of *The Sorry Tale*, an amazingly detailed biblical tale, set in the time of Christ, that became a best-seller during the early 1920s; and of *Telka*, an eighteenth-century pastoral written in a strange Anglo-Saxon variant of English.

It is unclear today whether automatic writing comes wholly from the subconscious of the person who is doing the writing or whether it stems from some outside agent using the subconscious of the individual. Modern psychological theory favors an origin wholly within the individual and suggests that the subconscious can, indeed, supply characteristics, and possibly knowledge, much different than expected from the conscious behavior of the individual. Regardless of its origins, automatic writing illustrates the hidden complexity lurking within the subconscious. Automatic writing is a remarkable phenomenon. We would urge the reader to beware of easy answers here. This is a field that requires continued, serious scientific research.

NERVOUS PLANTS

The keenness of the senses of both humans and animals is quite extraordinary. But recent work by Cleve Backster suggests that this sensitivity in perception extends beyond the animal kingdom to plants and, indeed, even to *the individual cells* from which life derives.[7] We mention at the start, however, that even more recent work by other investigators has not succeeded in duplicating Backster's results. On the contrary, his claims are disputed by working biologists in the field, and Backster stands alone. The burden of proof remains on him.

Cleve Backster is a renowned polygraph (lie-detector) expert. The polygraph measures subtle changes in a person's breathing, blood pressure, pulse rate, and skin resistance. In a normal person, lying induces an emotional stress that changes the electrochemical balance of the body. When a shot of vodka is downed an imbalance shows up in a Kirlian photograph; when a lie is told a similar imbalance affects the heart rate, breathing pattern, and skin resistance— all monitored by the polygraph. The changes in these three functions are considered at least 70-percent accurate in the detection of lies.

When connected to a plant the polygraph is sensitive to very slight changes within the plant. By measuring plant resistance on the polygraph, Backster claimed some results which, if reproduced by other independent researchers, would have a startling implication.

Backster claimed that plants seemed to anticipate his actions, as if reading his thoughts. One of the first tests Backster made was on a *Draena massangeana* plant. Backster decided to burn one leaf of the plant—and at that instant, *before* he actually burned the leaf, the polygraph responded. In fact, the response to the intent exceeded the response to the fact.

Further exploring this alleged eerie sensitivity of his plants, Backster devised a brine shrimp experiment. He set up an automated apparatus which dumped live brine shrimp into boiling water. After hooking his polygraph apparatus to three philodendra, Backster would leave for home. All night long, shrimp would be dumped at random into the boiling water while, all alone, the polygraph watched the plants. Analyzing the data afterwards, Backster noted a burst of plant activity five to seven seconds after the shrimp were actually dumped into the water. Those bursts of plant activity occurred at a level five times greater than that to be expected by chance.

Backster assiduously carried out further investigations. He concluded that a "primary perception" exists, in a yet undefined sensory system, in all forms of life; down, even, to the life within individual cells. He has conducted tests which point to this primary perception in fresh fruits and vegetables, in *paramecium*, mold cultures, yeasts, blood samples, amoeba, and even in spermatazoa. Distance, surprisingly, does not seem to affect some of the aspects of the perception, implying a nonelectromagnetic origin of this effect.

To Backster, the perception in plants appears attuned to individual persons. Plants, according to him, seem to respond particularly well to special, happy individuals— those with a green thumb. Also, they appreciate watering; but they detest dogs.

With all the shrimp and lobsters that are being dropped into boiling water in Chinese restaurants all over this country, how, one wonders, do plants get any peace? Backster feels that the answer lies in tuning. The plants, he says, can tune in delicately to things nearby; and they can also tune in to certain very selective things—to a special person, say—even if far away; but everything in between these extremes can be tuned out in some manner.

The experiments of Backster, if verified, would point to a strange, electrochemical, sentient life within plants, organisms, and, indeed, cells of all types. That life exists within a cell is an understandable fact; but a sentient character in single cells—that requires real proof.

There is a line of research into the sentient life of plants and cells, however, that threads back at least six decades. In 1917 Jagadis Chandra Bose was knighted for his invention of the crescograph, a device capable of magnifying minute motions 10 million times. Using this device, Bose found that plants seemed to respond emotionally, in tiny motions, to a variety of stimuli. At the Bose Institute, in Calcutta, his work led him to conclude that "plants have a sensitive nervous system and a varied emotional life. Love, hate, joy, fear, pleasure, pain. . . ."

For the past 60 years Dr. Harold Saxton Burr, a physician, has mapped the minute bioelectrical field patterns of humans, animals, and vegetables which arise within the protoplasm circulating inside each cell.[8] And recently Dr. Marcel

Vogel, a chemist studying these fields, found that the penetration of outside fields into the cell produced a "primary awareness." So the hunt continues. Within a few years we should know whether sentient cells, or plants, make sense.

FACT OR FICTION?

Records of the miraculous and the magical persist throughout all history. Faced with obstinacy, so the story in the Old Testament tells us, God visited Egypt with ten plagues. The water turned to blood; frogs, gnats, and flies were everywhere; and so forth. Were these stories invented by the people who wrote the Bible? Or were they simple accounts of real events?

Thirteen centuries later, according to the New Testament, Jesus Christ turned water to wine; He opened the eyes of the blind and the ears of the deaf; He straightened the cripples; He fed 5,000 people with five loaves and two fishes; He cleansed lepers; and He raised up the dead Lazarus—and, finally, Himself.

In looking back many thousands of years our judgment of the truth of such miraculous events cannot help but suffer: our vision of the reality blurs under the veil of time. The temptation grows, as time passes, to classify these reports as exaggeration or myth, as obviously wrong because they are so incredible.

How are we to assess such accounts of magic? There is no doubt that the prevalent view among scientists today is one of skepticism. Many are agnostics or atheists; very few believe in witchcraft or magic. Professor Freeman Dyson of the Institute for Advanced Study in Princeton, New Jersey, says, "There are a lot of scientists who consider religion as a childhood disease from which one is recovering."

But the truth—of God, of miracles, of magic, or of science—is established neither by an authoritative dictate nor by a democratic vote. It is not really pertinent whether or not this view is representative of the vast majority of scientists. That majority view may be ephemeral, to be replaced by a different majority view many years from now. The French Academy of Science once announced that reports of stones falling from heaven were completely erroneous, thereby banning meteors and meteorites from their science. The fact is that the truth or falsity of miraculous or magical events is very difficult to test experimentally. Until science provides conclusive evidence, it all comes down to a question of belief. Somewhere in a wide spectrum, ranging from complete belief to complete disbelief, each individual takes a position.

A sublime hope was expressed in an article in *Time*:

Beyond all the charlatanism, there is a genuine realm of magic, a yet undiscovered territory between man and the universe. Perhaps it can once more be accepted as a legitimate pursuit of knowledge, no longer hedged in by bell, book and candle. Perhaps, eventually, religion, science, and magic could come mutually to respect and supplement one another. That is a fond vision and one that is pinned to a fragile and perpetually unprovable faith: that the universe itself is a whole, with purpose and promise beneath the mystery. [9]

CHAPTER THREE
THE WITCH'S CAULDRON

■ *The Witch* ■ *The Mystery Religions*

■ *The Gods* ■ *Satanism*

■ *That Old-Time Religion* ■ *Witch Hunts*

■ *Tribal Witchcraft* ■ *Shamans, Medicine Men, Witch Doctors*

■ *Voodoo and Zombies* ■ *Modern Witchcraft*

■ *Magic or Miracle?*

THE WITCH

A hag mounting a broom in the sky, cackling at the full moon . . . a simmering cauldron, bearing a woeful spell . . . demons at one's command . . . the walking dead . . . merry dancers circling a midnight fire. . . Witchcraft invokes images of strange, fearful doings; and a surge of interest in the occult has stirred our dim knowledge of this craft. Popular myths surrounding witches, previously persistent in fables and gossip, now abound in playful television. But the popular view of witchcraft differs strongly from the view held by those who practice this hidden art.

Witchcraft derives its name from the Anglo-Saxon word *wicca* (akin to *witan*, to know); and witchcraft is often termed the craft of the wise. It has many sides, and is seen through many eyes. The Britannica considers witchcraft "the human exercise of alleged supernatural powers for antisocial, evil purposes,"[1] thus associating witchcraft with black magic. But within the craft itself there are witches such as Sybil Leek to whom "witchcraft, as any religion, involves the acceptance of certain tenets which are based on faith and acceptance of a Supreme Being. . . . From this Supreme Being comes life, and by many incarnations . . . a spiral of spiritual development."[2] Paul Huson sees witches practicing "with weapons forged from the darkness itself . . . to know the ways in and out of the unseen world." He warns, "Witchcraft is witchcraft. The seeds of success or destruction lie within you, and you alone."[3]

Common to all varieties of witchcraft is a promise of secret knowledge, a hidden mastery of nature. As judged from outside, witchcraft used for good is often termed white witchcraft, while its use for evil is termed black witchcraft. These days the attraction of witchcraft stems, in part, from the promise of a hidden, novel—but paradoxically, old—art that offers escape from the ring of technology that encompasses our culture, an art which seeks a oneness within all of nature.

Pragmatically, a witch is any one who claims to practice witchcraft. The term includes both males and females, although the terms wizard or warlock are sometimes used to indicate the male witch. The terms witch and sorcerer are often interchangeable in common language, but we will find it useful to make this arbitrary distinction: a witch is someone believed to have been born with special powers; while a sorcerer is someone whose powers are believed to have been acquired from without, by learning, or (in our imagination) by a pact with the devil.

Religion is ancient, but people continually found new churches. So it is with witchcraft. A modern practitioner, Anton LaVey, has set up a modern-day witch cult in California, where such things seem to happen naturally. There are five degrees of membership: apprentice, warlock or witch, wizard or enchantress, sorcerer or sorceress, and the highest magus—LaVey himself. LaVey uses witch, wizard, warlock, and sorcerer as convenient labels to help fill up his list, as needed.

The term "magus," derived from the same root as Magi, is often reserved for the supreme magician. The Magi were the ancient Babylonian or Chaldean sages-priests-astrologers whom we shall meet again when discussing astrology. Their occult learning and practice earned them a reputation as supreme magicians in the ancient world beyond their borders. There, their true learning was only dimly grasped. Their legacy survives in the word "magic": applying natural causes to produce surprising effects. In common lore, witchcraft and magic go hand in hand. But magical practice occurs, as well, in all religions: the saints and their miracles in the Catholic church, the patriarch Moses and the plagues, the mystical cabalistic tradition of the Hebrew religion, Mohammed moving his mountain.

In a broad sense, witchcraft appears in many guises: the ancient, pagan mystery religions of Egypt, Greece, and Rome; the tribal witchcraft from Africa; Voodoo, the descendant of tribal witchcraft in the Americas; satanism; and modern witchcraft. So magicians—Sabani, Home, and St. Joseph are examples—are called by many names: witch doctor, commoner, holy saint, mystic, shaman, fakir, and just plain witch.

The word "pagan" originally referred to people living outside the city—the uncivilized. In a certain sense this word describes many believers in today's witchcraft: they are people who simply do not accept today's depersonalized science and technology. So in a narrower sense, witchcraft is a pagan religion. As with any religion, it has a doctrine, rituals, and a priesthood. The priesthood protects and propagates the doctrines, and it conducts the rituals. In witchcraft the priesthood is made up of the witches and the high priestess, the rituals are their ceremonies, and the doctrine expresses a theology of the universe describing a principle responsible for life. All of life is a unity with nature, and there is postulated a continuing sequence of reincarnations which foster a spiritual development upward through nature.

Particulars in the theology vary among different sects. Depending on how far back a witch sect may trace its origins, various gods are found. Commonly, Diana (the moon goddess, the woodland goddess, and also the goddess of fertility) is the prime object of veneration. Female fertility goddesses corresponding to Diana, such as Isis, Minerva, Aphrodite, Ceres, Hecate, and the Virgin, are found throughout numerous religions and mythologies. Satanism, as distinct from witchcraft and the common religions, enters when worship centers upon an evil leader: Satan, Lucifer, Beelzebub, or Seth.

As with any legitimate religion, true witchcraft seeks out a sense of nature and right. Its practitioners strive to follow their own view of morality and truth. The concept of a white or a black witchcraft is imposed from without witchcraft and may simply express a limited knowledge, by those outside witchcraft, of the witchcraft religions. There are, indeed, paths that lead to darkness and evil; Manson and his followers are not myths. To describe their art as evil is correct, but to impose their evil upon all who practice witchcraft by terming it "black witchcraft" would be unfair—as unfair as it would be to impose it upon all Christianity in the guise of "black Christianity."

We devote this chapter to a study of "witchcraft," taking the term broadly as it is widely used by those outside the various witchcraft sects. So we will be discussing a wide range of topics, far beyond the religious beliefs of those few who term themselves witches.

THE MYSTERY RELIGIONS

There are some suggestions that Anglo-Saxon witchcraft can trace its origins back, through the trials of the Inquisition, to the ancient mystery religions of Egypt, Greece, and Rome. Here "mystery" indicates mute, silent. The present-day Rosicrucian societies are a prime example of a mystery organization; they also purport to trace their secret wisdom back to ancient times. The canons of the ancient mystery religions were reserved only for the initiates, remaining mute to the outside world. This silence obviously leaves us with few records to assess the mystery religions in detail. The colossal Sphinx at Giza dates from about 2500 B.C. An Egyptian standing in front of it, 1500 years before Christ, would have considered the Sphinx already ageless. Our discussion of Egyptian witchcraft can only be a small sample of the complex variations found in this monumental civilization.

Candidates for one particular sect of the mystery religions had to undergo a series of steps before being admitted to its ranks. A preliminary period of purification was demanded, the purification being a sign of good faith. Sometimes this involved severe fasting and ascetic practices; but at other times substantial donations were sufficient to evidence good intentions. Actually, of course, the rich needed the fasting more than the poor did; but such is the human way, both ancient and modern.

A confession of one's sins might then follow, with the candidates swearing that they had not committed any grave evil. In a surprisingly contemporary echo, they might be required to swear to never having laid waste either the land or the waters. After this an initiation ceremony would take place, in the best hazing fashion of college fraternities of the 1920s. The candidates might undergo trials testing their faith, perseverance, and belief in the efficacy of the gods. If successful, the candidates were then initiated in that particular mystery religion, and their education and further progress within the religion could then begin.

The importance attributed to the literal word itself is a keynote to the Egyptian mind. When an Egyptian child was born he or she was given two names, the true name and the good name. Only the good name was made public. The true name belonged to the *Ka*, a mysterious life force or spirit interspersed in the body's matter. This was considered an etheric double, but not the "soul." The *Ka* survived death in a "magical reflection of life in the grave." The images, tools, utensils, and small houses which were entombed for eternity with the deceased assured a mystical reality for the *Ka*.

The name, its word, was more than a sound: it was a part of the thing—its being, its extension. If one knew the true name of a person, one had power over that person. The gods themselves had a true name; and if an individual called a god by that true name, the god then had to abide that person's command. In an effort to find the true name of the gods, many incomprehensible, often foreign, words were used to address the gods. The following incantation comes from the times of Ramses II, before 1200 B.C.:

O Valpaga, O Kemmara, O Kamolo, O Karkemu

O Asmagaa. The Vana. The Uthun of the sun.

This is to order those who are in your midst. . . .[4]

The address was to the gods of the underworld. The magic proceeded from the words themselves, precisely said: to command—not to ask—these gods to do the speaker's bidding. Power came, indeed, from the word. So much so, that the words themselves made things magically true. The magician might then deceive the gods, or deceive the evil spirits. To guard against evil spirits at night the speaker would lie, and lie powerfully: "The beauties of (the speaker's name) are those of Osiris. His upper lip is that of Isis, his under lip is that of Nepthis. . . . His arms are those of the gods."[5]

J. G. Frazer has deduced two principles of thought that underlie much of magical practice. These principles are the *law of similarity*, through which the magician seeks to produce an effect by imitating the effect; and the *law of contagion*, by which the magician attempts to affect a person by acting upon a thing that belongs to the person. These principles are cardinal in explaining widespread practices carried on by magicians and witches throughout history, up to the very present.

The two laws are illustrated by the following love potion. Take the sweat of the body, mix it with flour, and form it into a small cake. Then mix either hair or nail clippings of the loved one into the cake; and bake. Give it to the loved one and if the cake is eaten, the loved one is yours. The love potion acts upon the lovers by intermingling (the law of similarity) the sweat of one with the hair or nail clippings of the other (the law of contagion) and instills loves in the heart of the indifferent one when he or she eats the cake (again, the law of similarity).

These laws emphasize the importance of the name and the word to the Egyptians. Nothing was so close to people as their name; and, if known, nothing so easily affected them. A whispered command to the true name could devastate the person behind the name. The precise word, correctly said, worked miracles— "In the beginning was the Word and the Word was with God; and the Word was God." (John i,1)

THE GODS

The doctrines of the ancient mystery religions revolved about their mythical gods. The main mystery religions centered on various dieties: Demeter, Kone, Hekate, Mithras, Attis, Dionysus, or, especially in Egypt, Isis. The myths concerning these gods changed with time and place throughout the Mediterranean areas. In a later Isis myth (see Fig. 3–1) the male gods Osiris and Seth and the female gods Isis and Nepthis were all offspring of Geb, the god of earth, and of Nut, the goddess of the heavens. Osiris was born to save the world. His brother Seth became jealous and, through trickery, enclosed him in a chest which he then threw into the Nile. Isis, both the sister and wife of Osiris, wandered far in search of him and finally found his coffin near Byblos, in Syria. She returned to Egypt with the body; but Seth stole it, dismembered it, and scattered it about the earth. Isis, again resuming her search, found it and reunited the parts with the help of sundry other gods. Osiris was resurrected, and he reigned as king of the dead. Horus, the son of Isis and Osiris, now sought to avenge his father and, in a titanic battle that raged across the sky, Horus finally overcame Seth.

In mythology Seth is identified with the Greek god Typhon, and the names are often joined as Seth-Typhon. Pliny writes, "A terrible comet was seen by the people of Ethiopia and Egypt, to which Typhon, the king of that period, gave his name; it had a fiery appearance . . . and was twisted like a coil, and it was very

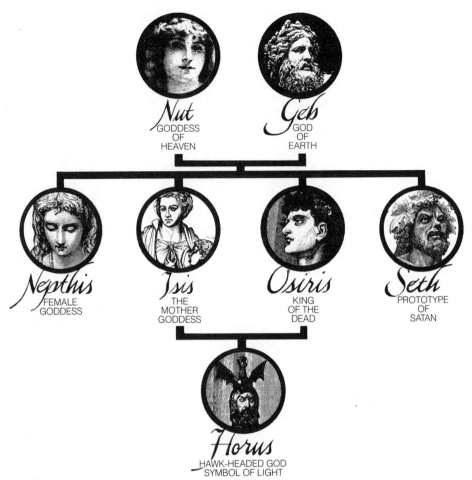

Fig. 3–1. The Isis myth. Note that Osiris and Isis, brother and sister, were the parents of Horus. Incest was widely practiced among the ruling classes of ancient Egypt.

grim to behold: it was not really a star so much as what might be called a ball of fire.'' Velikovsky, whom we shall discuss in a later chapter, suggests that the mythological battle of Horus and Seth may, indeed, describe the awesome near collision of a comet with the earth.

Seth was initially an ancient patron god of the eleventh district of upper Egypt. But as times change so do myths, and the gods sometimes have the devil's time trying to keep their status. Political vicissitudes plagued Seth's role, and he eventually became the adversary of Horus. The changing roles of gods among the myths reflect the twisted paths by which *the gods of the displaced religions often became the devils of the new religions.* A corollary of this rule is at play today in the case of some modern satanic sects which adopt the devils of the established religions as their own gods.

The myth of Osiris parallels a strong element of the Christian theology, as found in the New Testament of Christ—a savior destroyed and resurrected. The promise of redemption during life and of resurrection afterwards had a strong appeal to many in ancient Egypt. The mystery religions offered this promise of spiritual uplifting and salvation to the initiates, drawing many to their mysteries. Others came to the mystery religions, as some people come now to the occult, for many other reasons: the attraction of the unknown, novelty, the lure of the mysterious, hope for material gain, the temptation of sexual exploitation.

The importance of the mystery religions of Egypt to the historical development of witchcraft lies in their development of various magic arts. One such Egyptian art was their control over animals. They could, for example, cause snakes to become rigid. Their priests wore masks of all sorts of birds and animals in an attempt to understand and influence them. Another of their magic arts was the development, for themselves, of various altered states of consciousness. Suspended animation, immunity to pain, and hypnotic trance were all well known to these ancient Egyptians. Passed on for millenia, through numerous other civilizations, these magical practices eventually constituted one of the main ingredients prominent in the formulation of the European witchcraft of the Middle Ages.

SATANISM

The worship of the powers of evil—or of Satan, the Devil himself—forms satanism. Various reasons are given for the choice of the devil as the object of worship and veneration. At each age, undoubtedly, rebellion against an existing religious orthodoxy brings out a worship of the evil gods of that religion. Earmarks of such practice appear in the rituals used; they take their cues from the old religion, adopting distortions, reversals, or desecrations of the existing rituals for the satanic rituals. Thus, the altar may be approached backwards; the cross may be turned upside down, to form a satanic cross; profanities and illicit actions may be introduced into the ceremonies and Black Masses. Our present-day "hocus-pocus" is derived from just such an inversion, a play on the Latin *Hoc est Corpus*—Here is the body.

Satan is represented in many fashions: as a horned god, or with cloven feet, or with a tail, or in the form of a goat. He is worshipped under many names: Lucifer (the light bearer, Satan's name before his fall from God's graces), the Devil (from the Greek *diabalos*—accuser, slanderer), Beelzebub (in reality, an obscure Persian god of flies, incorporated into the succeeding Judeo-Christian religion as a devil). The role of Satan underwent a number of changes in recorded history. In Job, Satan is God's agent, the eye of the Lord, who seeks to test the true allegiance of humanity to God. God allows Satan to test Job's true allegiance by inflicting pain and sorrow. Satan's role in the Old Testament thereafter changes slowly until, in the New Testament, he is an active antagonist of God—powerful, but still subject to God's will.

Needless to say, the reality of Satan and of demons has never been experimentally established. Science, slowly handling and exposing so many uncertainties of nature, has gradually pressed the demonic hosts further beyond our reach. During the recent decades religion has sensed more embarrassment than reality from Satan, and has quietly veiled him in silence. But, in a recent statement, Pope Paul reaffirmed the more traditional belief: "We thus know that this obscure and disturbing being really exists and he still operates with treacherous cunning."

Whatever the reality of Satan, the satanic philosophy offers a wide scope for evil. These evils existed even before Roman times. During the days of Rome a law against human sacrifice was instituted and, on the basis of this law, Apollonius of Tyana was brought to trial in the first century A.D. But the harm has continued. There was, for example, a notorious case of satanism in seventeenth-century France—the case of a mistress of Louis XIV who had fallen from his favor. As a ritual to regain Louis' love, the mistress commissioned a renegade priest to perform a series of Black Masses over her nude body. Inquisition records state that the Black Masses were actually performed, and at each Black Mass the climax was the sacrifice of a living child.

The following are a few samples of the beliefs expressed by Anton LaVey, the magus of the "Church of Satan":

- I break away from all conventions that do not lead to my earthly success and happiness.
- Death to the weakling, wealth to the strong!
- Hate your enemies with a whole heart.
- There is no heaven . . . and no hell. . . . Here and now is our opportunity.
- Blessed are the victorious, for victory is the basis of right.
- Praying does absolutely no good—in fact, it actually lessens the chance of success.[6]

There are many others in the same vein. By our standards they are unqualifiedly evil; though they are self-consistent. These principles work for the benefit of a few. It is interesting that those who advocate them are always, somehow, in that small group. But any society that existed by such a code could certainly not long survive; remember Adolf Hitler's 1,000-year Reich.

THAT OLD-TIME RELIGION

The popular conception of a witch is that of an old woman dressed in black rags and wearing a tall, conical hat who has a jutting jaw that almost meets her long, hooked nose. A black cat is at her side, she is mounted on a broomstick, and a boiling cauldron is not far away as she wends her way through *Grimm's Fairy Tales*. What are the origins of such fabled imaginings? What sources prompted these stories in our Western lore? We have to go back beyond the Middle Ages in Europe and look at the historical evidence.

The witchcraft known in the European countries is a religion that gained prominence during the period from roughly 1000 to 1500 A.D., reached its peak in the years between 1500 and 1700 A.D., and still exists in various forms today. The religion formed by the confluence of two important factors which, in the Middle Ages (400–1500 A.D.), made it appear a serious threat to Christianity. The Church, in responding, exerted itself most vigorously—in fact, too vigorously—to repel it. It is interesting to note that this vigorous exercise, the Inquisition, took place not in the Dark Ages but in the Age of Enlightenment.

Lines of evidence suggest that the first ingredient in the brew that became Western witchcraft was a *fertility cult*.[7] This was the pagan religion of the Neolithic people who inhabited Western Europe for two millenia before the Christian Era. These people, the last representatives of the Stone Age, had been ruthlessly shoved aside by the Celtic, Teutonic, and Nordic tribes, all warlike and all eventually converted to Christianity, who descended on them from the north and the east. The original Neolithic people differed from their conquerors in appearance (they were shorter and darker) and this was reflected in the names given them. Race memories of these earlier people enshrine them as the Little People or leprechauns in Ireland; trolls or dwarfs in Scandinavia; goblins, fairies, or elves in England; and other distinctive names in Germany and France. Whatever their later names, these people were shoved into dismal swamps or remote islands where they continued to live with their animals.

Inferior in size and culture, they loathed the agriculture, churches, and iron technology of the new tribes and hung onto their own customs and festivals. Many of these centered about the dance, one of the earliest emotional expressions of group tribal unity in the development of civilization. The dances were follow-the-leader type, ring or circle type, or couple dances. In any case they were joyous expressions timed to various events—hunting ceremonies, times of animal mating, etc.—closely associated with nature. There was much animal symbolism. Goats, bulls, rams, and wolves played the most prominent roles. The least common denominator in the gods they worshipped was a horned figure, half man and half animal. Fertility was important, and phallic symbols abounded.

Over the centuries these Little People disappeared, whether by assimilation or erosion. Their memory lives on in folk tales which have been popularized by many writers, most notably the Grimm brothers, Shakespeare, and Walt Disney —though Tinker Bell and Robin Hood made it by other means.

The Little People gradually became worshippers of Christianity as well as of their own pagan fertility cults, but in this long process some of their own beliefs rubbed off on the peoples of the majority. There they remain to this day, altered into our superstitions. Their own *witchlore*, viewed as magic by us, was the second big ingredient in the development of medieval witchcraft.

Many different practices were probably employed in the ancient cult rituals. Psychedelic herbs and ointments, breath control, and concentration were all meant to alter the consciousness; natural ointments and medicine were for healing; sexual play and exciting ritual dances added their spell. In an earlier, pre-civilized, closer-to-nature state these practices had played a much greater role in people's lives than they did by the sixteenth century. This sort of magic had an allure which, when combined with the joys of eating, drinking, dancing, and sexuality of the witchcraft festivals, contrasted markedly with the self-abnega-tion, conscience, and postponed gratification of Christianity. The result was an irresistible attraction to many, steeped in lives of hard work and no reward; and the ranks of witchcraft swelled with converts from Christianity.

These converts included the remnants of the Little People; women seeking escape from oppressive conditions; peasants and intellectuals seeking to exchange the joys of the afterlife promised by Christianity for the present pleasantries of witchcraft; and others seeking magic cures. Whoever they were and whatever the reason, by 1500 A.D. the Church regarded them as dangerous heretics. For 500 years the Church had warned them, tried to isolate them, and used excom-munication as a weapon—all to no avail. The joys of heresy proved increasingly enchanting. So the Church eventually moved to harsher means of persuasion.

Before we recount some of these means, it is interesting to consider the mean-ing of the different characteristics which go to make up the popular conception of the witch. First: a witch is a woman. This probably stems from the fact that the vast preponderance of the converts to witchcraft from Christianity were, indeed, women. But the impression that the woman is old is incorrect. A study of the case histories of women dealt with in the witch hunts shows there were as many young and desirable ones as old and ugly ones. The black cat is certainly symbolic of the close relationship that existed between witches and animals, all animals. The boiling cauldron is connected both with food, dispensed by females in the early martriarchal societies, and with various herbs and plants having psychedelic powers. Here, too, it was women who were the repository of knowledge.

The broomstick is connected with the alleged ability of witches to fly. The explanations attempted for this, coming down to the effects of psychedelic drugs, are highly conjectural. Suppose we just say this is a reflection of the magical powers attributed to witches. As for the tatters, the ugliness, and the other evil attributes—would it not seem plausible that this is the revenge that the final victor takes on the victim? Is Christianity, the final conqueror in the contest with Western witchcraft, to be expected to be more charitable, more compassion-ate, or more comprehending than other victors in other contests? The popular image of the black, evil witch shows that, in this case, the Church was not.

WITCH HUNTS

Periodically societies are convulsed by the seeming necessity to heap their woes upon the heads of a strange few. In times of crisis, imagined evils must be uprooted and blame must be placed. These are the times when the witch hunts commence.

For 1,000 years European Christianity lived in uneven peace with the pagan, the Jewish, and the Muslim religions in its midst and on its borders. Within the pagan religions lay hidden a fertility cult of witchcraft. By the thirteenth century the Church felt threatened by the dangers of heresy among its members, and it saw the horned fertility god of the witchcraft cult as the Devil himself.

In a desperate effort to root out the dangers of heresy from its membership, the Church began a Papal Inquisition, and its actions slowly became both more arbitrary and more extensive. In 1484 Pope Innocent VIII issued a papal bull which openly attacked witchcraft as a serious source of heresy. Thereupon the floodgates to hell, not to heaven, were opened: everywhere witches were sought, found, tortured to obtain confessions, and then either hung or burned at the stake. The estimates of the number of people killed in the witch hunts range from 300,000 to well over a million people. All in the name of good uprooting evil, in the name of God.

It is worth emphasizing that the crime of which the witches were accused was not the practice of magic; it was heresy. All through this period magicians, such as astrologers and alchemists, were left relatively unmolested.

The judicial procedures of the Inquisition were similar to the common judicial procedures of the times. Torture, though common among the Greeks and Romans, had fallen into blessed disuse in the preceding 1,000 years of relative peace. Now it was gradually reinstituted. At the beginning the torture was mild and was performed only in the presence of an official observer. It was permitted once, and then only in a continuous fashion. Eventually, however, long recesses were allowed in the torture, so the restriction to a single torture became a meaningless legality. Those accused of witchcraft had no right to confront the accuser, often had no knowledge of the alleged crime, and were represented by attorneys who were mere tools of the court. The accused were presumed guilty until they proved themselves innocent. Confessed witches were required to name their accomplices, and the torture resulted in a constant supply of names of new accused witches. Confiscation of the property of a confessed witch came into use, at first only to defray legal costs; but this acted as a goad to unscrupulous inquisitors. Graft became common.

Witch trials were prevalent in France, Germany, and Scotland. Opposition to the injustices of the Inquisition rose time and time again during these trials, but to no avail. Italy suffered to some extent; but Holland, Scandinavia, and Ireland escaped the main brunt of the witch hunt. Of course, even the side effects were brutal: witness the expulsion from Spain in 1492 by Queen Isabella of the Jews, resident there for centuries.

The evidence of witchcraft acceptable to the clerical witch hunters degenerated to the most commonplace things: a mole, or an unusual scar, became certitude that the possessor was a witch. Pet birds, dogs, or cats might harbor a spirit. Gossip and rumor could bring about an accusation. A few samples of some infamous injustices follow.

• A woman in Scotland is burned as a witch for stroking a cat at an open window, at the same time that a householder found his brew of beer turning sour.

- A mother and daughter in England are executed as witches on the accusation, by a ten-year-old girl, of bewitching her with fits.
- A witness in a witch trial in France makes a dying confession that his evidence had been dictated by the prosecutor; nothing is done to reopen the case and the accused, a nun, dies in solitary confinement.
- A woman in Scotland is convicted as a witch for curing unhealthy children by washing them.*

The contagious disease of witch hunting eventually spread from the Old World to the New. In North America the most notorious case was the Salem witch trials. The epidemic began in February 1692 in colonial Massachusetts, at that time a theocracy. Elizabeth Parris, aged 9, and her cousin Abigail William, aged 11, began displaying attacks of uncontrollable sobbing that soon became convulsions. The girls had been listening to occult tales of the West Indian Islands from Tituba, a slave of Rev. Parris, Elizabeth's father. Their fits gained considerable notoriety, and soon a number of other young girls in the town suffered such attacks. Gradually the hysteria spread.

Rumors of satanic possession sprang up. Naturally, the source of the torment had to be sought. Under prompting, the girls accused the obvious scapegoat—the weak and the out-of-the-ordinary: Tituba, the slave; Sarah Good, a pipe-smoking woman; Sarah Osborne, a cripple who was remiss at church attendance; Martha Corey, the village midwife and mother of an illegitimate son. The cases grew: torture extracted confessions and more candidates' names. The young girls continued their accusations, caught in a whirlwind they had started with a sob.

Altogether, over 150 people were imprisoned. Confession meant reprieve—and 55 confessed and obtained reprieves. But others valued their honor more highly. Giles Corey, the 80-year-old husband of Martha Corey, was accused and "pressed." A board was placed over his body, and rocks were added while he was asked to confess. But Giles staunchly defied his accusers, going to his death as he stubbornly muttered "More weight, more weight."

In all, 30 persons were condemned to death. Pardons reduced this amount; still, 19 people were actually put to death. The trials stretched into 1693, but sanity began to return and the trials abated. On January 15, 1697, the colony kept a day of fasting in order to repent the wrongdoing of the trials. This infamous witch hunt then passed into history.

TRIBAL WITCHCRAFT

The beliefs and practices of primitive tribes give us an idea of the origins of witchcraft and magic among all peoples. The beliefs of most tribal peoples show varying degrees of two important concepts that underlie the religious practices which form the base of witchcraft—animism and totemism.

---

* From *The Encyclopedia of Witchcraft and Demonology* by Rossell Hope Robbins. © 1959 by Crown Publishers, Inc. Used by permission of Crown Publishers, Inc.

Animism attributes a soul, or spirit, to all things—both living and inanimate. The Abron people on the Ivory Coast of Africa offered sacrifice to the earth god, to their river deities, and to their ancestors. North American Indians would take the heart from the dead body of a courageous enemy and eat it in hopes of gaining the courage living there. Indeed, there may be some biological basis to the idea that special properties reside in the organs of the body; for various organs do, indeed, have unique combinations of nutrients and specialized RNA. Consider the following case. Experimenters on minute *planaria* have trained them to respond to light. These *planaria* have then been cut up and fed to other *planaria*, whereupon the new *planaria* were found to respond more rapidly to light: they had acquired some of the learning of the dead *planaria* on which they had fed.

In tribes practicing totemism, groups within the tribe bound themselves to a specific totem—an animal or, less frequently, a plant or tree. Taboos grow up about the totem, emphasizing the sacred power in the animal and linking this power to the members of the group. Thus, Alaskan totem poles are carved in masks resembling their totems; and, by the mystical law of similarity, they are considered to house the spirits of these totems.

The actual witchcraft and magic found among tribal peoples is best illustrated by examples. We will consider the Azande of Central Africa.

The Azande are a Sudanic-speaking, ethnically mixed, amalgam of tribes united by the Avongara conquest of the eighteenth century. The tribes have practiced cannibalism in the past, are inclined to warfare, and have strongly resisted the intrusions of Arab slave traders from the Southwest Sudan. The Azande are totemic: they believe that at death the body-soul, one of the two souls of a deceased, departs into a totemic animal of the clan. The concept of a god is unimportant to the Azande, but witchcraft beliefs play a strong role in the community.

The Azande see a clear distinction between witchcraft, *mangu*, and magic or sorcery, *ngwa*, which is related to medicine. Not all tribal groups see the clear distinction between witchcraft and sorcery displayed by the Azande. The Azande also see the witch, *iwa*, as hereditary, with the spirit of *mangu* real within the stomach of the witch. After death they often extract a blackish sac—perhaps the gall bladder—from the witch and hang it as a totem. To the Azande the witches emit a bright light as they walk through the jungle at night; but only another witch can see this light in the daytime. While sleeping, the witch can dispatch his *mangu* spirit to harm others. The witches form covens in which the elders instruct the novices. Sorcerers accomplish their works by harmful medicine, by rites, or by spells that can be learned by anyone; they do not require inherited powers.

Witchcraft is such a prevalent notion among the Azande that they have evolved an elaborate ritual to discover and confront the witch. A father may have a sick child who, he thinks, has been bewitched. His concern will drive him to seek the witch's name. He first consults the *iwa* oracle, who conjures for him the names of possible suspects. Then the father consults a second oracle, who takes a chicken, poisons it with strychnine, and ritually recites the suspected names. The death of the chicken at the mention of one name confirms the identity of the witch. The witch must then be confronted and accused—a wing of the chicken is cut off and placed before the hut of the accused by a deputy of the chief. The suspected witch has the choice either of refuting the accusation or of stopping the witchery of the child. The father will await the recovery of the child, and if the child does not recover, the father may himself enlist witchcraft or magic against his enemy.

Several common factors can be distilled from the potpourri of investigations of tribal witchcraft beliefs. It should be noted that these beliefs are usually held by nonwitches; not all witches share these beliefs.

- Belief in witchcraft is widely distributed geographically, but it does not appear in all tribes or in all cultures.
- The accusation of witchcraft, and also its persecution, arises during times of stress—personal, social, or psychological—within a society.
- A witch mythology exists. The witch is always adult, and usually female. The powers are inherited. A witch bears physical stigma—red hair, a birthmark, a limp, or some physical defect. A witch is unpleasant—reserved, stingy, quarrelsome.
- The witch turns against his or her own people, thereby causing sickness, death, drought, and all forms of natural havoc.
- The witch is driven by personal envy, malice, and spite more than by a desire for gain.
- Witches break conventions and tribal taboos—they dig up the dead, eat human flesh, go naked, ride animals backwards, and sacrifice children.
- Although sorcery may be seen as substantially natural, witchcraft implies a paranatural element. Witches also have a spirit fellow, called a familiar, often appearing as a pet animal, to do their bidding. As a corollary, a way to combat witchcraft is with other witchcraft.

SHAMANS, MEDICINE MEN, WITCH DOCTORS

Commonly the three terms shaman, medicine man, and witch doctor are used somewhat interchangeably. The Australian *medicine man* initiates tribal members into the myths, rituals, and secrets of the tribe. He is a combination seer and doctor. Versed in meditation and telepathy, he also protects the tribe against black magic. The *shaman*, a dignitary of some Siberian tribes, is both a medicine man and a priest. He is expert in the technique of ritualized ecstasy. He claims the power to leave his body at will, to journey in the spirit world for the benefit of his tribe. He guards the tribal lore, heals, controls the weather, and defends against sorcery. The shaman is sometimes hereditary, but he always requires an initiation by elders within the tribe. In South America he may himself practice black magic. The *witch doctor* is a more popular term, combining the attributes of the medicine man and the shaman.

The shamans, medicine men, and witch doctors are expert in altering their consciousness into a trance state induced by meditation or ecstasy. They are reported to see the future, to know present events, to heal, to read minds, and to control inanimate objects. Except in unusual circumstances, their magic powers are inherently weak. Psychic healing, or psychic damning, usually takes a considerable time. Dr. Turnbull's sickness apparently took some time to develop— antibiotics and poison work much faster.

A word should be said about the curative role of medicine men. Their curative methods often pale in comparison to the methods of the medical doctor; but in one way they are vastly superior. The medicine man treats the whole patient as best he can—not only the bodily ailment, but also the mind and the soul. He will devote his whole time—hours or days, as needed—to support the patient through visible ritual and prayer. And though he will take sustenance, the medicine man takes no fee but simply plays out his role as an honored member of the tribe.

VOODOO AND ZOMBIES

Popularly, Voodoo is the infamous black witchcraft of Haiti associated with *Zombies,* the "living dead." In common lore it is black magic to the *nth* degree. Technically, Voodoo is the religion of Haiti, recognized by the state in 1945 and believed in by perhaps 95 percent of the population. In reality, Voodoo represents a composite of a public religion, a private witchcraft, and a magical practice. Voodoo mixes together parts of the native West Indian tribal practices, parts of Roman Catholic liturgy and worship, and parts of the religious beliefs of the black slaves taken to the West Indies from Guinea and Dahomey between the seventeenth and early nineteenth centuries. The word "voodoo" is probably a corruption of *Vodun,* meaning god or spirit in the four languages spoken in Dahomey. Sister cults exist in New Orleans, in Cuba as Santeria, in Jamaica as Obeah, and in Brazil as Orisha. As befits a religion, Voodoo has a characteristic priesthood, theology, and ritual practice.

Voodoo theology centers on the *Loas,* divine spirits who are deified ancestors; some of these are loosely identified with the saints of the Roman Catholic religion. There is usually one place, a mythical paradise lost, the land of the gods, to which the worshippers travel in their rites. Damballah, the supreme god represented by a snake, is the leader of the *Radas,* the good gods. The goddess Erzulie is a black Venus, the Virgin of Voodoo, with one beautiful face and one ugly face: sexually insatiable but devoured with jealousy. She is the dispenser of love, beauty, and health—but also of vengeance and discord. The lower world of the *Petros,* the evil gods, is led both by Baron Samedi, the Lord of the cemetery, and by Prefect Duffant, the Devil.

The priest of Voodoo is the *hun'gan;* the priestess is the *mambo.* Like the shamans and medicine men, the priests have apparent powers as seers and clairvoyants, and they act as mediums in the trance state, which is basic to the rituals practiced. By repetitive drum beating and by ritual dancing an initiate of the religion becomes entranced. He or she is possessed by a Loa, who shows this possession by producing a characteristic movement in the initiate. The Loa then becomes incarnate—to dance briefly but gaily, to give supernatural counsel, and to accept sacrifices from the worshippers. In Voodoo, one person may be possessed by many Loas during a lifetime, although the family Loa tends to dominate—a remnant of an ancestral African totemism.

In a procedure reminiscent of the ancient mystery religions, the candidates must first study the Voodoo doctrine, and they must demonstrate their faith before entering the religion. They are initiated, during special Voodoo rites, into the lowest order of membership. Intermediate stages must be passed through before the baptism, which then serves as introduction for a hun'gan or mambo (highest) stage. Only the Petro rites initiate the members into the magical practices of Voodoo. The priests provide a sanctuary as a place of worship. It may only be a shed, supplied with a wooden table; an altar, decorated with pictures of the saints; and a center post, about which mystical geometric symbols are drawn on the floor with white meal and ashes.

In Haitian lore the psychic powers of the hun'gan can be so great as to produce the Zombie. Zombies are commonly thought to be dead people who walk about, as if they were alive. This ghoulish aspect of the black magic associated with Voodoo is believed to owe its existence to the herbal knowledge possessed by the witch doctors in Haiti. Zombies are not truly walking dead. They are thought to be live people poisoned, in secret, with an herb that destroys the mind and will, but leaves the body healthy. The immediate effect of the drug is to produce apparent death; actually, it is a state of minimal life. The families of the stricken persons, believing them dead, bury them. Later the drugged persons are dug up and revived. Their state now, however, is that of a Zombie, their minds destroyed—perhaps by the lack of oxygen intake during the interval of apparent death.

Some unscrupulous witch doctors in the past have used these Zombies to prove to their naive followers a power to raise the dead. Zombies are also believed to act as magical charms who can insure continued prosperity for businesses. Families are forced to guard the graves of their dead ones to prevent the evil practice of digging them up for prosperity insurance. Voodoo worshippers regard the Loas as a source of protection to themselves both against the Zombie practice and against the other evils that may exist in the Voodoo magic.

MODERN WITCHCRAFT

Like other religions, the pagan witchcraft sects perform a variety of ceremonies. From the descriptions of a number of self-professed witches we can piece together some features that are apparently common to the practice of modern

Anglo-Saxon witchcraft. Within the practices outlined we can expect to see wide variations.

The witches perform their rituals either singly or in groups. The witchcraft groups, called covens, vary widely in size. An ideal size is sometimes considered to be thirteen; six men, six women, and one leader—usually a woman. Worship is often directed toward a female principal. Monthly meetings, *esbats*, are held on the night of the full moon. There are also meetings held at the witching hour, midnight, on certain holidays called *sabbats*. The apparent connection to the Hebrew word sabbath is uncertain, and some authorities suggest the origin of sabbat is from "*s'esbettre*," to frolic.

The covens perform group ceremonies which worship and beseech aid from their gods and goddesses. In some older groups the mother goddess is usually called Hecate or Diana and the horned god is Pan or just the God of the Hunt. The rituals are religious ceremonies. In some sects spells, divination, and communication with the unseen may be practiced—all the elements commonly considered as magic. The asceticism common to traditional religions is rarely found in witchcraft sects.

There are two holidays which are especially important:

• The evening of October 31—Halloween, the feast of the dead, and

• The evening before May 1—Beltane, the fertility festival.

Witches often celebrate six other holidays:

• March 21—New Year's Day. This day stems from the ancient practice of astrology, where the vernal equinox was taken to be the start of the sun's annual journey through the signs of the zodiac.

• The evening before June 22—the Eve of St. John, midsummer night's eve.

• August 1—Lammas, the summer festival, or bread feast.

• September 22—the autumn festival.

• December 21—St. Thomas Day. Although the names St. Thomas and St. John suggest Christian saints, the origins of the witch festivals were older than Christianity and these holidays were sacred long before Christ.

• The evening of February 1—Candlemas, the winter festival.

• Halloween, Beltane, Lamma, and Candlemas are often treated as major sabbats.

The ceremonies at esbats and sabbats are both religious services and feasts. In some sects nudity, sexuality, and varied drugs play roles in their ceremonies and an altered state of consciousness is sought in order to make the psychic attainment of magical powers easier.

Many witchcraft sects still stay close to nature and have an intimate knowledge of her secrets. The witches are familiar with herbs for healing purposes as well as their possibilities as deadly poisons. In some sects no knowledge is written; it is passed on by word of mouth. The members learn about breath control as a means of inducing trance states. The habits of animals are among the secrets that may be passed down among the members of a particular coven. Some witches claim an ability to "call" wild animals from deep within the forest, and some keep an animal—a bird, a cat, a snake, a dog—as a constant companion. This leads to stories that the animal is the host for a *familiar*, a spirit that accompanies the witch.

The moon and stars dominate the night sky of the esbats and sabbats and, in a witchcraft close to nature, astrology becomes a natural counterpart in the magic of nature. Indeed, in today's explosion of interest in the occult it is common to find the greatest curiosity about both these topics.

Sybil Leek, who claims to be a witch, does not claim to ride a broom, nor can she turn someone into a toad. But she does claim to possess second sight—the ability to foresee the future, to foresee death. Indeed, witches claim to know the time of their own death, and arrangements are made in advance to distribute their craft possessions to a close relative who practices witchcraft. Otherwise their possessions must be burned.

A circle with a diameter of nine feet, drawn clockwise on the ground, plays a central part in witchcraft ceremonies and rites. Only within this circle do the witches operate; here they call on their gods or demons, and no breaks in the circle may be permitted: otherwise opposing forces could penetrate into the interior. Within this circle the witches and warlocks chant and dance nude, outdoors in a forest for those sects which really believe in back-to-nature, but indoors for the more comfort-loving sects.

MAGIC OR MIRACLE?

Religions, witchcraft included, play many roles within society. They establish a moral tone, often seeking to codify morality into a doctrine that expresses their view of good. At the core of religion is a mystic view of what lies beyond the apparent, a glimpse into the darkness on the other side, the supernatural.

Seemingly in all religions, there are found a few gifted experimentalists who explore the unknown to test that mystic vision, to verify old beliefs, to shape new ones. The psychic shamans send themselves outside their own bodies to discover unknown lands; the ecstatic St. Teresa of Avila sought and reported a mystic union with God; the cabalist Luria voyaged on the astral plane above the physical and named its pathways; the meditative Hindu mystics still search within, as they have done for thousands of years, and discover a cosmic consciousness without.

But, beyond these explorations, religions seek to bring back proofs which justify their beliefs. They seek, by producing unusual effects beyond natural explanation, to verify their view of nature and the supernatural: the saintliness of St. Joseph of Copertino is attested to by his levitation; the existence of the Voodoo Loas is shown when they possess the entranced worshipers; the power of good is revealed by the faith healer's power of restoration; God establishes the validity of Moses's mission with the plagues. Are these real? If so, are they magic? Are they miracles?

The answer seems to be, mostly, a point of view. The magic in our own religions forms the miraculous; the miracle of witchcraft is its magic. The scientific exploration of this miraculous magic will carry us through the next several chapters, where this magic appears in many different forms. It is strange to say that in its original form, in witchcraft, the magic seems not to have been a field for much scientific study. Perhaps, because of its mystery and secretiveness, the data are hard to acquire.

We have lectured to numerous students on the topics in this book, and a strange fact emerged. Of all the subjects we discuss, witchcraft is the one that fascinates them most. Yet, despite this deep interest that they display, witchcraft is the one topic that they believe in least. Time after time they have voted witchcraft top in interest and bottom in belief. Is it that the craft of the wise holds for them only the lure of the obscure? Is it the grip of the primitive on the sophisticated? Is it a yearning for a simpler set of beliefs, less demanding and more fulfilling than the ones we now possess?

CHAPTER FOUR
PSYCHIC PHENOMENA

PSI

Most people have experienced, at some time, an incident which has forced them to wonder whether there were not at play forces of a strange, perplexing quality, forces they simply could not understand. *Déjà vu* is an example. We step into a room that we are certain we have never visited previously; yet in our mind's eye we recognize familiar details, or remember incidents, that could only be associated with an earlier visit to this very room. As another, less common, example—a pervasive sense of uneasiness overcomes one, vague and unresolvable; later one learns that a critical event occurred at that moment to some loved one, perhaps far away.

These are simple illustrations of psychic phenomena. Stories of such a nature have come down through all history, everywhere in the world. Most ordinary people pragmatically accept such brushes with the unknown that lies beyond our physical senses. Perplexing and difficult to understand, but true. Why not?

Many facts, scientifically proven facts, are also perplexing and difficult to understand.

But scientists have a different reaction to such psychic events, phenomena which seemingly defy the laws of nature. These laws were first established as natural philosophy by the careful application of reason and experiment to the physical world around us. The fact that psychic phenomena seem to defy these rules has brought scientists face to face with a dilemma: *either* ignore these psychic events, pretend they do not exist, perhaps even assert that they are based on misinformation or chicanery—for they do not yield to reason; *or* acknowledge that there is a shadow world, one beyond the horizon of our present knowledge, senses, and reason. If we accept the second possibility then it is at present unclear how far this psychic shadow land of the unconscious, a paranatural domain beyond the border of what we now call physical reality, extends into the supposed realm of the supernatural.

By way of analogy, we might consider those early scientists who were experimenters in the field of optics. They were familiar enough with visible light but they were just beginning to wonder about the possibility of ultraviolet and infrared radiation. They had no apparatus for detecting or for measuring ultraviolet or infrared, both invisible to the human eye. They were faced with a similar hard dilemma. Are there such things? How can you tell? Maybe one but not the other? Maybe neither?

The psychic phenomena we discuss in this chapter fall into two broad groups. One is referred to as extrasensory perception, ESP; the other is psychokinesis, PK. We define these words immediately below in terms of some rather outlandish ideas.

EXTRASENSORY PERCEPTION

Extrasensory perception, ESP, is the ability to perceive or sense by means other than the known physical senses. Strictly speaking, for complete skeptics, we should say "presumed ability." The known senses, usually listed as the five traditional senses of sight, sound, touch, smell, and taste, actually include a number of other, more obscure, senses; for example, the sense of balance. ESP itself stands for three separate but linked paranatural phenomena: telepathy, clairvoyance, and precognition.

Telepathy refers to the ability of one mind to reach out and somehow communicate with another mind directly, but by means unknown. There is an obvious analogy here to a radio transmitter and receiver; except that, as we shall see, there is no known wave and no known terminal equipment.

Clairvoyance denotes the ability of a mind to make contact with a physical object by means not utilizing the senses. Only one mind is involved here. Clairvoyance, like telepathy, is an ESP of the present.

Precognition, however, is an ESP of the future. It is the faculty of knowing, or prophesying, the occurrence of future events. Prophets throughout history have claimed to have this ability, a fearful one.

To be complete one might also postulate retrocognition—the ability to know the past without recourse to memory or the senses. Clairvoyance, precognition, and retrocognition form a logical set of ESP abilities concerned with present, future, and past events. Retrocognition has sometimes been offered as the explanation of ghosts or apparitions.

Psychokinesis, PK, is the ability of a mind to control the motion of a physical object by paranormal means. Since it requires the "transmission" of a considerable force rather than a mere idea or vision, it would seem to be even further removed from normal reality than the telepathic or clairvoyant forms of ESP.

Both PK and ESP operate by means not presently known, means quite apart from the normal. This is why both are called paranormal phenomena. Their investigation is usually undertaken in the branch of psychology termed parapsychology. The composite set of PK and ESP phenomena are also referred to by the generic term Psi, derived from the Greek letter ψ. (The "psi" sound is similar to that in the words psychic, or psychology, the p being silent.)

The study of psychic phenomena splits quite naturally into cases that are produced in the laboratory and cases that occur spontaneously, outside the laboratory. The spontaneous cases form the great wealth of psychic lore that has prompted and still supplements laboratory studies. By their very nature spontaneous cases are difficult to document properly. They cannot be proven satisfactorily to outside parties. Of course, a psychic event, if it actually occurs, is as real without documentation as it would be with documentation. In an area of knowledge so far outside the normal, accepted sciences, however, documentation is absolutely necessary if one wishes to establish the trustworthiness of such phenomena.

Reports of spontaneous cases of ESP contain numerous instances claiming that this phenomenon occurred over great distances, or over wide spans of time, or both. Spontaneous PK is apparently present in *poltergeist* (German: playful ghost) phenomena. Here quite heavy objects are claimed to move about, sometimes in a violent fashion, without any obvious physical means producing the motion. The authenticity of such reported cases must be thoroughly checked.

In the laboratory, it is extremely difficult to distinguish between telepathy and clairvoyance. Indeed, it is quite possible that no laboratory experiment yet devised has succeeded in distinguishing, unambiguously, between these two capabilities. It has been suggested that they are merely two different facets of one phenomenon. Some tests we will describe later—those with Eileen Garrett—suggest, however, that there is a real difference between telepathy and clairvoyance. So we will keep the separate, individual names.

SPONTANEOUS CASES

There are many, many reports of spontaneous psychic experiences. Here are several cases which give the flavor of such reports.

• A four-year-old boy awoke screaming from a nightmare in Springfield, N. J.[1] He dreamt that his father was struggling to prevent himself from drowning in water, where he was surrounded by tall grass. His father soothed the boy as the lad told him his dream. Two days later the father and his brother-in-law were hunting in a marsh. The boat capsized and the brother-in-law drowned. But the father managed to attain land. As he struggled through the tall marsh grass, the father vividly remembered his son's dream.

• In Philadelphia, during World War II, a middle-aged woman dreamt that the S.S. *Oregon* was rammed by a vessel off Nantucket. She saw her son clinging to a raft with several other survivors and she woke screaming. That morning's paper pictured such an event, very much as she saw it. Her son, happily, was among the few survivors.

• In Ohio a woman, her husband, and their five-year-old child moved into a two-year-old house at a ridiculously low rent.[2] During their first night there they heard a terrific crash in the basement. This was followed by a noise like that of a metal tub rolling over. When they looked in the cellar the next morning they could find nothing that had fallen.

Subsequently, the woman—but not the husband—began to feel a monstrous "presence"; however, she never saw anything. The presence became so terrifying to her that the woman would wake up at night, shaking and hugging her child. The family stayed six months and then moved out. Just before they left the owner took the husband aside and asked him if anything unusual had happened to them during their stay. The owner then said the house was haunted by the first tenant who had lived there. He was a criminal who was being pursued by the police. He had stood on a metal tub in the basement and he had hanged himself by kicking the tub away.

• The husband of a California woman was killed in a car accident in February 1966.[3] The woman was grief stricken. She prayed for a sign that her husband's spirit lived on. Once, a week after the husband's death, the woman was standing in the nursery, looking at her youngest child who was only 2½ years old. Suddenly the mobile over the baby's crib began to turn at full swing, its music box playing; and it continued to turn for a full five minutes. The baby, asleep, had not moved. The mobile needed to be turned by a hand in order to play its music, yet no hand had turned it. The woman was filled with a feeling of deep assurance.

• Two brothers had recently worked on building construction in New York City. One brother, who was working overtime alone, became trapped in a ditch when a portable concrete mixer overturned on him. He attempted to send mental messages for help to his brother. His brother did, in fact, arrive unexpectedly several hours later. The brother had felt a premonition that something was wrong.

The first story, the dream of the father drowning, illustrates a case of precognition of an event two days distant. The second, of the collision of a vessel, is an example of clairvoyance over a distance of 300 miles. The haunting in the third case could be interpreted as retrocognition. The story of the woman widowed by a car accident is a *poltergeist* experience, in this case a friendly one. The last story, of the brother smothering in concrete, apparently demonstrates telepathy. It may, however, be as easily interpreted as clairvoyance. This story illustrates how difficult it is to separate the two phenomena.

Many of the stories containing spontaneous psychic reports deal with crises. But hauntings, although frightening at times, are often just unsettling. Sometimes, indeed, they are quite benign—and people seem to be able to put up with them for months, even years. We suspect that only the more dramatic psychic events get reported. Possibly many more such events occur, events that are not deemed worth reporting and that, in fact, may not even have been noticed. There is no doubt that the reports of some psychic events have no crisis content. They are not dramatic and are sometimes just humdrum.

The difficulty with believing the spontaneous cases of psychic phenomena is obvious. How can we tell whether the person reporting the case is lying or is telling the truth? Since there are usually no witnesses the events cannot be reproduced and it comes down to a question of faith in the integrity of the reporters. Only trained scientific investigators could be entrusted with the job of studying such cases. It is to be expected that if this type of hearsay evidence is the only evidence available then there will be many skeptics and disbelievers. The skepticism would exist not only among scientists, who are trained to be skeptical, but also among ordinary citizens, who have a great deal of common sense.

For many years to come the percentage of skeptical, doubting, or disbelieving scientists among those who study this field will probably remain high. This is because of two general characteristics pertaining to psychic events.

1. The psychic, or Psi, faculty operates substantially independent of space and time; it lies outside the conventional forces of nature.

2. Most individuals report experiencing psychic events only a very few times. This indicates that the faculty is either inherently weak or that it is strongly masked by our other senses and faculties.

A possible explanation of these two characteristics must be mentioned: that the Psi faculty does not exist. We, ourselves, think that the laboratory evidence we present below rules this explanation out. We agree it is inexplicable; but to us the evidence that it does exist is overwhelming.

INTO THE LABORATORY

The introduction of the study of ESP to the laboratory was a very important step into the occult land of the psychic. Laboratory ESP is inextricably linked with the name of Dr. J. B. Rhine (Fig. 4–1) who was the director, until 1965, of the Parapsychology Laboratory of Duke University in Durham, North Carolina. Since 1965, and until quite recently, Dr. Rhine was the director of an independent organization, the Institute for Parapsychology, which was sponsored by the Foundation For Research on the Nature of Man. As early as 1927, when he first came

Fig. 4-1. Dr. J. B. Rhine. Dr. Rhine has been a seminal figure in converting the study of psychic phenomena into a laboratory science. (Photo courtesy of the Foundation for Research in the Nature of Man.)

to Duke, Dr. Rhine decided that it was pointless to attempt to investigate the authenticity of various stories of psychic phenomena. By the time the investigator arrived either the conditions had changed, and there was nothing to investigate, or one had to estimate the credibility of various witnesses. In either event, there was then only an isolated tale, not a body of fact.

Dr. Rhine wanted to apply the standard techniques of a laboratory science to the investigation of psychic phenomena. He sought a reproducible experiment. If he could find conditions such that other scientists could duplicate an experiment of his and arrive at similar results, then he could hope to secure both their interest and their belief in the existence of these psychic phenomena. In other words, he wanted to move the study of such occurrences out of the primitive, descriptive, anecdotal stage into the experimental stage characteristic, say, of physics. It was the lack of reproducible experiments that kept both the scientists' interest and the belief in occult phenomena at a minimal level.

Dr. Rhine was not the first academic figure to work in this field—there were many others before him. As early as 1917 Professor John E. Coover of Stanford University published a voluminous statistical report on various psychic phenomena. Other, later researchers in the United States were Dr. E. B. Tichener of Cornell, Dr. William McDougall of Harvard and Duke, and Dr. Gardner Murphy of Harvard. Abroad, the names of Professors Charles Richet of the University of Paris, Henri Brugmans of the University of Groningen in the Netherlands, and S. G. Soal at Queen Mary College, London, stand out.

Even earlier, the world-famous physicist Sir Oliver Lodge of the University of Liverpool had become interested in the investigation of spiritualism. The Society for Psychical Research had been founded in 1882 in England to foster the dissemination of knowledge in this field, mainly through the study of spontaneous cases. But the originality and persistence of Dr. Rhine were outstanding. His insistence on the highest standards has made his results, and the entire field, much more interesting to the body of physical scientists whose respect he sought. The easy, gullible approval of the masses was something Dr. Rhine avoided.

In company with many pioneers in science, Dr. Rhine's work has sometimes been damned. Even his honesty has been questioned. In the 26 August 1955 issue of *Science* (p. 359), there appeared an article by George R. Price, then a research associate in the Department of Medicine of the University of Minnesota. Dr. Price stated quite frankly his opinion that the results of Dr. Rhine's work could best be accounted for by the assumption of fraud. Yes, fraud. Not Freud—fraud; and in nine pages of text he proceeded to support this view.

Sixteen and a half years later, there appeared the following letter to the editor of *Science*:[4]

> During the past year I have had some correspondence with J. B. Rhine which has convinced me that I was highly unfair to him in what I said in an article entitled, "Science and the Supernatural" published in *Science* in 1955 (26 Aug., p. 359). The article discussed possible fraud in extrasensory perception experiments. I suspect that I was similarly unfair in what I said about S. G. Soal in that paper.
>
> George R. Price

It is of some mild interest to note, in passing, that both of Dr. Price's communications—appearing 16½ years apart—began on the same page, page 359.

ESP CARDS

The initial means that Dr. Rhine adopted for his clairvoyance experiments were very simple. He made a special deck of 25 cards, designed by Dr. Zener of the Duke psychology department. Five cards had the symbol of a circle printed on one side, five had a cross, five a rectangle, five a star, and five an array of wavy lines. (See Fig. 4–2).

The experimenter shuffled the deck thoroughly and then placed it, face down, on the center of a table top. Seated at the table, in addition to the experimenter, was a subject who undertook to name the symbol on the underside of the top card of the deck. The experimenter recorded the subject's choice. After recording

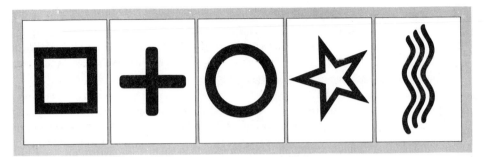

Fig. 4–2. The Zener deck of cards. They were widely used in early card testing for clairvoyance, telepathy, and precognition. (© J. B. Rhine, F.R.N.M.)

the subject's estimate for the top card, this card was removed, without exposure, and was placed nearby, also face down. Then the subject tried to guess the second card, which was now on top of the original stack. This choice was recorded and, without exposure, this card was transferred on top of the first one, also face down. The next cards were treated in a similar fashion. When the entire pack of cards had been dealt, and only then, the experimenter turned the stack over, revealing the first card on top, the second card next, and so on. He then made a comparison of the actual symbols with the subject's estimates. This was called a run. One run consisted of 25 estimates, guesses, surmises—call them "calls."

It is clear that just on the basis of mere chance a subject should guess one fifth of the cards correctly. The "subject" could be a machine generating random guesses, or a chimpanzee, or anything instead of a human being. It would still be expected to score 20 percent hits merely on the basis of probability, without involving any special powers.

At the beginning Dr. Rhine did not set out to test the entire population for possession of ESP; he only wanted to prove the existence of the ability by determining if *anyone* had it. So if, after several runs, a subject did not score appreciably above 20 percent of the number of guesses, the test was stopped. This, of course, left Dr. Rhine vulnerable to the charge that he was keeping a record of the high-percentage hits and throwing away all the low-percentage hits, and that if runs on poor subjects were included the results would be those of pure chance. We will treat this objection later.

The testing procedure is simple and open to a number of variations. After shuffling thoroughly, the deck can be placed face down on a table; the subject is asked to guess the cards from the top down through the deck. This test checks for clairvoyance. Precognition is tested by having the subject guess, ahead of time, the order of a deck of cards that will be shuffled and stacked subsequently. If the experimenter, or an aide, looks at the cards one at a time, from the top down, and attempts to project their images to the subject's mind, that is a test of telepathy; but really, we have no sure way of distinguishing these results from clairvoyance. For most subjects the scores above chance on telepathy, clairvoyance, and precognition tests are remarkably similar.

The card test is so simple that it is still widely used in many informal tests of ESP, although scientific tests have now evolved well beyond this card-guessing technique. A few simple precautions should be taken in such a card test. A new Zener deck should be very thoroughly shuffled, while a used pack may only require four to five dovetail shuffles. The cards should be screened from the subject at all times. The subject's success or failure in a forced test should be disclosed only at the end of a complete run. The subject should relax rather than try to concentrate. Only the experimenter should handle the cards and records, but the subject should double-check the recording of the results. A decision should be made before a run concerning the determination of a score: if a run is "for fun"—to get used to the procedure—decide that beforehand; do not use the data to draw a conclusion. All the runs that are "for real" must be used to determine the final outcome of a test. None should be discarded.

SMALL CHANCE

Before we can determine whether the Psi faculty is indicated in a subject's score, we must know the probability that the result of a test for ESP or PK is due to pure chance rather than to the Psi faculty being tested. This requires some analysis of statistics. Some results are summarized in Table 4–1, which lists the minimum number of hits one must make in a given number of runs in order to beat various odds against this happening by pure chance. With this table one can test oneself to see if there is any significance to the results—to see if there is likely to be a psychic factor present or if the results are such as to be reasonably expected by chance.

Suppose, for example, that we tested ourselves in one run and obtained 10 hits. Remember, the expected number of hits in one run, by pure chance, is 5 hits out of 25 calls; so if we actually obtained 10 hits it might seem, at first blush, that we had made a remarkable score. But, actually, it is found that any number of hits can be obtained by luck alone, with no psychic powers postulated, if we only try long enough. In fact, it is to be expected that out of 100 runs there should be 1 run in which 10 hits, instead of 5, are obtained by pure luck. So, as the table shows, the odds are 100:1 against getting 10 hits in one run by pure chance—and odds of 100 to 1 are of little significance. So after the first blush had faded we would be faced with dull reality—a rather mediocre score, signifying little. The table shows, in the first column opposite 1 run, that 10 hits are needed to obtain odds against chance of 100:1.

To discover how many hits are needed in one run to give odds of 1,000:1 (still odds of just fair significance) against it happening by chance, look at the second column opposite 1 run. Twelve hits are needed: this means that almost half the deck has to be called correctly. Now if just more than half the deck is called cor-

TABLE 4–1

NUMBER OF HITS NEEDED FOR ODDS (AGAINST CHANCE RESULT)

Number of Runs	100:1 Little Significance	1,000:1 Fair Significance	10,000:1 Good Significance
1	10	12	13
2	17	19	21
3	24	26	28
4	30	33	35
5	36	39	42
6	42	46	49
7	48	52	55
8	54	58	61
9	59	64	68
10	65	70	74
11	71	76	80
12	77	82	86
13	82	88	92
14	88	94	98
15	93	99	104
16	99	105	110
17	105	111	116
18	110	117	122
19	116	122	128
20	121	128	133

rectly, 13 hits in 25 calls, the odds against this happening by pure chance increase dramatically, to 10,000:1.

Similar situations arise with more than one run. One important feature of the statistics of chance is quite valuable to the experimenter: the greater the number of runs the smaller the relative increase in the number of hits needed to yield given odds against chance.

The ESP tests outlined above have produced some very startling results for Dr. Rhine. One of his best subjects in the very early thirties was a Duke student, A. J. Linzmayer, who later became his assistant. Dr. Rhine hynotized him one day and, while in this state, Linzmayer called 9 successive hits. The odds against this occurring by pure chance are about 2 million to 1. This is, of course, most unlikely. But it will happen. Then, the very next day, Linzmayer again scored 9 straight hits. Later that day, however, he began falling off on the percentage of hits and he was only guessing at the chance level of 20 percent after a total of 300 calls through the ESP deck. The third day, Linzmayer's last as a student at Duke, he obtained a very low score. But later in the day, after a relaxing auto ride, he scored 84 percent hits in a run, 21 correct guesses in 25 attempts. This was, of course, phenomenal. The probability of this occurring is incomprehensibly small: the odds are better than trillions to one against it happening by chance.

Dr. Rhine's most important subject was a divinity student, Hubert Pearce. Pearce, who incidentally believed his mother had psychic powers, was tested by an assistant of Dr. Rhine's, J. G. Pratt. The reports of some Pearce-Pratt distance tests, which will be mentioned subsequently, later achieved much notoriety. In the first 5,000 trials Pearce scored nearly 40 percent hits, for truly astronomical odds against chance. Pearce continued the tests daily over a period of two years with consistently high results. In one spectacular run, administered by Rhine himself, Pearce scored 25 hits in a run of 25 trials. In another set of runs, Pearce scored consistently high with a special deck of cards on which the printed symbols were particularly small, just to show that ordinary sight was not involved.

Toward the end of two years of consistently high scoring, however, Pearce's hits began to fall. A pattern was emerging: in laboratory tests, ESP declines with time. In the years since leaving Duke, his hits have remained consistently at chance level. The decline phenomenon seems common to all subjects, and its existence plagues all Psi tests. Subjects eventually find it very difficult to maintain interest over long time periods, and this psychological factor has often been suggested as a reason for the decline effect.

Rhine found numerous other students who scored a consistently high percentage of hits for long periods of time.

- June Bailey scored 32 percent and 40 percent hits in several thousand trials.

- May Frances Turner scored 36 percent in thousands of trials.

- Sara Ownbey consistently hit 32 percent to 44 percent. (In testing herself, previously, she had reached 60 percent.)

- George Zirkle not only hit 32 percent–36 percent average, over a long period in which occasionally there were stretches of 60 percent–65 percent hits, but once even equaled Pearce's record: 25 hits in a row. Incidentally, Zirkle and Ownbey subsequently married each other.

Dr. Rhine estimates that about one-fifth of the general population has a degree of ESP ability; other experimenters agree. One survey of 17,000 people found that 10 percent had had an unexplained psychic experience. In all the cases mentioned above, it is important to note the psychic power did not continue indefinitely. Some of the subjects just discontinued testing for one reason or another, while with the others the percentage of hits just dropped off and stayed at chance thereafter. It was noted very early that psychological factors strongly affect Psi scores. When subjects become distracted, tired, or disinterested their scores seem to move toward chance.

DISTANCE AND ESP

In order to test the effect of distance on ESP, as well as to eliminate any possible claim of error and fraud, Dr. Rhine instituted the now famous Pearce-Pratt test. Separated by a distance of 100 yards, in different buildings, Pratt would take the top card from the deck and lay it on the center of a table, face down, for one minute; then he would put it aside and put the next card in its place. Pearce was located in a reading cubicle in the Duke University Library. Their watches synchronized before the test, Pearce recorded his impressions of the card at the midpoints of each minute. After 50 cards the decks and the records were brought separately to Rhine. He first checked the results, and he was then double-checked by Pratt and Pearce.

In the first two days Pearce's hit percentages were 12 percent, 32 percent, and 20 percent—not very impressive; but the third day he hit 36 percent and 40 percent. His *average* for days 3, 4, 5, and 6 was 45.6 percent hits; the last day was his best—50.7 percent hits in 75 trials.

Rhine then increased the separation to 200 yards. Over a five-day span, the percentage hits varied from a low of 8 percent to a high of 48 percent. Altogether, in 1,100 guesses Pearce scored 26.8 percent hits. The odds against this happening by chance alone are 70 million to 1.

Many other investigations since the Pearce-Pratt test have demonstrated that Psi is substantially independent of distance, at least for several thousand miles. This agrees with the results obtained from various spontaneous cases of psychic phenomena. Though this is quite unlike most physical results, the tests seem to be unassailable. They must be accepted as fact, whether they are palatable or not.

THE BRITISH SECOND-GUESS

The outstanding British ESP experimenter is S. G. Soal, a former mathematician. After many years of laboratory card-testing for precognition, he was skeptical of its existence. Here, in precognition, the 25 guesses were all made first, in a sequence; then the cards were shuffled thoroughly and the pack was laid face down; finally the cards were examined one at a time, starting with the top card; and a comparison was made with the guesses. However, in reexamining the many data he had gathered with his outstanding subject, Basil Shackleton, Soal noted a pattern—the so-called displacement effect. Shackleton's scores were quite high if his guesses were compared with the second-next-card rather than with the one that was his target. In one run of 764 cards, Shackleton made 236 displaced precognition hits. The odds against achieving such a score by pure chance are far beyond our imagination—about a trillion to one.

To verify the displacement effect further Dr. Soal, together with Mrs. K. M. Goldney, an officer of the Society for Psychical Research, then carried on two and one half years of testing a former subject under very strict conditions. The displacement effect continued, and after 11,378 trials they obtained astounding odds against chance of 36 digits to 1!

This result is a remarkable, independent, laboratory verification of psychic precognitive ability. Numerous other investigations, aside from Duke University and outside the United States, have since demonstrated the Psi faculty.

THE TOSS OF A COIN

PK tests are most easily accomplished by coin flips or dice rolls. Here a person throws, say, six dice at a time and wills one number—for example, the 3—to be on top. This is done many times and the number of 3's is compared with the chance expectation of 1/6 the number of rolls of the dice. Or, as a variation, a coin is flipped 1,000 times and it is willed to fall heads up. By chance alone there should be 500 heads. The odds are that close to 500 heads will actually occur if chance is the only effect in evidence. The deviation from 500 is given by the actual number of heads minus the 500 expected heads.

In Germany a 17-year-old high-school boy, Kastor Seibel, had indicated significant PK ability in preliminary tests. At the beginning of further tests his mother, a widow, requested that the experiments be stopped. "For generations there has been in my family a hereditary . . . second sight . . . to foresee accidents and deaths . . . a heavy psychical burden for some members of my family."[5] Mrs. S. Seibel, though, was persuaded to allow further experiments, and Kastor had an excess deviation of 584 hits in 10,000 coin tosses—almost 12 percent above chance. This corresponds to odds greater than 10 billion to 1 against such a result occurring by chance alone. In 10 billion trials this result could be expected to happen just once.

If one considers that in PK a force is transmitted over some distance by an as yet unknown, nonphysical means then PK would seem to differ substantially from ESP, where only the transmission of some signal is required—not the transmission of substantial power.

Poltergeist phenomena do seem to involve the transmission of power but rarely over large distances. Here, apparently, heavy objects can be made to move, jump, or fall. These happenings have rarely been duplicated in the laboratory.

A wide variety of PK tests have been made and are summarized in Louisa Rhine's *Mind Over Matter*. The highest average above chance for PK has never approached the highest ESP scores above chance. But, averaged over many, many experiments, the averages above chance are similar. In Kastor Seibel's case, as in Pearce's case, we apparently see a strong inherited factor in Psi. This is something which is also indicated in the lore surrounding the many reports of spontaneous psychic phenomena.

CLAIRVOYANT MICE

A psychic sense has long been attributed to animals. Pierre Duval (a pseudonym for a famous French bioscientist) and Evelyn Montredon disclosed strong confirmation of this, at the end of 1967, by their careful work on mice.[6] Mice were placed, one at a time, into a cage six inches high, eight inches wide, and seventeen inches deep. A small partition, over which the mice could jump, separated the cage into two halves. Each half of the cage was separately connected to an electrical generator which, in a *random* fashion, delivered a mild electrical shock of five seconds duration once a minute. The point was to determine if a mouse had any precognitive faculty; for if it did, it could determine which half of the cage was to be shocked and jump the barrier to avoid the shock. Here random guessing, like coin guessing, will give the correct result once every two trials, just on the basis of pure chance.

Three types of mouse response occurred. Some mice, the stubborn ones, did not jump at all, disdaining the shock. Other mice, the lazy ones, jumped to the opposite side—but only after they had been shocked. And there they sat until they were shocked again. These were completely patterned responses —they depended on no outside influences. But a third type of response occurred among other mice, the "psychic" ones. These mice jumped in advance of the application of voltage, as if they were guessing the outcome. We will ignore the stubborn and lazy ones, concentrating only on the "psychic" ones.

In preliminary tests of 612 trials the "psychic" mice avoided the shock 53 times more than the chance expectation of 306 times—17 percent above chance. On a subsequent test of 8,314 trials, wild mice produced 258 more hits than called for by chance. This was 6 percent above chance; and for such a large number of trials this gave odds greater than 10 million to 1 against chance.

This experiment was done with great care. Typical of modern experiments, the location of the mice and the number of hits were recorded automatically. No person or device knew which half of the cage was the next one to be supplied with the shock voltage. The mice were isolated, and about half the trials took place when no one was around, so that there would be little chance of the mice picking up human cues. This experiment opened up a vast area of research, and preliminary confirmation of the experiment has already been obtained in this country. But an everpresent danger has jarred investigators of Psi powers in animals and, indeed, parapsychologists in general.

For over a year researchers at Dr. Rhine's parapsychology laboratory had attempted to extend the French investigations of animal Psi. Experimenters had implemented electrodes into brain areas of mice such that an electrical voltage applied to the electrodes gave the mice a very pleasant sensation. The stimulation was produced randomly, using a special electronic generator. Early results indicated that the mice could influence the otherwise random stimulation of the generator to produce stimulations whose number was above that to be expected by chance. Independent verification of these early results, however, showed only a chance level of stimulation.

At this point other experimenters noticed that the senior investigator, Dr. W. L., was manipulating the apparatus to obtain results above chance. They reported their results to Dr. Rhine, who confronted the senior researcher with the evidence. The investigator admitted his guilt and resigned. Thereupon Dr. Rhine notified the community of psychic investigators of the fraudulent occurrence, which was, of course, unrelated to the earlier French work.

As we have noted earlier and will reiterate later, the possibility of fraud is a stumbling block in all psychic investigations. But this possibility plagues all human endeavors. Indeed, another recent case of fraudulent research, also on mice but in the conventional area of genetic biology, was carried out at the Sloan-Kettering Center in New York City. It drew widespread attention just a few months before the case of Dr. W. L. But parapsychology is a less established, and a less accepted, science than is biology. It works with a more elusive set of effects than any other science, so the danger of fraud poses a much more serious threat to the life of this newborn science.

TESTING A "MEDIUM"

Dr. Rhine investigated the ESP ability of a group of people variously known as oracles or mediums. For three weeks he was able to test the well-known British spiritualist "medium," Mrs. Eileen Garrett, who had a reputation, like the magician Harry Houdini before her, for exposing fakes and frauds in the world of the occult. Actually, both Houdini and Mrs. Garrett wanted, more than anything else, to uncover unassailable evidence for the existence of occult phenomena; but they were honest enough to feel it their duty to reveal duplicity when they found it—and they were both very knowledgeable in this area.

After 8,000 trials with Mrs. Garrett, Dr. Rhine found her to be gifted, indeed, and in a unique way: she showed a large discrepancy between her telepathic and clairvoyant abilities, the only case where he ever encountered such a difference. The results below show her percentage hits both in her normal and trance states.[7] It should be understood there are few reliable data specifying just what is meant by a trance state.

	Telepathy	*Clairvoyance*
Awake	40.4 percent	22.8 percent
Trance	36.4 percent	22.4 percent

Mrs. Garrett was much better at telepathy. The overwhelming evidence, however, is that people score about equally well in telepathy and in clairvoyance.

Mediums and professional psychics do not necessarily do well in laboratory tests. The test surroundings are quite different from the environment in which they normally exercise their powers; and if trickery is normally used, close observation is evidently inhibiting. Indeed, Rhine's laboratory employs the services of a professional stage magician to guard its testing procedure against possible artifacts.

THE RANDOM GENERATOR

The mental attitude of a subject has a great effect on scoring ability. If subjects are tired, or distracted, or uninterested, or pressed to do well, or forced to adopt suggestions, they will not do well. Human errors in recording and transcription produce mistakes and can leave the way open for conscious or unconscious deception. Modern Psi testing procedures have largely succeeded in making the testing interesting, relaxing, and free of error and the possibility of deception. The recent work of Dr. Helmut Schmidt, a physicist and now Dr. Rhine's successor as head of FRNM, demonstrates these testing advances dramatically.[8]

The equipment for the Psi testing is a small, sealed, aluminum box containing four bright lights—a red, a green, a yellow, and a blue one. One light at a time will be lit, *randomly*. The subjects press a button under the lamp they think will light. The light chosen is determined by the time of emission of beta particles from a harmless, but radioactive, strontium 90 source enclosed in the box. The quantum processes which govern the time of emission ensure that it is random. Computer evaluation of 5 million automatic trials verified the random lighting. The subjects make guesses by pressing a button while, through internal computer circuits, emission of the very next beta particle selects the light. Counters on the box advance to register the trial and score the hit, if a hit is made.

The selection is open-ended: no set number of red, green, yellow, or blue lights must appear. So the subjects are allowed to see the score immediately and are continually kept challenged and interested. The subjects can proceed at their own pace on the sealed unit and work whenever the mood strikes, without direct supervision. The mood is purposely kept informal. No human errors can affect the recording.

One test utilizing this equipment involved a student psychic and two mediums, all chosen for the abilities they showed on preliminary tests. The three subjects underwent 63,066 trials, producing 691 extra hits: 5.8 percent above chance. This test can be interpreted either as one involving precognitive ESP or as one involving PK. The probability of a hit here is, of course, 1 in 4. The odds against chance in this test calculate out to be 500 million to 1. To disregard such results because they do not fit into our scheme of logic does not seem sensible.

SHAPING A DREAM

Seeing these golden stars . . . the night sky with the gold stars in it . . . Sort of some more light mood or more holidayish . . . when I was on the island . . . It seemed there were a few small plants here and there . . . I think one of the men is wearing a shirt with alternating stripes which might be like the bees and the stripes they had on. And it would be a foreign land . . . .[9]

The words are those of Dr. Robert Van de Castle, summarizing his night's dreams, on his fourth night as a subject in the dream telepathy experiments of Ullman and Krippner. These experiments were part of a series that had long been conducted at the Dream Laboratory of the Maimonides Medical Center, in Brooklyn, New York.

Once each night, for eight nights, after Dr. Van de Castle had gone to sleep, one target picture was chosen, at random, from eight art pictures. A compatible young woman viewed the target picture and attempted to transmit her view to the sleeping Dr. Van de Castle by concentrating on the target during the long night. She hoped to shape Van de Castle's dreams to various portions of the picture. This particular night the target was "Kathak Dancing Girls," a picture showing two girls dancing in a meadow in India, robed in brightly striped costumes. Overhead, the blue sky held golden star-like objects in the background.

After the night's session at the Dream Laboratory the subject reported his dreams. He was then shown all the eight pictures from which the one selected had been taken and he was asked to rank them in accordance with his dreams, from one to eight. A rank of one signified the highest correspondence, while eight represented the least. A "hit" was recorded if the picture actually used for the telepathy was ranked either 1, 2, 3, or 4. A "miss" was recorded if the projected picture was ranked 5, 6, 7, or 8. Then a set of independent judges made a separate evaluation, based on the subject's report of his dreams.

Robert Van de Castle was an extraordinary subject. Many people remember but a few fragments of their dreams upon awakening. But Van de Castle had unusual dream recall and remembered a surprisingly large range of details from his dreams. On earlier occasions, elsewhere, he had displayed a strong telepathic (clairvoyant?) content in his dreams, and he was anxious to test himself in the Maimonides experiments. Van de Castle's performance there was outstanding. In the eight nights of testing, Van de Castle achieved the following scores in his ranking of the target pictures: 1, 4, 3, 2, 3, 2, 3, 1—eight hits and no misses. There were two direct hits (number one rank) which came on the first and last nights. The odds against this overall scoring by chance alone were 256 to 1. The independent judges, using Van de Castle's dream descriptions, obtained only six hits and two misses; but five of the six hits were direct hits!

The Maimonides dream-telepathy experiments have investigated a number of other subjects in tests of varying lengths. In 40 complete sets of scores, 15 by the subjects themselves and 25 by the independent judges, the target pictures scored more hits than the other pictures 30 times out of the 40. In 12 of these 30 times of higher scoring the number of excess hits was considered statistically strong enough to confirm the existence of ESP. In the whole series of tests, hits exceeded misses 414 to 253, a result to be expected by chance only 1 time out of every 140,000 times that such a whole series is run.

These tests have gone a long way toward confirming the belief that the dream state of sleep is an altered state of consciousness which possesses psychic overtones. The idea of prophetic revelations in dreams is, of course, an old one. The Bible, for example, has many instances. But until the Maimonides experiments there was nothing approaching a scientific verification.

TWO MODERN PSYCHICS

People sometimes harbor a puzzled question in their minds about psychic phenomena. Why are there no psychic prodigies nowadays with talents to rival Fr. Joseph, D. D. Home, Eileen Garrett, or Hubert Pearce? Or to rival those great psychic mediums, Eusapia Palladino and Mrs. Piper, whom we shall discuss in later chapters? The answer is: if we only look, the prodigies are here. Time confers a halo of mystery on the past and we seem to grant it a greater wealth of talent than we are ready to acknowledge for the present. But if we look about we do find many psychic prodigies in our own time. We discuss here two possible candidates for historical recognition as psychics: the Russian, Madam Nina Kulagina, and the Israeli, Uri Geller.

Nina Kulagina has been studied for over 10 years by Professor Sergeyev of Leningrad University.[10] She had initially demonstrated an ability at skin reading—she could sense and read, while blindfolded, printed material on paper placed under her fingers. She experimented with her talent and found that she could make the paper move. After considerable practice Madam Kulagina developed an ability to make small objects move without touching them. Often she concentrated deeply and rotated her hands vigorously above the objects, but without touching the objects. In rarer instances she needed only to focus her attention and eyes upon the object in order to make it move. She usually warms up by causing a compass needle to rotate without touching the compass. Films show her moving compasses, matches, fountain pens, and other small objects without contact. The objects are commonly of less than 5 grams mass, although she has moved objects of more than 20 grams.

The mental strain involved in her psychokinesis often leaves Madam Kulagina exhausted. Curiously, she also possesses a negative healing power. She can inflict a serious burn on a person's skin simply by holding the skin or by putting some object in contact with the skin. This power seems to involve no mental strain. It is also said to affect photographic film.

Experiments give us only a rudimentary hint as to the source of Madam Kulagina's ability. The electrostatic field about her body is not unusually large and, indeed, seems only about three quarters as large as that of other people. There is a suggestion, in experiments, that her psychokinetic ability depends upon ionization effects. Professor Sergeyev suggests that ultraviolet radiation, originating in some manner from Madam Kulagina when she concentrates, produces the ionization and the skin burning.

Madam Kulagina has made herself available to numerous researchers and thorough investigation has left almost no room for trickery. One investigator writes "Madam K. is the answer to a parapsychologist's prayer—she will submit to any test, any condition . . . she realizes it is our duty to make sure that no tricks are used. She does not require reduced illumination nor any means for subterfuge."[11]

Our second candidate has had a more mixed appraisal of the reality of his talents. The Israeli sensitive, Uri Geller, is famous for his "mental" ability to bend keys and spoons and to cause broken watches to run again. He has appeared successfully—and unsuccessfully—on numerous American and foreign television shows. And beyond psychokinesis his apparent talents extend to telepathy, clairvoyance, and teleportation. The young Uri, who left Israel under uncertain circumstances and now lives in the United States, tours widely and is an accomplished and personable stage performer. Many people have pointed out that many of the effects Geller has demonstrated on television and on stage are well within the ability of a competent stage magician. Is there more to his ability?

Two physicists, Russell Targ and Dr. Harold Puthoff, have carried out rigorous experiments with Geller at the Stanford Research Institute. Great pains were taken to avoid the possibility of trickery and cheating. The results were reported both in a conference proceedings, edited by the astronaut, Edgar Mitchell,[12] and in the highly respected British Science journal, *Nature*.[13] The fact that *Nature* published such an article, by the way, was in itself a notable achievement for the whole field of psychic research. *Nature* did much soul searching before it took this step, and it printed a full-page editorial in the same issue as that in which the article appeared, explaining the reasoning behind such a radical step.

The two experiments reported in the conference procedure were set up to test Geller's ESP and PK abilities. The protocol of the ESP experiments allowed Geller to "pass" any trial in which he was uncertain of his perception.

In a double-blind experiment a single die was placed in a closed metal box, which was then shaken by an experimenter and set down. Geller looked at the box and, without touching it, called out his guess as to which face was uppermost. Ten trials were made. In two of these Geller passed his guess; but he correctly guessed the die number on *all* of the eight remaining trials. The chance probability of this occurrence is nearly one in a million.

In a different experiment Geller was asked to identify which one of ten cans contained an object. The cans were prearranged by a laboratory assistant before Geller, with the experimenters, entered the room. In fourteen trials, Geller declined to guess twice. And, again, *all* of Geller's guesses proved to be correct. The olds against this being pure chance are enormous—one in a trillion.

In the set of careful tests reported in *Nature* Geller attempted to draw a picture corresponding to that drawn by an experimenter in an outside room. Uri was seated in a metal, shielded room. The experimenter outside chose, at random, a word from a dictionary and set out to draw a picture suggested to him by the word. Geller, inside the shielded room, sought to reproduce the picture. Geller chose not to submit a drawing three times; but the ten drawings he did produce showed some remarkable correspondences to the original drawings. In several cases the correspondence was actually startling. Independent judges were asked to match Geller's drawings to the originals. They did so without a miss. The odds against a chance correspondence here are three million to one.

And yet other experiments suggested that Geller could mentally influence a test balance and a magnetometer—a device to measure a magnetic field.

The overall results of these experiments are almost unbelievable. The odds are overwhelming that chance was not the factor operating with Geller. A unique psychic ability or deception are alternative explanations.[14] If the stringent precautions of Targ and Puthoff against fraud were efficacious then their tests on Uri Geller place Geller's psychic powers on a par with those of the most famous psychic prodigies of all time.

PSI SUMMARIZED

We present here a general summary of the findings of extensive Psi tests. Some of these effects are now so well established that they may be considered psychic laws. True, some of these psychic laws seem to be at variance with long-established laws in other fields. Precognitive tests bear witness that Psi is independent of time, and this conflicts with our present concept of causality derived both from science and from our everyday experience. Again, the Psi decline effect makes it difficult to design the definitely reproducible experiment which Rhine sought. Nevertheless, the evidence is now so overwhelming that any open-minded person must consider these parapsychological laws as laws of a still-obscure part of nature. We do not yet understand them—but they are true, nevertheless.

• Psi is an inherently unconscious attribute. In laboratory tests a subject does not know when he or she is scoring well, or when poorly. In the reports of spontaneous cases a strong conviction does occur in over half the cases; the conviction, however, is based on unconscious feelings that emerge to the conscious level—intuition.

• The average scores of gifted people may range as high as 5–6 percent above chance on extended ESP tests, and a bit less than this on PK tests. The extraordinary results presented earlier are the *very* exceptional cases found with ESP; they are almost never found with PK.

• PK has been confirmed in the laboratory mainly on moving items. *Poltergeist* phenomena suggest that PK may occur with stationary items as well.

• On the average, people's scores are very close to the chance expectation; but the variation from the chance value appears to be different from what one would expect chance to produce. Psi scores sometimes are much too low to be due to chance alone: this is referred to as *Psi missing*, and it can balance off *Psi hitting* in a test, to give an average score in a nonchance way. For normal people ESP gives scores close to the average, but with differences from some of the more subtle characteristics that chance must have. In these cases ESP appears very much as nonchance masquerading as chance.

• On the average, Psi hitting is highest at the beginning of a run and declines toward the end of the run. The first runs in a test score highest, and scores drop off toward chance as the test proceeds. Sometimes upturns in the scores occur before the end of the run and before the end of the test. This overall pattern is characteristic of both ESP and PK tests.

• Heredity may play a strong role in conferring an unusual psychic ability on people.

• Animals, as well as humans, display psychic abilities. Tests on lower animal forms suggest they have a paranormal sense, but these tests require fuller confirmation.

• Mood strongly affects scores. Those who believe in ESP do better, by a few percent, than those who do not.[15] Interest is vital for good scores.

• Many factors do not strongly affect average ESP scores. Some of these are sex, intelligence, practice, and ethnic background. Biofeedback techniques seem effective at times.

• Alcohol, drugs, lack of confidence, all tend to depress the scores. Hypnosis sometimes seems to affect the scores. It is the frame of mind while under hypnosis that seems to be decisive.[16]

• ESP acts substantially independent of distance (up to thousands of miles) and also of time.[17] This is a *major* empirical result of Psi research. It is not explainable at present. It seems to contradict much of what we presently understand within the natural sciences. PK, however, appears to drop off strongly with distance.

• Psi has been confirmed, time and again, by numerous investigators, in different laboratories throughout the world, with a certitude outside any reasonable possibility of error or chance expectation. As early as 1937 Dr. Rhine asserted: Psi has been conclusively demonstrated. Further extensive work has certainly made this statement true in 1976.

THE PROSECUTION

As told above, the story of ESP is not a completely balanced account; it is more nearly like the brief of a lawyer in a defense case charged with outlining the case for ESP. In many respects a convincing case has been made. Now it is necessary to bring in the other side. We will list some of the objections that can be raised to Psi research. In each of the following paragraphs there is, after each objection, a reply to the objection, made on behalf of the defense.

What are the complete figures, not only on those subjects who have a high percentage of hits but also on those with a low percentage? Even with pure chance, without the operation of any supernatural force, one would expect streaks of luck; some individuals would score high, others low. Maybe the high scores presented are balanced by the subjects you have chosen to ignore.

Apply this argument to the quantum-computerized random generator experiment of Dr. Schmidt, as an example. The odds against this outcome, by chance alone, are 500 million to one. This means that 500 million additional experiments, each covering over 63,066 trials would have to be run, and come out as chance dictates, before the outcome found by Dr. Schmidt could be attributed to insignificant chance. Suppose, instead, that only *two* experiments were run; and that the second came out with the same percentage *below* chance as Dr. Schmidt found above chance for the first. Then, surprisingly, the case for Psi would be *reinforced* rather than demolished, even though the average of the two experiments would now be at chance. This second result would, itself, be so far outside chance (again, 500 million to one) as to demand a nonchance explanation. All of the unreported tests so far carried out on Psi, if scoring at chance, can only go a fraction of the way to offsetting this one experiment; they cannot possibly offset just the few positive results presented above.

Unfair as it may seem, it is part of the scientific system that the burden of proof is on the innovator. Part of the necessary proof, whether in physics or medicine, is some inkling of an idea as to a mechanism. The mere collection of data is insufficient to give convincing proof of the existence of a psychic force. How is the force propagated? Without a plausible explanation few sophisticated scientists will find Psi acceptable. For example, in physics the Davisson-Germer experiment revealed that electrons reflected from a metal surface just as if they were waves instead of particles. But the very article presenting the data also showed what the wavelength of the electrons must be if they were, indeed, waves and then showed that the electrons actually existed at those places where the waves reinforced each other. This radical idea could not then be logically resisted, and it was not. Without such a theory to back up the data of Psi— which have such unorthodox implications—scientists find it quite easy to discount Psi. The burden of proof is on anyone trying to show the existence of ESP. Part of this burden is the suggestion of a mechanism.

Many important scientific results were announced without any theory to support them; the theory was developed later, often by others. For example, in 1831 Michael Faraday announced his law of the induction of voltage. It was only in 1905 that Albert Einstein, in his theory of special relativity, gave an explanation for this effect. Should Faraday have allowed this data to be unpublished for lack of a theory? Our whole technology of electrical power is based on Faraday's results.

From the outset, scientists studying the psychic sought a reproducible experiment. They have not produced one. The subjects who showed this supposed psychic power to an outstanding extent have, one by one, at some point or another, ceased displaying it. Evidence based on the experience of these subjects is no better than hearsay, or folklore, or an unsubstantiable tale.

The decline effect does, indeed, make Psi studies frustrating. However, its very presence in the data presents a structure that chance would not produce: a nonchance effect is at work, governed by some still unclear law, an effect that produces this nonchance decline phenomenon. The vagaries of ESP and PK testing irk the natural scientists, accustomed to working with things, objects, and ideas —inanimate nature. These uncertainties, however, are familiar to psychologists and scientists who are used to working with humans. Results like the decline effect may eventually find their origin in the psychological laws governing Psi in human subjects. Although experiments demonstrating Psi are not reproducible at will, they have nevertheless been reproduced repeatedly, up to the very present, in numerous independent laboratories.

One likely explanation for the ESP data is that they simply show correlations of an extrachance effect which are as yet not well understood. Nevertheless, they will be understood eventually and will not require a paranatural hypothesis.

This argument appeals to not-yet-understood correlations which produce extrachance results. How does this differ from not-yet-understood ESP which produces extrachance results? It does not differ at all. Once an explanation of the paranatural emerges then our arena of reality will enlarge—the paranatural will no longer be outside the natural.

Dr. Rhine never allowed "ringers" in his ESP tests. He did not require his subjects to guess the supposed values of a face-down Zener deck when some or all of the cards were blank or had designs of some extraneous kind. It is clear he does not have any confidence in their ability to detect this deviation. Why should anyone have confidence?

Psi phenomena are very weak effects and they can be detected only with difficulty, at best. Why make the situation far from best? Why make it, in fact, worst? Psychological factors like confidence are absolutely essential to the success of such tests. A subject who thinks he or she may be a victim is not likely to gain confidence. Such a procedure of introducing ringers would be conducive to failure.

THE FUTURE

Precognition is a phenomenon which, a priori, seems to be impossible without violating our commonsense ideas of cause and effect. Critics often raise this question concerning the implications of precognition: If one knew in advance that something were going to happen, could one not take steps to circumvent the occurrence? But if one took such steps, and the event that was foreseen did not happen, then what was foreseen was false. A mother dreamt that at 4:15 A.M. the chandelier in her baby's room would fall and kill her baby. The dream was so frightening that the woman woke her husband, and he moved the baby. At 4:15 A.M. the chandelier fell. But the baby was safe. And the dream was false. If we accept the dream as precognition, what future did it precognize? Are there many futures we can sense while we live but one? Can we, then, use the present to sense the future and so alter the future sensed? But what, then, is cause and effect if the future alters the present and, also, itself? We will meet these questions once again in our last chapter. Scientists in quantum mechanics have confronted similar paradoxes.

Fatalists might argue that fate can not be parried, nor the future altered. The following excerpt from the play *Sheppey*, by W. Somerset Maugham, illustrates this point rather well.

DEATH SPEAKS: There was a merchant in Baghdad who sent his servant to market to buy provisions and in a little while the servant came back, white and trembling, and said, Master, just now when I was in the market-place I was jostled by a woman in the crowd and when I turned I saw it was Death that jostled me. She looked at me and made a threatening gesture; now, lend me your horse, and I will ride away from this city and avoid my fate. I will go to Samarra and there Death will not find me. The merchant lent him his horse, and the servant mounted it, and he dug his spurs in its flanks and as fast as the horse could gallop he went. Then the merchant went down to the market-place and he saw me standing in the crowd and he came to me and said, Why did you make a threatening gesture to my servant when you saw him this morning? That was not a threatening gesture, I said, it was only a start of surprise. I was astonished to see him in Baghdad, for I had an appointment with him tonight in Samarra.*

So, predestination takes precognition off the hook of logic. If all events have been programmed on an IBM card, this includes the precognition, the vision of the future. It was *the movement of the child that was fated, not the death seen in the vision.* However, predestination hoists humanity on another petard which is even worse than that caused by precognition: morality. For if all events are predestined then we are not responsible for our actions. Why punish anyone for a crime if it is not really his or her fault? If society does not like what someone does, why blame that person?—blame God. Or fate. People can feel free to do whatever they wish, for it is predestined—it is the will of Allah. Even the punishment, unfair as it is, must then be predetermined. But the feeling of freedom is illusory, for there is no free will if predestination reigns.

Experimental evidence of precognition raises troublesome questions, indeed. But the evidence is there. It should not be dismissed. As for the questions—they remain to be answered.

THE PERPLEXING PRESENT

The experimental evidence for Psi raises other puzzles for scientists. This weak psychic faculty does not fall off substantially with time or space—it seems independent of both. If we ascribe some particular degree of strength to our Psi faculty, that strength is then found to be, usually, quite small; nevertheless, it does not diminish when probing events at great distances or other times.

Yet, paradoxically, the faculty is amazingly precise. Pearce was able to sense the characters on the single card laid out by Pratt 100 yards away—despite not only the 24 other cards not to be sensed but, also, the hundreds of millions of characters in all the surrounding written material in the Duke University Library.

---

* From *Sheppey*, copyright 1933 by W. Somerset Maugham. Reprinted by permission of Doubleday & Co., Inc.

Still, a subject could probably not detect a ringer injected into the card deck, nor, in fact, a whole deck of blank cards. In that sense the faculty is a very fuzzy, diffuse one. So Psi is both precise and diffuse.

The paradoxical precise-diffuse character of Psi should strike a responsive chord in the hearts of physicists. It is this schizoid character which has bedeviled several generations of physicists seeking an understanding of one of the cornerstones of modern quantum theory, the wave function. This is used to describe, among other things, the wave properties of an electron, which is usually considered a particle. By a strange coincidence, the wave function is also described by the greek letter, psi.

The quantum psi function determines the probability of finding a particle, say an electron, at some place and time. The function is itself diffuse (although not as diffuse as Rhine's Psi is), but the particle it describes is quite precise. An electron within a radioactive atom may interact with the atom's nucleus, even though the volume of the nucleus is less than one tenth of a billionth of that of the electron's psi function. The paradoxes, and causality have troubled physicists inquiring into the nature of the psi function. The psi function is physically real, beyond doubt; though mathematically it is not real but complex, containing an imaginary component. Today we can write equations to predict its behavior, and two generations of physicists, chemists, and engineers have found these equations, though difficult, correct.[18]

How do we sum up our feelings concerning the validity of ESP? These unexplained phenomena do exist, and they cannot be explained by chance. Yet we, also, must listen to the critics. One cannot simply assert that the laws of physical science do not apply to ESP. One does not easily discard the relation between cause and effect, nor our sense of free will. If Psi is independent of *all* space and time, is the *whole* universe held in *one* mind? The facts of Psi place a difficult burden on a rational approach.

Perhaps the old Jewish folk tale of the rabbi listening to the quarreling couple best gives our view.

"He is lazy. He plays cards all the time. He runs around with other women. No man should do that," said the wife.

"You are right," said the rabbi.

"She is very sloppy. She can't cook anything. She spends too much money on her clothes. How can a man live with that?" said the husband.

"You are right," said the rabbi.

The rabbi's wife interrupted. "How can they both be right? Either she is right or he is right. Take your choice. You can't have both."

The rabbi thought a while.

"You know," he said, finally, "you are right too."

CHAPTER FIVE

BRAIN WAVES, DREAMS, & DRUGS

■ Altered States of Consciousness   ■ Entranced
■ Brain Waves   ■ To Sleep . . . to Dream   ■ The Dream People
■ Nicotine and Dr. Freud   ■ My Cup of Tea   ■ Alcohol and the Barbiturates
■ Marijuana   ■ The Amphetamines and Cocaine
■ Narcotics   ■ The Psychedelics

ALTERED STATES OF CONSCIOUSNESS

Consciousness means awareness. The normal state of awareness or consciousness is characterized by normal sensations, emotions, thoughts, and other mental attributes. But what is normal? Certainly, what is normal consciousness for one person may be far from normal for another; in fact, what is normal awareness for one person today may be abnormal for that person tomorrow.

Is a dog conscious? Since dogs can and do respond to complex stimuli they must be aware of them. But if a dog may be said to be conscious, is a tree conscious? Shine light on it from one direction and the leaves will turn, be it ever so slowly, that way. Few would care to make the definition so broad that plants, in responding to simple stimuli, would be said to be conscious. Suppose we try to limit the range of applicability by saying that introspective thought is a necessary component of consciousness. An inward turning of the mind, especially the power of judgment and reason, then becomes a criterion for the determination of normal consciousness. So this grants no normal consciousness to the baby exploring its new world on its hands and knees.

Between the two extremes of a simple, living response to stimuli and of life complex enough to support introspection lies a spectrum of mental functioning in the upper part of which lies the range for the normal state of consciousness of a human mind. Having thus, unsatisfactorily, disposed of the problem of defining a normal state of consciousness, we can now define an altered state of consciousness as "a qualitative alteration in the overall pattern of mental functioning."[1]

We all know of one state of awareness which differs from our normal state of consciousness: the dream state, during which the mind orchestrates a rich variety of sounds, sights, and emotions while blocking off most normal senses. Not all outside stimuli are blocked off, however: a loud cry or an unaccustomed cough from a child in the next room will instantly waken a sleeping parent.

In this chapter we discuss a few of the many states of consciousness. A complete list of different altered states of consciousness would be awesome both in length and variety. Such states can differ greatly, one from another; but since consciousness is a property of the mind and there is yet only the vaguest inkling of the working of the mind, all these altered states of consciousness have one thing in common—though we have some slight knowledge of them, more is hidden than is revealed.

Everyone experiences not only the normal, awake state of consciousness but also the dream, hypnagogic, and hypnopompic states found in sleep. (The hypnagogic state is the transitional state experienced when entering the sleep state, while the hypnopompic state is the one encountered when emerging from sleep.) Alcoholic intoxication and various other drug-induced states of consciousness are encountered less frequently; they carry potential dangers to the individual. The schizophrenic state is associated with mental illness. We will treat the ecstatic and meditative states more fully in the next chapter. The term "trance state" commonly refers to either one of these two distinct sets of states of consciousness. Strangely, the hypnotic state of consciousness, like the autohypnotic one, seems to be only slightly, if at all, different from the normal conscious state.

ENTRANCED

Outside reality enters our consciousness through our senses and is integrated via the central nervous system (mainly the brain) into the memory, the patterned behavior, and the other subconscious processes. This total, composite subjective picture of reality forms a state of consciousness. Most altered states of consciousness lead into one of two opposite directions. In one direction, external impressions understimulate the senses. This produces a tranquil, relaxed, meditative state of consciousness. In the opposite direction the senses are overstimulated. This leads to an aroused, hallucinogenic, consciousness-expanded, or ecstatic view of reality.

A wide variety of states of consciousness lie along these two paths, the meditative and the ecstatic. Such states of consciousness may be produced from without, by restricting or by enhancing the impressions assaulting the senses. Or they may be produced from within, by self-control—in ecstasy by favoring the sympathetic nervous system; and in meditation by favoring the parasympathetic nervous system. The ecstatic and meditative states of consciousness lie at the base of many psychic practices.

The altered states of consciousness due to extreme understimulation of the senses range from a mild variation or abnormality to a complete freaking out. An extreme example of the latter is given by the punishment of solitary confinement in jail. Nothing harmful is done to the prisoner; nothing good is done either. In fact, *nothing at all* happens—no variations of sight, sound, smell, or any other sensation. The frightening result is an altered state of consciousness that is so severe that it falls under the heading of torture.

A much milder variation of the same understimulation may be produced by sheer boredom or monotonous conditions. Travelers on the long, lonely desert, or sailors on a long, solitary sea voyage, or Eskimos hunting in the arctic tundra are all subject to the problems of hallucinatory mind derangements. A pilot flying alone, high in the sky, is subject to similar difficulties, and we wonder about Amelia Earhart's conscious state on her last, lonely flight over the endless South Pacific before her tragic disappearance. Driving an auto at night on the lonely, straight roads of the great midwestern plains also tends to produce such abnormal states of consciousness, which are the cause of many improbable accidents.

Hospitals provide several examples of the type of monotony which may lead patients to "go out of their minds." A victim of poliomyelitis who must live in a respirator tank is subject to sensory understimulation. So are patients whose head and limbs are in traction, or in plaster of paris casts. Any person whose head must be immobilized for a fairly long time is also subject to such an altered state.

The opposite type of abnormal state of consciousness is produced by extreme overstimulation of the senses. When prisoners in jail are given the "third degree" it is often possible to get them to say things that they would not conceivably say in a normal frame of mind (which is why the third degree is forbidden in civilized societies). Hundreds of thousands of people who died after confessing to witchcraft were victims of an altered state of consciousness induced by torture. The brainwashing techniques employed in the thirties in the Soviet Union were only a modern, sophisticated variation of this method. Arthur Koestler's *Darkness at Noon* provides many insights showing how dedicated communists are manipulated into a frame of mind that permits them to confess to crimes against communism of which they are innocent.

Certain religious revival meetings produce an extremely emotional ritual which batters the senses of the participants, thereby evoking an altered consciousness. This state is often brought on by loud, monotonous chanting in unison on the part of the congregation, combined with a back and forth interplay between the leader and the assembly that builds ultimately to an uncontrollable peak of frenzy and religious excitement. "Speaking in tongues" is a manifestation sometimes evoked in this altered state.

The whirling dervishes are members of an ancient Islamic religious sect who achieve a similar altered consciousness, a sense of communion with God, by a rhythmic and monotonous, intensely physical dance. The dancers are often well into the trance state from their chanting and flute playing even before they begin their continuous whirling. Many of the orgiastic witch ceremonies of the Middle Ages may have put the participants into a trance state suggesting possession by the Devil. The Voodoo dancers in Haiti end in a frenzy of spasmodic, jerking motions which are revered as a symptom of possession by a familial god.

A common example of an altered state of consciousness brought on by intense stimulation of the senses, though one seldom mentioned in public, is that achieved during sexual orgasm. An uncommon example is the fugue, which is characterized by unusual actions, such as wandering, of which the individual is not conscious afterward. Here an inner turbulence provides the intense stimulation. We have another uncommon example in the case of a person who suddenly goes berserk, shooting and killing innocent bystanders.

Fire walking in India, which has been carefully observed by scientists, is also an example that falls into this category of overstimulated states of consciousness. Here the Indian fakirs, often in a ritualistic ecstasy, can so control their senses and alter their consciousness that exposures to very intense heat cause them no pain and, perhaps more surprisingly, produce few burns or blisters. In one case studied [2] the fakir walked along a trench, 20 feet long, that was filled with glowing embers to a depth of several inches. The surface temperature was 806°F.; the interior temperature was 2,552°F.

Just as either a deficiency or an excess of stimulation of the senses can produce an alteration of the normal state of consciousness, so can a deficiency or excess of a person's attention form such an alteration. Meditation of the type practiced in the Far East, whether yoga or Zen Buddhist, is based on strongly diminished attention. The torpor and semisomnolence that often envelops sun bathers is another example. A spirit or medium who is in a meditative trance becomes almost completely unaware of the surroundings and retains only minimal alertness to their effects. On the other hand, when people listen to a charismatic speaker their intense absorption also leads to a change in their state of consciousness, tending toward hallucination and ecstasy. Intense absorption leads to the visions and mystical rapture of people engaged in fervent prayers. Similar effects assault people absorbed in prolonged observation of radar screens, as well as soldiers on prolonged sentry duty.

BRAIN WAVES

In the early 1920s, Dr. Hans Berger claimed, to the disbelief of his scientific contemporaries, that electrical impulses existed in the living brain. In 1924, using electroencephalography (EEG), he was able to demonstrate the existence of alpha waves in humans. Alpha waves were but the first of a number of types of electrical waves later found to exist in the brains of humans and animals.

The human body is a walking electrical generator. Low-voltage impulses pervade the body. These are triggered off by a variety of interior and exterior stimuli and are then transmitted over the body's circuit lines, the nerves. Electrodes, making good contact with the body's skin through an electrically conducting paste, pick up a jumble of electrical rhythms. Both the strength of these electrical waves and their frequency supply information on conditions within the body.

Brain waves can be picked up by placing two electrodes on the head, one on each side. The strength of these waves is very small, on the order of millionths of a volt. The brain-wave frequency, measured in cycles of variation per second, is found not to vary much with the location of the electrodes on the skull, and thus serves as an index of the brain activity.

Dr. Berger discovered both alpha and beta waves, the names coming from the first two letters in the Greek alphabet. An alpha wave has a frequency which falls in the range from about 8 to 13 cycles per second. It is closely connected with vision, for the presence of alpha waves is greatly enhanced when there are no signals from the optic nerve to the brain. Alpha waves are prominent when the mind is relaxed and the eyes are closed. A typical strength of an alpha wave detected by the electrodes is about 20 millionths of a volt. The alpha rhythm is associated most strongly with the brain's occipital lobe, where the nerves related to sight are located.

Visual sensations are the ones which are the most complex and the most important to the brain. When they are missing the brain is in a state of passive, relaxed anticipation; the absence or presence of other ordinary sensations is of secondary importance to visual sensation in influencing alpha waves and relaxation. It is for this reason that in transcendental meditation it is necessary to keep the eyes closed to achieve mind relaxation while it is not always required to retire to a quiet place. For even if all other nonvisual external sensations were missing, there would be signals of comparable amplitude reaching the brain from various internal organs. In Zen meditation, however, it is possible to achieve a relaxed, meditative state of consciousness with alpha waves present, even though the eyes are open; but this requires training and intense concentration over many years.

Attention abolishes the alpha rhythm and produces strong beta-wave activity. Beta waves permeate our normal waking state of consciousness and are associated with our critical abilities. Such waves have approximately half the amplitude of alpha waves. The beta rhythm is associated with creative activity and, less frequently, anxiety. Their frequencies lie in the range from 13 to perhaps 50 cycles per second. Beta waves are not really cyclic, however. They are, instead, conglomerates of cyclic waves which lie within this frequency range. So beta waves do not have a smooth, steady rhythm but, instead, come in clumps or bursts of activity.

Theta and delta waves were discovered later than alpha and beta waves. The theta and delta waves fill in the frequency range below 8 cycles per second: theta waves span the range from 4 to 8 cycles per second and delta waves, appearing almost exclusively in sleep, range below 4 cycles per second. Figure 5–1 illustrates the distribution of the brain-wave spectrum.

When the normal person falls asleep the brain rhythm quickly drops from beta activity, through alpha and theta, into delta. The pattern alters during the night. Alpha waves emerge mainly during dream states. The delta rhythm appears to be associated with a state of complete unconsciousness. Theta rhythms, although often associated with relaxation, have been correlated with alertness and some forms of motor activity.[3] Theta waves emerge in the conscious state of deep meditation, there often displacing the alpha state found in a more shallow state of meditation.

The brain waves of humans vary considerably. In an individual one half of the brain may be producing beta waves while the other half is generating alpha waves. One person's alpha pattern may differ considerably from another person's. Indeed, two to five percent of normal adults show no alpha pattern at all, yet display no perceptible physiological effects which are due to its absence.

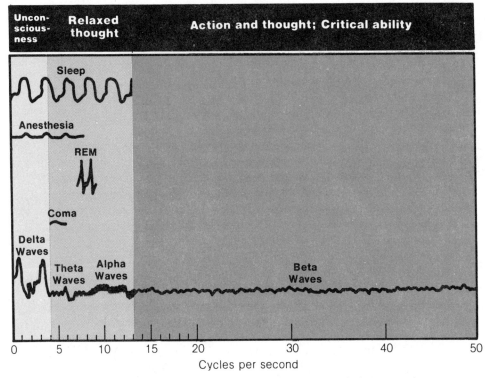

Fig. 5–1. The frequency spectrum of brain waves. Electroencephalograms of various brain waves are also shown, each pattern located in the appropriate range of frequencies.

The brain patterns of infants, from the unborn fetus to the four-year-old, are dominated by delta waves. As children grow so does the frequency range of their brain waves. Theta waves predominate between the ages of four and six years, while alpha waves assert themselves between the ages of seven and twelve years. Only then do beta waves arrive.

The alpha-wave activity of the brain has attracted wide popular attention. These waves are associated with a relaxed state. Even when the eyes are closed, for example, worries and mental attention will prevent alpha waves from appearing. Deeper relaxation, though, induces a theta-wave rhythm. Anesthesia eliminates the presence of alpha waves. Strangely, muscular activity accompanying blinking produces strong alpha bursts. Finally, and of special interest for us, several laboratory experiments suggest that the alpha and theta states, both of them, enhance psychic performance.

TO SLEEP . . . TO DREAM

Several times a night a strange presence invades our mind, there to cast its spell. Immobilized, we witness odd, fretful, or enchanting events, usually only dimly remembered by the time morning arrives. Sleep has worked its magic in some occult manner we only vaguely perceive.

For all of us sleep proceeds in a special rhythm of cycles of brain activity. Four or five complete cycles of sleep pass during the night, each cycle lasting roughly an hour and a half. A cycle consists of a number of different phases which can be distinguished from each other by the measurement of various physiological processes. Instruments of all kinds have been employed for this purpose, among them the EEG, sphygmomanometers, eye-movement monitors, respiratory ratemeters, skin-resistance measuring devices, and others.

The first stage of sleep sees bits of dreams and imagery floating to consciousness. In this twilight sleep the brain-wave pattern becomes irregular and small in amplitude, the breathing slows, and the blood pressure and body temperature drop. In the second stage the sleep has become so deep that the sleeper would "see" nothing even if his or her eyes were open. In the third stage the muscles become quite relaxed. The breathing and pulse rate slow down so much that the brain-wave frequency drops to one per second—slender delta waves have taken over. But the deepest sleep is still to come in the longer, fourth stage. It is difficult to arouse the sleeper now. Ultimately we reach the last stage, the dream stage.

When the sleeper first enters sleep, stages 1, 2, 3, and 4 follow in succession. This is an introductory sequence. Then stage 2 is repeated. Now it is followed by the dreaming stage, an hour and a half after sleep first began. Perhaps 50 percent of the time spent in sleep is in stage 2. That stage invariably precedes the dreams that repeat every 90–100 minutes (stage 2, dreams, stage 2, dreams, . . .) once the initial sequence is over.

All normal people dream four to five times each night during these successive cycles of sleep. The memories of these strange periods of altered consciousness fade rapidly; and in the morning we may dimly remember, at most, only one or two of them. Quite often we may recall none of them. People who believe they do not dream actually do dream; they have simply forgotten all their dreams by the time they waken. Studies of eye movements indicate that birds, cats, dogs, and sheep dream.

The dreaming stage of sleep is called REM (rapid eye movement). Volunteers in laboratories have been connected to equipment designed to measure their eye movements. When they first sleep, their eyes may be at rest or they may roll slowly under closed eyelids, but later the eyes begin to move rapidly. If awakened when their eyes are either still or moving slowly, subjects consistently assert they have not been dreaming. But if they are awakened later, during the period of rapid eye movement, the volunteers will clearly remember experiencing dreams. The pattern is definite: REM—dreams; no REM—no dreams. So the presence of REM is a sure indicator of a dream. Some recent work suggests, however, that nightmares work their terrors not in the REM period but, instead, during a disturbed fourth stage of sleep.

Dreams do not pass rapidly; they may last as long as 25 minutes. Studies conclude that two of every five dreams are frightening—dreamers are often trying to get away from someone who is chasing them. In some cultures things are even worse: there may be seven dreams of misfortune for each pleasant dream.

The first and last dreams of the night each involve very recent happenings, perhaps those of the day before, while the more distant past enters dreams only during the middle of the night. It is found that women dream with equal frequency about both sexes, but men dream more often about women. Alcohol, barbiturates, and most tranquilizers decrease the amount of dreaming; so does advancing age. Starting slowly at age 45 or so, REM sleep decreases from about 25 percent of the sleeping time to about 13 percent in very, very old age.

Sleep is, of course, essential to good psychological health. Early experiments indicated that when volunteers were awakened whenever REM set in so that they could not dream they showed psychological failings—irritability, hallucinations, and derangements—but later experiments have cast doubt on the special nature of dreaming sleep.[4] A few rare individuals apparently require almost no sleep—and no dreaming—at all.

A number of studies, and many anecdotes, point to a heightened psychic and creative ability in the dreaming states. Crises involving loved ones are, for example, often reported in dreams. The dream of the four-year-old boy and that of the middle-aged woman, which we mentioned in Chapter 3, are examples. To test the possibility of heightened psychic ability during dreams several laboratories have attempted, in the past few years, to project mental images, say of a picture, to sleeping subjects. Results indicate a definite correlation between the dreams some sleeping subjects experience and the images being projected, as we have indicated.

In a manner completely unknown to the conscious mind, the subconscious mind often works on knotty problems, and dreams sometimes yield the results. For example, the kernel of his metaphysical philosophy came to Descartes in a dream. A dream inspired the physicist Niels Bohr to form his Nobel Prize-winning concept of the structure of atoms. Robert Louis Stevenson is credited with dreaming the plot of *Dr. Jekyll and Mr. Hyde*. Samuel Taylor Coleridge is said to have composed "Kubla Khan" while dreaming. The famous chemist F. A. Kekule visioned the then unknown shape of the benzene molecule during a dream.

One of the biggest steps in the understanding of the nature of dreams was taken by Dr. Sigmund Freud in the first quarter of this century. It was, until then, a completely occult subject. Freud, a truly seminal figure, established the foundation for psychoanalysis by interpreting dreams as the play of the subconscious mind upon removal of the normal restraints of society, parents, spouse, children, and—most important—the conscious mind. According to Freud, sex was of overwhelming importance to the subconscious mind, but some of his followers have tended to modify this. Most people have neurotic difficulties at one time or another—some more, some less—and many people with neurotic difficulties have been helped by his methods and have been enabled to function in a fairly normal manner. Yet, the high hopes of half a century ago have not been fulfilled—the mental wards are filled with patients who have not been appreciably helped by psychoanalysis. The psychoanalytic interpretation of dreams as a guide to the working of the mind evidently has stringent limitations and the mind remains, as it was before Freud, an occult subject.

THE DREAM PEOPLE

On a lonely mountain peak in the Central Mountain Range of the Malay Peninsula there lives an isolated tribe of 12,000 people, the Senoi. Called the Dream People, the Senoi are reported to have been without violence for perhaps the past 300 years. This preliterate tribe is surprisingly free of crime, tribal warfare, and chronic mental or physical ailments. Their once patriarchal culture has developed an extraordinarily advanced dream psychology that blends their dreaming and waking lives.[5]

This strongly democratic tribe is guided by their *halaks*, primitive psychologists. Numerous tribal members are versed in the meditative states. Although the tribe does not practice black magic, it allows its foothill neighbors to think it does, thereby assuring the isolation and safety of the Senoi from tribal warfare.

While still quite young, the Senoi are initiated into the dream psychology of the tribe. Each morning every tribal member recounts his or her night's dreams, either in a family meeting or in a small tribal group. Here the elders interpret the dreams and teach the members how to meet the problems posed through the dreams.

The Senoi believe that individuals recreate features of the outside world in their own minds, and these features turn up in their dreams as disguised images and beings. Some dream images indicate conflicts, either within a member's mind or between tribal members. The Senoi feel that the dream images and figures can be understood and then put to use for the benefit of the tribe. The essence of the Senoi dream psychology is that dream consciousness should be mastered for the benefit of the waking consciousness.

To master their dreams children must first overcome their fears. Dreams of falling are quite common, and these are frightening to children. An elder can quickly calm a child who recounts such a dream. "Wonderful, this is the best of dreams. Where did you fall to? Everything has its purpose and falling is the quickest way to the power of the spiritual world." Soon the child learns to enjoy these dreams.

Dreams of dying are treated similarly—anyone who dreams this will surely wake with the power of the other world. Dreamers must always master the dream and call upon the images of other people when necessary. Pleasurable dreams should be carried to their natural end. Then dreamers should seek a useful prize from their dreaming companions or spirits—a song, a dance, a riddle—to use when awake.

When a Senoi harms the dream figure of another in a dream he or she must obtain this person's good will by presenting a gift. The Senoi feel that hostile spirits can only use the dream image of one whose good will toward the dreamer is low. Thus, on awakening, the dreamer seeks to repair the good will of the person whose image threatened the dreamer.

Pleasure is encouraged in the dream world, but only as a means toward a useful end—unproductive fantasy is discouraged. Although a rich sex life in dreams is a special favor of the spiritual universe, the dreamer so blessed must always bring something back from the dream world—the subconscious—that is of use to the waking world. For with the Senoi the altered state of consciousness must not control the normal conscious state but must serve it.

NICOTINE AND DR. FREUD

One of the easiest, though not necessarily the wisest, means for obtaining an altered state of consciousness involves the action of various chemicals which are either smelled, swallowed, or injected into the body—drugs. Drug stores which dispense chemicals on a doctor's prescription are to be found everywhere. Such drugs, used for pharmaceutical purposes to counteract different human ailments, are not our concern here. We are interested in the use of drugs for altering the normal state of consciousness. There are several broad categories of such drugs, and they must be sharply distinguished from each other. We will sketch a few of the main features, roughly proceeding from the drugs most commonly used for this purpose to those less common.

The most widely used mind-altering drug is nicotine. It is also the one drug which has the worst physical consequences for the body. Consider the following case history. Nobody ever knew as much about the working of the human mind as Sigmund Freud. He was a genius. Nevertheless, he was a human being, and he had his share of small human frailties. One of these petty shortcomings was his habit, throughout his adult life, of smoking 20 cigars a day. He loved his cigars; he needed them; and they made him feel good. Unfortunately, they did not agree with his system—they gave him palpitations of the heart. He tried to stop smoking a number of times, but each time the effort produced severe psychological symptoms, and he soon failed. He was addicted to smoking and, try as he would, he could not stop.

Freud's smoking also caused him to be continually hawking, bringing up phlegm, and spitting it out. This habit was most distressing to his visitors. He knew this, yet he continued to smoke 20 cigars a day; day in and day out, year in and year out. He could not even cut the quota down.

When he was 67 years old he contracted cancer of the jaw and right palate, an ominous disease that was probably a direct result of his addiction to tobacco. An operation was performed. Then another. And yet another. In the next 16 years of his life Freud suffered 32 additional operations on his jaw and oral cavity, all caused by his smoking. He was in constant pain; his whole jaw had to be replaced; he had difficulty chewing and swallowing; he often could not speak; and his heart arrhythmia continued to plague him, accompanied now by angina. Yet he continued to smoke. He was unable to stop and he finally died of cancer at age 83, after 16 years of constant pain.

Freud lacked neither willpower, nor understanding of the problem, nor understanding of his mind. What occult curse kept him tied to his bitter enemy, nicotine, for over half a century? The answer, to put it simply, is that he was hooked to the drug.

Every package of cigarettes sold in the United States must now carry the statement "Warning. The Surgeon General Has Determined That Cigarette Smoking Is Dangerous to Your Health." For we know that smoking is the primary cause of lung cancer and that it contributes both to emphysema and to problems with the heart's arteries. These effects are due both to the nicotine and to the tars and other chemicals contained in the smoke; the nicotine, however, serves as the agent that glues the victim to these chemicals.

Why, then, do people smoke? Aside from the fact that smoking is a habit, and like all habits hard to break, people smoke because of the effect of nicotine on the mind. So many people have smoked that its pleasure is well known. In some occult manner, nicotine can be either a stimulant or a depressant, an up or a down, as the need may be. And people smoke to obtain the benefits of the altered state of consciousness. Unfortunately, there are some side effects.

MY CUP OF TEA

Next on the list of best-loved drugs comes caffeine, the active ingredient in coffee, tea, and cocoa. (Coca-Cola has caffeine in it. Originally this caffeine came from an extract of the kola nut, but the efficacy of the drink as a stimulant rested chiefly on an extract from the leaf of the coca plant. Today's Coca-Cola has neither. Its caffeine is supplied synthetically, as a chemical additive.) A century-old description of tea captures the flavor of its hold, if not its taste. "The stomach is strengthened; it creates appetite, dissolves secretions, assuages the most burning thirst, checks colds, dispels vapours; in a word, the inner distempers and outer complaints are all allayed by this tea. Is it not divine?"[6]

Caffeine is a drug which stimulates the cerebral cortex of the brain. For this reason beverages which contain it are used all over the world as pick-me-ups and as breakfast drinks. Caffeine affects one's heartbeat, blood pressure, metabolism, flow of gastric juices, urination, and blood-capillary diameter. Caffeine overcomes sleepiness and fatigue, increases motor activity, clears one's thinking, and sharpens one's senses. One cup of coffee or tea contains about 200 milligrams of caffeine. Compare this with the one milligram of nicotine in a cigarette. Obviously, the effect of caffeine on the central nervous system is much less, per unit mass, than that of nicotine.

Taken in moderation caffeine does not seem to have harmful effects on the body. It is only when one habitually drinks five or more cups of tea per day that adverse effects become noticeable. This can result in heart palpitations, sleeplessness, and a high pulse rate. It can also lead to addiction. Once such a physical dependence has been acquired the typical symptom of tolerance appears—an increasing dose is required in order to achieve a given mental and physiological response. The characteristic withdrawal symptoms of users hooked to a drug also appear.

Individuals who drink coffee or tea daily and think that they do so because they like the taste are kidding themselves. They drink it because of the mind-altering qualities of the drug caffeine.

ALCOHOL AND THE BARBITURATES

Alcohol is a natural drug. Because it has no bad effects when taken in moderation it is dispensed, without a prescription, in 40,000 liquor stores throughout the country as well as in innumerable restaurants, bars, saloons, cocktail lounges, and honky tonks. People like alcohol. It relieves tension, overcomes anxieties, rids one of inhibitions.

The barbiturates, on the other hand, constitute several thousand different synthetic compounds which were first fashioned as sleeping pills in the late nineteenth century to replace the narcotic drugs. There are two broad classes, long-acting and short-acting. The best-known example of the former is phenobarbitol (Luminal), and it is used for strong sedation rather than for mild insomnia. The most common of the short-acting type are pentobarbitol (Nembutal) and secobarbitol (Seconal). In street language, the barbiturates are called either "barbs" or "downs." They are legally obtainable only with a doctor's prescription.

The effect of barbiturates in altering one's state of consciousness is very similar to that of alcohol. This is especially true of the short-acting variety. When downs are taken immoderately they produce all the symptoms of severe alcohol addiction—dizziness, vomiting, the need for ever-increasing doses, and with-drawal agonies. The easy but dangerous combination of booze and barbs has pro-duced numerous deaths. It does seem illogical to place such tight restrictions on one and such loose restrictions on the other.

Alcohol and the barbiturates are mainly depressants that act on the parasym-pathetic nervous system. Paradoxically, alcohol can act as a psychological stimu-lant by suppressing normal inhibitions. It is, indeed, a common sight to see some of the habitués in a bar as quiet, withdrawn, and, probably, depressed. On the other hand, just as many barflies are garrulous, hail-fellow-well-met people who will soon be offering you the shirt off their backs.

No. Alcohol taken in moderation is no problem. It has, instead, many virtues to recommend it. The same, however, cannot be said of alcohol taken immoder-ately—most emphatically not. For alcohol is an addicting drug and its victims do not know, cannot know, the meaning of the word moderation. For such addicts, and even for the occasional drunk, alcohol is a drug of the gravest consequences; and since about 5 million people in the United States are alcoholics, this is also a serious matter for society. One need consider only the following statistics—

• 40 percent of all arrests are for intoxication;
• there are ¼ of a million arrests annually for drunken driving;
• 28 percent of all homicides occur in a place where liquor is sold;
• 31 percent of all suicides are committed by alcoholics.

We could vastly expand our documentation of the danger of alcohol to society, but everyone is aware of these dangers. A bit less known, perhaps, is the danger to the individual. Mere occasional drunkenness is only a discomfort: perhaps a little nausea, vomiting, and reeling on one's feet. But prolonged drunkenness is much more serious. An initial up, a good and high one, is followed many hours later by a down—a deep one—the hangover. This requires a drink or a bar-biturate to steady the nerves and make one feel normal again. So the cycle is started, leading to a roaring drunk which may last for days, or even weeks. Should the inebriate then try to sober up, he or she then has to go through the classic withdrawal symptoms of any drug addict—the shakes, vomiting, convul-sions, and d.t.'s. For a chronic drinker who does not drink to excess at any one sitting, but who drinks steadily and to excess, the punishment is rather different: irreversible damage to the liver and the brain.

It is not generally recognized that withdrawal from alcohol or barbiturate ad-diction is more devastating physically and more dangerous to life than narcotic withdrawal, terrifying as that is. Such withdrawal symptoms may last several days, culminating in the d.t.'s and possibly death, if untreated.

Although not definitely established, it appears that the tendency to alcoholic addiction is an inherited, perhaps sex-linked, characteristic. Many more men than women become alcoholics; children with two alcoholic parents have an especially difficult time in handling alcohol.

Nature handles the narcotic- and alcohol-addiction problem of a society in brutal fashion. It mercilessly weeds out and prunes the addicted individuals, generation after generation, until the fraction of potential addicts drops to a level small enough to be manageable by the society. Perhaps 3–10 percent of the people in a culture that has had long-term contact with alcohol will end up as alcoholics. Those cultures which have not handled the problem earlier in their history bear the brunt of nature's onslaught—witness the American Indian's battle against the white man's whiskey.

MARIJUANA

Marijuana is the common name of a plant, *cannabis sativa*. It is also the name of the product which is obtained by drying the leaves and the flowering tops of this plant. The dried leaves and tops are called pot or, less frequently, grass. The drug obtained by drying the resin exuded by the marijuana plant is called hashish, or hash. Both pot and hash are usually smoked, though they can also be taken orally. Hash is five to eight times as potent as an equivalent amount of pot. Until recently it was not possible to make accurate quantitative statements or measurements concerning this drug, but in July 1973 a method was found for measuring the amount of THC (delta-9-tetrahydrocannabinol) in a person's bloodstream. Since THC is the active ingredient in both pot and hash, it should soon be feasible to make measurements concerning marijuana as accurate as those about alcohol.

Marijuana differs completely in its action from the drugs previously considered. At least 20 million Americans have smoked pot, and the alteration of the state of consciousness that makes it so popular, especially with teen-agers and college students, is a marked increase in the sensitivity of the sense organs. The spectrum of sounds that the ear perceives seems to be greatly extended, both in the low and high frequencies, so that recordings of rock artists seem to achieve a quality of high fidelity they do not otherwise possess. The smell and taste of foods are greatly enhanced so the foods seem to be eaten more slowly, the better to savor them. The sense of touch is much more delicate.

Accompanying the increased sensitivity of the sensory organs there is a perception by the user, whether it is actually so or not, of an increased alertness of the mind and an increased precision in various motor functions. It is for this reason that for decades jazz musicians became stoned on marijuana. Paradoxically, a group of students who have taken pot will usually be found to be sitting around, completely withdrawn into themselves. They do not talk much, they do not jump around, yet they claim to have a greatly expanded insight into the personalities and statements of their partners.

Marijuana—unlike nicotine, caffeine, or alcohol—has no physicially addicting properties. There is little evidence for either withdrawal symptoms or a tolerance effect; the dose required to produce a certain effect does not increase with use. No fatality has ever been recorded, to our knowledge, as a result of its use. It has never been proven that marijuana leads to stronger drugs; but recent evidence suggests that marijuana users are more likely to use alcohol. Yet the penalty for the possession of one marijuana joint in many states is the same as that for selling heroin. In Texas the law, at least until 1973, made it a felony to be found in possession of one joint of marijuana (two ounces or less) punishable by a sentence of two years to life in jail.[7] And the Louisiana Pardons and Paroles Board recommended against reducing the 50-year prison sentence given to Robert E. Apablaza, 35, of New York for selling five dollars worth of marijuana to an agent.[8]

There is great controversy among researchers as to whether marijuana, although probably nonaddictive, has other properties which are harmful. Reports cite evidence of cellular damage from the excessive use of marijuana,[9] of lowered white-cell reproduction among regular users, and of a reduction both of male sex hormones and sperm levels in heavy, long-term users.[10] In addition, the following effects seem possible: impotence, the growth of female-like breasts on men, debilitating effects on the bronchial tract and lungs, potentially irreversible brain damage, and sharp personality changes.[11] There is little or no evidence of any harmful effects from smoking a few, occasional joints; the potential dangers arise in the case of long-term, heavy use. Even then, there is only relative unanimity among the experts about the deleterious effects on the lungs, while there is sharp disagreement about the effects on the brain and the central nervous system.

On the other hand, marijuana opens the air passages of asthmatics, and may provide the basis for a new treatment of their ailment.[12] Reports suggest that marijuana is valuable as a sedative and pain killer, in the reduction of aggressive behavior, and in the treatment of glaucoma.[13] John Kaplan of the Stanford Law School writes that medical findings led him to conclude that "marijuana is not a very dangerous drug. That is not to say that the drug is completely safe. Indeed, if it were, it would be the only drug we know of that does not harm at least some of its users . . . it is impossible for any reasonable person to conclude that marijuana is more dangerous than alcohol."[14]

THE AMPHETAMINES AND COCAINE

The amphetamines are, like the barbiturates, synthetic drugs and they, too, are usually taken in the form of pills. They have found a pharmaceutical use because of their effects on the central nervous system, but the effects of amphetamines are diametrically opposite to the effects of the barbiturates. The amphetamines are stimulants used to combat melancholia and depression. As diet drugs, to ward off hunger, and as pep pills, ups, to fight sleepiness and produce extra stamina, they are well known to millions of housewives, students, athletes, and long-haul truck drivers. They affect consciousness and put one into a different-from-normal frame of mind.

The original chemical, amphetamine, was marketed under the trade name Benzedrine. Since then several new, widely accepted variants have appeared: dextroamphetamine (Dexedrine) and methoamphetamine (Methedrine and Desoxyn). Regardless of trade name, the pills are often called bennies. First synthesized in 1887 and first used medically in 1927, in recent years a conviction has been strengthened about the action of the amphetamines: they have an effect very similar to that of cocaine, a drug extracted from the leaves of the coca plant, found originally in South America. When taken orally in moderation, the effect on the nervous system is similar to that of drinking tea, coffee, or Coca-Cola and no more damaging to the body. Of course, an overdose will have drastic effects.

The name for amphetamines injected into one's veins is speed; and the people who do this are called speed freaks. At the very first freak-out they reach a state of ecstasy. "What have I been missing out on, all my previous life?" So a second freak-out is inevitable. Then a spree of freak-outs follows. The sprees get longer and they occur more frequently. The speed freak stays awake continuously, for as long as six days without sleeping, living in a constant high. Of course, this is not a normal state of consciousness; he or she is, as the saying goes, freaked out.

This high is followed by the crash: 24 or 48 hours of continuous sleep. Awake once more, the speed freak is ready to renew the cycle. Only now there is a strong tolerance effect, and the dose required is even stronger. Speed freaks lose appetite, lose weight, lose the desire for everything but the next fix to raise them from their despair, through despondency and melancholia, up, up and away— into euphoria. Out of obscurity into oblivion would be more accurate. Dr. Timothy Leary himself has denounced speed freaks as an abomination.

We mention the case of Dr. Max Jacobson, an elderly New York practitioner who for many years injected amphetamine into the veins of a large number of people, including famous artists, writers, and politicians.[15] What makes this a chilling story is the fact that two of the doctor's patients who had such treatments, patients of long standing, were President John Kennedy and Mrs. Jacqueline Kennedy. In 1961 Dr. Jacobson accompanied the President to his Vienna summit meeting with Khrushchev; and the doctor claimed he gave the President such injections there. Mrs. Jacqueline Kennedy Onassis later confirmed she had been treated by the doctor but refused to give details.

Chewing the leaf of the coca plant, *erythroxylon coca*, also has stimulating effects. The Indians of South America have done this for centuries to increase their stamina in high altitudes of the Andes Mountains; it also eased their chronic hunger. The chief ingredient in the coca plant that produces these effects is the drug cocaine, first obtained in its pure state in 1883. Cocaine is a white powder which is either sniffed or injected into the veins. It is not taken orally, for it is very bitter.

Cocaine is very expensive. It requires ever-increasing doses; in the end of a chain of continually increasing dependence it produces an effect similar to d.t.'s. Cocaine has suffered some loss of popularity recently, mainly because amphetamines injected into the veins (mainlining) are much more potent than cocaine. The high is higher; you get there faster; and it's much cheaper.

Sigmund Freud became enamored of cocaine not too long after it was first obtained, and he prescribed it as a panacea drug to some of his patients. In a letter to his fiancée he wrote, "I expect it will win its place in therapeutics side by side of morphine and superior to it. I have other hopes and intentions about it. I take very small doses of it regularly against indigestion, and with the most brilliant success."[16] Because of subsequent bitter experiences with it, he eventually renounced all drugs, preferring suffering—whether for himself or for his patients. Possibly because of his influence, cocaine has long held an unenviable reputation as an addictive drug—a narcotic.

NARCOTICS

If nicotine is the best loved of all the mind-altering drugs, the narcotics are the most feared. "Narcotic" is a generic term for an opiate or, sometimes, for any drug that acts like an opium derivative—one that is strongly addicting. Rigorously, despite its reputation, cocaine is not a narcotic. The basic narcotic is opium. This is the dried juice which is squeezed from an unripened capsule of the opium poppy, *papaver somniferum*. Opium can be taken orally or it can be heated to give off a vapor which is inhaled. Opium dens, where addicts "smoked" opium, were prevalent in prerevolutionary China and also in California in the nineteenth century, when the Chinese were imported as coolie labor for the railroads.

The chief active chemical ingredient in opium is morphine, and much greater efficiency is obtained in altering one's state of consciousness by using this drug. Morphine is taken either by sniffing it, by injecting it under the skin, or for maximum effect, by mainlining—injecting intravenously. The mind-altering property of morphine, and all the narcotics, is that of a very powerful tranquilizer. Anxieties are banished. Pain is relieved. There is no rush to do anything. Calm descends.

But all sorts of works of the imagination also take place. Thomas De Quincey wrote in "Confessions of an English Opium-Eater," (1822): "Whatsoever things capable of being visually represented I did but think of in the darkness, immediately shaped themselves into phantoms of the eye; and, by a process apparently no less inevitable, when thus once in faint and visionary colours, like writings in sympathetic ink, they were drawn out by the fierce chemistry of my dreams, into insufferable splendour that fretted my heart."[17]

Heroin is diacetylmorphine. It is made by heating morphine in the presence of acetic acid and it, too, is either sniffed, injected, or mainlined. The body then internally converts the heroin to morphine. Mainlining heroin is the chief means of taking narcotics today in the United States—progress, in the backward direction, from the opium "smoking" dens of a century ago.

There are other narcotics—codeine, methadone—but they are not as commonly used. They are all similar in their action on the central nervous system.

The dread of narcotics is due to only one of the properties they possess—they are so addictive that, practically speaking, once a person is hooked it is impossible to escape. For there are few proven harmful effects of any kind on the body of a narcotics addict. On the mind, yes: a female addict, of whatever background, will turn prostitute, casually, to obtain a fix; a male addict will lie, cheat, steal, or even kill, as required. But there are surprisingly few known physical effects on the liver, heart, or lungs.

The cause of such a strong addiction is a deep mystery. All attempts to cure it on a psychological or sociological basis in this country have been completely fruitless. One would be tempted to conclude it must have a chemical basis, some irreversible change in the body's biology.

The narcotics problem in the United States is plagued by two factors. First, until recently almost all narcotics addicts were blacks. Nobody seems to know why this is so; it is certainly not true in England; and lately an increasing, but still small, percent of the addicts have been suburban whites. So the treatment of narcotics has acquired racist overtones. Second, the price of a fix has jumped astronomically because of the fantastic penalties. The pushers, who take a chance, want a big incentive. This has brought organized crime into the narcotics traffic, since the profits are so high. Also, because the addicts generally cannot afford the high cost of addiction, $25.00 per day even in the late 1960s and much more now, they perform criminal acts to secure the money. Most of the jails today are filled with prisoners who were convicted of drug-related criminal acts; and many of these acts are due to the high prices caused by outlawing the drugs.

THE PSYCHEDELICS

I remember looking at a finely detailed photograph of the Swiss Alps. I had admired this photograph before, in my pre-LSD days an hour or an aeon ago, but now its precision became reality and the temperature plunged and fine crystals of snow whipped across my face and I circled like an eagle above the crags and snowy summits of the mountain top. An expedition of climbers waved up at me and I lifted one talon to wave back. I was called back to Greenwich Village by obscenity. A sound, a chant, lascivious and brutal, a whining pornography assaulted my ears and left me furious with moral indignation. "How dare you say things like that to me," said I to the disembodied chant. It suddenly ended, as quickly as it had begun, and I saw R removing a record which he explained to me was a recording of fertility mantras to the goddess Kali.[18]

So begins a journey into consciousness. This report is typical of the mind-expanding, hallucinatory experiences produced by the psychedelic drugs. Because there are such large differences in the effects produced on the human mind by the various drugs, we are treating them separately. In a book such as this one, where we deal primarily with very poorly understood subjects, there is no doubt that, of all the drug types, the psychedelic drugs are the ones most suitable for inclusion. For this reason, and also because this type is probably the least used variety of drug, we have saved it for the last.

The psychedelic drugs appear both naturally and synthetically. Peyote, certain types of morning glories, and various kinds of mushrooms exemplify the natural kind. Peyote is a cactus plant which has no spines. When properly harvested, dried, and swallowed one takes off on a mind trip. All sorts of hallucinatory effects may occur—kaleidoscopic visions, strange music, mystical insights. The Indians of the Southwest have used this plant for many years.

Mescaline is a psychedelic drug which is an active chemical ingredient of the peyote plant. It has also been synthesized in the laboratory. Two other synthetic psychedelic drugs are LSD and psilocybin. LSD is short for d-lysergic acid diethylamide; its street name is, simply, acid. It is 10 to 1,000 times as potent as the other drugs discussed in this chapter: where their doses are of the order of milligrams (thousandths of a gram) the doses of LSD are measured in micrograms (millionths of a gram). LSD is taken orally by dripping one drop of "acid" on a lump of sugar and swallowing it.

LSD was synthesized by Dr. Albert Hoffman in Switzerland in 1943 from ergot, a rye fungus that, itself, has strange mind-altering properties. Thinking a quarter of a milligram to be a small dose, he administered it to himself, and he soon took off on a trip. It proved to be a rough one, for it was actually a huge dose. But he was able, nevertheless, to record his feelings. He laughed uncontrollably. Space became contorted; time was spread out.

Now, thirty years later, we know a good deal more about trips. Some can be pleasant, some grotesque. The nature of the trip seems to be greatly affected by the expectations, but certain types of people seem to have extra difficulty in experiencing a good trip. People tripping have jumped out of windows, thinking they could fly; so people taking a trip should never be left alone. Also, after a person has had a bad trip another bad trip can reoccur to him, at some future time, even when he has not taken a drug, and he is forced to relive all the horrible experiences, perhaps without friends to help him.

There was considerable controversy until recently as to whether or not LSD had any harmful effects on the body. But an article in *Science* implicates LSD in a greatly increased rate of spontaneous abortions and birth defects among drug abusers; and it also suggests that LSD may disrupt the body's immunity system by interfering with the production of antibodies.[19]

LSD may also strongly affect an individual's psychic powers: unspoken feelings seem to be sensed with considerable accuracy. Nevertheless, since 1970 there seems to have been a lessening of interest in these very powerful, very unusual, and potentially very dangerous drugs. Dr. Timothy Leary, the charismatic propagandizer and popularizer of LSD, goes unheeded: there simply have been too many bad trips. Perhaps with these drugs, unlike the others, further experimentation in consciousness alteration will be left to the cautious scientist rather than the daring thrill seeker.

CHAPTER SIX THE PSYCHE

- *A Map of Consciousness*
- *Transcendental Meditation*
- *Yoga* *Zen, American Style*
- *Hypnosis* *Questions and Answers*

A MAP OF CONSCIOUSNESS

We have emphasized the separation of states of consciousness into two distinct branches: one terminating in an overstimulated, ecstatic state; the other in a deeply relaxed, understimulated, meditative state. The dervishes whirl along the ecstatic path, and LSD paints its hallucinogenic imagery there; the yoga master and the lethargic alcoholic relax on the meditative path. Vastly different practices lead to strongly similar states. St. Teresa of Avila, the talented mystic, joins both the Voodoo dancer, and Dr. Albert Hoffman, ingesting his newly discovered LSD, in an ecstatic trance; while the Zen master, the prisoner in solitary confinement, and the homecoming executive who downs a martini are at different stages of the meditative trance.

A map of the varied states of consciousness has been suggested by R. Fischer as a means of unifying the principles underlying them. (See Fig. 6–1). The normal waking state of consciousness, designated as the "I" state, is located in

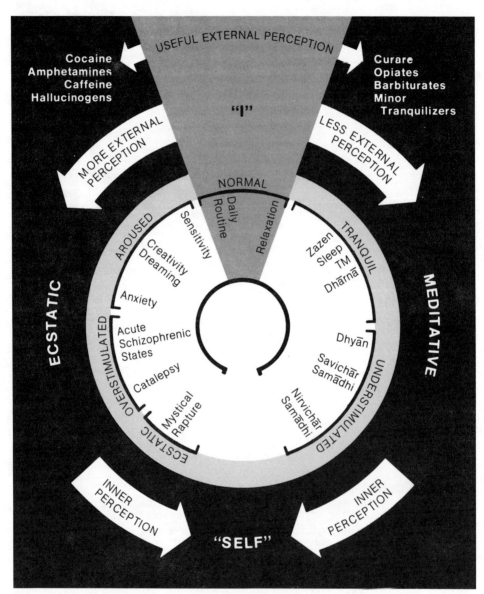

Fig. 6–1. A map of consciousness. A modification of the map proposed by Roland Fischer (Reprinted, by permission, from *Readings in Abnormal Psychology: Contemporary Perspectives,* ed. L. R. Allman and D. T. Jaffe, New York, Harper & Row, 1976, p. 250). As consciousness moves away from the normal state, less physical control exists on the ecstatic side, while less physical activity is desired on the meditative side. The activity of drugs is complicated, and only the main activity of some drugs is indicated. On the meditative side, drugs normally act only just beyond the boundary of the normal state. Marijuana, not shown, produces a composite state with elements of both the tranquil and the aroused states.

the center of the diagram. In the "I" state perception is balanced against both introspection and the need to exercise motor activity to meet the many large and small demands of life. Here perception is not at a maximum; rather, effectiveness in coping with or combating reality is a maximum. On a crowded stairway a quick dodge prevents a collision; at home a cut with a knife must slice a pickle neatly, not a finger badly. The demands of life vary, and the "I" state ranges between a harried routine and a relaxed daydream.

In the "I" state the sympathetic nervous system (SNS) and the parasympathetic nervous system (PSNS) are in balance. In those aroused states which ultimately lead to the ecstatic state and mystical rapture the SNS increases its activity at the expense of the PSNS.

Going to the left from the "I" state in the figure, as more sensory data is processed to the mind, the person becomes more aware of the outside world and his or her consciousness expands. More of the nervous system is used in perception and less is left to initiate motor activity. With increased excitation of the SNS in the aroused states there is a progressive loss of freedom to produce voluntary activity. Common here are feelings of being overpowered, or paralyzed, or hypnotized by the experience.

The hyperaroused states, still further to the left, include the states displayed by acute schizophrenic and catatonic patients. Catatonic persons are so overwhelmed by the sense data fed to the brain that the brain's computer-like circuits become jammed, freezing their motor responses.

Hallucinations (waking dreams) may claim the individual's consciousness along the ecstatic pathway. These produce intense sensations which the persons can neither verify nor discard because of their "frozen" motor activities.

The talented mystic can hurdle the schizophrenic and catatonic states and break through to the mystical rapture of ecstasy, where the entranced subject has neither the ability nor the necessity to verify the overpowering sensations. Here the mystic encounters the "Self." As ecstasy is approached the inner sensations are so strong that they require less and less intense outside stimuli to produce them. The senses merge and, finally, in the words of St. Teresa, "the soul neither hears nor sees nor feels; while it lasts, none of the senses perceives or knows what is taking place."[1] The boundary separating the inner person from outside reality dissolves, time and space disappear, and a mystic union of ONE with ALL takes place.

Going to the right from the normal "I" state in Fig. 6–1, the PSNS increasingly controls the body's activities. This direction leads to relaxation, diminution of expenditure of energy, and a decreased sensitivity to external stimuli. The tranquil states are the first ones encountered on the meditative path. Deep relaxation and Zen occur here, as well as the meditative state of transcendental meditation, TM. Again, as in ecstasy, motor activity is strongly diminished. Muscular activity is still possible but its appearance terminates the meditative journey. With further progression toward the right we attain first hypoarousal and finally the deep meditative states of yoga.

External stimuli are increasingly shut out along the meditative pathway. Yoga masters are adamant in their insistence that they notice no outside stimuli during deep *samadhi*, and laboratory experiments support their claims. The ears hear but, in some occult manner, the brain does not. The master experiences only an inner world, again a "Self," and nothing outside. A feeling of mystical unity, of oneness with the universe, may ensue in *samadhi*, as in ecstasy. Fischer, indeed, suggests that the "Self" in ecstasy and the "Self" in *samadhi* are the same state. He points to their similarities. In drug experiments cats respond to hyperarousal of the SNS with rage; but at the peak of hyperarousal, they yawn, curl up, and promptly fall asleep in deep understimulation.

The two pathways can be travelled by mystical techniques that allow mental control of each pathway. Later in this chapter we discuss the techniques of yoga and transcendental meditation. These mental techniques have the advantage of leaving control with the individual. Drugs also effect partial journeys along the pathways: tranquilizers, barbiturates, and the opiates act on the PSNS and produce states along the meditative path. LSD, mescalin, psilocybin, and other psychedelic drugs excite the SNS and produce states on the ecstatic pathway. The drug-induced states, once started, however, are no longer under the control of the individual.

On the ecstatic pathway of Fig. 6–1 lies a region where the "I" and the "Self" are in intimate connection. Fischer suggests that this is a state which leads to creative activity in the arts, science, literature, and religion. We have already seen that inspirations often occur in the dream-like state. This state is shown in Fig. 6–1 near the creative state where the reason and reality of the normal state may contact the illusions and inspirations of the ecstatic world.

While the creative region is indicated well within the ecstatic state, this does not imply that creativity does not exist in the normal state. Figure 6–1 is a useful simplification of the different states of awareness; however, points along the pathway need not be followed in succession, and individuals often skip long intervening regions. A mystic does not have to traverse intermediate states to reach rapture.

The normal state, itself, is a very broad mosaic. Indeed, for very short periods, continually repeated, the brain of a person in the normal state will dip into the creative state. It may be at these fleeting instances that many inspirations, flashes of genius, or hunches occur. Using these inspirations, however, requires an orderly, prepared mind in the normal state so that the creativity inspired on an excursion along an ecstatic path may be understood and exploited. There is a danger that an inspiration produced in a prolonged altered state may be either forgotten or misunderstood on one's return to the normal state. We are reminded of the Dream People, who placed a strong emphasis on utilizing their dreams in their waking states.

Various cultures have long adopted techniques that alter the state of consciousness: chanting, dancing, whirling, fasting, flagellation, breathing exercises, and concentration techniques. We have already met some of these techniques and we will discuss others shortly.

Precisely where in our physical make-up does the occult magic of altered consciousness cast its spell? Fischer suggests that these subjective, irrational, but often creative states of consciousness are seated mainly in the right hemisphere of the brain.[2] We know that in right-handed people the left hemisphere governs speech and analytical thinking. This hemisphere is cultivated by education and experience and, Fischer suggests, it dominates the right hemisphere in the normal consciousness. The right hemisphere is the seat of visual sensation and, Fischer thinks, also of the creative and artistic impulses. If he is correct, then the right hemisphere of the brain is the key both to altered states of consciousness and to creativity in the normal state. This creativity is generated, he argues, when the individual switches his or her thinking between the left and right hemispheres in the normal state, thereby generating a nonlogical spark through which the logical mind can glimpse a new path toward knowledge.

TRANSCENDENTAL MEDITATION

In the preceding chapter we discussed some chemically assisted methods for altering the state of consciousness. Here we will consider several methods which are self-induced. The first of these, which is now very popular in the West, is a variation of yoga.

The term "transcendental meditation" surely must have originated as a put on. This ponderous designation, popularly shortened to TM, refers to a process so simple that even a child can do it. One closes one's eyes while sitting in a comfortable position and repeats to oneself under one's breath a simple, meaningless syllable or sound, monotonously, over and over again. The sound is called a mantra, and the teacher of TM assigns a different mantra to each new pupil. In this country, a devotee of this variation of yoga philosophy is often sworn to keep secret his or her particular mantra—though nobody knows why, for mantras can be bought for a small coin in any market in India: hrim, phat, om, svasti—take your choice.

The meditation procedure is performed for two periods of 20 minutes each, once in the morning before breakfast and once in the evening before dinner. If necessary, it may be done at any other time, and in any place—even in uncomfortable positions, such as standing in a subway car while holding on to an overhead strap.

That is almost all there is to TM. Vast publicity attended a 1967 trip to India by the Beatles when they were personally taught the system by the teacher, or guru, Maharishi Mahesh Yogi. (A yogi is simply one who practices the Hindu discipline of yoga.) The public-relations work of this Hindu monk has been very effective and large numbers of people have taken up the practice, many of them in the United States. The Maharishi has since transferred most of his activities from India to America. In India there are many other forms of yoga and many other yogis. In India, also, few potential customers exist at $125 per head, the fee exacted here. (Students, however, pay less than this.)

Today there are over 4,000 trained teachers of TM, and the Maharishi is kept busy travelling about in his Lincoln Continental and in his own airplane supervising their activities. Many of these teachers are simple believers who listen breathlessly to the taped messages, direct from the Maharishi, which are an integral part of the course.

We have purposely hinted at some of the negative aspects of TM in our account above because we want to say, clearly and simply, that for many people this simpleton method does indeed work. TM makes many people more relaxed, yet more alert. The people for whom this technique is most effective are the very ones who need the relaxation the most: the tense, up-tight individuals with nervous stomachs or high blood pressure who are potential ulcer victims or cardiac cases. TM may be superfluous for relaxed, easy-going men or women.

Sometimes yawning after "awakening" from their 20-minute exercise in immobility, TM practitioners generally find themselves more efficient mentally and more energetic physically during their subsequent waking hours. And universities all over the country have opened their doors to the Students' International Meditation Society because of still another benefit of TM—there are reports that TM practitioners have a tendency to give up alcohol, tobacco, and drugs.

Transcendental meditation confers a state of consciousness which is different from the ordinary, normal state of consciousness. The state is not hypnosis, it is not sleep, but it apparently lies well along the meditative, understimulated path. We will outline below some experimental evidence which shows how this state of consciousness differs from the normal one. We also include a simple procedure for inducing TM for those interested in exploring it.

Since 1935 various investigators have measured the physiological effects occurring in the meditation practices of Hindu yoga and Buddhist Zen. These types of meditation are similar to TM, though they differ in the details. In TM the eyes are closed, enhancing the alpha-wave activity of the brain. Zen meditators keep their eyes half open, yet through learning and intense concentration they are still able to attain a large increase in the alpha-wave pattern of the electrical activity of their brains. This pattern, characteristic of a state of relaxation, ordinarily can be attained only when the eyes are closed—80 percent of the external signals to the 10 billion neurons in the brain come from the optic nerve.

Since 1970 scientists have made detailed studies of the physiological effects of TM. Two Harvard medical researchers, Herbert Benson and R. K. Wallace, decided to study TM because of the large number of practitioners from whom they could pick their subjects, because the TM technique was much more uniform than either yoga or Zen, and because there was not as great a distinction between expert and novice in TM.[3] In a study of 36 meditators they monitored the blood pressure, heart rate, rectal temperature, skin resistance, oxygen consumption, carbon-dioxide elimination, and EEG waves.

Figure 6–2 shows how the oxygen intake varies with time—before, during, and after TM. Both it and the CO_2 elimination drop by about 15 percent during the TM period. Both effects are due to a decrease in the metabolism rate. This results

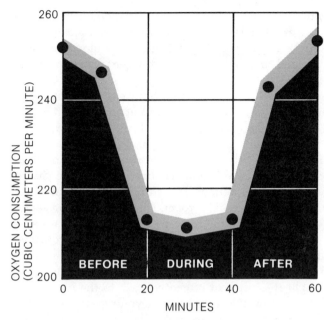

Fig. 6–2. Decrease in oxygen consumption during transcendental meditation. A drop of 17 percent is indicated here. (Reprinted by permission from Robert Keith Wallace and Herbert Benson, "The Physiology of Meditation." Copyright © 1972 by *Scientific American*, Inc. All rights reserved.)

in a decrease in the rate of respiration of roughly two breaths per minute and a decrease in the volume of air breathed of one liter per minute. The blood pressure does not change significantly during meditation. This is also true of the partial pressures of O_2 and CO_2 in the blood during meditation, though there is a slight increase in its acidity. On the other hand, there is a sharp decrease in blood lactate during TM. Lactate is produced by anaerobic metabolism, or the chemical life processes that occur in the absence of free oxygen. This decline in lactate production is due to increased blood flow as measured, for example, in the forearms during TM. The greater blood flow brings excess oxygen, despite the lowered O_2 consumption, to the skeletal muscles where the lactate is produced; and increased oxidative metabolism diminishes the demand for anaerobic metabolism. This lactate decrease is significant, for it is well known that patients with an anxiety neurosis respond to stress with a rise in the blood lactate, and it has even been shown that lactate infusion into the bloodstream produces anxiety symptoms. Patients with hypertension have higher blood lactate levels than normal patients. Thus, the lowering of the lactate level by TM tends to produce relaxation even though the practitioner is fully awake.

A very great increase in skin resistance also accompanies TM. The resistance increases by a factor of about ten in the 20-minute interval of meditation. Accompanying this is a decrease in the average heartbeat of perhaps three beats per minute. The EEG recordings monitoring the meditators' brain waves show, after computer analysis, that the slow waves in the brain are markedly increased during TM.

The physiological effects of TM bear the trademarks of the dominance of the PSNS: the decreased heart rate and the decreased O_2 consumption accompanying constriction of the bronchi and slower breathing. The increased blood flow may follow relaxation of the arterial muscles produced by the parasympathetic system.

The state of consciousness of TM is distinct from both sleep and hypnosis. In TM the percentage change in the O_2 consumption is completely different, and much larger, than that in either of the other two cases. Hypnosis shows an O_2 consumption almost identical with that in the normal state.

We close this discussion of TM with a few words directed toward those readers who might want to try it on a do-it-yourself basis. Unlike the case of hypnosis, we see no danger in this exploration. First sit down, on a chair or on the floor, in a comfortable manner. Pick a quiet room. Don't lie down or get too comfortable—you don't want to fall asleep. Now we will give you a special mantra, "OM," pronounced like "home" without the h. Next, close your eyes and start repeating the mantra aloud, in time with your breathing. Try to empty your mind, gently, by the monotony of the mantra rhythm; but if it fills with extraneous thoughts, don't fight it—just lead it, gently, back to the mantra. Let the mind dwell on the mantra and let the body relax as you repeat the mantra.

Almost automatically, the relaxation you have already produced will cause you to repeat the mantra more and more quietly, slower and slower; just let everything ease down. After a few minutes the mantra will become almost inaudible. Finally, it may be repeated wholly within the head. Thoughts will come to intrude, but just guide the mind gently back to the mantra. The breathing will gradually slow down, and deep relaxation will envelop the whole body.

The practice should be carried out before a meal for a period of 15 to 20 minutes, preferably twice a day. All physical movements should be minimized, although if you feel a bad itch while meditating, don't suffer: scratch it slowly and return to the mantra. If the telephone rings, ignore it; if you are spoken to, ignore it. Meanwhile, and throughout everything, keep your eyes closed, do not talk, and keep repeating the mantra. As with anything, don't overdo meditation. Twenty minutes is plenty; don't purposely exceed it. If you can't estimate the time reliably, set an alarm clock or carry a watch and look at it. Boredom may set in during the practice; bear with it.

With a little practice there is no need to begin the meditation with a spoken mantra—the mantra can be "spoken" in the mind. The mantra itself seems to be a device that focuses the mind narrowly, shutting down the senses and the SNS, thus allowing the PSNS to produce deep relaxation, while the attention to the mantra maintains consciousness. Just about any pleasing and simple nonsense syllable will serve as a decent mantra.

To some individuals TM and similar meditative techniques present a path to inner knowledge. The meditator can learn to focus attention on an inner sense that perceives the real, outside world in a new manner. The path from this sense leads to the mind that records the sense. Having met the mind, the meditator slowly learns its workings: the emotions, thoughts, ideas that well up, spill over, and drain away during the confrontation between reality and the senses. With deeper searching the talented meditator, the mind, and reality all merge into the completely embracing union sought so avidly by the mystic. The "I" is lost, its ego surrendered to a universal "Self."

One of the two authors of this text found TM interesting for a while, but then forgot it. The other author feels that all the effort required in writing the book was well spent, if only for the benefit he derived from this simpleton exercise. Perhaps this is a crude measure of the probability of TM successfully providing relaxation, yet invigoration, to the newcomer.

YOGA

The literal meaning of the word yoga is "to yoke"; both words are akin to Latin *jugum.* Yoga refers to a Hindu ethical and religious system which attempts to achieve a closer bond between a person and some higher, all-encompassing entity—call it the Universe, or God, or the Supreme Reality. There are a number of different yoga systems, differing from each other in stressing one phase or another of their common features.

Altogether there are eight aspects which are more or less common to all the yoga systems. Table 6–1 lists them by their Indian names and gives a brief description of each. TM, which we just considered, is a particular type of yoga emphasizing the *dhyana* feature to the exclusion of all the others.

In the Occident the word yoga has come to be associated in the public mind with the physical postures and, to a lesser extent, the breathing exercises. The practice of only these two aspects, *asana* and *pranayama*, by yoga devotees here in the West is, therefore, quite different from the practice of yoga in the Orient.

The term yogi is also used differently in the Orient and in the Occident. In the Orient it refers to one who has achieved the goal of a complete union between the self and the universe. This is attained in the trance state of *samadhi.*

TABLE 6–1
THE EIGHT FEATURES COMMON TO MANY YOGA SYSTEMS

Aspects of Yoga

Yama	self-control
Niyama	religious observances
Asana	physical postures
Pranayama	breathing exercises
Pratyahara	suppression of external stimuli
Dharana	concentration state
Samadhi	trance state
Dhyana	meditation state

Sometimes such a yogi becomes a teacher, a guru, but this is not necessary. The meaning of the word yogi is somewhat watered down here in the West, where it simply refers to one who is a follower of any Western type of yoga.

The physical postures of yoga produce in the person practicing them a state of relaxation not very different from that obtained after an intensive workout in a gymnasium, but without the sweat. This state is a form of drugless tranquilization. The means by which the postures induce this feeling of well-being in a person remain unknown. Some of the physiological changes that occur are quite the opposite of those in meditation—the uptake of oxygen increases during *asana* and *pranayama* yoga.

Along with the postures and exercises, there are also certain other cleansing concomitants. The diet is very strict; no tobacco, drugs, alcohol, meat, or spices are permitted. Sex is to be avoided. So are noise, laughter, or quick movement, including the warding off of a blow.

The feats of physical endurance which are sometimes attributed to yogis, such as walking about with huge pins stuck through parts of the body, or being buried alive for several days, or walking on hot coals, are feats possible to, but avoided by, true yogis. Such feats are generally performed by people seeking notoriety, or alms, or self-satisfaction. Yogis, on the other hand, avoid all these and seek to lead only quiet, retiring, meditative lives.

Yoga is a part of the Hindu tradition which traces itself back to the invasion of India by the Aryans, almost two millenia before the birth of Christianity. The Aryans introduced four books, the Vedas, which are largely collections of sacrificial hymns sung on religious occasions. The Vedas, which greatly advanced the development of mythology, magic, and religion from their previous primitive states, were followed by a number of treatises, the Upanishads, which dealt with philosophical topics. These gave birth to all the subsequent Indian schools of philosophy which were largely concerned with the nature of the supreme soul.

One of the basic beliefs of these philosophies is termed *karma*. According to *karma* all acts are related to each other. What we do now is determined, to some extent, by our past habits; and what we do now will affect, in some way, our future behavior. By present good conduct we may undo some of the effects of past bad behavior; evil conduct today will only lead to future entanglements, not necessarily as a punishment but as the inevitable outcome of events set into motion by our actions.

Another basic doctrine in yoga is rebirth; we are reincarnated in an endless sequence of successive lives. In future lives we may suffer the drastic consequences of our deeds in this one, and the way we live now is largely attributable to our past *karma*.

One Westerner, Jane Hamilton, detailed some of her experiences in a Buddhist *wat* in Thailand, where she practiced meditation in intensive fashion.[4] A *wat* is a religious compound that is normally restricted to males; she was, however, able to find one which had facilities for women. To be accepted she first had to agree to refrain from:

- killing—anything live, including mosquitoes.
- asking for anything; she could take only what was freely offered.
- sexual intercourse, or even any sexual activity.
- lying, or gossip, or put-downs.
- liquor or drugs.
- eating between noon of any day and the dawn of the next one.
- amusements, including shows or dances.
- sleeping on a soft bed.

All the time of the initiates was occupied in studying Buddhist writings, going to classes where the teachings of Buddha were taught, and practicing meditation. This occupied them 18 hours a day. The *samadhi* meditation was practiced all day, but the study of it was restricted to evening sessions in the Abbott's room. This room was lit only by saffron candles burning in front of the altar, but the atmosphere was suffused with fragrant incense and the sound of tinkling bells filled the air. All the meditators sat on the floor in the half-lotus position.

The day began at 4 A.M., with the ringing of a temple gong. The monks and novices then joined in morning chanting. At dawn the monks, in their saffron robes, left the compound to beg for food from the faithful, for whom the giving of alms is a holy deed. Women, not allowed to seek alms, were given their food, a rice soup, by the *wat* at about 6:30 A.M. Then meditation was practiced until 11 A.M., when the initiates took their second meal of the day. Then more meditation until late in the afternoon. Between 5 P.M. and 8 P.M. the meditators were called in, one by one, to the room of the meditation monk to report their progress in meditation. They asked questions, were given explanations, and received a new assignment for the next day.

Jane became a virtual hermit, not talking more than one hour each day. After ten days of constant meditation she was unable to talk, eat, or walk fast. Yet she reported a calm, a happiness, an understanding that she had never known before. The price was high, but so evidently were the rewards.

ZEN, AMERICAN STYLE

Buddhism spread through India 500 years before the birth of Christ, 1,000 years before the birth of Mohammed. Although the scriptures of Buddhism were already being translated into Chinese at the time of the first century of the Christian Era, its essence was first carried from India to China in 520 A.D. by Bodhidharma. The latter is generally associated with the birth of the Zen philosophy. The word *Zen* is a corruption of the Chinese word *Ch'an*, which comes from the Sanskrit word *dhyana,* meaning meditation. Actually, Zen Buddhism originated in China with Hiu-neng (638–713). It is a modification of the teachings of Buddha, placing much more emphasis on intuition and *inarticulate* understanding than on the meditation characteristic both of other brands of Buddhism and of the Hindu yoga. From the seventeenth century on, the Zen influence in China was on the decline. A strain of it was transported to Japan earlier, in the twelfth century, and there it is still a vital force, with some 5 million adherents.

Buddhism preaches the impermanence of existence, of the self. Since things are transient, they can only possess minimal importance. The devotee seeks the permanent in existence. In Theravada Buddhism, there is only one permanent measure—the release from continual rebirth. The resulting philosophy shapes a way of life.

Zen Buddhism stresses a personal path to knowledge and enlightenment. The Zen monk's awareness of life and living is heightened through concentration and discipline. In Zen Buddhism there is no creed or dogma, either to guide or to block one's path toward knowing. There is only a lonely, monastic life which supplies the inner seeds for an inspiration, an intuitive flash that points the way to inward knowledge.

Since World War II there has been considerable interest in Zen in the West. Partly this was due to our increased involvement with Asia; partly it was produced by our reaction against science and toward the occult. Of course, America could not take over the difficult practice of Zen without alteration. The lack of a dogma to be learned, of a creed to be believed, eases the path toward instant Eastern mysticism. The asceticism of the Zen monks is conveniently forgotten by the Beats who followed Zen searching for quick enlightenment through the uncertain embrace of drugs and alcohol. An American, Peter Hyun, born in Korea, has described this Zen, American style:

> They know nothing about Far Eastern culture and civilization, so it is convenient for them to speak in vague riddles. Not long ago, on the terrace of the Café Les Deux Magots, I had a typical experience with a young American Beat Zen poet.
>
> "What gives," he said.
>
> "What a lovely weather we're having today," I said.
>
> "Christ Almighty," he exclaimed, joyously, "you know. You know, my enlightened one."
>
> Then we both ordered Pernod.
>
> "Gotta light?" he said.
>
> "Yes," I said, offering to light a match for him.
>
> "Jesus," he said, furiously. "No, man, I meant the light of the wisdom of the East! How prosaic can you get, man?"
>
> "Man," he went on, "you failed my test!"[5]

HYPNOSIS

Considerable controversy surrounds the question of whether there is or is not a specific altered state of consciousness, the hypnotic state.[6] There is no doubt, however, that there is an *effect* called hypnosis; that it is induced in an individual by the power of suggestion; and that a hypnotized person will perform extra-ordinary actions which are not characteristic of his ordinary, normal, waking state of consciousness.

Hypnotism undoubtedly belongs in the paranatural class of occult phenomena, and its mechanism still remains hidden, long after its introduction by Franz Anton Mesmer over 200 years ago.

Hypnosis may be induced either individually or simultaneously, in a group of people. Hypnotists usually instruct their subjects to close their eyes, though this is not necessary. Then they may strongly suggest that the subjects, though not asleep, pay strict attention to what the hypnotist says, while disregarding all extraneous stimuli, suggestions, people, and distractions. Eighty to ninety per-cent of all people can be hypnotized to some extent; the others either will not or can not be hypnotized by anyone. Beginning hypnotists can hypnotize about 40 percent of their subjects. People differ in the depths of hypnosis they can attain and only 10 percent of all subjects can reach the deepest levels.

Hypnotism usually involves a monotonous repetition of a limited number of phrases which understimulate the senses in such a way as to affect the suscep-tible subject. The crux of the matter is suggestion. But the necessity and the exact action of the induction are still uncertain; hypnotism can also be accomplished without the utterance of a single word. Once a susceptible subject has been hyp-notized, by one procedure or another, the subject can be made to perform a number of unusual acts. Some examples follow.

• The hypnotized subject is told there is a dog standing next to him; after he opens his eyes he is to pet the dog, say a few kind words to it, lift it, and put it on a chair. Whereupon, the subject gives a performance indistinguishable from what it would be if a dog were actually present. The subject is undergoing a *positive hallucination*.

• Priscilla is hypnotized and the hypnotist tells her that her boy friend, John, is *not* in the audience. Then he tells her to open her eyes, look about, notice everyone in the room carefully, and tell him whether she recognizes anyone. She reports that she does not see anyone she knows. He directs her attention to John and asks if she recognizes him. Priscilla answers "no." She is under-going a *negative hallucination:* her eyes see but her brain does not.

• "Your eyes are shut," the hypnotist says to the subject, "and no matter how hard you try you will be unable to open them. Try to open them for yourself, and see. I dare you." The subject struggles to open his eyes, and finds he cannot. The eye muscles are locked by *paralysis*, under the hypnotist's control.

• *Anesthesia* can be induced by hypnosis. Many dentists have extracted teeth in this manner, without the use of drug anesthetics. Unfortunately this technique is neither fool-proof nor fail-safe. Some people cannot be hypnotized at all, and many cannot be hypnotized deeply enough or for the necessary length of time.

• One of the most enticing hypnotic phenomena is called *regression*. A girl is asked, "Who was your teacher in the third grade?" She does not know; she cannot remember. She is then hypnotized and told to imagine that she is going back in time, getting younger, until she reaches the age when she was in the third grade. "What was your teacher's name in the third grade?" she is now asked. "Mrs. Brown," she replies, unhesitatingly.

The hypnotist tells the girl to open her eyes and, still imagining herself to be in the third grade, to write her own name on a piece of paper. Holding the pencil stiffly, in the manner of a child, she writes her name in large, crude letters that must have been typical of her handwriting then.

• Still another astonishing facet of hypnosis is *posthypnotic suggestion*. A hypnotized subject is told that he will soon be asked to open his eyes. Then, the hypnotist says, he will casually say the word "butterflies" in some context, and the subject will promptly fall asleep. And so it happens. The particular word or signal is immaterial—it could just as well have been any other word, or a tug at the ear, or the tapping of a pencil.

One of the dangers of hypnosis is illustrated by this case. For if it should happen that the hypnotist does not remove the posthypnotic suggestion before dismissing the subject then the suggestion will last for some period of time—several hours usually, but sometimes much longer. The subject may be driving home in an automobile, listening to the radio. If by chance the word "butterflies" is spoken he may very well fall sound asleep while driving and possibly cause a serious accident. This danger, however, has been overworked. People have a built-in safety system, it seems, that removes the suggestibility when personal danger is involved.

An interesting corollary to the phenomenon of posthypnotic suggestion is the idea that kleptomaniacs or pyromaniacs act the way they do because of some compulsive suggestion which was given them at some earlier time—not by a hypnotist, but by some event in their lives. Claustrophobia, fear of cats, and many other.types of "irrational" behavior may be attributable to a type of posthypnotic behavior.

Another facet of the posthypnotic suggestion, a fascinating one but not without dangers, is the fact that a hypnotist, using it, may erase from the subjects all knowledge of their ever having been hypnotized. And a hypnotist may also make it difficult for any other individual to ever hypnotize this subject in the future. The subject will later deny having ever been hypnotized, and will become a difficult subject for other hypnotists. One shudders to think of the power this has given the hypnotist. For example, it may be quite impossible to convince a subject that he or she was not reincarnated, when this was suggested at an erased hypnotic session.

• A variation of hypnosis—suggestion by a hypnotist—is the important phenomenon of *autohypnosis*, hypnotizing oneself. This may take some difficult practice, but eventually it is possible to produce on oneself, by oneself, almost all the effects that can be produced by another person. Hallucinations, paralysis, anesthesia, regression, may all be self-produced. Some uses of autohypnosis can be beneficial: one can learn how to fall asleep at night instead of turning and tossing miserably in bed for hours. But some may be self-defeating: such as the delusion that one is the best lover in New Jersey.

A distinction should be made between autosuggestion and autohypnosis. Autohypnosis requires deep hypnosis. An example of autosuggestion is the Coué craze that swept the country in the 1920s. Daily people charmed themselves: "Every day, in every way, I am getting better and better."

In extreme cases autosuggestion may lead to a psychological phenomenon termed dissociation: the breaking up of the personality to such an extent that two completely different personalities may replace the initial one. Some people who personally commune with God, or with St. Augustine, or the Devil, may have gradually degenerated over a period of time from a mild case of autosuggestion.

Because of people's usual inability to determine the direction of their autosuggestion objectively rather than subjectively, this entire area is fraught with danger. Difficulties which might arise are not easily recognized by oneself, though they might be obvious to a trained outside observer. Good advice concerning autosuggestion is to be careful: this is something to be reserved for trained professionals.

QUESTIONS AND ANSWERS

• *Is a person asleep during hypnosis?* No. In many ways the hypnotic state is no different than the normal state. It is definitely not a sleep state, and it may prove, eventually, to be not even a trance state.

• *Can the hypnotist make a person do things that he would not do in his normal state?* That is a question that every teacher of the subject is asked by some student, sooner or later. Of course, what the student is really asking is, "Can the hypnotist make a person do things that *she* would not do in her normal state?" The subject cannot be forced to do anything under hypnosis, and if the hypnotist makes the attempt nevertheless, then the subject will come out of the hypnotic state. The answer to the question, then, is "no."

• *Can a person be hypnotized by a phonograph record, or radio, or TV?* Definitely "yes." In fact, tests of hypnosis by TV were so successful that broadcasts of this kind are forbidden.

• *Does hypnotic susceptibility vary with age?* Yes. Hypnotic susceptibility is present in five-year olds, rises to a peak in preadolescence, declines very slowly until the middle thirties, and declines more rapidly thereafter.

• *Will subjects obey a posthypnotic signal if they know they have been hypnotized?* The following report by Marcuse should answer this question:

The case is told of a young man who was told in hypnosis that at the count of three he would tug his ear-lobe. When awakened, he stated quite sarcastically that he wasn't even "near" being hypnotized, and then he proceeded to describe in detail the posthypnotic suggestion that he had been given. During this tirade by the subject, the hypnotist quietly counted to three, whereupon the subject was described as saying "aw shucks" and pulling his ear-lobe.[7]

• *How long is a posthypnotic suggestion effective?* It depends. The remembrance of nonsense syllables has been reported 20 years later; the remembrance of a buried traumatic experience has been forgotten in 20 minutes. The effects of most hypnotic suggestions wear off in a few hours. The danger comes from the few that last longer.

• *Are there different levels of hypnosis?* Any attempt to set depth levels in hypnosis is arbitrary. Some hypnotists use three levels, some try to distinguish among thirty. The following scheme of six levels seems a practical compromise.

Level	Characteristics	Percent Hypnotized Reaching Level
1	Catalepsy (rigidity) of small muscles. Swallowing. Can be induced to be unable to open eyes.	100
2	Catalepsy of medium-sized muscles. Can be induced to be unable to bend or lower arm.	90
3	Catalepsy of entire body. Can be induced to forget name, or to count 1,2,3,4,5,6,8,9,10; or to be unable to rise from a chair, or to walk.	60
4	True amnesia, not merely difficulty with articulation. Can be induced to feel no pain, though sensation of touch remains.	30
5	Positive hallucinations. Can be induced to feel neither pain nor sensation of touch; or to tell the time shown by a nonpresent clock on wall.	20
6	Negative hallucinations. Can be induced to be unable to see an object directly ahead.	10

• *Are there any personality factors that may be related to susceptibility to hypnosis?* Perhaps, but they do not include intelligence, gullibility, sex, psychic powers, or submissiveness. People who exhibited an imaginative childhood, sometimes as an outlet for stern parents, show greater susceptibility.

• *Can hypnosis increase one's muscular strength?* Yes, up to very close to the maximum possible.

• *Can hypnosis improve one's memory?* Despite the recall which is possible under hypnotic regression, the subject's memory in his or her normal state is not improved by a previous hypnosis. Neither is posthypnotic suggestion effective here. But some hypnotists claim that autohypnosis over an extended period is effective in improving memory.

• *Can persons be hypnotized against their will?* Ordinarily not. The will to cooperate with the hypnotist is central to the success of hypnosis, and if persons do not wish to be hypnotized they cannot be hypnotized. Through trickery, however, subjects may be hypnotized without their knowledge.

• *Do people reveal their own, true nature under hypnosis?* No. People under hypnosis will not do what they do not want to do.

• *Is hypnosis effective in treating mental illness?* Mental illness, which fills a large proportion of the hospital beds throughout the country, is frequently connected with a phenomenon which Sigmund Freud discovered, the complex. A complex is a repression, often dating back to one's early childhood, in which the subconscious mind withholds some knowledge from the conscious mind because of a conflict and because the conscious mind rejects the information. The real difficulty arises when the repression itself causes a conflict between the conscious and the subconscious. There is little doubt that many physical diseases also have a psychosomatic origin and can be traced back to a complex. It appears that the Freudian complex can, in a manner of speaking, be considered a posthypnotic suggestion—with the modification that it is caused by life instead of by a hypnotist.

It seemed to Freud that hypnosis should be able both to uncover the basic conflict and to resolve it; but this turns out to be a most difficult task indeed. The neurosis or psychosis built up by the patient over a long period of time is so strong that he or she very strongly resists attempts to uncover it; and, unfortunately, deep hypnosis works on only a minority of people. Freud himself tried hypnosis as a method of combatting mental disease. But he gave it up, favoring psychoanalysis—a method which is drawn-out and expensive and does not always work.

• *Are there dangers in hypnotizing a subject?* It is extremely important that the hypnotist refrain from negative suggestions that might lead the subject to feel inferior or deficient. Such suggestions may enter the subject's subconscious and produce psychological damage.

It is also very important to dehypnotize a subject thoroughly at the end of each session. Although the hypnosis itself would wear off eventually (the required time varying with the individual), and there is no danger of the subject remaining attached by invisible bonds to the hypnotist in Svengali fashion, it is necessary to remove any posthypnotic suggestions that the subject may retain.

In closing a session, the hypnotist eases the subject back from the journey through consciousness. The following is typical of dehypnosis:

You will begin to waken. Your sleep will get lighter and lighter. You are now beginning to awake. Your sleep is now becoming lighter; much lighter, much lighter. You are beginning to waken. I will count from one to ten, and as I count from one to ten your sleep will become lighter and lighter. And at the count of ten you will be wide awake, wide awake. Wide awake. One-two-three—your sleep is becoming lighter, much lighter, much lighter; four-five-six —you are starting to waken, starting to waken. Seven-eight-nine—you are almost awake now, almost awake. Ten. You are now wide awake, wide awake, and feeling fine. You feel just fine and you're wide awake.

CHAPTER SEVEN

SEERS AND THE MYSTIC ARTS

■ *Foretelling the Unknown* ■ *Ancient Divination*
■ *Nostradamus* ■ *J. W. Dunne* ■ *Catching a Premonition*
■ *Edgar Cayce* ■ *Dowsing* ■ *The Table Turns*
■ *Phrenology* ■ *Graphology* ■ *Numerology*
■ *I Ching* ■ *The Meaning*

FORETELLING THE UNKNOWN

A branch of the occult most difficult for a rational person to accept is that of prophecy. The idea that a person can predict the future seems to demand that the future be preordained. People and events become, in this view, merely convenient bearers of computer cards—like actors and props in a very complicated play which merely unfolds according to a script by a supernatural playwright. But can the future then be altered? We touched upon this issue in Chapter 4, where we presented some of the modern statistical evidence that seems to favor a degree of precognitive ability. Like it or not, understand it or not, this evidence that strains one's credibility cannot logically be ignored.

Still another fact makes the study of this phenomenon a worthwhile activity rather than a mere regurgitation of age-old superstitions. There seem to have always been a number of individuals who possessed a mystical self-assurance in their gift of prophecy. Were they self-deluded? Were they conscious frauds? Is there any hard evidence to convince a man from Missouri one way or the other? Some of these prophets convinced multitudes of people of the reality of their extraordinary gifts, and thereby affected the course of history.

In this chapter we will also treat a few of the many methods of divination, arts of foretelling the future or revealing the unknown present. These have come down to us from the past and are in use today. One of these methods, astrology, has achieved such a degree of popularity that we have accorded it a special study of its own in Chapter 12. In the present chapter we discuss prophecy and prophets, the art of dowsing, the pseudoscience of phrenology, the almost-science of graphology, the nonscience of numerology and, finally, the mystic art of the *I Ching*. There are many other prophetic systems extant which we unfortunately do not have the time to study. So the reader who is interested in learning about Tarot cards, palmistry, tea leaves, or crystal balls will have to seek elsewhere.

ANCIENT DIVINATION

The record of prophecy among our distant ancestors goes back some 5,000 years, to China, Babylon, Sumeria, Assyria. The fabric of which their divination was constituted was mostly threads of dreams and stars; yet this flimsy cloth was strong enough to survive the ravages of five millenia of time.

One thread which did *not* survive is a method of prediction known as hepatoscopy. This consisted of an examination of the liver of an animal, usually a sheep, to advise the king of the probable consequences of some proposed action. Was a proposed trade mission a good idea? Would it succeed? Gradually a special group of seers arose, trained in the art of reading the omens shown by the liver. Sometimes the intestines or other organs were used. Eventually the seers learned to couch their omens in generalities—the better to survive the wrath of the ruler. We have no account of what percent of the predictions actually came true. From the hindsight of 5,000 years, it just looks weird.

Neither dreams, nor stars, nor livers played much of a role in prophecy among the ancient Hebrews, the people of the Bible. In fact, such methods were anathema to devout Jews, who associated them with the polytheistic beliefs of their neighbors, all of them spiritual enemies. Prophecy in the Bible is associated with prophets who claimed to be passing on, directly to the people rather than to the king, revelations obtained straight from God. Usually they placed blame rather than foretold happiness; and the blame was placed on the Hebrews rather than on their enemies. As a result, the lives of these prophets were not especially secure. The people then, as now, preferred happy prophets to prophets of doom.

Why, therefore, didn't the prophets court the favor of the masses? Perhaps it is simply that they preferred the ultimate security of the truth they glimpsed.

In ancient Egypt the art of divination was given a magical, mumbo-jumbo content. Statues of the gods with movable jaws were employed to address the people directly. Necromancy, divination of the future by the exhumed dead, was practiced. Although this art was widely practiced elsewhere, it is perhaps most easily understood in connection with the early Egyptians, who seemed to embrace a mystic rendezvous with the dead. Dreams also played a large role in Egyptian divination, but their divining was done for the pharaoh rather than for the people.

The ancient Greeks were wise believers in dumb luck. Life to them was not something that could be planned but was more nearly a collection, in time, of a series of accidents—illogical, implacable, and doomed to tragedy in the end, try to escape as one would. The very history of this people—superior in almost everything to all their contemporaries but, nevertheless, unable to survive—lends credence to their beliefs. So it is perhaps surprising that this logical people, knowing they could do nothing to influence their destiny, should illogically implore the fates and the furies to avoid their destiny.

One of their principal means of augury was consulting with the oracles. There were many oracles in ancient Greece but the most famous, by far, was the oracle at Delphi. Originally Delphi, because of a scenic setting, served as a sort of tourist center; but it began to achieve special notoriety and accumulate special wealth as a result of a growing conviction that there was an especial accuracy in the prognostication of the Delphic oracle. The peak of its fame was probably reached in the sixth century b.c., but its influence extended over a period of almost 1,000 years.

One particular cave in Delphi was situated directly behind a golden statue of Apollo and was set in the temple of Apollo before Mt. Parnassus. Towering cliffs and a deep gorge gave a spectacular aura of mystery to the place. Within a cleft in the cave, according to legend, gases escaped from the bowels of the earth; the gases induced a trance state in anyone breathing them deeply. Here a priestess, the pythia, would be brought once a month to go into a trance and utter obscure sounds which were, however, full of meaning for specially trained priests. The priests were all well-educated men, of noble descent; the pythia was an ignorant commoner on whom a special constraint was placed—she had to be a virgin. For hundreds of years only beautiful young girls were selected as pythias, but after one was seduced by a client the priests henceforth decided to pick only elderly, and homely, candidates.

Among the other peoples of the Mediterranean basin, the cradle of Western civilization, the role of prophecy varied. The Romans, to whom sibyls were very important, had a Sibyl of Cumae whose oracles were consulted in the Temple of Jupiter, in Rome, on the eve of great decisions. To the Arabs, who played a primary role in transporting and developing the ideas of mathematics, science, and astrology from the Orient to the West, prophecy was of negligible importance except for their veneration of the Prophet Mohammed. And the early Christians were opposed to prophecy because of its heathen connections. "No art at all is involved in soothsaying, and only accident makes some of its predictions come true," wrote St. Augustine.[1]

NOSTRADAMUS

The Renaissance produced possibly the outstanding prophet of all time. Michel de Notredame (1503–1566), known to us as Nostradamus, was a French physician who delivered his prophecies in a poetic form which has great charm, even in English translation. The prophesies were mostly concerned with political events, but were usually couched in such general terms that their implications often remained either obscure or ambiguous, capable of being employed to justify any point of view.

A few of his predictions, however, were sharp and to the point. Various of his proponents have selected quatrains from Nostradamus claiming to show that he predicted the French Revolution, Napoleon, atom bombs, Hitler. . . During World War II the Nazis used selected writings of Nostradamus, in leaflets dropped behind the French lines, to undermine the enemy's morale. The selections were made by a Swiss astrologer, Karl Ernst Krafft, who had come to the attention of Dr. Joseph Goebbels because of a correct prediction of Krafft's that Hitler's life would be endangered during early November 1939. We do not doubt that a British astrologer could have selected other verses showing that the Nazis would most certainly lose the war.

Nostradamus's parents were Jews who had converted to Roman Catholicism and he, himself, remained a devout Catholic all his life. He led an uneventful early life, learning Latin, Greek, Hebrew, and a great deal about herbs and magic. At the age of 26 he became a physician, and he soon made a considerable reputation counteracting the plague which was then ravishing Provence. Nevertheless, his wife and two sons soon fell victims of the scourge, and he was helpless to save them. It was after this, while he wandered for eight years in the desert of his sorrow, that he began to develop psychic powers.

We will detail only one of the many tales of prophecy attributed to Nostradamus in this period, stories which eventually made him famous throughout all France. He saw a young monk walking toward him. Kneeling before the unknown, common-born youngster, Nostradamus said, "I kneel before his Holiness," a statement which his companions treated as a joke. Some 45 years later this monk became Pope Sixtus V, and the story of Nostradamus was recalled. Is the story a true one? If it is, is it mere coincidence? We cannot know, for sure; and this, of course, makes it all the more intriguing.

In 1547 Nostradamus remarried; he also published his prophecies, *Centuries*, which were said to have been made when he was in a trance. Queen Catherine, the wife of King Henri II, had an overwhelming interest in the occult and summoned him, in 1556, to learn the fate of her seven children. As it turned out, they all, uniformly, met disastrous ends; but Nostradamus, knowing this in advance, was said only to have foretold, "They will all be kings." They were. But such a story does not advance the fame of Nostradamus substantially.

Nostradamus foretold his own death in 1566; and he predicted terrible catastrophies for the years 1999 and 7000. So we have to wait less than a quarter century for a test of the accuracy of this prophet.

J. W. DUNNE

With Nostradamus prophecy occurred when he was in a state of trance; and he certainly recognized that his gift of prophecy, real or imagined, was a most unusual one. Coming much closer to our own time, we find a dreamer who not only claimed that his dreams were premonitory, but who believed that this was quite ordinary. Everybody had such dreams, he thought; it was just a question of remembering them.

The dreamer was J. W. Dunne, an English airplane pilot and experimenter in aeronautics, and a Fellow of the Royal Aeronautical Society. In 1927 he wrote a book, *An Experiment with Time*, which recounted some of his experiences. It is worth noting that the world's outstanding authority on dreams, Sigmund Freud, discounted any possibility of their being prophetic:

> I am therefore of opinion that after one has taken into account the untrustworthiness, credulity, and unconvincingness of most of these reports, together with the possibility of falsifications of memory facilitated by emotional causes and the inevitability of a few lucky shots, it may be anticipated that the spectre of veridical prophetic dreams will disappear into nothing.[2]

Nevertheless, what were some of Dunne's dreams? Once, in South Africa in 1902, he dreamt he was on a hilly island on which jets of vapor issued from cracks in the ground. He knew it would soon blow up from volcanic action, and he tried to warn French authorities that 4,000 people would perish unless an immediate evacuation took place. The next boat to arrive from England carried news of the eruption of Mont Pelee on Martinique in the West Indies: 40,000 people lost their lives. (Dunne read this as 4,000 in the newspaper account. Only 15 years later did he recognize the discrepancy.)

Again, he dreamt of a fire in a fog. The jet of water from a fire engine had scarcely any effect. People were choking, gasping, dropping dead everywhere. Smoke covered everything. He awoke, frightened, and went for the morning papers. They contained no news of such a catastrophe. But the evening papers did. There had been a disastrous fire in a rubber factory in Paris, and the details fit his dream.

What are we to make of J. W. Dunne today, with the hindsight of half a century? Simply this: ex post facto storytelling is not convincing. Make a prediction. Give all the details, being as specific as possible. Then give it to some trustworthy agent to hold, to ensure it is not tampered with. Finally, when the predicted event occurs, bring the prediction to the attention of impartial observers. Let them check the facts against the predictions. Only then can there be any credibility. Anything less has the makings of a myth.

CATCHING A PREMONITION

The need to judge, more scientifically, the quality of prophecy has led to the founding of a number of premonition registries. Registries have been set up in London, Toronto, and New York City. The Central Premonitions Registry in New York (Box 482, Times Square Station, New York, N.Y. 10036), which was begun in 1968 by R. D. Nelson and Stanley Krippner, is patterned on the *Evening Standard* Premonitions Bureau of London, founded by the late J. C. Barker. The New York Registry presently carries 13 categories of premonitions, including Prominent Personalities, Natural Disasters, and War and International Relations.

Premonitions can be documented as valid only if they are first recorded and handed to an objective party, such as one of the Registries, *before* the occurrence of the subsequent events which they predict. The New York Registry considers a premonition as correct only if it is registered a short time before the event, if the details fit closely, and if coincidence is unlikely. Predicting the outcome of a presidential race or a sporting event is hardly considered a feat of prophecy. But one person, Rex Coile, did register, on June 10, 1969, his prediction that the New York Mets, then with odds 100–1 against them, would win the 1969 World Series.

Several other predictions registered with the Central Premonitions Registry follow[3]:

- Alan Vaughan, June 10, 1969: "I see tragedy coming soon for Bob Hope, possibly even death." Ivor Hope, Bob's brother, died of a heart attack five days later.

- On July 29, 1969, Lorna Middleton sent, from London, a sketch of a plane crash on a lake. On August 3, a picture of a crashed, half submerged airline was run in a London newspaper.

- Thomas Casa of New York wrote on May 12, 1969: "In my dream I saw what appeared to be a Piper-type plane. The rudder was painted blue and the number was N129N, N429N, or N29N. . . I saw the craft make a bumpy landing and the craft nosed over." A Piper-type aircraft, serial number N3149X, crashed on August 31, 1969, carrying Rocky Marciano to his death. The photo ran in a New York newspaper.

The registries find that premonitions often come in dreams. Those who work at remembering their dreams seem to be able to develop their premonitory powers. Here are a few helpful pointers for the reader who wishes to improve in this respect. The method is actually a form of self-hypnosis. Just before going to sleep say to yourself, 20 times: "I will wake up after a dream. I will remember the dream." Say it to yourself, under your breath. Each time you say it, tuck in a finger; that is, use your fingers to do the counting. Repeat this procedure night after night without fail, going twice completely through the fingers of both hands, so that it becomes a regular part of your falling-asleep pattern. Keep a pad and pencil handy at the bedside or under the pillow. Upon waking, and while still in bed, immediately review the feelings and thoughts of any dreams you have had. Then, at once, write down all the details, starting from the most recent images and working your way backward toward the earlier ones.

The considerable number of well-documented premonitions published in the various parapsychology journals point up the fact that premonitions are often quite accurate. Rarely, however, do they agree with the eventual facts in full detail. Of the first 3,500 premonitions received by the New York Registry, only about one percent were eventually considered to have come true. But within this small fraction sufficient details were given to enable the registry to exclude chance agreement as a likely explanation.

Another factor tending to eliminate coincidence as a plausible explanation is the fact that the true predictions are not evenly distributed. There are a few gifted individuals who consistently score ten times as high as the average score attained in all the registered predictions. Yet even these sensitive prophets are by no means infallible.

We have checked the public predictions made by 16 famous psychics in the *National Enquirer* during 1973 and 1974.[4] We excluded all predictions which were obvious extrapolations of current events—for example, President Nixon's resignation. We also excluded predictions about events which could not be easily checked. We found we had 49 predictions remaining. Of these we judged that 40 were incorrect and 9 correct. But most of these 9 predictions were in no way unusual. They fell into the class of predictions typified by "Two internationally known Hollywood film stars will die suddenly this year."

We certainly see, both in the registry studies and in the laboratory, that precognition or prophecy is not a strong faculty. Even among those few who claim its bold gifts, the art of prophecy is a chancy wonderment at best.

EDGAR CAYCE

The most famous seer of modern times is Edgar Cayce (pronounced Casey), and numerous books have been written about him. Born in 1877 near Hopkinsville, Kentucky, his training was rudimentary. His education terminated in the sixth grade but he retained a lifelong affection for literature.

Cayce's first occult experience occurred when he was only eight. He saw visions of his dead grandfather, and shortly thereafter he gave some medical advice to his parents, advising them on the preparation of a poultice to be applied to his own neck as a remedy for a condition caused when a baseball hit him in the head. This was the first of 30,000 readings which he subsequently gave, readings he continued until his death in 1945. The Cayce Foundation in Virginia Beach, Virginia, has classified almost 15,000 of them, those given from 1901 on. They are predominantly of a medical nature, and the ones that relate to prophecy are of strictly secondary importance.

Before Cayce gave a reading he put himself into a trance state by means that strongly suggest autohypnosis. The plausibility of this is strengthened by the fact that he never knew, after he came out of his trance state, what he had said in his reading. In fact, he was often completely unaware, in his normal state, of facts, languages, and figures that he had employed in his psychic state. Cayce was known, therefore, as the sleeping prophet.

He was a devoutly religious man and read the Bible constantly throughout his life. His oft-stated aim in life was to help other people, and he exhausted himself with health readings and divination aimed toward this end. He had no interest in material things, and his family often lived close to poverty. A few times he tried to utilize his psychic power for personal gain, but he invariably fell ill as a result and soon gave up these attempts. He was, however, normal in other ways: he worked very hard, but he enjoyed cards, gardening, and fishing; and though he loved his wife dearly, he did enjoy being in the presence of beautiful women.

As a healer, Cayce often suggested the application of castor-oil packs. He prescribed gold chloride for "any condition wherein there is any form of the condition bordering on rheumatics, or of rejuvenating any organ of the system delinquent in action." He recommended "three almonds a day" to guard against cancer. Cayce often ascribed spinal lesions as the basic source of various difficulties. Needless to say, his efforts as a healer won him the bitter enmity of the American Medical Association. They considered him an uneducated, dangerous quack. As a result, when Cayce advocated the use of a specialist it was usually an osteopath or a chiropractor.

What is one to make of the many tales having psychic overtones which surround this man? While in a trance Cayce would describe the symptoms of a man whom he did not know and had never seen, a man who at that moment could be hundreds of miles away. This is alleged to have happened not once but hundreds of times. And, according to the patients, the descriptions were accurate and Cayce's prescriptions worked.

On one occasion Cayce treated a doctor's wife. Her physician had diagnosed a tumor in her stomach as the source of her problems. Cayce's diagnosis was succinct: pregnancy, with an attendant bowel disorder. Successful delivery of the child cured the illness. On another occasion Cayce diagnosed the ailment afflicting Dr. Wesley Ketchum, a homeopath, as a spinal disorder. Ketchum, himself, had believed the symptoms indicated appendicitis. Cayce proved correct, and Dr. Ketchum reported the case favorably to the American Society of Clinical Research at Boston. The *New York Times* ran a story on this on October 9, 1910 and, as a result, people flocked to Cayce.

Some of Cayce's readings in the trance state dealt with prophecy. These were predominantly concerned with world events rather than with the future of a particular individual. One item that kept recurring over a 20-year period was the lost continent of Atlantis. This continent, according to Cayce, would rise again from the waters where it had been buried for 12,000 years. The turgid style of Cayce's readings is evident in the following passage describing his vision of Atlantis:

> With the continued disregard of those that were keeping all those laws as applicable to the Sons of God, man brought in the destructive forces that combined with those natural resources of the gases, of the electrical forces, that made the first of the eruptions that awoke from the depth of the slow-cooling earth, and that portion now near what would be termed the Sargasso Sea first went into the depths.[5]

In 1940 Cayce predicted that a portion of Atlantis would rise again, first in the area near Bimini, off the Florida east coast; and he gave 1968 or 1969 as the date. In this he was most assuredly wrong. He also predicted that evidence concerning Atlantis would eventually be found, hidden away in Egypt among other places, but he gave no date for the find.

Another subject that appeared time and again in Cayce's prophecies was that of geological cataclysms. His predictions were sometimes general, sometimes very specific, and often quite wrong. Among his predictions are the following: Los Angeles, New York, and San Francisco would suffer destruction some time after 1958 and before 2000; parts of Japan would slide into the sea in this period; the earth's axis would be tilted; the Great Lakes would empty into the Gulf of Mexico instead of the St. Lawrence River; and northern Europe would suffer drastic changes. None of these predictions have yet come true but, of course, there is still time left.

All in all, Cayce's record in prophecy is quite unimpressive, and the assertions of his followers that some of his predictions have already been fulfilled seem to be very strained. His record in healing, on the other hand, seems extraordinary. Despite his arrests for practicing medicine without a license, despite the learned opposition of the AMA, despite his lack of education or training, there is no dearth of individuals who testified that Cayce helped them where everyone else failed. Call the cases psychosomatic, call the methods deplorably unscientific, call him anything one wishes—the fact remains that thousands of people swore that he helped them back to health. Nobody pretends to know how he did this, least of all Cayce himself, who was always amazed at his trance statements.

DOWSING

One type of divination that is practiced by a comparatively large group of people is variously called dowsing, water witching, or water divination. Its practitioners are predominantly either farmers, well diggers, or retired people, most of whom practice their art as a hobby. People of many other trades and professions engage in it also, and it is found that there is little, if any, correlation with education. There are fees charged for the dowsing service, but these are generally minimal. One piece of equipment is an integral part of the practice: the divining rod. It is often a forked twig in the shape of a Y, made of the wood of almost any kind of tree. However, a bent metal rod, a swinging pendulum, or even a radio tube will do. These have all been used by one dowser or another.

Dowsing divines something that presently exists. Various forms of dowsing were common among the ancient Medes, Persians, Scythians, Greeks, and Romans. In his travels during the late thirteenth and early fourteenth centuries Marco Polo encountered dowsing among the Orientals. And in 1556 Georgius Agricola wrote about the application of dowsing to mining in his substantial work *De Re Metallica.*

The modern-day use of divining rods began in Germany in the early sixteenth century. They were employed in an effort to detect veins of metal ore and were of interest only to small groups of people. It was only when the rod began to be employed for finding water that it became popular among a wider slice of the population.

Figure 7–1 shows how the divining rod is held in the hands when a dowser seeks water. The knuckles are down, the palms face up, and the twig or rod

Fig. 7–1. Divining rod and dowser. (Reproduced from the collection of the Library of Congress.)

points either partly forward or straight up. The dowser paces back and forth over a field, gripping the rod tightly. Absorbed in this work, the dowser is oblivious to distracting stimuli and experiences considerable muscular tension. Then, at a certain point in the dowser's peregrinations, presumably at a point where there is water flowing in a vein or stream underneath the ground on which the dowser is standing, the rod suddenly points downward. According to all dowsers, this motion occurs spontaneously and quite independent of any conscious thought or movement on the part of the dowser.

The dowser notes this special spot in the field, and a well is subsequently dug there. Usually the dowser attributes the movement of the divining rod to an external force or pull exerted on the rod by the flowing water, and estimates the depth of the spring by the intensity of the pull on the rod. The depth is important, for often it is not just the location of water that is required of the dowser but also an estimate of the cost of digging the well.

The interest in dowsing among the general public in America was greatly enhanced by the books written by Kenneth Roberts about his personal experiences with the Maine dowser Henry Gross. Roberts listed one dowsing ability that he said Gross possessed, one that few other dowsers claimed: long-distance dowsing. Given a map of some land in England, Henry Gross in America moved his divining rod back and forth over the map until the rod dipped. Roberts declared that when wells were dug at the points indicated by Henry Gross water was found. A remarkable similarity is seen to exist between this claim and the previous one noted for Edgar Cayce and long-distance healing.

There are two questions of outstanding interest with respect to the subject of dowsing. First of all, does the effect actually exist? Is it self-delusion or does the divining rod actually dip, by some mechanism beyond the control of the dowser? Second, if the effect does exist, then just what is it? What is the mechanism by which it works?

A fact agreed to by all investigators of the subject is the honesty and sincerity of the vast majority of dowsers. There is no conspiracy to hoodwink the public. Dowsers do believe they possess such an ability; they feel they need the rod to find the water; they know that they do not knowingly produce the dip in the dowsing rod. However, most laboratory tests on dowsers, to date, have revealed little unusual ability for finding water under the confines of laboratory conditions.

A large indoor area is divided into squares of equal size and one container is placed under each square. Half the containers are empty; half are filled with water. A flip of a coin determines, in a random fashion, whether a particular container is to be filled or not. So the probability for just guessing whether there is water under a particular square is $1/2$. No extended tests of this kind have ever been reported where dowsers have achieved significantly better than chance expectations. And when a comparison is made of the success achieved in well sinkings at divined as opposed to nondivined sites the results are almost indistinguishable.[6]

But the results are not always negative. In 1968 a part-time dowser, Robert Leftwich, was tested publicly on British TV.[7] Professor John Cohen, a critic of dowsing, had buried some cans containing water, one knife, and several dummy containers at places unknown to anyone else. There were no visual clues to the locations. In the presence of Professor Cohen, the dipping of Leftwich's rod located three of the hidden water cans. He did not find the knife. Professor Cohen openly admitted that he was impressed; but Leftwich, himself, was disappointed that he had missed the knife and the other two cans.

Various experiments have been performed on the rods themselves. One rod was suspended horizontally from a vertical string which supported it. Tests were made to see if the rod would dip when water was placed beneath one end. No motion was noted. One may conclude that the dip of the dowsing rod is not caused by a physical attraction between the water and the rod. Regardless of what most dowsers think, the rod is not pulled down by the water. We, ourselves, conclude that the dip of the dowsing rod is a real effect. Regardless of what sceptics think, the rod does dip involuntarily.

An objection has been raised to the types of experiments described above: the water in the containers was still water, while the water flowing in underground streams is moving water. This objection, however, is based on a misconception. The water under the surface of the earth does not generally exist in the form of streams or rivers. There is a layer, within the ground, where the earth is completely water-logged. This extends up to a certain level called the water table. The water is static. It is this water table that one seeks in drilling a new well.

What, then, is responsible for causing the dowser's stick to dip? The dowsing stick *does* dip, but not because the water pulls it. We undoubtedly have, in dowsing, an automatism similar to the one we have already encountered in automatic writing and in trance speech. The rod moves because of unconscious muscular activity on the part of the dowser. It is only after intense concentration, with a tight grip on the two forks of the rod for a long time, that the rod becomes active. Then the muscular nerves become deactivated; and even a slight motion of the wrists will produce a rapid jerk of the twig, which is normally in an equilibrium state under high tension.

One's interest then shifts to the unconscious nervous system of the dowser. What influences it to trigger the automatism? Chance? Visual cues from the surroundings? Some subtle physical force of water on the central nervous system? Some form of ESP? It would seem plausible to suggest that there is an intimate connection between dowsing and clairvoyance. Clairvoyance is so complicated that it is usually only studied on a statistical basis; but dowsing is more complex in that it also involves an automatism.

One complication that hinders attempts to test dowsing ability in the field rests on the fact that the pure-chance odds for finding a well are not easily determined. In some places digging a hole anywhere will bring in a well; but in other places there is no spot where digging a hole will bring in a well. So the odds are not necessarily 50–50, nor are they any other figure. So far, nobody has been able to suggest a method for determining what this chance level is. Only when this has been found will it be possible to state whether dowsers are more effective than geologists in finding water. We do know that oil companies seem to prefer geologists to dowsers.

Dowsing does involve an automatism. Its source is one we can partly see, but its full origin is still puzzling. Nevertheless, the automatism itself is so interesting that it deserves another look in a very different guise; and it is to this that we now proceed.

THE TABLE TURNS

Over a century ago, a most gifted physicist, Michael Faraday, then already world famous for his many discoveries in electromagnetism, investigated a spiritualist effect called table turning. This craze, which had sprung up in England in the wake of the spiritualism started by the Fox sisters in America in 1848, placed a number of people about a round table with the palms of their hands on the table top. There they sat quietly, sometimes for several hours, in deep concentration, waiting for the table to turn in some predetermined direction as a sign of communication with the spirit world. Eventually the table would begin to move randomly, and ever so slightly; but then it would turn decisively in the wished-for direction. If the people continued to sit, the table would continue to turn until the sitters had their hands completely stretched out; but if the sitters arose to follow the revolving table, then the table would continue to revolve faster, and still faster. Eventually the table would be spinning so fast that the people could not run fast enough to keep up, and they would be forced to drop out by the exuberant spirits.

The participants in table turning were all completely convinced that the table turned independently of their own wishes or forces. Faraday decided to test this.[8] By arranging several layers of thick paper with a soft cement between them he was able to prove that the uppermost layer, the one touched by the hands of the participants, was shifted in the direction of rotation from its original position; and it was displaced by a larger amount than the shift of the lowest layer of paper, the one soft-cemented to the table top. In other words, the sitters were not following the revolution of the table—the hands were causing the table to turn. And this was unknown to the participants, who swore they were followers and not leaders.

Faraday then made an arrangement of levers that actuated a pointer to indicate whether the upper paper layer was turning clockwise, say, before the lower paper layers did. If the pointer went to the left, that meant the table was turning first; if to the right, the hands were turning before the table. If the indicator was hidden from the participants its readings merely substantiated Faraday's previous results; but if the participants were permitted to see the indicator while seated about the table waiting for it to turn, then all motion of the table ceased. The feedback of information to the sitters inhibited them. Their unconscious muscular efforts, which had provided the motive power for the revolution of the table when they could not see the indicator, disappeared when visual feedback supplied their brains with the information of these muscular efforts. Evidently the normal feedback, by the nerves attached to the muscles themselves, was inoperative in this automatism. Whether this lack of feedback was caused by autosuggestion or by fatigue, the participants had no way of knowing their muscles were doing the pushing. They all swore they were merely following the rotation manifested by the spirits.

We turn now, from this aside into automatism, to discuss some of the mystic arts of divination.

PHRENOLOGY

Phrenology is a mystic art, now long aborted, that served society well. A German doctor born in 1758, Franz Joseph Gall, had observed among his fellow medical students a correlation between good memories and prominent eyes. Gall concluded that a certain part of the brain, that concerned with memory, was located behind the eyeballs. Another part of the brain, that dealing with self-esteem, was located at the top of the head toward the back; and destructiveness was located near the ears. He divided the functioning of the brain into 37 distinct faculties, each localized as a separate organ in a different part of the cranium. The size and the contour of the head was, thus, very much affected by the relative development of these different faculties, and to one who was expert in such matters it ought to be possible to judge a person's character by making measurements of his or her cranium or, in the case of a dead person, of the skull. A large head would, of course, be associated with a full development of many of the faculties.

Gall was a very serious experimental scientist and a very competent physiologist. Until his death in 1828, he tried to perfect his theory, and he was not ashamed to admit ignorance. Figure 7–2, which illustrates the location of the various faculties in the brain, was completed by his followers. Gall, himself, left various portions of this chart blank since he had insufficient experimental evidence. Between 1810 and 1819 he published four large volumes of a book titled *Anatomy and Physiology of the Nervous System in General, and of the Brain in Particular;* later this was followed by *On the Functions of the Brain and on Each of Its Parts.* He was a pioneer in the study of the physiology of the brain.

To his studies of the structure of the brain and the cranium Gall added theories of psychology and social philosophy. Though he was an elitist who considered most people mediocrities in need of wise leaders, preferably strong geniuses, his theories appealed mostly to the reformers and radicals of his day. For his theories, that humans had potentialities that could not only be measured but improved, soon found a wide application that fit the democratic belief that all persons are created equal.

Although Gall was a medical researcher of the highest quality, he was not very

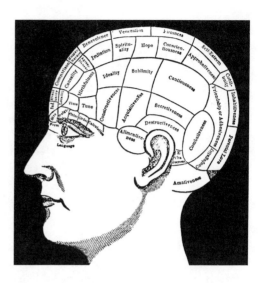

Fig. 7–2. Phrenology. Promoters of this belief claimed that various psychological traits are governed by different sections of the brain. They also advocated cheerfulness, fresh air, brown bread, and cold showers. (Reprinted, by permission of the author, from John D. Davies, *Phrenology: Fad and Science*, Hamden, Ct., Shoestring Press, 1971, p. 6.)

competent in public-relations work, and it remained for a former pupil of his, Johann Spurzheim, to popularize his ideas. Starting in 1802, Spurzheim found application of Gall's ideas to the treatment of three groups: pupils, prisoners, and the insane. In the course of this work a growing estrangement occurred between the two men as Spurzheim gradually altered his master's ideas. Some of the brain's faculties, as assigned by Gall, were of an evil nature; but Spurzheim did not believe in original sin and thought that all human propensities were good, only needing the perfection of phrenology to bring them out.

In one of Spurzheim's lectures in Edinburgh he had a listener, George Combe, whose instant conversion had an important bearing on the future of phrenology. Combe had no medical training, but was an excellent lecturer. For him phrenology became an optimistic religious substitute for the pessimistic Calvinism in which he had been raised. He quickly learned both to dissect the brain and to lecture on the reform of human affairs; but more important, from an organizational viewpoint, he started the first society of phrenology. The society published a 500-page volume of transactions and soon instituted a Phrenological Journal. Combe also wrote numerous books, of which one, *The Constitution of Man*, published in 1828, enjoyed a very wide sale. By the 1830s there were a dozen prenological societies in England. These, however, were small and appealed mostly to the upper classes. The 66 books that had been written by then on phrenology also were directed primarily to this group.

The conversion of phrenology to a popular cause, a mass movement, took place not in England or Europe, where it was born, but in the United States. It had been brought here in the 1820s by English books and American travellers returning from Europe, and was given great momentum by Spurzheim's New England tour in 1832. Spurzheim died in the midst of the tour, after arousing tremendous interest in phrenology. There were 3,000 marchers at his funeral in

Boston. Another lecture tour, by George Combe between 1838 and 1840, also provided great impetus to the movement. He gave 158 lectures in many of the cities east of the Appalachians, and the audiences always numbered in the hundreds.

The tour of George Combe may have been the high-water mark of phrenology. Although Boston was the chief center of the organization, there were some 50 associations in different cities of the country at one time or another. Yet phrenology appealed to only a limited group of people, and was mainly of medical and scientific concern until Orson Fowler and his brother Lorenzo transformed it into a movement with wide popular interest. These brothers had neither a background nor an interest in medicine. They took the lumps and the bumps on the cranium and made craniology a system of divination that gave advice on love, health, marriage, happiness, and child-rearing. Orson Fowler was just what phrenology needed to become a "growth stock," for he had those highly developed Yankee skills found in the evangelist and the peddler.

Orson Fowler, a practical man, replaced the scientific and philosophical approach of Gall and Spurzheim with a pragmatic approach to phrenology as a business. He established an agency which trained lecturers, at a fee, then sent them out in the field as his representatives. They held big, free public meetings where they read heads blindfolded. Private consultations, afterwards, did require a fee. There they engaged in a primitive psychoanalysis, and they told fortunes. A day-by-day, do-it-yourself chart was sold, to help customers grade their own improvement of their faculties. Fowler opened a so-called Phrenological Cabinet in New York City which he stocked with thousands of skulls, skeletons, and paintings. Admittance, of course, required a fee. To help those for whom a personal appearance at the Cabinet was difficult he had a special service requiring only the submission of a daguerreotype of the head, three-quarters pose preferred. He also held a convention. He wrote books. In short, he was a big-time operator.

As phrenology abandoned its original, research-oriented birthright for quick generalizations and the tenacious pursuit of money it lost much support among the intelligentsia of the country, though a few, like Edgar Allan Poe, Walt Whitman, Horace Greeley, and Alfred Russell Wallace, gave it their support nevertheless. But some of its pragmatic ideas won a gradually widening acceptance, until today they are taken for granted. For example, it was an age when the hickory stick was considered a necessary adjunct for education, when learning by rote was the rule, and when the three R's were considered sufficient for the masses, with Latin and Greek for higher education. Along came phrenology which held that the carrot for reward was more effective than the stick for punishment, that one learned better by doing than by memorizing, and that practical subjects were more important than classic literature. At that time these were all radical ideas. So, also, was the insistence on short school days, fresh air, and lots of play. It should be added, in fairness, that not all of the ideas of phrenology are accepted today. Phrenologists also taught that night air was bad; that mental exercise at too early an age weakened the brain; that tea, coffee, masturbation, and concentration on religion led to disease; and that brown bread, cold showers, and cheerfulness were healthful.

In those days insane people were often considered as possessed by evil spirits and were treated with cruelty. Phrenology, claiming that insanity was a disease of the brain and no more deserving of opprobrium than a disease of the heart, or the lungs, or the liver, urged the removal of chains, straitjackets, and punishment; and gradually this was done, to be replaced by an elementary type of psychiatric theory.

In medicine, phrenology had been introduced in text books as based on solid research. At the time American experimental work on the brain was nonexistent, and these texts were widely used in medical schools. It was not long, however, until the foundations of craniology came under strong attack from the medical profession. Doctors pointed out that varying thickness of the bones of the skull in different individuals made a determination of brain size and formation difficult from measurements of the cranium alone. The logic of phrenology would imply that a big brain meant a full development of many faculties, yet there were many very intelligent, even famous, people with small heads. And soon it was discovered that various sections of the brain could be removed without destroying its supposed faculties.

The net result of these attacks was that support of phrenology among intellectuals had largely withered away by 1850. Among the reformers and radicals of that time, too, there was a steady erosion of interest—a new idea had come to the scene, abolition. Besides, many of the liberal ideas advocated by phrenology had been increasingly accepted, so new battlefields had to be found. With the intellectual and liberal leadership gone, the interest of the masses in the toy of craniology diminished and, by 1861, was gone completely.

Phrenology left its mark on the American scene in the acceptance of the idea that the human mind is a fit subject for study, the idea that freedoms may be better for students than restrictions, and the idea that punishment is not always the answer for the insane or for criminals. So it is perhaps easier to eliminate the quick sneer that often rises to people's minds at the mere mention of the word phrenology.

GRAPHOLOGY

In the third century B.C. Aristotle wrote "Spoken words are symbols of mental experience; written words, the symbols of spoken words. Just as all men do not have the same speech sounds, neither do they all have the same writing." So began the long history of graphology.

In the second century A.D., G. Suetonius Tranquillus studied the handwriting of Emperor Octavius Augustus and noted idiosyncracies in his script. The Chinese philosopher Kuo Jo-hsu pointed out the relation between handwriting and personality in the eleventh century. But the first systematic studies of handwriting were performed in the early 1600s by two Italians, Prosper and Baldi. In the late 1800s a French abbé, Jean-Hippolyte Michon of Paris, a member of a group which made many systematic studies of the subject, coined the word graphology to denote handwriting analysis. Jules Crepieux-Jamin, a follower of Michon, emphasized that handwriting displayed the psychological traits of a writer, not the physiological characteristics. Michon persuaded Alfred Binet, founder of the intelligence test, to test the claims of graphology scientifically. Binet's positive findings eventually made handwriting analysis respectable.

Graphologists have taken great pains to avoid the path followed by phrenologists. Graphologists regard their field as that part of psychology which studies a demonstrable relation between handwriting and personality. They do not claim to foretell the future, predict the outcome of a love affair, or predict success in business.

Handwriting can reveal the sex of the writer, although not with accuracy sufficient for use in court. Binet tested Crepieux-Jamin and another graphologist against 15 untrained participants by asking them to determine the sex of the writers of 180 samples. The graphologists far surpassed the untrained participants. By chance alone one should score 50 percent. Crepieux-Jamin scored the highest, with 79 percent. Scientific tests show discernible differences between neurotic and normal writers, between delinquent and nondelinquent adolescents, and between sick and well people. But times change. Graphologists now find they are less and less able to tell the sex of a writer—a comment on graphology or society?

In their analyses graphologists utilize many factors: the size of the letters, their width, their slant, their angularity, their spacing, the connectivity between letters and words, the writing speed, the pressure, the rhythm. They do this to help determine the innate personality of an individual. A rising script shows optimism, a falling one pessimism. A backward slant indicates self-consciousness, a forward slant sympathy. Writing that fluctuates in height and slant suggests lack of control over impulses. An "i" with the dot placed behind shows hesitancy and caution. The large pronoun "I" shows an overdeveloped ego. Figure 7–3 gives a quick review of many graphological interpretations.

Handwriting is highly individualistic. Among related kin, for example, their differences in handwriting are much greater than their differences in height, weight, or intelligence. Handwriting does not remain constant throughout a person's life but changes as the person changes. And amazingly, if writers change their style of writing, this in turn produces changes both within the individual and in his or her self-perception.

The final judgment of the scientific value of graphology has not yet been made. But in graphology, unlike phrenology, we see the edge of knowledge slowly advancing toward its acceptance as a science.

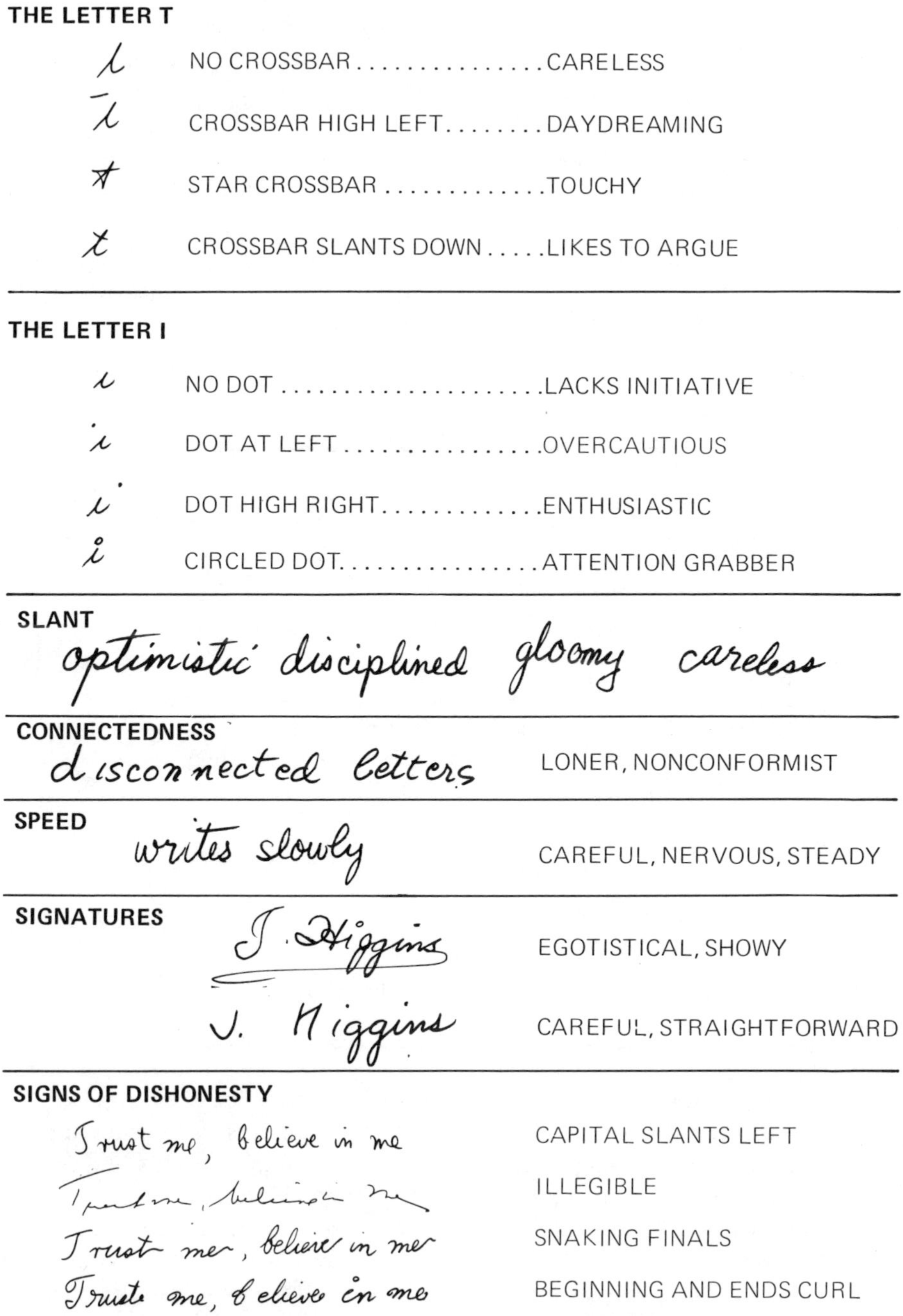

THE LETTER T

𝓁   NO CROSSBAR . . . . CARELESS

𝓁̄   CROSSBAR HIGH LEFT . . . . DAYDREAMING

⋆𝓉   STAR CROSSBAR . . . . TOUCHY

𝓉   CROSSBAR SLANTS DOWN . . . . . LIKES TO ARGUE

THE LETTER I

𝓁   NO DOT . . . . LACKS INITIATIVE

𝓲   DOT AT LEFT . . . . OVERCAUTIOUS

𝓲   DOT HIGH RIGHT . . . . ENTHUSIASTIC

𝓲   CIRCLED DOT . . . . ATTENTION GRABBER

SLANT

optimistic disciplined gloomy careless

CONNECTEDNESS

disconnected letters   LONER, NONCONFORMIST

SPEED

writes slowly   CAREFUL, NERVOUS, STEADY

SIGNATURES

J. Higgins   EGOTISTICAL, SHOWY

J. Higgins   CAREFUL, STRAIGHTFORWARD

SIGNS OF DISHONESTY

Trust me, believe in me   CAPITAL SLANTS LEFT

Trust me, believe in me   ILLEGIBLE

Trust me, believe in me   SNAKING FINALS

Trust me, believe in me   BEGINNING AND ENDS CURL

Fig. 7–3. Handwriting analysis. Many other features, in addition to those shown here, need to be considered in order to evaluate a person's character fully.

NUMEROLOGY

The next art, numerology, is really a pseudoscience. The art of divination through numbers is based upon two underlying beliefs. The first principle, "Numbers are all," goes back to the ancient Greeks. The second principle, "The name is all," is more ancient still, its origin buried in Egyptian antiquity. To combine these two principles, first assign numbers to the letters of a name; then decide how these numbers are to be read. Presto! Numerology is born.

The workings of numerology are best illustrated through example. Take your name, in the form by which you prefer to have it written, and then, from Table 7–1, assign a number to each letter. Finally, add the numbers. Thus, using

TABLE 7–1
NUMEROLOGY TABLE

1	2	3	4	5	6	7	8
A	B	C	D	E	U	O	F
I	K	G	M	H	V	Z	P
Q	R	L	T	N	W		
J		S		X			
Y							

(a.) The letter-number relations are here based on the Hebrew alphabet. Latin letters such as E and X fill in letters that do not exist in the Hebrew alphabet. The number values follow the common ordering of the Hebrew letters.

1	2	3	4	5	6	7	8	9
A	B	C	D	E	F	G	H	I
J	K	L	M	N	O	P	Q	R
S	T	U	V	W	X	Y	Z	

(b.) This shows a modern form which uses our Latin alphabet, in sequence.

Table 7–1a, one of the two forms of this table, JOHN LENNON becomes $1 + 7 + 5 + 5 + 3 + 5 + 5 + 5 + 7 + 5 = 48$. Now, add the numbers in the sum and repeat if necessary to get a single number between 1 and 9. Thus, in 48 add 4 and 8: $4 + 8 = 12$. And once more: $1 + 2 = 3$. John Lennon is a three.

It is sometimes easier to work with the names separately, but the result is the same. For JOHN is nine; LENNON is three (30 gives $3 + 0 = 3$); and the sum of 9 and 3 is 12, which yields three again. This, by the way, illustrates the fact that numbers which add to nine may be disregarded in obtaining the final sum. They cannot influence the final sum. If JOHN $= 9$ had been omitted the LENNON $= 30 \rightarrow 3$ would yield the same answer.

Once the number corresponding to the name is found then the interpretation, shown in Table 7–2, is assumed to give the person's character. No justification is given for this association other than, presumably, experience. Threes are lucky, charming, highly talented; but they lavish their efforts in too many directions. Looking from afar, does this seem a reasonable description of John Lennon? Perhaps. It must also be true, then, of Percival Percy, whoever and wherever he is.

How can we assess the scientific validity of numerology? There is almost no hard, scientific evidence on numerology. Those practicing the art have their experience to guide them, but they have done little real testing to check their predictions. Scientists shy away from this area completely, considering it patently unscientific. Widespread testing of numerology is quite feasible at present, with the aid of fast computers.

A few words should be said on the problems numerology faces, since its adherents claim to divine a knowledge from nature. Graphology, a semiacceptable science, has grown from its original birth as an empirical art. One charitable view might classify numerology—along with phrenology, palmistry, Tarot cards, and astrology—as an empirical art in which esoteric knowledge, gained slowly over the years and centuries, has fashioned the content of the art. In numerology, then, the relation between letter and number, as between number and meaning, might have been learned in centuries of experience by numerologists reading the numbers, casting predictions, and improving their knowledge by observation of the outcome. Some support, for example, might be given along these lines for astrology's assignment of a manic influence to the moon. There is no evidence, however, that the art of numerology was fashioned empirically.

The existence of several number-letter assignments (two of which are shown in Table 7–1) is rather an embarrassment to any possible empirical basis for numerology. The assignment of numbers according to the position in our alpha-

TABLE 7–2
CHARACTERISTICS COMMONLY ASSOCIATED WITH NUMBERS

Number	Positive and Negative Characteristics
1	leader; arrogant; inferiority complex
2	tactful; over-sensitive; unsure
3	lucky; extroverted; creative; romantic; superficial
4	self-disciplined; hard-working; honest; stubborn; conservative
5	resourceful; sensual; adventurous; irresponsible; short-sighted
6	responsible; warm-hearted; peaceful; narrow-minded
7	intellectual; self-controlled; pessimistic; skeptical
8	practical; efficient; greedy; ruthless
9	selfless; visionary; compassionate; extremely selfish
11	idealistic; inventive; intuitive; fanatic; perverse
22	practically idealistic; creative; abusive of power; vicious

bet, Table 7–1b, is obviously convenient, but it is quite arbitrary. This betrays no empirical origin to a specific value for a given number. In fact, the letters I and R, corresponding to the number 9, lose significance completely in this assignment since they cannot influence a sum. Hence they have no influence on the person's number. The more ancient system is free of this defect, and the number values appear to be assigned by means other than order. In actual fact, the numbers are assigned according to the common order in the Hebrew alphabet. This happens, accidentally, to vary from our own common order. Again we see no hint of an empirical basis where nature itself, and not the intruding observer, has dictated an assignment of number to letter by some unknown underlying scheme.

I CHING

I Ching (pronounced Yee Jing) means "the oracle of change." Legend places its beginnings in Chinese antiquity more than 4,000 years ago. About 1200 B.C., King Wen wrote summaries of the oracle for his son, the founder of the Chou dynasty. It has been revised many times since then. It has been affected both by Lao-tse and Confucius, and has since been passed down for millennia from one generation to the next. Accepted for so long by so many, it is today frowned on by the Communist government, which is, in general, trying to root out many of the ancient beliefs.

I Ching is not a specific oracle for one person. It is a general philosophy. It holds that nothing is static, that all things are constantly in flux, and that there are cycles in the affairs of humanity and the universe. If we follow these patterns, then we can adjust our private lives to be in harmony with the tide, making it easier for ourselves. Otherwise, we are likely to be similar to the wanderer in the Arctic tundra in summertime—with each step we sink into the soggy turf and, whichever way we go, we are walking uphill. A hard way to travel, especially since we all carry a pack of one kind or another on our backs. Better to learn the patterns, avoid hiking the tundra in the summer thaw.

When we come to a crisis in our lives, or when we have a deep perplexing question to which we wish an answer, then we must learn the rhythm of nature. How do we learn the pattern to live by at any given moment? By chance. But by chance in a special manner—that specified by the book, *I Ching*. There is a factor that diminishes the role of the occult in *I Ching*; the wording of the oracles is so general, so vague, that the same revelation of the hidden facets of the rhythm of the world will be translated to mean one concrete fact by one person and something completely different by another. Evidently the subconscious mind of the person consulting the oracle is intended to play as large a role as the occult "mind" of the oracle. This throws a new light on the occult facet of the book *I Ching*. Possibly it has very little of an occult nature; possibly there is *only* the subconscious mind of the mortal.

There is an ancient, conventional method for determining which one of the 64 pages of the *I Ching* is to be applicable at any given moment. This approved method uses piles of yarrow stalks and a time consuming ritualistic procedure for letting chance, finally, decide which page to pick. This technique possibly induces an altered state of consciousness in the operator, making him or her especially open to use the promptings of the *I Ching* for probing subconscious desires. We will not describe this elaborate procedure. A much simpler method for determining the page of the *I Ching* follows.

A group of three similar coins is tossed into the air six times. Depending on the number of heads and tails which appear at each throw, the thrower is led to consider just one of the 64 pages in the book, *I Ching*. Each page is characterized by a specific figure called a hexagram, and each page has five successive texts giving the meaning of its hexagram. The first one is called the *Decision*. It is a brief interpretation of the hexagram, given originally by the feudal Lord Wen, who ruled the western province of Chou toward the end of the Shang dynasty, about 1143 B.C. The second text is a *Commentary*. This was given either by Confucious or by other followers of his school of philosophy, on the text of Lord (later King) Wen. It is perhaps four or five times as long as the first. Next comes a text called the *Image* which is, again, a terse interpretation. The fourth text, called *The Lines*, is applicable only in those special cases when there are moving lines, as explained below. Finally, each of these special cases has a brief *Interpretation*.

The 64 hexagrams in the book of *I Ching* are based exclusively on lines of two lengths—a long one (yang) and a short one (yin)—something like the dit and da of the Morse code, with the short ones only used in pairs. One long line has the same length as two short lines plus the space between them. A trigram is made up of three rows, one above the other, each row containing either one long line or two short lines. A hexagram is made, very simply, by placing one trigram above another. Since the top half can be made in 8 ways and the bottom half can be made in 8 ways, a hexagram can be made in 64 different ways. This accounts for the 64 pages in the book of *I Ching*. A key to the page location in the *I Ching* is made up of a chart which lists the upper trigrams in 8 columns and gives the lower trigrams in 8 rows.

Let us assign a value of 2 points to a coin when it falls heads; and 3 to a coin when it falls tails. Three heads will then give 6 points; three tails will give 9; two heads and a tail equal 7; two tails and a head equal 8. These are the possibilities on a single throw of the three coins: 6, 7, 8, or 9 points.

The 9, the larger of the higher pair, corresponds to a yang (long line), the 8 to a yin (two short lines); the 7, the larger of the lower pair, corresponds also to a yang, the 6 to a yin. The first throw of the three coins gives the bottom row of the hexagram, the first place. The second throw gives the second row up, or the second place; six throws of the coins gives all six rows. Thus one specific hexagram is determined.

The 6 and 9 are called *old* yin and *old* yang, respectively; while 8 is a *young* yin and 7 is a *young* yang. The names old and young rest on the probabilities of their occurrence. The various possibilities for the coins, letting H = heads and T = tails, are as follows:

```
H H H H T T T T
H H T T H H T T
H T H T H T H T
— — — — — — — —
6 7 7 8 7 8 8 9
```

Of the total of eight cases, the 6 and 9 are comparatively rare. They are called old. The 7 and the 8, on the other hand, are comparatively plentiful, and these are called young. The results are summarized as follows, where the asterisk designates "old."

9   old yang   ———*
8   young yin   — —
7   young yang ———
6   old yin   — —*

If a hexagram consists of all young lines, whether young yang or young yin, then it is only necessary to read the first three texts of the page for that hexagram—the *Decision, Commentary,* and *Image.* If a hexagram contains any old lines, then the fourth and fifth texts pertaining to those old lines must also be read.

The old lines are also known as the *moving lines.* When they occur it is necessary to make a change after the fifth text of the hexagram has been read. These moving lines, and they alone, are now transformed into their opposites: old yang → young yin, old yin → young yang. This gives a new, additional hexagram. When moving lines occur, one must read all five texts pertaining to the original hexagram plus the three additional texts of the transformed (or moved) hexagram.

We illustrate this procedure by an example. Let the six throws of the three coins be such that the sums were, in sequence: 9, 7, 8, 6, 8, 7. The bottom line (first place) is, from the 9, old yang. The second place is, from the 7, young yang. The third is young yin. The fourth is old yin. The fifth is young yin. And the top line (sixth place) is young yang. The original hexagram is shown to the left in Fig. 7–4, while the transformed hexagram is given at the right.

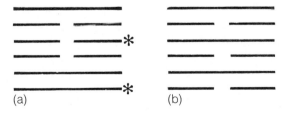

Fig. 7–4. (a) Hexagram for an assumed six throws of the coins. The asterisks designate the old yang and the old yin: moving lines. (b) The transformed hexagram. The moving lines have been changed to their opposites.

(a)   (b)

Suppose we refer to the *I Ching*. Figure 7–4a has yang-yang-yin for the lower trigram, yin-yin-yang for the upper one. This is hexagram 41, where we read:

The Decision

Decrease. A decrease of what is in excess brings great good fortune if it is carried out with Sincerity. It results in freedom from error, firm correctness which can be maintained, and advantage in every action that is undertaken. In what circumstances should this gainful decrease be employed? Even when making sacrifices to Heaven; two baskets of grain are a better offering than insincere munificence.

Commentary

Here the lower trigram is diminished and the lower added to. The power of the hexagram proceeds upwards.

There is a time when the strong should be diminished and the weak strengthened. Diminution and increase, fullness and emptiness; all these take place in harmony with the conditions of the time . . . .[9]

This gives the flavor of the hexagram. The *Image* is also read, as are *The Lines* for nine in the first place and for six in the fourth place (the two moving lines). Then we refer to the second hexagram, which is listed as number 64. This time only the *Decision*, *Commentary*, and the *Image* are read, without any *Lines*.

THE MEANING

The *I Ching* is one example that illustrates the typical embroidery which accompanies a mystic art. The advice is often given that the Book of Changes be wrapped in silk and stored away high in a room—although sometimes it is under a pillow—and that persons prostrate themselves three times before addressing the oracle. Interestingly enough, similar instructions are often given for the use of the Tarot cards; and, indeed, ceremonies of all types are encountered in palm readings, fortune-telling with a crystal ball, and spiritualist seances. What, then, is necessary for any modicum of success and what is just mumbo jumbo? If there is any truth, where does its source lie, in the ceremony or in the deed? In tossing the coins? In the text? In the unconscious, itself? Or is there simply no truth, whatever, either in the ceremony preceding the reading or in the reading itself?

• Freud's rival in psychology, Karl Jung, proposed one answer. The future might be divined, he suggested, not through any causal relation but by a synchronism of nonrational coincidences whose meanings are glimpsed by the unconscious mind of the seer, whether utilizing the *I Ching* or any other mystic art, such as palm readings. If we accept such a nonrational approach then the particular embroidery attending any of these arts hardly seems important and, indeed, one art may have little, if any, preference over another.

• Other answers vary. For example, in the *I Ching* perhaps one's psychokinesis faculty unconsciously determines the outcome of a throw of the coins and leads the reader to the precise passage necessary to answer his or her problems. Psychokinesis, however, is a very weak faculty—certainly in laboratory tests—and, even in the strongest *poltergeist* phenomena, does not show the purposeful intelligence this answer requires. So, many would prefer an answer within the other unconscious or psychic abilities of the mind.

• Another possibility suggested is that the person posing a question may, unconsciously, already know the answer. The ceremonies simply prepare the unconscious mind for questioning, and the text simply presents cues that the unconscious mind uses in raising the answer to the level of consciousness. If the texts are sufficiently broad, and if the psychological preparation is effective, then the unconscious mind will see its answers in any one of a wide range of texts, any one of which could be just as effective as another.

• Still a different possibility is this: the *I Ching* reader, the numerologist, the palmist, and the astrologer may use clairvoyance, telepathy, or precognition in attaining their interpretation. The particular mechanism utilized, whether the *I Ching*, numbers, the hand, or a horoscope, may simply act to cue ideas that the unconscious mind sorts through in arriving at a psychically derived answer. In laboratories these psychic abilities are quite weak, even in gifted persons; and we would be forced to assume that the psychological trappings used in the readings enhance these faculties substantially.

We must always keep in mind, however, the fact that astrologers, palmists, or fortune-tellers usually meet their subjects and talk with them at length before proceeding with the divination. In this meeting the diviners gain important impressions and cues to use in their readings. Competent readers are not aiming to prove the authenticity of an art to a subject. They want to answer specific questions as accurately as they can, and they will use all the information they have available. Part of divination, then, will just be psychological insight.

So we conclude that .the outcome of any reading given in a mystic art is enhanced by the individual reader, as well as by his or her response to its ceremonies. A computer can be taught the discipline of an art and can even be programmed to make predictions. But, at least so far, computers do not have an unconscious mind, nor do they possess psychic abilities to trigger a response. Gifted seers can, evidently, tap sources far beneath the surface of the discipline itself and there search out occult knowledge and frame their divination. There may be no content, whatever, to the mystic art itself; there may only be the mystic artist.

CHAPTER EIGHT CROSSING OVER

MODERN SPIRITUALISM

What glimpses do we have of the spirit world, if there is one, that lies beyond that great natural barrier, death? We will examine the evidence, and some of the nonsense, connected with the spirit world, real or phantom, on the other side. We will let the facts tell us, as best they can, the truth about the land of spirits.

The evidence has, historically, included many physical effects—rappings, table tipping, voices, the sound of musical instruments—as well as the apparitions themselves. The apparitions have usually been described as veiled, ghostly figures, or blobs of ectoplasm. But in rare instances there have also been reports of solid hands, torsos, heads. The first tales of communication with the dead are quite ancient. The Old Testament describes the materialization of Samuel's spirit by a medium in Endor, at the request of the distraught Saul, seeking help against the Philistines then menacing Israel.

The term spiritualism has acquired a very narrow sense. We will use it to refer only to the belief, practices, and outward evidence concerned with spirit communications. The term, for us, has no connection with the soul, or morality, or intellectuality. The birth of modern-day spiritualism, in March 1848, is connected with two young girls. The Fox family, who occupied a farmhouse in Arcadia, Wayne County, New York, had long been bothered by strange knocking sounds. One day the youngest daughter of the family, Kate, then 12 years old, decided to challenge the strange sounds. Speaking to nobody, but talking in the direction from which the sounds came, she asked the maker of the sounds to match the number of times she snapped her fingers. The offer was accepted— and spiritualism was born.

A code was soon established with the intelligence behind the sound. The sounds claimed to be the spirit of a peddler who had been murdered for his money in the house the Fox family later occupied. In April of that year the "spirit" behind the knocking noises instructed Kate to dig in the cellar. Some obscure remains were, indeed, found. The news of the rappings spread about the neighborhood and was, naturally, greeted with skepticism. But Kate was soon joined in the communication with the spirit by her close sister, Maggie, and they found that the sounds followed them even to other houses, to other towns. Within a short time they were giving demonstrations in various nearby localities. Subsequently the Fox sisters went on tour, joined by their much older sister, Leah. Leah had little talent for soliciting the sounds, but she had great talent for handling financial arrangements.

The rappings were taken, both by the Fox sisters and by other listeners, as manifestations of spirits from another world, or another plane. These spirit manifestations seemed most contagious; for soon others, both in this country and in England, were producing them. Ira and William Davenport successfully commanded spirits to play musical instruments. Florence Cook actually materialized one spirit, Katie King. D. D. Home carried out some amazing feats which we have already described. Eusapia Palladino, whose feats we will describe later in this chapter, tantalized a battery of scientists with a combination of displays, some fraudulent but some apparently genuine. It seemed that seances, table tipping, rappings, levitation, and the Ouija Board had become very much in vogue.

The Fox sisters toured widely and successfully, and an interest in spiritualism overwhelmed the country. Kate and Maggie, young and untutored, produced impressive demonstrations, both in open-stage presentations and in closely monitored private sessions. In many of the latter, the rappings gave remarkably accurate answers to very private questions. The rappings were loud and often came in long, closely spaced spurts, the sound seeming to fill the entire room. The assumption grew that intelligent spirits guided the sounds. In his diary George Templeton Strong recorded his observations:

The production of the sounds is hard to explain, and still stranger is the accuracy with which ghosts guess of whom one is thinking—his age, his residence,

vocations, and the like. They do this correctly nine times out of ten at least. . . .
A systematic trick and deliberate legerdemain producing these results is about
as incomprehensible and as difficult to believe.[1]

Kate gave seances at which unusual *poltergeist* phenomena occurred: tables
moved, a guitar floated in the room, books flew about. Throughout much of their
careers, the two youngest Fox sisters acted as mediums, and during their seances
they displayed a curious mental ability. They could enhance the weight of a
table so much that a strong man had difficulty lifting it from the floor.

An oft-repeated "explanation" that has been offered for the rappings, but not
for their strange intelligence, is this: that the two sisters could dislocate their
knee joints, rapidly and with such force as to produce loud sounds. Sometimes
it was said to be the joint of the big toe. If so the sisters had a very unusual and
durable bone structure, one that kept making these sounds for 10 to 12 hours
daily and for weeks on end.

Eventually the two youngest sisters came upon hard times. Alcohol plagued
them during the latter part of their lives; and they ended up destitute and jealous
of their older sister, Leah, who continued to fare well to the end. Then, 38 years
after their first rappings, the two sisters publicly confessed to fraud. Although
this seemed to be an obvious attempt to earn some badly needed money, their
confession clouds the interpretation of their feats. Margaret later recanted and
it is claimed that Kate did also. Kate died in 1892, Margaret a year later. The
era they began faded, but it did not end; spiritualism is with us even today.
There are mediums, still, who claim to communicate with the spirit world; there
are psychics who claim to summon the spirits to produce physical effects beyond
our knowledge; there are strange voices, from the unknown, on tapes; and there
are strange memories of other lives in some unsuspecting young people. We will
have more to say about all of these.

THE MENTALISTS

Any judgment of the reality behind spiritualism and its psychical effects must
be based on the truth of the effects themselves. Some knowledge of the standard
illusions that are employed by professional stage magicians is helpful here, for
these illusions have often been used in illegitimate practices by people claiming
to be mediums.

First the obvious. A stage magician, a professional mentalist (one who claims
only the illusion of psychic ability), a fake medium, may all have years of experience behind them. They have worked hard at their art, perfecting it daily. They
are professionals at their tasks and, indeed, they have a deep well of information
from their own experiences and from others to draw on. Close cooperation often
exists among members of the profession. Moreover, there is no ethical code that
prohibits assistance, on or off stage.

A novice investigator who devotes a few hours to testing a diligent fraud
cannot hope to cope with all the illusions the professional can produce. It takes

a thief to catch a thief; it takes a magician to snare a magician; it takes a medium to trap a medium. A good psychical or spiritualist investigator must know all the tricks of the trade to separate the fakes from the true psychics. The great Houdini travelled widely exposing fraud. The renowned psychic investigator Hereward Carrington was an experienced amateur magician, and he exposed many fake mediums throughout his career. The gifted medium Eileen Garrett exposed much commonplace fakery, while herself demonstrating very rare psychic powers.

We will review a few of the effects that can be simulated in order to become better acquainted with those effects that cannot be. In general, the more control of a situation the performer has, the more difficult it is to exclude trickery. Stage magicians, of course, claim no real magic. They entertain an audience that is fully aware of the fact that their eyes are betrayed by skillful illusions. In a stage performance purporting to demonstrate psychic or spiritualist phenomena, however, it is most difficult to exclude the possibility of connivance. For the control is in the hands of the performer, who can prepare the set, screen the audience, plant assistants, and direct the program.

Consider the following time-honored mentalist demonstration. Pieces of paper are passed to the audience and the participants are asked to write down a phrase that has deep significance to them. The papers are then folded and collected, to be placed in front of the mentalist. The mentalist selects one paper at random, presses it to his forehead, exhorts the audience to think hard about their written messages, and then invokes the assistance of a spirit communicator. With halting voice, the mentalist bumbles out the phrase, "Frank, why did you leave?" and a woman's surprised gasp is heard. The mentalist unfolds the paper, checks the message, and the woman stands to acknowledge its contents. One by one, *every* single message is correctly perceived, with but minor mistakes, to the amazed audience.

To perform the demonstration above requires no psychic ability. All it requires is a shill in the audience. The shill folds, or marks, his or her paper in a characteristic way. The mentalist picks from the pile, one by one, every message but the marked one, leaving that one for last. The first message is acknowledged by the shill, whatever its content. In apparently checking the paper, the mentalist *reads* the next message, in full view of the audience. No less! The mentalist proceeds down the line of messages, with a few mistakes and bumbling attempts in the phrasing in order to lend reality to the theatrics.

But the mentalist can perform even without a shill. In the solo variation of this demonstration, the people in the audience are instructed to slip their messages into envelopes, seal them, and pass them up front. The mentalist standing at the lectern then proceeds to read the *sealed* messages! By dipping the envelopes into a fluid (just about any colorless liquid) the paper becomes transparent. So, at the lectern, the mentalist rubs some alcohol onto the chosen envelope while going through the normal motions of handling the envelope. The reading can be made even easier by means of a small flashlight to illuminate the back of the envelope. In a few minutes the alcohol evaporates, and all traces of deception have vanished.

A practised mentalist can find, by muscle reading, a hidden message previously secreted in a room by someone else. The mentalist, blindfolded and holding the arm of one who witnessed the hiding of the message, is led about the room by this witness. The mentalist "reads" minute muscular cues in the unwitting witness and is thereby led to the hiding place. The muscular cues are merely a form of automatism, similar to the automatic writing we have encountered in Mrs. Curran's prolific output.

Much equipment is available to the enterprising magician or mentalist: miniature lapel mikes, to communicate with a shill planted in an audience; impression clipboards using old-fashioned carbon paper, to copy a volunteer's secret message; Deluxe Spirit Slates, to capture a spirit's message at a seance.

If the clairvoyant reading of written messages can be faked, can true mind reading (telepathy), where there is nothing written down for the performer to look at, also be faked? Yes and no. In a large audience of 1,000 the performer asks people to think hard about a date that has special meaning to them. The hushed audience concentrates. "March, the twelfth," announces the telepathist, and a young man quickly stands up near the front of the impressed audience. A moment's thought, however, should convince one that the chances are strong that three people out of 1,000 will actually think of any given day of the year, regardless of which particular date the performer mentions. And if an inquisitive eye had looked around the large hall, it might, indeed, have seen three people stand up, not just one.

In any prepared performance a little searching can go a long way to identify events in people's lives and uncover their aspirations and friendships. The performer, or assistants, can garner quite a bit of information from a telephone book, from the registration book, from the local paper, and from the line waiting in the lobby before the performance. And the performer needs detailed information about only a few of the people there, not about everyone. So that's the "yes" side of the answer to "Can mind reading be faked?"

A GREAT MEDIUM

But not everything can be faked—even in a prepared audience. An unscheduled visitor who silently phrases questions only in his or her mind will not be answered by fakery; however, there is then no check for others, for the audience will not have heard the unspoken words. When, either by chance or by design, we do come to know that the unspoken words were, indeed, answered then suspicions of fakery must be transmuted into convictions of truth. That process seems to be difficult for some people.

The knowledgeable Hereward Carrington, an experimenter in psychic research for over half a century, termed Leonore Piper the greatest mental medium he had ever known. Mrs Piper *knew* things about the sitters in her seances: open things, hidden facts, intimate secrets. Dr. Richard Hodgson, then secretary of the Society for Psychical Research, who had previously exposed a number of fake mediums, used his techniques to investigate Mrs. Piper. She was trailed by detectives; her mail was searched; her actions were closely watched; but no physical means could be identified as the source of Mrs. Piper's knowledge. And Dr. Hodgson, who began as a skeptic, slowly became convinced of the reality of Mrs. Piper's mental powers.

Mediums often have spirit controls—their supposed spirit companions—whose knowledge is transferred to the mediums. Mrs. Piper had several spirit controls at various times: Phiniut, Imperator, Rector, Prudens, . . . At first they spoke through her while she was in a trance state; later they used her hand in automatic writing, again in trance, with her head fallen forward on cushions while a pencil was thrust into her hand.

One of the reasons for Carrington's, and Dr. Hodgson's, belief in Mrs. Piper's power lay in the outcome of a special series of seances arranged for her in north Boston.[2] At these seances, an early investigator of psychics, Professor James H. Hyslop, would arrive, masked and completely unannounced and unknown to the entranced Mrs. Piper. Hyslop would sit silently during the seances, and he would depart before Mrs. Piper "awoke." Even if Mrs. Piper were awake during the seances, she could not have known of Professor Hyslop's presence. Yet during these seances, Mrs. Piper, through her supposed spiritual communicators, continually referred to Professor Hyslop, although not asked to do so by anyone. She supplied the audience with much detailed information about family happenings, some of which had occurred 70 years previously in the distant midwest, about much of which even Professor Hyslop was unaware. Professor Hyslop spent more than six months in continual investigation afterward, finally determining that the information had, indeed, been true. Trickery or fraud is not a plausible explanation in this case. Almost all of Mrs. Piper's life was spent in Boston, and much of the information supplied to the unspoken questions was not known even to the unseen visitor.

The question of the legitimacy of Mrs. Piper's mentalist powers boils down to the question of the integrity of Hereward Carrington, Dr. Richard Hodgson, and Professor James Hyslop. Here it is necessary to rely on the testimony of their friends, including the famous psychologist William James, as well as on their writings, and on their lives. We, ourselves, are inclined toward belief.

INTRIGUE IN THE DARKENED ROOM

Private seances are the opposites of open performances, but again the performer, usually the medium, is in control and has a surprising range of physical tricks to display. Let us discuss the intrigues that are possible, even in a seance where the medium is held under stringent physical control.

The room is usually *dark* as a seance begins. One corner is curtained off. The medium is held, both arms and both legs, by outside investigators. As the medium, usually a woman, enters a deep trance, her body goes into convulsions and she utters strange words. Her arms and legs thrash about; perhaps they are temporarily loosed from the hold of the investigators; then the medium is quickly brought under control again. After further convulsions, the medium quiets down and the spirits arrive. The table in front tilts uncertainly, a bell rings, and a guitar materializes in the air while unseen hands strum the strings.

An accomplished cheat needs no help to orchestrate such a seance. The trick is to free one arm and one leg during the writhing. While undergoing the rapid convulsions in the dark, the skillful medium can transfer the arm of a momentarily distracted investigator to the leg that is held by the other guardian. The freed leg then lifts one side of the table, tilting it precariously, and objects slide on the table. The free hand, meanwhile, acquires a hidden telescoping, black tube of about the same size as a long pen. But when opened, this tube extends to a three-foot length. It is used to ring a bell hidden in the curtained section of the room; and also to raise the phantom guitar. Meanwhile, the freed foot depresses a button which begins the spirit music. If both a hand and foot are not successfully freed, then the audience has to settle for a bit less of the spirit display—the spirit contact is poor. And when neither hand nor foot is freed, an educated toe can always lift the table's leg in salute to the hidden spirits.

EUSAPIA PALLADINO

An illiterate peasant, Eusapia Palladino, born in Bari, Italy in 1854, displayed an ability to produce a large variety of inexplicable physical phenomena. She was investigated by many knowledgeable psychic investigators about the turn of this century. They attested to her genuine ability to move and levitate objects in bright daylight and to materialize forms and shapes from nothing; but they also attested to her penchant for faking an effect, just for the heck of it. The toe lift was one of her favorites. But when a skilled investigator openly expressed displeasure, Eusapia would often get down to serious work.

Eusapia's physical manifestations were quite impressive. They were very different from the mental abilities of Mrs. Piper, and seemed to share, in part, the physical deeds of D. D. Home. Strangely, Dr. Hodgson was unconvinced by Eusapia; but Carrington firmly believed in her ability. We will let Carrington tell of one of the most striking physical phenomena he ever witnessed. Eusapia had been trying to materialize a Professor Lambroso, whom she dearly loved. Carrington records:

> As a matter of fact Lambroso did *not* appear nor did anyone else, but a most curious and striking phenomenon occurred, which is almost unique in psychic annals. As the seance progressed, there formed over the center of the seance table what I can only describe as a sort of psychic water-spout—a whirlpool of invisible energy, felt by everyone at the table, and affecting them so much that several of the sitters had to leave the table and go to the window to get

fresh air. As one receded from the table, this power became less and less noticeable, and as one approached it, the force became stronger and stronger. Nothing could be seen, nothing heard, but over the center of that table a power was operative, sensed by everyone present, which was most impressive and indicative of the reality of the invisible.[3]

Which is correct—the skepticism of Dr. Hodgson, who still believed in Mrs. Piper, or the conviction of Hereward Carrington? Among the mediums fraud often exists; but the question remains—Is there a residue of truth? None at all? How can we be certain?

A STRANGE REMEMBRANCE

Laxmi Narain was born in 1886, the son of a wealthy landowner who lived near the town of Pilibhit in India. He grew up the center of family attention, waited upon by servants in a palatial home. Laxmi attended school garbed in fine silk garments, but displayed little prowess in schooling and left at the age of 17, several years behind in his studies. A penchant for pleasurable distractions, rather than a lack of intelligence, was apparently the cause of his difficulties. The lad had the wit to learn enough of the alien Urdu language to earn a position in government service. His distractions, incidentally, were understandable: parties, music, beautiful women, wine, meat on a platter. The youth showed an inclination toward neither marriage nor a settled life.

His father died. Laxmi acquired the family wealth, but only after a bitter lawsuit against his close relatives. Spoiled and quick tempered, Laxmi nevertheless displayed a generous nature. He shared his meals with beggars. He once advanced 500 rupees to a Muslim watch dealer in order to help the dealer begin his own business. And from his deeply religious mother, Laxmi apparently acquired a reverence toward the Hindu religious services.

But Laxmi's personality weaknesses prevailed. He gradually dissipated the family wealth. The family home fell into disrepair. He took a mistress, Padna, a prostitute whom he jealously regarded as his private love. Padna's profession, however, was at odds with Laxmi's possessiveness. Arriving at Padna's apartment one day, Laxmi encountered a departing visitor. In a fit of rage, Laxmi seized a gun and shot the man dead. Murky legal maneuvers ensued. The result left Laxmi free, but he was forced to move to a nearby town. A short time thereafter a sudden illness struck him. It persisted, and it grew worse, and five months later he succumbed to a high fever and chronic lung trouble. The date: December 1918. His age: 32. He left his mother lonely and impoverished.

A little more than two years later, on February 7, 1921, one Bishen Chand was born, the fourth and youngest child of a poor railway clerk in the village of Bareilly, 35 miles from Pilibhit. At the age of ten months, barely learning to speak, the boy uttered the word "Pilvit," or "Philivit." As the baby grew, his parents were presented with a case of baffling behavior, for Bishen began to speak of a previous life in the town of Pilibhit. It was a life in a wealthy family, one completely unknown to Bishen Chand's family. Bishen claimed that his previous name was Laxmi Narain.

The lad displayed a quick temper and a haughty attitude. He disliked the poor food he was given, the only food that the impoverished family could afford. "Even my servants would not take the food cooked here." He despised the meager clothes he was forced to wear, speaking of the silken clothes of a previous life. Every day the child would speak with his elder sister, Kamla, of this previous life. Once, four years old and riding through the village of Pilibhit with his family by train, he demanded to get off there, stating that he "used to live here."

When he was five years of age Kamla caught Bishen drinking medicinal brandy. "I am used to drinking it," he explained matter-of-factly. Bishen's family were teetotalers.

Again, meat was forbidden to their Kattri sect; but Bishen soon developed a strong, hidden craving for meat.

Embarrassingly, when but five and a half years of age, the precocious youth asked his father, "Papa, why don't you keep a mistress? You will have great pleasure from her." And, worst of all, the little boy boasted of killing the lover of his previous mistress.

The bewildered parents handled Bishen Chand's behavior with a combination of understanding and tolerance that can only be termed inspired. His statements were neither belittled nor suppressed. In fact, they were later recorded. Thus the parents' previously private bewilderment has now been bestowed upon a much wider audience.

When Bishen Chand was getting on toward the age of six a lawyer, K. K. N. Sahay, heard of Bishen's claims. Interested in reincarnation, Sahay visited Chand, carefully recorded a number of his statements, and then arranged a visit—together with Bishen's father, his brother, Bipan, and Bishen himself—to Pilibhit. This took place on August 1, 1926. Prior to the visit to Pilibhit, the small child advised his father not to buy a watch. "When I go to Pilibhit I shall get you three watches from the Muslim watch dealer whom I established there."

In Pilibhit Bishen recognized Laxmi's home, now in a terrible state of disrepair. He knew, in advance, the location of the staircase, buried in rubble, and the female quarters. Laxmi's mother suspected that a treasure lay hidden somewhere in the house, and Bishen Chand led her to a room where, subsequently, some considerable amount was, indeed, found.

Bishen Chand correctly identified the gate belonging to a neighbor of Laxmi, and also the house of another neighbor. He picked out the boy, Laxmi Narain, in a photograph taken with Laxmi's father. The boy correctly described Laxmi's classrooms, and teacher, and a nearby river. Given a pair of drums, the boy played them with ease although he had never been instructed in the use of drums. When pressed to give the name of his mistress in the previous life, Bishen reluctantly replied, "Padna."

When the relatives of Laxmi who had been involved in the lawsuit entertained Bishen, he remained remarkably cool. They offered the child candy and a few rupees. "You wanted to take my blood," replied the not quite six-year-old child, "and now you are tempting me with money."

Before the day ended the child attempted to get for his father the watch he had promised him, but he was unable to do so. The Muslim dealer, who was well remembered in the neighborhood, had moved away a year ago.

The case of Bishen Chand was further investigated, much later, by Ian Stevenson, who carefully supplemented Sahay's original work.[4] Dr. Stevenson, of the Psychiatry Department, School of Medicine, of the University of Virginia, has long investigated a number of types of psychic behavior. Fortunately, many of Bishen's statements were recorded by Sahay *before* any attempt at verification. More detailed information was subsequently obtained by Stevenson. Out of 46 statements made by Bishen, 34 were verified; 10 were unverified, although some seemed to be certainly true; and only 2 proved incorrect. Oddly, Bishen believed that he had died at the age of twenty in his previous existence.

As the young Bishen got a little older his memories of a previous life faded, undoubtedly to the relief of his parents. By the age of seven most of the memories had gone. The strange facility with the drums disappeared with disuse. His temper moderated slowly, as did his leaning toward alcohol and meat. The memory of Padna lingered. Indeed, in his early adulthood, Bishen paid her a visit. Padna, older and wiser, did not allow this to progress beyond poignancy. Before the age of five Bishen had, improbably, interspersed Urdu words into his native dialect. This ability was *not* moderated; it was enhanced by Bishen's later study of Urdu in school, and by his use of it in government service.

Bishen Chand is still alive today. He has a family and is a respected member of his village. The only vivid memory he has left of the previous existence he claimed is that of the killing of Laxmi's rival. This is a memory which Bishen now recounts remorsefully. Some nostalgia does remain for his previous life, however. Who can blame him? Wine, women, song , . . .

BRIDEY MURPHY

We will shortly consider some of the evidence for reincarnation collected over many years in the Near East and the Middle East, where cultural factors encourage belief in such phenomena. But first we would like to outline a case of supposed reincarnation that took place in Pueblo, Colorado in 1952–1953.

The story was brought to the attention of the public by Morey Bernstein, a businessman in Pueblo who was also an amateur hypnotist. He had twice hypnotized a young woman from his town, Ruth Simmons, and by means of the well-known technique of age regression had induced her to recall memories of the days when she was seven years old, and then when she was five and in kindergarten. Ruth Simmons was 29 years old, married to an insurance salesman, and apparently quite normal in every way except one—she was extremely suggestible and was one of the best subjects for hypnosis that Bernstein had ever met. So he decided that he would extend the age regression under hypnosis to times that were even earlier. He hypnotized her six other times, extending over a period from November 29, 1952 to October 1, 1953, always in the presence of her husband and a number of other acquaintances and always with a tape recorder making a permanent record of the proceedings.

The narrative presented by Ruth Simmons under hypnotic age regression was written a year later in *Empire*, the Sunday magazine of the *Denver Post*.[5] On January 1, 1956, Morey Bernstein's book, *The Search for Bridey Murphy*, was published. Over a long period of time the story was written up by many papers and magazines, some attacking and some defending, but all helping to sell *The Search for Bridey Murphy*.

The story that emerged from the deep, hypnotic trance of Ruth Simmons was that she had once lived in an earlier life in Cork, Ireland where she was known as Bridey Murphy. She claimed to have been born December 20, 1798. Her mother, whose name was Kathleen, was of medium height, with black hair. Her father's name was Duncan. He was a barrister and he was tall, with red hair. She had a brother, Duncan, who was two years older than she. She remembered playing house with him. She had another brother who had died, when she was four, of a "black something." They lived in a wooden house, painted white, which had two floors. There were no neighbors nearby, for they lived outside the village in a place called the Meadows.

At age 15, Bridey went to Mrs. Strayne's Day School, staying away from home during the week. At age 20, she married Sean Brian MacCarthy, the son of a barrister. She was Protestant, he was Catholic. The marriage was a Protestant one; but after they moved to Belfast, living in a cottage given to them by his grandmother while he went to school, they had another, Catholic ceremony. They had a happy marriage, though there were no children. She remembered that they often went to the home of their friends, Kevin and Mary Catherine Moore, for they liked to play with their children. Also, they attended a church called St. Theresa's where the priest was Father John Gorman, the man who had married them.

She recalled that she had died at the age of 66, after a long burdensome illness that resulted from a fall down the stairs in which she had broken her hip. Brian was in church at the time, on a Sunday. After she died she didn't go to purgatory, but her spirit remained in the house until, eventually, Father John died. "She" didn't wait until Brian died but "went" to Cork, where she stayed in her brother Duncan's house. She couldn't describe how she actually went—it was sufficient that she willed it, and she found herself there. When she talked to Duncan, however, he wouldn't answer her.

Asked to describe the conditions of "life" in her waiting period, Ruth Simmons (Bridey Murphy) was somewhat vague. She had liked it, but actually it wasn't better than life on Earth; for there was no sense of accomplishment, no emotion, no tiredness, no time, no sex, no talking to friends for very long. One could, however, read the thoughts of the living. She finally left that life in 1923, to be reborn as Ruth Mills, in Wisconsin. Mills was her maiden name before she married Rex Simmons and moved to Colorado.

Morey Bernstein tried to probe into any hypnotic memories Ruth Simmons might have of any existence prior to that as Bridey Murphy; and Mrs. Simmons did recall one. She remembered herself as a little baby, dying, in New Amsterdam in the American colonies. Her mother's name was Vera, her father's was John Jamieson. That's all she could remember of that existence; and she simply could not recollect anything about any earlier ones.

In an effort to obtain any facts which could be corroborated, now, in Ireland, Morey Bernstein proceeded to question Bridey Murphy at length about any facts which had been recorded. She said her husband had taught at Queen's University in Belfast. Also, Brian had written a number of articles for the Belfast *News-Letter*, but she didn't know whether he had his by-line over the stories. There was a marriage certificate, she remembered. People danced at her wedding and slipped coins into Brian's pocket, as was the custom, for good luck. She could not recall her address in Belfast. She remembered having read a book called *The Sorrows of Deirdre* as a child, and shopping at a grocer's named Farr. She remembered passing through a place called Bailey's Crossing, and a port called Galway. She was once punished for pulling straw from the thatched roof of her father's barn. She remembered some songs, an Irish jig, the denominations of money, a fairy tale, a few Irish words (*banshee*).

Subsequent attempts to check her story in Ireland were essentially inconclusive. There were no catalogs at Queen's University in those days. The stories in the Belfast *News-Letter* were unsigned. Yes, Galway was a city on the west coast of Ireland. There was a grocer's named Farr. There were no registers of births, deaths, or marriages in Cork before 1864. Based on the records, some reputable people believed the story of Bridey Murphy to be corroborated while others believed the whole thing was a fabrication. Bridey's tale intrigues the imagination, but it lacks the compelling verification of Bishen Chand's remembrances; and we, ourselves, view it with a most skeptical eye.

REINCARNATION

The baffling case of Bishen Chand is scarcely an isolated example. The belief in reincarnation is widespread and is ingrained in both Eastern religions and in Western occult beliefs. And the belief is buttressed by seemingly inexplicable events, of which the experience of the child Bishen Chand is but one of many.

Dr. Ian Stevenson has collected a large number of cases, some extraordinarily detailed, that suggest reincarnation.[6] To date, his catalog numbers nearly 1200 cases—from regions throughout the world, from India, Brazil, Ceylon, Alaska, Europe. Supplementing the work of earlier investigators, these cases display very definite characteristics, as if they obey some very concrete laws of nature. Do these laws reflect a natural explanation, embedded in the psychology of the child and the environment, or a supernatural explanation indicating survival in rebirth after death? We can supply no answers. The consistency and detail of the reports suggest that neither understandable error, nor misunderstanding by the child, nor exaggeration, nor fanciful imagination are likely explanations.

A typical reincarnation report involves a child, at a very early age, claiming to have memories of an earlier life as a different individual; and there is evidence which suggests that an individual as described by the child actually lived. Some strong similarities run through the many reports which have been analyzed in detail.

• The child's remembrance of a previous life begins at a very early age, as soon as the child begins to speak. The remembrances are sometimes clear, sometimes confused. They affect the child's attitude toward others. It is difficult to see how the child, at its young age, could have picked up these "remembrances" from family members or acquaintances.

• The child's character is sometimes strongly at odds with the family's characteristics. In many ways the character seems that of an adult trapped in a child.

• The child's remembrances of a previous life gradually fade as he or she matures. As soon as a child begins schooling the remembrances start to fade. They may almost completely disappear by the age of six or seven. The personality attending the memories fades in adolescence and disappears in adulthood.

• Culture affects the remembrances. Among Buddhists and Hindus changes in sex are culturally acceptable in stories of reincarnation. Perhaps 20 percent of all cases reported in these groups show a change in sex between the remembered life and the life of the child. In Lebanon and Turkey, and among the Tlingit Indians of Alaska, such sex changes are considered impossible. Not even one case has been reported there of a change.

• The child's birthplace and remembered death place are geographically close. As a very general rule, the place of death of the individual remembered by the child and the birthplace of the child are within a day's journey of each other.

• The time between the child's birth and the remembered death averages less than five years, the child being born after the death. There are exceptions, though. Laure Reynaud remembered an earlier life ending 59 years before birth. And in at least one case the birth occurred before the death of the remembered individual! There is an average span of seven to ten years between the previous death and the disintegration of the remembrances.

• A very large percentage of children remembered details of the previous death; and between 50 and 75 percent of those details, depending on cultures, were violent.

• The children remembering a previous life rarely show unexpected psychic power.

The findings in this embryo investigation of reincarnation, like those encountered in the strange chain of remembered facts linking the dead Laxmi Narain with the young Bishen Chand, are met by a natural skepticism, on our part, of things beyond our present vision of nature. One has only to read several of the many case histories collected by Dr. Ian Stevenson, however, to realize that if even a few of these facts are subsequently verified we will have no alternative to changing our view of what constitutes common sense. In the meantime we could use further study of this field, which is presently shrouded in embarrassed titters. The future alone will decide this conflict; one where outlandish evidence confronts a skeptical, commonsense dogma.

In the next section we encounter another subject, the haunted house, which is also the butt of amused pokes among the sophisticated. But where reincarnation belongs to a foreign culture, hauntings are part of our own Western culture.

THE HAUNTED HOUSE

I had gone up to my room, but was not yet in bed when I heard someone at the door, and went to it thinking it might be my mother. On opening the door, I saw no one, but on going a few steps along the passage, I saw the figure of a tall lady, dressed in black standing at the head of the stairs. . . .[7]

The words, not from a tale of fiction but from the diary of Rose Despart, are supposedly an account of events that actually occurred. We may associate haunted houses with the past or with a good entertaining story—mixed with a bit of fear, even terror—but new hauntings arise continuously. They are very much with us, all the time and in all parts of the world; and they are the subject of numerous investigations. Sometimes they are reported in an old, decrepit mansion; sometimes in the sleek, far-away home of a movie star; sometimes in a simple frame house crowded into a five-year-old development project.

A surprising number of houses are, this very day, reported as haunted. Often there is only the feeling of a presence; sometimes there are the sounds of footsteps, of rappings; and, rarely, there are sightings of the apparition itself. One member of a family may feel the presence while another may feel nothing. A large fraction of the people reporting a haunting simply endure it. They take the haunted house along with its other faults, like drafty windows and a leaking roof. But some people are genuinely frightened, and soon seek a less "populated" home. Most reported hauntings seem harmless enough—footsteps making their way down the back steps, perhaps. But a few are threatening—hands pulling the bedcovers or actually shaking the bed. Some psychics indicate feeling that at times there is more than one presence disturbing a house.

There was a widespread belief, in the past, that hauntings were caused by some tragedy. Present-day investigations, however, tend to discount this belief, at least in part. Indeed, hauntings are often intermittent, the ghosts coming and going periodically, regardless of tragedy, banality, or mirth.

A phantom is sometimes seen in places where the predeceased, living individual had neither died nor lived. Quite often, however, the phantom seems to prefer a particular locality in the house it is haunting. Dr. Gertrude R. Schmeidler, a professor of psychology at the City University of New York, has tried to use this fact in carrying out her investigations. In one case Dr. Schmeidler assembled a group of four sensitives who visited the haunted house of a friend of hers. They were asked to locate the focus of the haunting from a floor plan, and to describe its personality from a descriptive checklist.[8] The same information was then asked of three family members who had experienced the haunting. Two of the four sensitives agreed with the three family members concerning the location of the presence; and all seven were in agreement concerning its personality. The results argue for a separate entity—a real ghost—inhabiting the house. Unfortunately, insofar as a definitive test of haunting is concerned, this could also be interpreted as an example of clairvoyance and telepathy among the seven people.

Dr. Robert Morris investigated a haunted house in Kentucky in a different fashion—with a crew of animal investigators; namely, a dog, a cat, and a rattlesnake. When placed in one room in the haunted house the menagerie acted nonchalantly. But, when they were carried a few feet away, into a room where a tragedy had once occurred, then, he reported,

> The dog . . . immediately snarled at its owner and backed out the door. No amount of cajoling could prevent the dog from struggling to get out and it refused to reenter. . . . (The cat) immediately leaped upon the owner's shoulder, dug in, then leaped to the ground, orienting itself toward a chair. It spent several minutes hissing and spitting and staring at the unoccupied chair. . . . (The rattlesnake) assumed an attack posture focused on the same chair.[9]

There has not been much corroborative experimentation by others of this type of sensitiveness to the presence of ghosts. So we will leave it as is and turn, instead, to a more playful specter.

PLAYFUL GHOSTS

The *poltergeist*, or playful ghost, is one particular type of haunting, one which wreaks havoc (usually minor, but sometimes major) in a house. Often this is done by overturning furniture, pitching dishes to the floor, sailing cutlery through the air. Very often the fitfulness is merely prankish and disorganized, but occasionally it is definitely destructive and malevolent, appearing to be guided by a hurtful intelligence.

Reports of *poltergeists* are widespread, but only a small fraction of such cases have been thoroughly investigated and documented. Still, the number of such cases is sufficiently large to suggest that the phenomenon is worth study. The majority, but certainly not all, of the cases seem centered about a troubled adolescent. Confronted with too much of life's burden at the time he or she is

changing from fuzzy caterpillar to charming butterfly, the adolescent's unconscious seeks release. The age of the youngster in transformation may vary over
quite a range—from six or seven up to the early twenties.

Poltergeist phenomena centered about the Fox sisters, Maggie and Kate, renowned for their spiritualism, and also about the extraordinary D. D. Home. A
tentative parapsychological interpretation of the *poltergeist* attributes it to a re-
current spontaneous psychokinesis (RSPK). Then the solution to this perplexing
phenomenon should be sought within the adolescent, not in any lingering external spirit. The burden of explanation here is only shifted to the nature of
psychokinesis.

Consider the case of the young black child, Jeremy, now sixteen. His is a well-
witnessed and documented case, though that is not his real name.[10] At the age
of ten, Jeremy lived with his elderly foster parents in the rural South, near his
grandmother but quite far from his mother. Jeremy was finding school difficult
and troublesome.

Early in December 1971, Jeremy and his foster parents heard strange stompings coming from the basement of their house. The noises were disquieting, but
nothing really untoward happened until one day toward the end of the month.
As Jeremy walked through the kitchen, late in the afternoon on December 30,
things on the kitchen table began to move and fall off, almost as if they were
following Jeremy. That frightened the foster parents, and, together with the
stompings, proved enough for them: they packed Jeremy off to his grandmother.

At his grandmother's house everything was peaceful, until the following Monday, January 3. Then, it appears, Jeremy became a walking disaster area. That
afternoon Jeremy and his foster father were walking from the barn to the house
when a three-foot long wooden stick was hurled, from a considerable distance,
across their path. A metal stove, a large wheelbarrow, and a heavy feeding
trough all fell over as Jeremy passed by. Three fence posts fell backward, away
from him, as he came near. A five-pound brick dislodged itself from the well,
landing three feet away. And, just as Jeremy walked past the kitchen door, the
large garbage can toppled over. A neighbor, visiting that afternoon, saw a heavy
metal lawn chair rise one foot off the ground and then settle down. Jeremy was
six feet away.

That same afternoon Jeremy, his grandmother, and a great aunt were seated
inside the grandmother's house when a stomping noise was heard. Soon the
flower vase fell over; then two dinette chairs rocked sideways and fell over.
Jeremy set them right but they toppled over again. Two sofa pillows flew twelve
feet through the air. This was followed by an afghan shawl, which landed on
the grandmother's startled head. Then two more pillows whizzed off. Now the
extremely heavy sofa jumped about a foot forward, toward Jeremy, in two
bounds. Two heavy padded chairs turned over, and a small wooden chair lurched
to join them. Jeremy was ordered to leave the house. As he passed through the
dining room, a metal stool slid seven feet across the kitchen entrance.

Similar *poltergeist* activity repeated itself a number of times during the following days. In all, 50 separate incidents were reported, attested to by 11 separate witnesses. These witnesses were interviewed within a week of the most intense activity. Most of the *poltergeist* activity occurred within a distance of five feet from the adolescent Jeremy. This is consistent with the findings of W. G. Roll, head of the Psychical Research Foundation, Durham, North Carolina, that *poltergeist* effects fall off sharply with increasing distance from the agent. This finding places RSPK in a different category from the various types of ESP. Although it is conceivable that Jeremy may have used trickery in some of the instances reported, it is rather improbable—he should have been easily detected. Trickery was scarcely possible in those instances involving the movement of heavy objects. Incidentally, Jeremy was examined physically and no neurological abnormalities of any kind were found.

On January 10, 1971, Jeremy's foster father, who interpreted the events as a portent from God, decided it was best for Jeremy that he return to live with his mother. Jeremy has stayed with her ever since and, strangely enough, the *poltergeist* has never returned.

THE OTHER SIDE

Few stories of communication with the spirits of the dead have received as much publicity as those connected with Bishop James Pike and his son, James, Jr. The Bishop, born a Roman Catholic in 1913, went through law school and taught law in three different schools. But he was always more interested in theological and philosophical questions, and he switched both his occupational and his religious interests to the Episcopal Church and taught in three theological seminaries. Other highlights of his career include serving as senior trial attorney for the U.S. Securities and Exchange Commission, Rector of Christ Church in Poughkeepsie, N.Y., chairman of the Department of Religion and chaplain at Columbia University, Dean of the Cathedral of St. John the Divine, and Episcopal Bishop of California.

One would think that life would be one long round of tea and crumpets for a man to whom accomplishment came so easily, but this was not so. For, somehow, Bishop Pike was connected with tragedy and notoriety throughout his life. He was a complex, contradictory man, with a constant propensity toward stirring things up. He felt his church should be involved in social problems, and he became involved in trying to improve the situation of American blacks; but he did this long before it was acceptable for middle-class whites to do so. As a result he incurred the enmity of the southern Bishops of his church; and the feeling was widespread, among his friends at least, that this was the basic reason behind the accusation of heresy that was eventually levelled at him. Bishop Pike did, in fact, question the dogmatism in his church, though he highly approved its rituals. And he increasingly became a firm believer in the existence of psychic phenomena.

The Bishop's mother was said to have possessed certain psychic powers; and a number of psychic events occurred to him in his early life, to which he paid little attention. One series of such events took place in the rectory of Christ Church in Poughkeepsie. The typical things usually reported in connection with a haunting were said to have happened to him here; a light switch, and the lights, being turned on and off by invisible hands; the sound of books being dragged along the floor of an upper story; sudden gusts of wind, from nowhere, blowing out candles; phones that went dead and subsequently recovered by themselves; a dog that stiffened and whined at a presence; a bat that suddenly appeared, and attacked him. But he accepted these phenomena as more or less normal.

The psychic occurrences that changed his life were all connected with his son, Jim, who went to study in England at the Cambridge College of Technology, after having spent a year at San Francisco State College. Jim had been a bit of a problem to his father, having had a number of bad LSD trips; but they got along very well. Bishop Pike, who was also spending some time in England, decided to take a short trip back to the States, together with his son. While they were in New York, on their way back to England, young Jim rented a hotel room, took LSD, had a very bad trip, and committed suicide.

A little more than two weeks after his son's death Bishop Pike experienced a great many psychic events. Safety pins and postcards were found arranged like the hands of a clock at 8:19, the time of Jim's death. Objects moved around, unpushed, while Bishop Pike was looking at them. Things fell off tables and shelves; milk turned sour in two bottles in the refrigerator and also in one outside in the cold.

Soon afterward Bishop Pike started trying to communicate with his dead son in seances, via three separate mediums. One of them, Mrs. Ena Twigg, had been educated in a Roman Catholic convent and had a long history as a medium. She did this on a nonprofit basis, strictly to help various people who found themselves in difficulty. She did not know of Bishop Pike or his son, but she told the Bishop many things, both about him and his son, that he either knew, or learned later, to be true. His son reportedly said through Mrs. Twigg as medium, "I wanted out and found there is no out."

A second medium who made supposed contact with his son was the Rev. George Daisley of Santa Barbara, a minister and member of the Spiritual Frontiers Fellowship. According to Bishop Pike, his messages consisted of a combination of ordinary statements, such as could be made by any clergyman; other statements of facts that were not known by him, and must have been picked up by ESP; and a small number of statements that reflected the personality of his son, as it was before he died and also, now, in transition.

The third medium, Dr. Arthur Ford, was also an ordained minister. He is the one who attained the greatest notoriety for Bishop Pike's efforts to contact his dead son. Among other things, he held one of his seances on TV. Originally broadcast from Toronto, the tape was later shown throughout the United States and Europe, so the seance was seen by millions. Dr. Ford was blindfolded and when he spoke it was with the voice of "Fletcher," his spirit control. Fletcher, in the broadcast, mentioned a number of the people—Jim's grandfather, Elias; a long-dead ancestor, Marvin Halverson; Louis Pitt, a chaplain at Columbia University before Bishop Pike—about whom Dr. Ford was presumably ignorant. Bishop Pike was convinced that the contact with his son was genuine. In 1968 he wrote a book, *The Other Side,* with Diane Kennedy, his secretary, outlining in detail the seances held in the attempt to communicate with his dead son. And soon, on December 20, 1968, Diane Kennedy, 25 years his junior, became his third wife.

The Episcopal church did not take kindly to Bishop Pike's third marriage, for in its eyes his previous marriage was not invalid. So three days after the marriage Bishop Myers, the Sixth Bishop of California, Bishop Pike's successor and old friend, issued a personal request to see his clergy and bishops, asking them not to invite Bishop Pike to perform any priestly functions. Bishop Pike had two alternatives open: to start trial proceedings or to resign. In April 1969, he chose the latter.

For many years Bishop Pike had been fascinated with the origins of Christianity, and he took many trips to Israel to examine the sources personally. In August 1969, he and his wife decided to visit the Judean desert, to try to retrace the actual steps of Jesus into this barren wilderness, then as now devoid of inhabitants but possibly a refuge for contemplation and insight. On Monday, September 1, they started out in a rented car from Jerusalem. Neither speaking the language nor being able to read the signs, they groped ahead by instinct. The roads became increasingly bad. They were in boiling, desolate country, completely isolated from humanity, and travelling impassable roads. Tuesday evening their car broke down. They walked two hours, not retracing their steps to civilization but going forward into the unknown. Then Bishop Pike collapsed. Mrs. Pike decided to go on, and she walked all night. The following morning, bruised and exhausted, she came on some road builders.

Bishop Pike's predicament was reported to the police later that day, and it produced headlines around the world. A massive search for him was initiated by cars and helicopters, but days passed without news. Mediums throughout the world gave reassuring news of knowing him to be alive. Dr. Arthur Ford had visions of him alive in a cave not far from the spot where his wife had left him. An Israeli medium, Margot Klausner, described in detail the area to search, claiming information obtained both by swinging a pendulum and automatic writing. She also sent along a message from Edgar Cayce saying the Bishop was in a coma and could be saved. The English psychic and witch, Sybil Leek, said on September 3 that Bishop Pike was still alive and in the hands of Bedouins. He was being held by two dark people in loose garments for political reasons; nevertheless, he would show up.

The mediums, it turned out, were all wrong. On Sunday, September 8, the body of Bishop Pike was found on a most inaccessible crag. He had obviously fallen from a cliff, at least 60 feet above, and his death was instantaneous. To remove him it was necessary to use helicopters; it was difficult to see how anybody could have reached this spot. His body was found in a kneeling position, his head lying on the stone. An autopsy subsequently showed that he died only a few hours after his wife left him to seek help. The spot where he was found was less than three miles from the automobile.

On March 11, 1973, according to a *New York Times* article, two biographers of the late Rev. Arthur A. Ford reported they had found evidence he had cheated in the celebrated 1967 TV seance that had so impressed Bishop Pike because of the intimate and unknown details there revealed. In going through his papers they found that Ford had done advance research. All the details of messages said to have come from various ecclesiastical dignitaries, as well as from James Pike, Jr., were found in clippings that Rev. Ford had studied before the TV seance. Despite their findings that Rev. Ford had resorted to chicanery, the biographers concluded that he, nevertheless, had authentic and extraordinary psychic powers.

OUT OF THE BODY

A night storm whipped up the sea around a lonely steamer cutting its way across the Atlantic Ocean. Two men lay in their cabin bunks. One of them, William Tait, was startled to "see," in his set-back upper berth, a woman lean over the lower bunk and kiss its occupant. A wry thought crossed Tait's mind.

In Connecticut, Mrs. Wilmot roused herself from a strange experience. That evening she had gone to bed very troubled in mind, for her husband was a passenger on a steamer at sea during a storm. Sleep, when it came, had been fitful. Somehow, by means she didn't understand, she found herself aboard the pitching steamer. Working her way through the corridor, she found her husband's room and entered it. She saw him in the lower bunk and started to approach, but stopped when the passenger in the upper bunk caught her eye. She continued, then, to her husband, kissed him and departed, sure of his safety. The next morning, on the steamer, Mr. Wilmot claimed to Tait that his wife had come to him and kissed him in a vision.

This kind of report is classified as an out-of-body experience (OOBE). The details of this particular experience were gathered and verified by Mrs. Eleanor Sidgwick, a pioneer member of the Society for Psychical Research.[11] Out-of-body experiences have been recorded throughout history, going back at least to ancient Egyptian times. Peoples of very different cultures describe similar experiences in which persons feel and see themselves moving outside the physical body.

The experience is a rare one. Although most people who have an OOBE have it just once in a lifetime, there do exist some extraordinary individuals who have experienced hundreds of these strange voyages. Sylvan Muldoon, in ill health both as a child and as a young man, reported that he had repeated out-of-body experiences. These abated in frequency with the onset of good health in later years. Another case is that of Robert Monroe, who was suddenly seized with a severe, but temporary, stomach cramp. Shortly afterward he began to have out-of-body experiences. And then, like Muldoon, he learned to control the flights of his consciousness, and also their onset.

The more common, once in a lifetime, out-of-body experience is sometimes caused by some shock. In a car crash, for example, the driver may experience being above the wreck, looking at his or her own struggling body, and seeing help arrive. The experience may also be brought on by extreme sickness or emotional stress. The person usually finds himself or herself floating, near the ceiling if in a room and clothed. When accustomed to this new state the person is often surprised when, reaching for a knob, his or her hand passes through the door! The experience may last up to half an hour.

The vast majority of people who go through such experiences are profoundly affected and find them joyful. They now "know" that life can exist after death. Such experience may completely alter their perception of nature, which is now experienced and appreciated on a different level, one that no rational discussion can capture back. Those who undergo an out-of-body experience do *not* feel that they are dreaming, and they describe their experience as distinctly different from a dream. The description of events observed in the experience seems to be accurate beyond chance. It is rare, however, for other people to observe the out-of-body phantom in a manner similar to that reported by Wilmot and Tait.

A British researcher, Dr. Robert Crookall, has carried out a study of many data he accumulated on out-of-body experiences. Whatever the eventual explanation, Crookall sees a large number of consistencies among reports from many different people, young and old and in different cultures. Such consistencies argue for a common, underlying phenomenon, and this implies some definite laws of behavior governing such experiences.

Crookall finds that a blackout usually occurs upon release of the consciousness from the confines of the physical body. There is some confusion and vagueness as this out-of-body consciousness hovers over the physical body, but the vagueness clears as the experience continues. People commonly report a heavenly world, and joyous experiences differing from any worldly experience. A very strange, but persistent, element reported is a cord connecting the ephemeral body to the real body. The cord is mentioned repeatedly in independent reports. Often it is said to be silvery, sometimes it is substantial (several inches thick); but also, in other reports, it is said to be filmy and inconsequential.

The OOBE often ends as a mirror image of its beginning: a returning vagueness, a hovering over the physical body, and a blackout upon reentry.

A comparison to the out-of-body experience appears in the revelations of people who have had a close shave with death. Dr. Russell Noyes, at the University of Iowa College of Medicine, has studied 80 cases of near encounters with sudden death, 80 people who may be said to have returned to life.[12] Sixty of these cases were taken from the medical literature, and 20 cases concerned people whom he interviewed directly. His work also shows a consistent pattern emerging from these unexpected, face-to-face confrontations with death.

The studies show that three stages may develop. First a violent struggle to escape the danger, with the body and the mind alert and possessing unexpected, enormous reserves of energy. Then, if the danger is too strong to be overcome, a sense of resignation and deep serenity may follow. Apparently we observe with detachment our forthcoming doom. A third of the cases report that, as in popular myth, the past flashes by in review.

The final stage awaits those whose introduction to death comes still closer to acceptance. Reverie, visions, and deep peace encompass the individual in about one quarter of the cases. The feeling of an outside presence, or of a fusion with nature, is sometimes reported. The experience is joyful. Only a few of these escapees from death report a vision of hell or damnation.

The pattern displayed seems to show the individual first undergoing an incipient ecstatic, altered state of consciousness. This quickly develops into an out-of-body experience prior to, or perhaps in place of, the full ecstatic state experience. The final experience appears to be an extraordinary altered state of consciousness, preparatory to the ultimate experience which all living beings must confront.

THE RAUDIVE TAPES

In *Breakthrough: An Amazing Experiment in Electronic Communication with the Dead*, Dr. Konstantin Raudive recounts his communication with the dead. Using only a microphone and a tape recorder, sometimes augmented with a radio, Dr. Raudive addressed questions to various friends and relatives who were dead. With the questions recorded on magnetic tape, he would then switch from "Record" to "Playback," listening intently for any disembodied voices that might have chosen to answer his questions. It was as simple as that. And he heard the voices.

Using this method Dr. Raudive has recorded over 72,000 messages. Most were in mixed Latvian and German. What was surprising was the fact that the voices claimed to be not only those of people known by him but also those of Gorky, Jung, Tolstoy, Hitler, Trotsky. . . .

Dr. Raudive claims that more than 400 people participated in his recording sessions and that each one of them eventually became aware of the voices, though at first most of them had difficulty. He has analyzed 25,000 messages according to their content, rhythm, and language. Of these, several hundred were outstanding: they could be heard and identified by anyone with normal hearing and knowledge of the language spoken. His advice for people attempting to perform such tests themselves is to record, at a tape speed of 3¾ inches per second, for a period of not more than 15 minutes. This limitation arises from the many hours that must be spent in analyzing a 15-minute recording.

Some comments should be made here about the possibility that the words perceived are not transmitted but are actually generated by the random white noise that is recorded. Random noise will generate random cues that an ear can pick up, cues that the mind can interpret as syllables. The brain is a great pattern detector. Given practice and a fortunate arrangement of syllables, it will fashion scattered words from the noise, dropping a prefix or reinterpreting a consonant as necessary. When, by chance, several words fit correctly then a rare, short, distorted sentence will appear out of the gibberish recorded. Attention and time are all that is needed.

Indeed, the recorded voices seldom say complete, fully grammatical sentences. The word endings are often improper and words are often completely missing, in the fashion of a shortened telegram. A listener fluent in a different language may sometimes hear a different word in the other language, and this can result in an altered sense to the message.

Several variations of the microphone technique have been employed by Dr. Raudive. In one he employs a radio receiver which has its electrical output fed directly to the tape recorder. The output also goes to a loud speaker, which permits him to monitor the recording. He tunes the receiver slowly from one end of the band to the other, seeking a frequency which gives him random static, so-called white noise. This receiver frequency must be far removed from the carrier frequencies of any transmitting stations. Occasionally he has found himself helped by a mediator, a voice which tells him where to stay tuned for recording the voices. He claims there are definite advantages to the radio voices over the microphone voices: they have a clearer pronunciation, their messages are longer, and they convey more meaning.

Dr. Raudive's book contains 240 pages of excerpts from some of the 72,000 messages Dr. Raudive had recorded as of 1970. We list a few.

"Jundahl can walk by himself, the old pot. Tie him to the death bed."

"Leader, I am naked."

"At nights we are always fearful."

"Matilda is just looking through the diary."

"Real frost. Here is the arctic. Frozen through to the bones."

"The soul exists." Dr. Raudive then remarks that the soul is free of the body after death. A voice answers "It is not so, Kosti."

"I want water."

"Please, a bathroom."

Here, for once, we have a method of testing the claimed results of one observer by other, completely independent, experiments. The method is clear and straightforward. Independent verification of claimed results is imperative if one hopes to convince the scientific community.

VAMPIRES

The legend of vampires, although found also in Asia and Europe, arose and became widespread in the Eastern Orthodox lands. The concept of vampires is not part of the Eastern Orthodox religion; it is a superstition that arose primarily in those Slavic lands where this religion was predominant. Vampires supposedly drank blood from the veins of living people in order to obtain the vitality, the sustenance, that the living obtained from food. They were supposed to be like drug addicts—when they needed their fix they would move heaven and earth to obtain it; and they had many terrible powers denied to ordinary mortals.

In some societies it was believed that the bodies of certain cursed people would not be received by the earth upon their death: their bodies would not decay. People who were excommunicated, for example, would not "die." Although they would spend their days in a tomb, at night they would fare out, wandering aimlessly, their bodies whole. They were doomed—either unto eternity or until absolution. They were vampires: dead, yet not dead. They were the undead. Other societies imagined the vampires as people who had actually died and had come back to life again to plague the living.

The legend of vampires probably would have been restricted to the general area of its birth if an English author had not written a novel based on vampires. *Dracula*, written by Bram Stoker in 1897, has never been out of print in the twentieth century, and it is still going strong. Over 100 movies about Dracula have been made, the most famous one being the 1931 version which starred Bela Lugosi. It has become a standard, classic, horror film—in the same league with Mary Shelley's robot gone berserk, *Frankenstein*, which was made into the movie starring Boris Karloff.

The Count Dracula of the novel was named after a fifteenth-century prince who had actually lived. The real Dracula was a warrior from Transylvania, the "land beyond the forests" in the Carpathian Mountains. This was part of Hungary for 1,000 years, but it has belonged to Rumania since World War I.

The historical Dracula was a ferocious freedom fighter protecting Wallachia and Moldavia from the invading Turks; a devout defender of the faith against the infidel Mohammedans. He combined the expediency of a Machiavelli with the bold bravery of a Robin Hood—he was a hero.

The real Dracula was a terror, a psychopath. His name was Vlad Tepes—Vlad Dracula—Vlad the Impaler. For Vlad achieved his fame by impaling. He impaled all the enemies he could reach, dead or alive; and many on his own side as well. He was cruel beyond belief. The impalements were often performed in sight, while he ate. He once had a live foe's hat nailed to his skull. Sometimes he had noses cut off, and ears, and sex organs. Occasionally he boiled his victims alive. Often he had his victims pulled apart by horses. But, mostly, he impaled. Tens of thousands at a time. And his victims lay exposed on their stakes, for as long as half a year. It has been estimated that he killed 100,000 men on his own side alone by the time he died in 1476. This constituted over 20 percent of the people in his principality. That must really have scared the Turks.

It should be said that these were violent times. Vlad's father was murdered, his older brother was murdered, and his only son was murdered. He, himself, was framed, and spent 12 years in jail, as the result of fake letters implicating him in a plot of which he was innocent. And when he was killed in battle, at the age of 45, he was decapitated.

How does one account for the long-lasting popularity of this fairy tale? Or of other fairy tales in which a person becomes an animal, the were-animal? There are myths that center not only upon the transfer to a werewolf but also to a bear in Europe, to a tiger in India, to a hyena or leopard in Africa, and to a jaguar in South America. Indeed, the myths at times appear to turn into facts, at least in people's minds. There is a psychiatric term, lycanthropy, used to accommodate those real cases where persons believe themselves to have changed into animals.

Vampires do not exist. They are a product of the imagination; but there are two slight connections between vampires and the real world. First, there *are* animals called vampire bats, found in Mexico and South America, which live exclusively on the blood they suck from the veins of living cattle. The scientific name of the most common species is *Desmodus rotundus*. Their common name was given them by Cortez on one of his expeditions to Mexico. Second, there was a wealthy seventeeth-century Hungarian countess, Elizabeth Bathory, who almost played the role of a vampire. She drained the blood of young girls so she could bathe in it to keep her youth. She did this over a period of ten years, but was finally caught; whereupon her accomplices were beheaded while she was made a prisoner in a castle—being, after all, a countess.

HOW CAN IT BE?

What can we make of hauntings and *poltergeists*, of reincarnation, of spirits in flight and on tape, of the powers that might conceivably exist in mediums and spiritualists? What ties an apparition to one place? In reincarnation the survival time during which the "remembrance" lasts averages near seven years; while in spirit communication with the dead the information reported becomes less and less reliable beyond seven years from the death of the person "contacted." Why? What are the possible explanations for these occurrences that seem so extraordinary?

Two extreme answers immediately present themselves. These effects may be completely *natural* within our present understanding of nature; or they may imply the existence of a *spirit* world, but one that is somehow in contact with our present world.

A completely natural explanation within our present understanding of nature may be acceptable for vampire myths and, perhaps, the Raudive tapes; but it can hardly explain mediums, hauntings, *poltergeists*, or the reincarnation data. Of course, our understanding of nature is by no means complete; and, even in those areas where our technical knowledge is quite certain, we often do not comprehend its origin. Science certainly will progress beyond its present boundaries. It must progress further, even if all we wish is to make our present knowledge comprehensible. To ban anything outside our present knowledge closes the boundaries of science forevermore. It seems more reasonable to accept all well-verified phenomena that we cannot yet explain and to be frank about our lack of understanding. Here stands the real frontier of knowledge.

A spirit world may exist. But even if we knew it existed, that would scarcely be satisfactory: we need to know more than just whether or not it exists. Until we know how it operates we cannot relate a spirit world to any of its manifestations in our own world.

When we fathom an explanation for a particular phenomenon, any one of those we have discussed, we are fashioning a bridge between natural and supernatural phenomena, between our natural world and a "spirit" world. We are expanding our present limited view of nature to a more inclusive one. There are many explanations, all in their fashion attempting to bridge this gap by supplying, to some degree, mechanisms and laws. We will very briefly mention five theories concerning various aspects of the spirit phenomena.

• The *psychometric* theory accepts both ESP and psychometry as real phenomena. Psychometry is the supposed ability of some especially sensitive persons to look at or feel certain objects—keys, wallets, handkerchiefs—and receive from them impressions about their owners. When applied to a haunted house, for example, the psychometric theory would hold that a sensitive occupant "feels" the impression of a former occupant of the house, one in which some unusual occurrences starkly etched themselves. The haunting is thus subjective. This theory cannot explain those cases of hauntings where the phantom visits a place to which the dead person had never been.

• The *psychic-ether* theory is a more detailed form of the psychometric theory. It assumes that a "psychic ether," something containing both matter and the mind, exists. A tragic event might etch mental images upon this psychic ether and remain trapped there, only to be picked up by a sensitive, as a phantom, at a later date. The intermittent nature of some hauntings raises difficulties with this theory.

• The *psychon* theory postulates that the mind consists solely of psychons (sensations, images, etc.) which tend to link together. Some degree of consciousness results whenever two or more psychons link together. It is assumed that psychons are not limited spatially. Upon death a person's psychon system may survive for years, and it may even travel; but eventually it will be dispersed. This theory cannot easily explain *poltergeist* phenomena, but it does offer some description of many aspects of other psychic occurrences.

• The *spirit* theory presumes the existence of at least one nonphysical element associated with the body of a spirit. Dead spirits may be trapped (perhaps through an unexpected tragedy) between this physical world and the next, spiritual one. This accounts for hauntings. If we substitute psychon for trapped personality we see that there is much in common between these two theories. The psychon theory does not, however, assume another world.

• The theory of *alternative universes* may actually be a wide range of theories, depending on the number of alternative universes imagined. For example, two universes might be imagined. This would refer to this world and the "spirit" world, with a mind or soul connecting the two worlds. Death releases the soul from this world to the other world, unless it becomes trapped.

Some physicists propose that, on the basis of the quantum mechanical laws of nature, there exist vast numbers of universes connected through the very nature of space itself. We will discuss this interpretation in the last chapter. Here we note only that in some universe "you"—more precisely, your counterpart—may have just finished reading that last chapter, while in another "you" have just picked up the book to read it. In some universe there is no living earth, only a long-dead sun with its equally dead planets. There are huge numbers of in-between universes, spanning all possibilities. A sensitive person may somehow peer through the connection to another universe, one ahead of us, and seemingly read our future. Similarly, a haunting may represent a view, glimpsed through a dim connection to a universe behind us in time, of the counterperson dead in our universe but in agony in the other. Although weird, it is not logically impossible. It may even be true.

One must distinguish carefully between the facts and the conjectures. There is no proof, whatever, for any of the various theories mentioned above. They are all, each in its own way, way out. But they are designed to explain facts. It does no good to deny the facts because the theories seem outlandish. The facts of hauntings, the cases suggestive of reincarnation, and *poltergeist* phenomena cannot *all* be discarded simply because they do not fit our scheme of things, or even because there are many hoaxes and frauds. Facts are facts. Any theory which deals with facts of this kind is going to be off the beaten path; it is going to be disturbing. It may even be disturbing to Dr. J. B. Rhine. So we cannot blame other scientists too much if they become upset when confronted with implausible theories that attempt to explain those seemingly improbable events that cross the boundary to an unknown world.

THE EXTERNAL WORLD

PART TWO

CHAPTER NINE
THE AWESOME VOID

QUESTIONS

An investigation of the hidden aspects of nature divides naturally into two parts. So in Part 1 we considered various poorly understood phenomena that relate to the inner world of the human mind. Here, in Part 2, we will focus our attention on the external world. This dark outer world is vast, and we comprehend many of its characteristics only dimly.

In order to illuminate the role played by the occult in nature outside our earth we need to have some familiarity with the nature of our universe. We will treat some topics here that are truly at the very edge of our knowledge. How big is the universe? Is it finite or infinite? Is the universe expanding? If so, what is it into which it expands? How old is the universe? What was there, then, before its beginning? How was the Earth formed? How was the universe formed? Is there intelligent life elsewhere than here on Earth? How did life on Earth arise? Is it likely that there have been visitations to Earth by extraterrestrial beings? Can we hope to be able to communicate with them?

We attempt to answer only a few of these questions. The answers will only be educated guesses since we can, as yet, perform few experiments to test the theories. But this does not mean that one guess is as good as any other; inner consistency demands that the logical consequences of theory must be in agreement with our observations of the way nature works.

THE EXPANDING UNIVERSE

Our understanding of the physical universe has changed enormously even within the last half century. In the early 1920s our view of the universe extended only as far as our own galaxy, the Milky Way; within our own Solar System, the planet Pluto circled undiscovered; and the source of the enormous energy of our own Sun was still hidden. The chemical processes we then knew could scarcely keep the Sun burning millions of years, let alone the billions of years needed for life's evolution. The nuclear chemistry which would explain the Sun's long life still remained in darkness. During these years the astronomer Edwin Hubble aimed the newly built 100-inch telescope on Mount Wilson at the heavens. In 1924 he announced that other galaxies existed beyond our Milky Way, and the known size of the universe expanded a thousand-fold. What is our present view of this universe?

Large distances on Earth are measured in terms of miles or kilometers. But these units are far too small to be useful for measuring the huge distances, incomprehensible to the human mind, that stretch between stars and galaxies. The unit used for measuring astronomical distances is the light-year, the distance travelled by light in one year. The speed of light in vacuum is 186,000 miles *per second;* and in one day light travels more than 16 *billion* miles, or one light-day; while in one year light travels 5.88 million million miles. So one light-year is a distance, a short way of saying 5.88 million million miles, nearly six trillion miles.

When we speak of "the universe" we mean all matter, everywhere. We still do not know for sure, but at present it is thought that matter has a finite extent. In one of several possible versions of a finite universe, if we started a journey in a given direction and kept going indefinitely then, given sufficient time, we would arrive back at our starting point from the opposite direction, much as we do when we circumnavigate the Earth. Present thinking says, also, that the universe is expanding. Practically all astronomers and cosmologists think the expansion to be true.

The "big-bang" theory states that, sometime in the past, all matter and energy that is presently in the universe was concentrated into some very small volume. An explosion occurred (Why? How?) sending energy out in all directions; the energy condensed into matter, and the universe has been expanding ever since. A variant of this, the oscillating universe theory, holds that the expansion will not last forever. Eventually, the rate of expansion will slow down, stop, and a maximum radius will be attained. Subsequently, the universe will start to contract until, finally, it will not only come back to its present size but will continue to contract until all matter is again contained in a volume of submicroscopic size. Then the cycle will start once again.

Still another theory—the steady-state theory, or the theory of continuous creation—asserts that the universe is presently expanding in order to accommodate new matter that is continually being created everywhere. This creation of matter is *not* similar to that observed by physicists in nuclear processes, where it is created by the conversion of energy according to the famous Einstein formula, $E = mc^2$. This creation of matter follows a completely new, and unknown, path—it does not occur at the expense of the existing energy supply. The ad hoc assumption is made that the creation occurs at the expense of no other energy or matter.

Observations tend to favor a big-bang theory, with the possibility that the expansion will eventually turn into a contraction. But all the theories that are now generally accepted agree that the universe is expanding. This conclusion arises from just one set of evidence: the observation of a color shift in the light coming from stars in other galaxies, which indicates that these other galaxies are moving with greater speeds the farther they lie from us.

A few other possible causes of this shift in the light pattern from the galaxies have been suggested, but these explanations do not seem too plausible. We conclude that there is relative motion between the other galaxies and our own. Further, since the light patterns shift in color toward the red, we can pick out one direction for this velocity. A separation speed between a galaxy and Earth would cause a red shift in the stellar light; a violet shift would be caused by an approach. It is found that the stellar light from other galaxies is shifted to the red. The other galaxies in the universe seem to be moving away from us.

Years ago, because of an apparent motion of all the galaxies in the universe away from us, we might have been tempted to conclude that they were fleeing *us*, as if *we* had some plague. But we have learned, through the efforts of Copernicus and Galileo, the folly of taking an anthropomorphic view of our planet as the center of the universe. So we now conclude that all the galaxies are receding not only from our Galaxy but also from each other. We are not picked out; we are typical. A standard simile is employed here: that of a balloon painted with tiny polka dots. If the balloon is being filled with air, any one tiny polka dot would see all the other small polka dots moving away from it. The polka dots farther away from any given polka dot would seem to be receding faster than those that were closer, the velocity of recession being directly proportional to the separation. And that is what is found for the galaxies—those that are farthest from us are receding fastest. That's why we believe the universe is expanding.

OUR TINY ISLAND

The matter that is distributed throughout the known universe is not distributed evenly, like water in a jug, but is clustered into clumps. And the clumps themselves are not filled uniformly but are mostly vast reaches of emptiness, with small lumps inside them. The biggest clumps are called supergalaxies, and they are separated from each other by inconceivably large distances. Within each supergalaxy the matter is clustered in galaxies.

The farthest galaxies we have yet discovered are at the utterly incomprehensible distance of 10 to 20 billion light-years away. Within a sphere of that radius we estimate there are about 10 billion galaxies. The average distance between galaxies in a cluster of galaxies is estimated at 5 million light-years. Our Galaxy, the Milky Way, is an island in space containing over 100 billion stars and resembling a flying saucer in shape. It is 100,000 light-years in diameter, and we are in its interior, some 30,000 light-years from the center. Nothing special. We glimpse our own Galaxy, the Milky Way, as a long, tenuous streak spread across the night sky, centered on the constellation Sagittarius but spreading out in both directions in a milky, white path that is really a dense accumulation of star points.

The Sun is thus only one of 100 billion stars in one galaxy. As far as we know, neither the Milky Way nor our Sun are particularly exceptional. The star nearest our Solar Sytem, Alpha Centauri, is actually three stars, 4.3 light-years away. To gain an idea of the density of stars in our neighborhood, there are 15 stars within a distance of 12 light-years from the Sun; while there are 4,000,000 stars, each of them a sun also, within a distance of 10,000 light-years. Almost half of all the stars, which we see only as single dots, are actually double stars or triple stars.

The Sun is the major object in the Solar System and serves, very nearly, as the center about which the other objects revolve—the planets (with their moons), the asteroids, and the comets. These are all bathed in the Solar wind which blows from the Sun's surface. The Solar System—like an atom, like a human brain, like a galaxy, like the universe—is mostly empty space. The nine major planets in order from the Sun, are Mercury, Venus, Earth, Mars, Jupiter, Saturn, Uranus, Neptune, and Pluto. They are mere pinpoints in a vast void.

Mercury is both the smallest planet and the one nearest to the Sun. Its rotation about its own axis is locked in, by gravitation, to the rate at which it revolves about the Sun, in such a way that the length of Mercury's day equals two-thirds the length of its year. Mercury is so small that it has lost its atmosphere; like our Moon, its surface is pockmarked with craters. When it is cold there, during its long night, it is very cold; but when it is hot, it is hot enough to melt lead. Life here is most implausible.

Venus was once thought to be a planetary twin of Earth. But it is continuously cloaked in a dense cloud cover and we cannot see its surface, so until recently we could not even measure its temperature. Today, as a result both of close flybys and of instrument landings on its surface, we know that its surface temperature is about 900° F. Its surface pressure is 90 atmospheres. The Sun could never be seen from the surface, even if there were no clouds, because of the intensive scattering of light produced by the dense atmosphere. In fact, the light scattering would cause the surface to appear bright red. Venus is thus a reasonable approximation to Hades—a hell hole.

Mars, the planet just beyond us going outward from the Sun, is considerably smaller than Earth but has long been favored, in the public mind, as the most likely home for other life in the Solar System: Martians. But the November 1971 flyby of Mars by Mariner 9 completely disproved earlier notions of straight, regular canals on its surface. There are just many irregular details of various geological faults. There are huge volcanoes and impact craters, one volcano being hundreds of miles wide and 20 miles high. There are "ice" caps, but there are no oceans. The recent Viking 1 spacecraft has sighted tear-drop shaped "islands" in meandering channels of what may prove to be ancient rivers.

Edgar Rice Burroughs and his tales about Martians notwithstanding, there is no civilization on Mars. For, like Mercury and our Moon, there is only a trace of an atmosphere on its cratered surface. No free water has yet been detected on its surface; and the mean temperature is about −47°F, well below the freezing point of water. There are hints, however, that water did flow at some time in the past history of Mars.

The ultraviolet rays from the Sun are so intense that Earthlike life would not survive their harmful chemical effects very long; and even resistant microorganisms would shrivel up and die in a period as short as one second, except when the surface of Mars was being ravaged by one of the tremendous, global dust storms to which it is prey. The dust is then so dense that the killer, ultraviolet rays are completely obliterated: an ill wind that blows good. Tests by instruments landed on Mars in July 1976 by Viking 1 should soon tell us if there is even *any* primitive form of life there, buried in the sand beneath the surface.

It was thought that Mars was once like Earth but gradually lost its atmosphere and shriveled up and died. Today some scientists believe just the opposite: that Mars most likely was once like the Moon, but is now becoming more and more Earthlike as it heats up from internal radioactivity. It is even considered possible that an appreciable atmosphere may eventually be formed by the volatile gases emanating from its volcanoes. But by now everyone agrees that if there is life on Mars it is of an exceedingly rudimentary kind.

The next planet beyond Mars is Jupiter. It is completely different from the inner planets: its diameter is eleven times that of Earth. It has a very thick atmosphere consisting predominantly of hydrogen and helium, methane and ammonia—a poisonous combination. Being so far from the Sun, Jupiter receives very little heat from that source; but being so massive, it generates considerable heat internally both from radioactivity and gravitational contraction. We know that Jupiter emits radio frequency radiation in surprising quantities.

Recent data from the Pioneer 10 satellite cast light upon Jupiter's turbulent interior. Scientists who have examined these data feel that, 600 miles below the top of the heavily clouded atmosphere, the immense pressure squeezes the lower atmosphere into liquid hydrogen, despite a large increase in temperature. Fifteen thousand miles below the cloud cover the pressure may be 3 million times that of Earth's atmosphere! And the liquid hydrogen there turns to liquid, metallic hydrogen. At its core, Jupiter's temperature may be six times that at the Sun's surface. Yet, high above the surface a frigid atmosphere circulates at hurricane velocities, and lethal radiation belts spread far into space. There is nothing here to lead us to believe that life on Jupiter can be jovial.

Saturn, Uranus, and Neptune—the next three planets beyond Jupiter—mimic Jupiter in most features, but to a lesser extent. They are very, very cold by our standards. On one of Saturn's moons, Titan, there may possibly exist a low order of life. Titan, a moon as large as the planet Mercury, has an atmosphere that apparently consists of hydrogen, methane, and ammonia—possibly spewed up by volcanic activity. These gases are the necessary ingredients for the complex molecules, including sugars and amino acids, which are the precursors to the first stages of life. Titan seems to trap more heat from the Sun under its clouds than it radiates back. Through this greenhouse effect it manages to obtain a bitter, subarctic temperature that may allow for life's development, as it may have started on Earth in the far distant past. This is also true of two of Jupiter's twelve moons, Europa and Ganymede, which may be covered by large areas of water ice-frost.

Pluto, the last planet, is a frigid midget 40 times as far from the Sun as we are. Figure 9–1 is an artist's impression of the planets circling our Sun—the major parts of our Solar System.

Fig. 9–1. Solar System. Our Earth is the third planet from the Sun, with its Moon nearby. In this dramatic view, distances and sizes are only approximate. The asteroid belt is between Mars and Jupiter. (Figure adapted, by permission, from Robert Jastrow and Malcolm H. Thompson, *Astronomy: Fundamentals and Frontiers*, New York, Wiley, 1974, 2d ed., p. 4.)

The possibility of the intelligent life we know existing on any Solar planet seems limited to just one planet—our Earth. For one reason or another, none of the other planets qualify as the lucky ones.

The astronomer Harlow Shapley has offered an interesting conjecture concerning a different possibility of life.[1] It would occur not on some satellite of a star, but on a body whose size falls somewhere between that of a star and that of a planet. Shapley believes there are many such substars, too small to shine or be seen, but large enough to emit heat and support life. Our Earth emits such heat; Jupiter emits much more. An object in space ten times bigger than Jupiter (but not too much bigger than that) could have the sort of surface temperature we need for life. Shapley did not believe there was any such object near our Solar system, but he did think there was a good possibility that there are many of them about, elsewhere. We would need orbiting satellite telescopes, searching the deep infrared, to discover these substar candidates for life.

THE SPEED BARRIER

If a spacecraft could travel with the speed of light it would take 4.3 years to come to Earth from Alpha Centauri, the star nearest the Sun. But according to the theory of relativity and our experience in high-energy accelerators, it is not possible for a body having a real, greater-than-zero mass to travel at the speed of light. Only massless bodies, such as light photons, can do this; and only bodies with an imaginary mass could go faster than this. As far as we know, the speed of light is a remorseless barrier hindering any widespread *insterstellar* travel by massive beings. By interstellar, of course, we mean between our Sun and another star; interstellar is to be distinguished from *interplanetary*, which means between one planet and another within our own Solar System.

Even travelling at the speed of light to Alpha Centauri, at least 8.4 years must elapse on Earth before the completion of a round-trip interstellar expedition. For widespread travel hundreds of years would pass before an expedition, setting out to investigate a handful of stars, would return to its home planet, even if the speed of light could be attained.

The distance to nearby stars is a factor that is crucial even to the possibility of communication with centers of intelligence elsewhere in the universe, let alone the possibility of visitations. As an illustration: the diameter of the Earth is 8,000 miles, or 43/1000 of a light-second; that is, light takes 43/1000 of a second to go 8,000 miles. The Moon is at a distance of, roughly, 250,000 miles from Earth: 1.3 light-seconds. The Sun is 93 million miles, or 8.3 light-minutes, from the Earth. A two-way conversation with somebody this far requires the patience of a monk. There is a delay of 8.3 minutes before a spoken phrase reaches the other end; a delay of indeterminate duration is needed to allow comprehension and formulation of an answer; and another delay of 8.3 minutes awaits the return journey. So an exchange of messages would, of necessity, be like a very tedious conversation by telegraph, with a minimum gap of 17 minutes between successive transmissions. Alpha Centauri is 272,000 times as far away from the Earth as the Sun is; and, if we wished to communicate with somebody on a planet near Alpha Centauri, there would be, of necessity, an 8.6 *year* delay between successive transmissions. One wonders: could telepathy bridge the gap faster? But we have no evidence, one way or the other.

Between start and return of an interstellar expedition, then, the time span passed on the home planet is, indeed, very large. A paradoxical time effect would, however, take place for the members of any fast-travelling expedition from Earth. The flow of time for these travellers could be much slower than for people on Earth, the people they left behind them. If their speed were very close to the speed of light, the travellers could age only several years while hundreds of years passed on the home planet. We will discuss this time shortening, which is really a wondrous—and occult—aspect of science, in the last chapter.

To take advantage of this paradoxical time effect, a vehicle would have to travel at a velocity close to the speed of light. To attain such a speed is, however, very difficult; in fact, the closer we approach the speed of light, the more difficult it becomes to approach it further. So what is a reasonable figure to assume for a high-speed space vehicle sent out from the Earth? The very fast space vehicle, Pioneer 10, was launched March 3, 1972, toward Jupiter and it will eventually escape the Solar System to pursue an endless trek among the stars. Its initial velocity was 31,413 miles per hour. Let us envisage a dramatic increase by a factor slightly more than ten, making speeds of 335,000 miles per hour possible. Since the speed of light in vacuum is 670,000,000 miles per hour, this means we would then be travelling at only 1/20 of 1 percent of the speed of light. The one-way journey between Alpha Centauri and Earth would take this super-Pioneer 10 spacecraft 8,600 years! At such slow speeds the time effect mentioned above would be quite trivial.

Suppose the speed could be increased by a factor of 100 instead of by a factor of ten. This is, of course, easier said than done. But even then, travelling at 3,350,000 mph (or half of one percent of the speed of light), the journey would take 860 years. Except for science fiction writers, an interstellar journey *by us* is incredibly improbable in the near future. However, at an acceleration of 1g (the gravity we feel on earth) it would take us about one year to approach the velocity of light. Hence, time dilation could affect our journey to Alpha Centauri—*if* we had the extraordinary power source needed.

Is an interstellar journey equally improbable for the humanoids of another world? If their laws of physics are the same as ours then it is. They, too, would have to contend with the difficulty of approaching 186,000 miles per second. But if, unknown to us, their science has superceded the laws of physics known to us, then it becomes conceivable that they could make such a journey. We think it not unreasonable, however, to hesitate a great deal before placing our faith in such a possibility of overcoming the barriers of nature known to us. We have no evidence, whatever, to support such a view. Of course, if an Unidentified Flying Object were to land on Earth and discharge some passengers from a distant star, we might obtain such evidence. This, in itself, makes the study of UFOs of great potential value. But so far this has never happened, at least to our knowledge. Again, if it were eventually to turn out, say, that the velocity of light is different in different galaxies, then such a journey would be again conceivable. For if the speed of light is ten times as high in some distant part of the universe as it is in this part, near Earth, then the speed barrier for all material objects there is also ten times as high. But so far we have no evidence whatever that the laws of physics are not the same everywhere.

The story is completely different for the times required in *interplanetary* travel, within our own Solar System. Pioneer 10 passed Mars, and then the asteroid belt, on its outward journey from Earth to Jupiter and beyond. Jupiter's distance from the Sun ranges out to 484 million miles and, for that great distance, the Sun's gravitational pull slowed Pioneer 10 on its outward race. But after laboring 21 months the spacecraft hurtled past Jupiter in December 1974; and now it is going out, at a steady pace, to its endless appointment with the stars. Time intervals of this scale to the other planets of our Sun are within our comprehension. The trouble is, there seems to be no intelligent life on our neighboring planets. So where the distances and times are reasonable, we have no compelling reason to make the journey.

THINK BIG

Sebastian von Hoerner[2] of the Astronomisches Rechen-Institut of Heidelberg, Germany, has studied the limits on space travel imposed by various factors: the energy content of different types of fuels, power-mass ratios, acceleration times, relativistic factors, payloads, and other such considerations. The results he arrived at are most discouraging for the possibility of space travel. To quote just one difficulty: It would require a power output of 600 million megawatts, in a power station of less than 10-tons mass, to give a 10-ton payload a speed 98 percent that of light within 2.3 years of the crew's time. The required power output is nearly 90 times the world's present total power output. He concludes that space travel for technologies like ours must be confined to our own planetary system. Unfortunately, the numbers say that VAST amounts of energy are needed for interstellar trips.

Still, Freeman J. Dyson, a physicist at the Institute for Advanced Study in Princeton, N.J., famous as the longtime home of Albert Einstein, has made a proposal of a completely different kind for mastering the energy crisis faced by any plan for interstellar travel. (Dyson is remarkable in that he is one of the few outstanding physicists in the past century to have reached a level of general recognition without ever having paused long enough to acquire a Ph.D.)

Dyson's proposal for obtaining the large amounts of energy needed for interstellar travel involves a simple principle: THINK BIG.[3] Forget about fuel—you can't get enough of it. Instead, he proposes to use the gravitational energy of passing stars—to become a free-loading hitchhiker. Assume that we could somehow get a space vehicle to a point in outer space not too far away from a double star which circles about a common center. These stars would preferably be of the type known as white dwarfs, with densities approaching 3,000 tons per cubic inch. The spacecraft is navigated to make a close approach to one of the stars at a place where spacecraft and star are moving in essentially opposite directions. The effect on the space craft will give it a huge acceleration, swinging it about like a sling shot. Starting with a negligible speed, the spacecraft would acquire an enormous velocity *without the expenditure of any fuel whatever*. This would be, in effect, a gravitational machine. The energy would come from the two stars: after the spacecraft passed they would be circling at a slightly smaller energy.

To achieve the huge increase in speed envisioned, Dyson's spacecraft would have to undergo an acceleration of 10,000g—ten thousand times the acceleration of gravity here on Earth! Could human beings survive such huge stresses? Now, the spaceship is in free fall toward the stars, with nothing tending to resist this fall; and in such a case *any* acceleration could be withstood, either by humans or by objects, *if* the acceleration were uniform. Because the spaceship and the human body have finite sizes, however, there are slightly different gravitational accelerations on different parts of these bodies; and this difference in gravity *would* produce a stress. This is very much like the case of the tides produced on Earth by the Moon; these are also produced by the differences in the gravitational field. It turns out that these tide-like forces for the spacecraft are quite reasonable. Humans and delicate teacups, alike, would scarcely be aware of the 10,000g. So this sling-shot gravitational accelerator may be a reasonable possibility some time in the future.

As long as we are THINKING BIG, we ought to mention two other proposals. The first of these, also credited to Freeman J. Dyson, is concerned not with interstellar travel, but with an alternative to it. Dyson notes that advanced civilizations know that their mother stars will grow old, cold, and die some day.[4] Our Sun will die, for example, some 5 billion years from now. Hence there is a need to develop space travel in the meantime—in order to escape to a young mother star where life could continue. Since it takes a very long time for a star to get cold a civilization may want to conserve, in the meantime, the heat that a star was emitting. How would it do so?

Dyson believes that the following procedure may already have been followed many times in the past by other civilizations; not only because their stars were getting cold, but also because of the Malthusian pressures of an ever-increasing population and a fixed energy supply. Dyson suggests that such a civilization might dissemble the material of a neighboring planet and redistribute it into a spherical shell revolving about the star. Thus, we might take Jupiter and form of it a shell about seven feet thick, revolving around the sun at twice the Earth's distance from it, trapping all the Sun's energy. Fantastic amounts of energy would be required to so redistribute Jupiter, but Dyson suggests this could come from the Sun's energy itself, collected over a period of 800 years. He believes a shell of this thickness could be made habitable and could utilize all the sun's emitted energy, where we now trap only a minute portion of it.

Dyson believes that we on Earth ought to start a search for any civilizations that may have taken this alternative. Since their stars would no longer be visible to us, how would we find them? We would have to look for dark objects, of size comparable to the Earth's orbit. The temperature of such an object would be about what we enjoy here on Earth, 300K (27°C. or 80°F.). Our Sun, with a surface temperature of 5500K, would be sending out, to the ring, radiant energy peaked in the green part of the spectrum. The ring would radiate out an equal amount of energy as heat to the outside world, but with a peak wavelength of 10 microns, in the infrared portion of the spectrum. Fortunately, the Earth's atmosphere is transparent from 8 to 12 microns, so we could photograph such infrared stars. We need some infrared telescopes and the time to search for these objects. It would probably take a long time, so the investigators would need to be driven, dedicated persons.

The last of our crazy, crazy BIG ideas concerns an idea that was proposed by I. S. Shklovskii, who coauthored (with Carl Sagan) *Intelligent Life in the Universe*. This idea is an interesting comment on the halting way in which things sometimes happen in science.

In 1944 B. P. Sharpless, of the U.S. Naval Observatory, published a paper in the Astronomical Journal reducing all the data then available, from 1877 on, concerning Phobos and Deimos, the moons of Mars. He found a slow, long-term deceleration of Phobos, the inner moon, which was similar to that of our present-day artificial satellites in the Earth's atmosphere. But the atmosphere of Mars is too rare to cause deceleration of the planet's inner moon, so Shklovskii proposed a novel thought. If the mass of the moon were very much smaller than assumed, then the attenuated atmosphere of Mars would be sufficient to drag the moon down. Shklovskii calculated the mass and density of the moon for this to occur: the moon had to be hollow!

On this basis Shklovskii came to the conclusion that the inner moon of Mars must be an artificial satellite constructed by an intelligent race of Martians to create an environment more hospitable to life than that on Mars. And, if Martians could have done this, then other civilizations could have constructed artificial satellite homes too. So, perhaps, should we if conditions on Earth ever become too inhospitable.

But some time subsequently the English astronomer G. A. Wilkins repeated all the calculations leading to the data on the inner moon of Mars, and found no evidence for the deceleration found by Sharpless. Shklovskii withdrew his imaginative proposal that Phobos was the site of a nearby civilization. Still, the possibility remains that other civilizations have constructed such homes for themselves elsewhere. Should we be seeking them?

And now, having taken the reader along a slight tangent, we gently return to our main trajectory.

EXTRATERRESTRIAL LIFE

The universe has a radius of some 10–20 billion light-years, and its age, as estimated on a big-bang model, is of the order of 10–20 billion years. As our knowledge has grown, that age has grown from a figure that was close to 3.3 billion years only some four decades ago.

Stars, or star-like objects, make up much of outer space (space outside the Solar System) that we can see. They fall into several categories which have definite life-styles: white dwarfs, main sequence, red giants, supergiants, pulsars, and quasars. The life history of our Sun is rather typical of stars: it was born roughly 5 billion years ago, and it is now in a mature stage; it will blaze up, then die to a dark cinder, perhaps 5 billion years in the future. We are now midstream—middle aged and wistful.

The method by which the Sun acquired its planets is still a source of controversy. Until the mid-1930's the dominant theory held that a catastrophic close encounter between the Sun and another star raised huge tides on the Sun's surface and spewed matter into its surroundings. This eventually conglomerated into lumps, then bigger ones, and so forth, until the planets were formed. James Jeans was an outstanding proponent of this view; but the astronomer H. N. Russell eventually showed that the theory was wrong. It could not explain the fact that 98 percent of the angular momentum of the Solar System was in the planets while 98 percent of its mass was in the Sun. Also, the planets would be much closer to the Sun than they actually are. So the theory was abandoned. Such a close encounter between two stars is a comparatively rare thing, and by this theory our planet would be a somewhat unique thing in the Universe.

According to another theory, small particles of dust as well as gases in the surrounding space were attracted to the Sun by gravitational forces and, in the process of accretion, were conglomerated into planets. But where did the gas and dust come from? The most widely held view at present is a modification of an earlier theory of Kant and Laplace that the planets and the Sun originated simultaneously out of the gas of our Galaxy. This is a long, slow process which occurs everywhere; so one would expect to find planets everywhere in the Universe.

Other theories have also been advanced. But all the theories that have been proposed so far have some strong objections that can be made against them, and we are not yet certain about any of them. We do know with good certainty, however, from the evidence of radioactive rocks, that the Earth is perhaps 5 billion years old and that fragmentary life existed on Earth over 3 billion years ago. The human being probably evolved from *Homo erectus* at least 1 million years ago. Nearer ancestors, not too different from ourselves, existed 100,000 years ago; but civilized humans, beings that can organize widely, communicate, and leave records, are not more than 10,000 years old. The age of human technological growth on Earth is much briefer—only 200 years or so. Figure 9–2 lists some of the scientifically significant events in the history of the Earth.

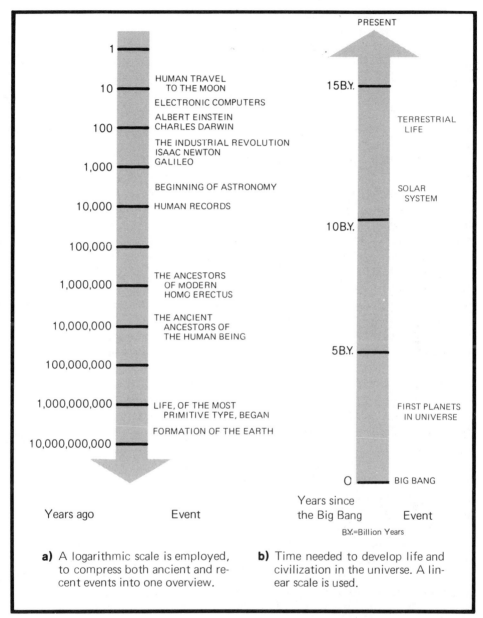

Fig. 9–2. Some scientifically significant events in the Earth's history.

One thing is certain: the life span of humanity on Earth is limited by the future, certain death of the Sun. It is possible that we will annihilate ourselves first, through our destructive technological weapons: ICBMs, MIRVs, and hydrogen bomb warheads. It is conceivable that we will be able to escape to a planet near some other sun and live happily ever after, or at least for quite a while. But in any event, our life span in this Solar System is finite.

What are the possibilities that life, approximately as we know it, exists elsewhere than on Earth? The story of Earth-like life must surely be closely intertwined with the story of a liquid, water. The liquid state is one of the four states in which matter exists. (The others are the gaseous state, the solid state, and the plasma, electrically charged, state). The liquid state is by far the least common one in the universe. But it is the one state that allows the existence of dense stable complexes, molecules, that can yet move about easily—an earmark of life.

Liquids do not exist in the vast reaches of "empty" space. Outer space, away from the stars, holds about half of all matter in the universe in the gaseous state. The tenuous matter that fills this empty space is predominantly hydrogen, about one atom per cubic centimeter. This is a "vacuum" at least a million times less dense than any we have yet created on Earth. No intelligent life could live in this gaseous state, far from solids. Most of the rest of the other half of matter is in the plasma state, within the stars themselves. Temperatures here range upward into the hundreds of millions of degrees, and the atoms are stripped of their electrons. No life as we know it can conceivably exist on the stars themselves.

So the existence of life at all akin to us is limited to the very small percent of matter remaining after the plasma stars and the gaseous "empty" space are eliminated. This is where the solid and liquid states enter—in and on the planets revolving about the stars. But not all planets have conditions of temperature and pressure that allow the existence of liquids; in particular, of water. Only in such places can life, as we know it, exist. For years astronomers have been making estimates of the number of planets where liquids like water, and life, can exist; over the past few decades these estimates have changed considerably, and we cannot yet have too much confidence in the values. Still, the numbers may come as a surprise.

One estimate,[5] made recently by I. S. Shklovskii, is based upon the following reasoning. The life-styles of stars are generally displayed on a graph known as a Hertzsprung-Russell diagram, on which most of the life of a star is spent in a phase known as the "Main Sequence." The H-R diagram classifies stars by surface temperature and intrinsic brightness. The classes range from the hottest and brightest, designated O, through B, A, F, G, and K intermediate categories, to the coolest and least bright M stars. (A mnemonic device that all students of astronomy learn in order to remember this is: Oh, Be A Fine Girl. Kiss Me.) The G, K, and M stars are characterized by low surface temperatures and very slow rotation about their axes. The slow rotation means that such stars have very little angular momentum; O, B, A, and F stars, on the other hand, have considerably greater rotation rates; and the change from one group to the other is sharp and discontinuous, not smooth, like the variation of most of the other parameters. Astronomers have come to the conclusion that G, K, and M stars probably have their angular momentum in a planetary system! Our own Sun is a G star, and it has planets. Now, such stars are quite common in the Main Sequence; therefore it seems quite plausible that of all the 100 billion stars in our Galaxy several percent, or several billion stars, have a planetary system.

If life is to exist on a planet a number of conditions must be met. The most obvious one is that the temperature must be neither too high nor too low: it defines an inhabitable zone in the vicinity of the star. Another condition is that the planetary mass not be too large (in which case the atmosphere would, like Jupiter's, contain too much hydrogen, and it must not be too small (in which case it would lose its atmosphere altogether, like Mars). Most planets which have a proper temperature would probably have a satisfactory mass.

Another requirement for life is that the star be sufficiently old to allow the time needed for evolution. About 3 billion years are needed for this process, if one judges by our own example. It turns out that the G, K, and M stars, the smallest in the Main Sequence, are old enough.

Two other criteria that must be met are fairly obvious. First, the star must be in a phase of its life cycle characterized by very stable conditions that do not change appreciably over long periods of time. For if the star's brightness, say, changed very much in a million years, we could not expect a given planet to remain suitable for life over this period. G, K, and M stars are very stable over billions of years. Second, the star must be a single, not a multiple, star. With a double or triple star, a planetary orbit cannot be expected to be stable over long periods. It is known that about half of all stars are single stars.

Thus we can expect that nearly a billion planets in our Galaxy would have conditions suitable for life. But of these planets, how many actually do have a civilization? Shklovskii makes the guess that the life of any civilization is finite. It takes a certain number of years for evolution to produce the civilization, starting with the organic primeval soup. Then there is a lifetime of, perhaps, a million years. Finally, for one reason or another, death. So in the lifetime of a star, a few billion years, a civilization flourishes for less than 0.1 of 1 percent of the time. This reasoning reduces the number of other civilizations in our Galaxy from a billion to a million.

Finally, these million civilizations in our Galaxy are distributed throughout a volume stretching over an extent of some hundred thousand light-years. How many of them are then not more than 100 light-years away from us? The answer, assuming the laws of probability to hold, is one or two. And so, if we were to start to search immediately among the closest million stars, only eavesdropping to pick up messages and not attempting the much more difficult communication, and spending one hour on each star, it would take a century until we found a star mothering a civilization. The cost and patience would, indeed, be astronomical.

GALACTIC CIVILIZATIONS

The spark of life is, presumably, spread far and wide throughout the universe. Our technological achievements here on Earth began perhaps 10,000 years ago, in the Neolithic age, and mushroomed only over the last 200 years of the 5 billion years of Earth's existence. If these developments are at all typical, then there must be many civilizations throughout the universe much more advanced than ours. A million years' advance is but a very small fraction of the span of life on a planet. Yet the advances we have still to make, granted another million years' survival, are awesome; indeed, terrifying. We must then expect that the universe is populated by many extremely advanced civilizations. And we must expect that they have advanced knowledge and technologies we cannot even imagine.

We can barely discuss the nature of these possible advanced civilizations since we ourselves do not have the knowledge that time has yet to unfold to us. There are two possibilities. If technology has inherent limitations there will be a large number of intelligent civilizations at a stage of stable, technical achievement well beyond ours. If technology is not inherently limiting there will be a wide spectrum of advanced civilizations, with the highest holding fantastic capabilities, perhaps capable of changing the universe.

Remember that our Solar System is a late comer in our galaxy and in the universe. Born perhaps 9 billion years after the original Big Bang, the Sun contains heavy elements which could only have been derived from the debris of long-extinct novas and supernovas that signaled the death of previous stars long, long ago. Planets and civilizations begun on more ancient stars have had billions of years of life before our Sun was born. (See Fig. 9–2b.) Should even a minute fraction of these societies still survive, perhaps now on a foster solar system, their type of civilization must be far advanced over our own.

A classification of the possible extraterrestrial civilizations has been attempted by scientists. Nature placed successive natural barriers about a planet in space: the planet's surface, its sun's planetary system, its parent galaxy. As a civilization matures its development is successively limited by the resources of its planet, then of its star, then of its galaxy.

Those civilizations which are well on the way toward fully using the resources of their planet are classed as Type I. We, ourselves, are becoming a Type I civilization. As we have learned painfully over the last decade, our planet's resources are finite. Yet we use less than one four-thousandth of the Sun's energy that falls on our planet's land.[6] At a three percent compounded annual growth rate we will not reach our planet's energy limit for 1200 years; and we still have to utilize the Sun's energy falling on the seas. But once a Type I civilization has grown to the limits of its planet's capabilities there begins a long hiatus in its further growth.

It is, perhaps, tens of thousands of years later before the next stage is fully underway. The planet's inhabitants crave their sun's *total* energy. Following Dyson, they seek to enshroud their sun, to catch its heat and light. The civilization is growing into Type II, slowly building itself around its sun, perhaps at the expense of an otherwise useless companion planet. Such a civilization comes to another stopping point when it has completed the encirclement of its sun. Its energy resources may now be 1 billion times as great as they were in its Type I phase.

Eons later the society, if it is still in existence, has sufficient mastery to step out among its neighboring stars to capture their prodigal resources. A Type III civilization is being born. Its final task: to entrap the resources of its galaxy. Slowly it works its way out of its corner in the galaxy, generation upon generation devoted to exploration and exploitation within its galaxy, whose stars offer 10 billion times the resources it tapped as a Type II civilization. Its final limit is the galaxy itself. The distances to the next galaxy are just too far . . . too far.

Looking throughout our own Milky Way we have seen, so far, no evidence of either a Type II or a Type III civilization. But we may not yet know how to read the evidence.

The classification above stops at the boundary of the galaxy. Is a Type IV civilization possible, limited by nothing but the universe itself? The command of nature by a Type IV civilization would seem godlike to nascent Type I civilizations like ours. Powers beyond our vision or belief would lie at their behest. Nature may, by edict, forbid the Type IV civilization—a rival to its very self. Or, the thought is irresistible: one Type IV civilization may reign, supreme.

CONTACT

If other civilizations of varying types lie beyond us in space, should we contact them? Have we, unknowingly, already contacted them? How would they react to us—favorably or unfavorably? Are we to assume that if we should ever encounter such a civilization they would accept us, at face value, for what we profess to be? "Love me. I'm an American." Would it help if we had freckles, a boyish grin, red hair, and a disarming candor? Perhaps. But so far we have not yet achieved that success even with other denizens of the Earth.

Is the barrier at the velocity of light one of technology's basic limitations to such a contact? If advanced knowledge shows that it is not, then advanced civilizations, free to probe the whole universe, have likely done so for millions of years. Our Earth may, then, have been probed many times throughout our history by such civilizations.

If, on the other hand, the barrier is forever impenetrable, then all civilizations, no matter how advanced, must be limited in exploration to their own small niches in the universe. Visitation to us from other intelligent civilizations, no matter how advanced, would then be—though possible—most unlikely.

On the basis of our knowledge to date, we have no evidence whatever to suppose that the speed of light can be surpassed. If we accept this lack of evidence as significant, then the chance of our having been observed by interstellar visitors is extremely remote, and the possibility of its occurrence in the future is also small. Probably, then, the 6 billion or so years remaining to our Sun's existence is too short a time period in which to expect such a visitation. Still, the probability is finite—it is not zero. The importance of serious, unprejudiced, evaluation of Unidentified Flying Objects is obvious if we are to attempt to answer questions concerning the existence of other intelligences, or questions concerning the speed barrier of nature.

PROJECTS OZMA AND CETI

In April 1960 a brief search of two of our nearest neighbors in the skies was started in an attempt to detect messages from other beings who might inhabit these worlds. None of the project's sponsors expected it to succeed. Still, it was certain that such attempts would be made increasingly in the future, so why not begin? The name picked for the project was, accordingly, taken from a never, never land—the Land of Oz.

The detector employed in this investigation was a radio telescope located in Green Bank, West Virginia, that had been completed only a year earlier. Its antenna was a metal dish, 85 feet in diameter, accurate to 1/16 of an inch and capable of scanning almost half of the celestial sphere. As the huge dish points toward one point in the sky, like a searchlight beam in reverse, it collects all the electromagnetic radiation impinging on the dish from that direction. The large size of the dish makes the antenna very sensitive to small radiation levels and some radio telescopes have still larger sizes. The movable antenna of the Jodrell Bank radio telescope near Manchester, England, is 250 feet in diameter; while in Arecibo, Puerto Rico, there is a fixed dish antenna (shaped to a valley in some hills) which has an area of 20 acres! (See Fig. 9–3.)

As the dish follows a star across the sky, a permanent record is made of the signals which emanate from that source. What the operator seeks is a direction where there are some cyclic variations of the signal strength, indicative of some purposeful design behind it.

The choice of the central frequency to which the radio telescope is tuned is important. For it may be that a signal is being sent to us and that we have turned a radio telescope in exactly the right direction to pick it up, but our amplifier is tuned to the wrong frequency. How do we know what the right frequency is? We don't. We can only make an educated guess, picking a frequency that has a minimum of background noise associated with it.

A frequency of 1,420 million cycles per second is associated with very strong radiation that reaches Earth from the extensive atomic hydrogen clouds that surround us in the "empty" space around us, in all directions. It is a frequency landmark in space. So the detector for Project Ozma was tuned to a frequency close to this value. This frequency is in the ultra high frequency (UHF) portion of the spectrum, somewhat higher than that of TV broadcasts.

The Green Bank radio telescope watched two stars systematically for Project Ozma, seeking some constantly repeated signal. Several directions were originally favored, for we know there are seven stars within 15 light-years of us which have a luminosity and lifetime making them likely candidates for seats

Fig. 9–3. Radio telescope at Arecibo, Puerto Rico. As the world's largest radio-telescope (its dish reflector covers an area of 20 acres), this huge instrument is able to listen in on an entire galaxy. At the same time, it can emit the most power-ful signal now leaving Earth. (Cornell University photograph by Russ Hamilton, courtesy of the National Astronomy and Ionosphere Center.)

of civilization. Some of these were discarded because they were in the southern hemisphere, some because they were multiple stars. Two stars were chosen: Tau Ceti in the constellation of Cetus (the whale) and Epsilon Eridani in the constellation of Eridanus (the river). Both are about 11 light-years from the Sun.

For 150 hours, altogether, in a period of three months of searching, no signal was found coming from these two stars. Operators tuned in a narrow frequency band for one minute, and then the adjacent band. A wide band of the radio spectrum, altogether 400,000 cycles per second wide and centered about 1,420.4 million per second, was slowly scanned this way. The results were completely negative. So in July 1960 the project was terminated and the radio telescope time was allocated to other projects. There are many misses for each success in the slow, halting progress of science.

Since Project Ozma there have been a few sporadic attempts, elsewhere, to listen for extraterrestrial signals. In the USSR, V. S. Troitskii of Gorki University spent a total of three weeks listening on two frequencies to the emanations from 12 separate stars. The results were negative. And, again at the National

Radio Astronomy Observatory in Green Bank, West Virginia, Dr. Verschuur made several efforts to detect signals.[7] Ten stars were listened to, no signals were detected.

Communication with Extraterrestrial Intelligence, edited by Carl Sagan (Cambridge: MIT Press, 1973), is an English translation of a conference held in 1971 in Soviet Armenia, that was attended by 32 scientists from the USSR and 18 from the USA. The conference was translated into both English and Russian. In reviewing the English version of the conference A. G. W. Cameron had an intriguing comment.[8] He noted that Freeman Dyson had suggested that the human race may in the future inhabit the interior of comets and had cited as one advantage the fact that people could thus get away from their government. Cameron's comment: "How had the Russians translated this in their edition?"

Partly as a result of this conference, the USA and the USSR have since embarked on a slow but steady long-range program for scanning the skies for signals from space. The project is called CETI, an acronym meaning "communication with extraterrestrial intelligence." The American effort is split into two parts. The first, using the Green Bank, West Virginia, facility, has already scanned 700 stars within 80 light-years of us. It will continue to examine hundreds of our nearest neighbors in space. So far, no news.

The second American effort is far more ambitious. Utilizing the Arecibo, Puerto Rico dish, this search is directed at a whole galaxy, thereby listening in on 100 billion stars at one time. It has already been directed at the five nearest galaxies. A serious obstacle is evident here, even if this search is successful. For, if we do detect such a signal, it will come from a civilization which is millions of light-years away; so the signal being examined was originally emitted millions of years ago. Even though we are now picking up its signal, that civilization may no longer exist. And to find out if it does exist we will first have to wait further millions of years until they receive our query and we receive their answer. How do we know they still exist after that, when we then receive their response?

The Soviet effort is also split into two parts. The first makes use of eight widely separated stations simultaneously scanning the entire sky available to them. By comparing the fluctuations in their signals, they are able to eliminate local signals and thereby greatly increase their signal-to-noise ratios. Not only do they scan the entire sky, rather than concentrate on one spot at a time, but they also scan a wide range of frequencies ranging from 1 million cycles per second to 100 million per second. This program, which is to run until 1985, will eventually make use of two space stations in addition to the network of stations on Earth. These may be artificial satellites circling the Earth; or they may be comparatively slow-moving observatories, situated at spots in the Solar System where there is an equilibrium of various gravitational forces.

The second Soviet program will also run for a decade, beginning in 1980. It will employ, in addition to satellite monitoring of the whole sky, two stations on Earth with very broad artificial dishes and artificial scanning capabilities made possible by the use of computers and movable reflectors.

THE ODDS

Given our brief survey of the universe and of the tiny region in our immediate neighborhood, what conclusions have we reached about the possibility of a visitation to Earth by extraterrestrial beings who seem likely to populate at least some of the vast void outside?

The information we have presented shows that interstellar space consists of regions which are incomprehensibly vast, with dimensions that are incomparably large compared to those with which we are familiar. *If* the laws of nature are the same throughout the universe and *if* we cannot find in nature immense power sources, as yet undreamed of, then any speeds which we are ever likely to achieve fall short, by a very wide margin, of the minimum range of values necessary to cover such distances in a reasonable time. We are willing to consider journeys lasting ten generations; but it makes no sense to consider a million generations dedicated to such a journey.

It is no wonder that most scientists are very wary of the suggestion that Earth has ever been visited by humanoids, robots, or UFOs from outer space. However, we do think it is a mistake to refuse even to consider the subject of UFOs, extraterrestrial travel, or visitations from outer space as respectable topics for investigation. There are, after all, big *ifs* connected with this conclusion of the impossibility of interstellar travel: *if* the laws of nature are the same everywhere and *if* there are no immense power sources awaiting discovery.

To be sure, extraterrestrial visitation is a premise that most scientists find difficult to accept. There is no hard evidence that makes such a premise inviting, they say, much less compelling. Why make it, then? In the next chapter, Unidentified Flying Objects, we present some evidence that is sufficiently convincing to some astronomers to make them believe that UFOs represent a real phenomenon outside our present understanding of nature. Is this phenomenon the visitation by extraterrestrial beings? The best attitude may simply be an unbiased mind.

Interstellar *communication*, on the other hand, is much more likely than interstellar *travel*. However they arrived at their opinions, all experts in the field are agreed that there are a very large number of advanced civilizations elsewhere in the universe. All except a very small number of these would be very far away from us—so far away, in fact, that for all practical purposes of communication they might as well not be there. But there should be some very small number of them within our signal range. We should be trying to listen to them, perhaps even trying to talk to them, via radio telescopes. One day we are bound to make contact with one.

Our recent explorations in our immediate neighborhood by interplanetary flybys and trips to the Moon have indicated that the possibility of finding intelligent life elsewhere in this Solar System is negligibly small. The other planets, for one reason or another, are quite inhospitable to advanced life as we know it. So, while the distances in interplanetary travel are fantastically more reasonable for us than those in interstellar travel, we have learned as a result of our recent space travels that the chance of finding an advanced civilization anywhere in our Solar System is nearly zero.

This is the background. The chances of contact are slim. Yet, we repeat, they are not zero. They are finite. Perhaps the best way of making contact with such a civilization is by trying to listen to them, and by letting them listen to us.

SCIENCE FICTION

We noted early in this chapter the dim and frail knowledge we possessed but 50 years ago about our universe. Who would have dared to guess the future and its vast changes, changes which many of us have witnessed within our own lifetime? Yet there *were* those who dared.

A century ago the novels of Jules Verne showed the fertile imagination needed to hold the interest of the public in the advances of science; yet his was an imagination that was disciplined and logical enough to withstand the scrutiny of scientists. *A Rocket to the Moon, 20,000 Leagues Under the Sea, Journey to the Center of the Earth, Around the World in Eighty Days*—these and many of his other books fed the fantasy life of countless boys and girls. Chock full of adventure and imaginative beings, they filled a need for excitement that would later in life be served, instead, by the fantasy worlds of sex, or power politics, or big business. Generations of youngsters imagined themselves roaming under the worldwide seas with Captain Nemo. Television then brought us Captain Video and "Star Trek."

After Verne came H. G. Wells, whose *War of the Worlds, The Invisible Man*, and *The Time Machine* were addressed to adults, as were the books of Jules Verne which are now read by kids. The two authors are remarkably similar. There is not much characterization in these books—one never really comes to know the individuals who roam its pages. Their emotions are subdued. Love and hate are occasionally mentioned; but the lesser passions such as sex, greed, betrayal, and hunger are practically ignored. The emotional vein of later science fiction still lay untapped.

In science fiction, as in the detective or wild west story, the author has an obsession, an *idée fixe*. The story centers about one point, some noncommon-sense assumption that the reader is asked to take for granted. It is the author's job to develop all the consequences that flow from this assumption. Attention to detail is necessary in order to make the incredible credible. Are the strangers from a small planet which is too weak, gravitationally, to hold much of an atmosphere? Then they must be barrel chested. Is it important for them to be able to see in all directions, not just forward? Then they must have their eyes on the tips of long, flexible antennas.

Verne and Wells were not the only ones to write books of this kind. Jonathan Swift's *Gulliver's Travels* could be classified in this genre, as well as H. Rider Haggard's *She*, S. L. Clemens' *A Connecticut Yankee in King Arthur's Court*, Edward Bellamy's *Looking Backward*, and Aldous Huxley's *Brave New World*. But the birth of the modern brand of science fiction is marked by the April 1926 appearance of the magazine *Amazing Stories*. This was edited by Hugo Gernsback, who was already the publisher of a magazine called *Science and Invention*. It is Hugo Gernsback who is the father of Sci-Fi, or S.F. (two variants of the words "science fiction"). The annual award for the best science fiction is called the Hugo. Since Hugo Gernsback, science fiction has flourished in the short story rather than in the novel.

Amazing Stories went under in the depression of 1929. But from the ashes, phoenix-like, Gernsback brought forth *Wonder Stories*, dedicated to the proposition that fiction is stranger than truth. And this new magazine lasted until 1936, when Gernsback left the field for other, greener pastures. In 1929, however, another magazine had established itself in S. F. Its name has undergone numerous metamorphoses—*Astounding Stories of Super Science*, *Astounding Stories*, *Astounding Science-Fiction*, *Analog Science Fact-Science Fiction*—but its particular title was not its important characteristic. Its relevance to the history of Sci-Fi lies in the fact that from 1933 on it had on its staff John W. Campbell, Jr. As editor from 1936 until his death in 1971, he played an important role in bringing a form of rigor and high standards to science fiction. Campbell wrote unsatisfactory short stories, but as an editor he was superb. Two other magazines that acquired a considerable following were *Galaxy Science Fiction* and the *Magazine of Fantasy and Science Fiction*.

Science fiction is relevant for us here because the imaginings of hundreds of authors in thousands of stories peer through the veil into the unknown. The nature of extraterrestrial visitors to Earth—whether from another planet in our Solar System or from the planet of some star outside our Galaxy—was predicted in manifold variations. The nature of life on other planets, far away or long ago, was examined in many mutant forms. Could life travel, over huge distances and time spans, from one galaxy to another via spores, one of the lowest but hardiest forms of life? Could they spawn life here on earth? A fit subject for innumerable stories. Could time be warped, so that we could instantaneously skip time intervals, to be transported forward or backward, by ten years or by millenia? That's one way of breaking through the limits of light's speed. Can a stellar-born twin age more slowly than his or her earthbound twin? Could I really be my own grandfather? What would it be like to live on a world dominated by another species, say ants? Are robots inevitable in advanced civilizations? What would it be like in a world where we could make ourselves invisible? Are mutants necessarily harmful? Where are the edges of our awesome void, and who guards those outposts? What were the beginnings of this universe, and what mystery witnessed its birth? Only the imagination limited the choice of topics, problems, and solutions.

ONE LAST QUESTION

Science fiction is limited by the imagination but science is limited by fact. One fact that dominates all of present science is causality: for any effect there is a cause. We see a universe; what caused it? And what caused the cause? There is either a continual succession of causes, on backward, with no beginning; or there is a first cause—a cause that finds its own origin in itself—an uncaused cause. Postulating a continual succession of causes only pushes backward the problem of finding the ultimate cause; or else it postulates the uncaused cause as the whole series itself. Either way, we arrive at the idea of an Ultimate Cause with no cause other than itself: The First Cause, God.

We have met many gods within the human mind and, once again, we meet God outside it. It seems unlikely that conventional science can give any definite answer about the ultimate nature of this God. New knowledge in science pushes back the frontiers of causality. But we only see what happened after the beginning, not what caused the beginning. The meaning of such thoughts must, of necessity, largely remain unclear and hidden. Indeed, the problem of the existence and nature of God may be the ultimate unknown, forever veiled and seen only dimly through our everchanging insights. And, if we choose to deny the existence of God, then the existence and nature of the other-than-God left becomes the ultimate unknown. Why? How? When? Where? Turn as we may, we are brought face to face with the narrow limits on the knowledge possessed by humans.

CHAPTER TEN

UNIDENTIFIED FLYING OBJECTS (UFOs)

■ *Flying Saucers* ■ *Some Early Case Histories*

■ *The Condon Investigation* ■ *Some Explanations*

■ *The Condon Report* ■ *The Findings* ■ *Dr. Hynek's Rebuttal*

■ *Nocturnal Lights* ■ *Daylight Discs*

■ *Radar-Visual Reports* ■ *Close Encounters*

■ *The Extraterrestrials?* ■ *The Lady or the Tiger?*

FLYING SAUCERS

On June 24, 1947, a Boise, Idaho businessman named Kenneth Arnold, piloting a private plane near Mt. Rainier, Washington, reported that he saw a line of flying objects which looked like pie plates skipping over the water. Newspapers all over the country immediately picked up the story and called the things he saw, or reported he saw, flying saucers. The wide publicity given this report triggered a spate of sightings of similar flying saucers, not only throughout the United States but all over the world.

Concern arose about the possibility that flying saucers might represent a threat to our national security: so many reports were turned in that, at times, some military communication channels were clogged. The government, seriously concerned over the possibility that an enemy contemplating a sneak attack might deliberately stimulate a wave of reports of flying saucers, became officially interested—in a very minor way. In September 1947 it commissioned a branch of the Air Force at Wright-Patterson Air Force Base in Dayton, Ohio, to make a study of reports of unidentified flying objects, or UFOs. Early in 1948 the study became Project Sign, but in February 1949 the name was changed to Project Grudge and in July 1951 it became Project Blue Book. This is the name it kept until the study was officially terminated in December 1969. The study had assigned to it the following personnel: one officer, one sergeant, and one secretary.

The government interest in UFOs was, thus, officially initiated by the Kenneth Arnold sightings in 1947. At first the results of these studies were considered classified information, but from 1952 until the project's end in 1969 the reports were declared available to everyone—though they were stored in a restricted area. The studies had convinced the Air Force that UFOs were not a threat to national security.

The number of reports of sightings of flying saucers would probably have declined rapidly after the initial wave of interest were it not for the vastly increased speed in communication made possible by our advanced technology. The intense public interest in UFOs was inevitably fed by many articles and books. In the January 1950 issue of *True* magazine "Flying Saucers are Real" by Donald E. Keyhoe introduced the hypothesis that UFOs were spacecraft either flown or controlled by intelligences from another world. The article asserted that these spacecraft were visiting our planet clandestinely.

The extraterrestrial premise seemed extremely attractive, not only to the general public but to many other writers; and this article opened the floodgates to a steady stream of articles on the extraterrestrial origin of UFOs. In time there were three national private societies (the National Investigation Committee for Aerial Phenomena—NICAP, the Aerial Phenomena Research Organization—APRO, and, later on, the Mutual UFO Network) with thousands of members devoted to tracking down, reporting, investigating, and photographing UFOs. Opinion surveys showed that several *million* Americans believed they had seen UFOs. And UFO sightings were by no means an American phenomenon, for widespread sightings have been reported in Canada, South America, Europe, Australia, and even the South Sea Islands. Sightings are continually, to this day, reported from most major areas of the world, and a great many people absolutely believe the extraterrestrial hypothesis of the nature of UFOs. The Air Force continually tried to deemphasize both UFOs and the extraterrestrial theory; but after the Central Intelligence Agency secretly tried to debunk UFOs in 1953, many people became convinced that there was a plot on the part of the Establishment to keep the facts hidden from the American people. It was well known to those in power, so one story went, that UFOs were spies from other worlds intent on ferreting out our secrets, especially our military secrets. The military and the political/industrial complex were in cahoots to keep this knowledge from the people, in order to prevent the panic certain to occur with the knowledge. This "theory" was bolstered by the fact that in 1952 there was an unusually large number of sightings near Washington, D.C.; and at other times there were many reports around remote New Mexico military bases. The Air Force still has in effect a regulation establishing a UFO officer at each Air Force base responsible for accepting and investigating sightings.[1] Through a wry twist, the money paid that officer comes from the government out of its *Foreign* Technology Division!

SOME EARLY CASE HISTORIES

In order to give the reader the flavor of some UFO sightings we will present, from among the many, a selected number of the early case histories which initiated the subsequent wide public fascination with UFOs. These reports will not be typical of all UFO observations, a group now estimated to contain 100,000 individual reports. Among the whole group there would certainly be a number of hoaxes and frauds, well-intended but misguided illusions, and simple misinterpretations. The small group selected here is restricted to reports by airplane pilots, people who are not amateurs in the identification of airplanes. In identifying UFO events the customary reports are extremely specific. This is quite unlike ESP identifications, which are often very vague. Here we give name, rank, place, and time. The actual case studies are, of course, much more detailed.[2]

• Less than six months after Kenneth Arnold's sighting, early in the afternoon, on January 7, 1948, a huge, round, glowing object (sighted earlier by hundreds at Madisonville, Kentucky) flew over Godman Air Force Base, near Fort Knox. It hovered over the field, alternately glowing red and white. Capt. Thomas Mantell, flying past with three other F-51 pilots, was asked to investigate by the Godman tower. Sighting what appeared to be a huge metallic object, he started to follow it on a climb, maintaining radio contact with the tower. After a while his reports ceased. Later that day his wrecked plane was found, his body not far away. No reason for the crash was evident.

• Two Eastern Air Lines pilots, Capt. C. S. Chiles and First Officer John B. Whitted, saw a brilliant cigar-shaped craft at 2:45 A.M., July 24, 1948, near Montgomery, Alabama, heading southwest directly toward them and going very fast. Both vessels veered, then passed each other only 800 feet apart. The pilots claimed they saw two rows of windows on the UFO, and said it gave off an intensive blue glow from the inside while it trailed a red-orange exhaust. As it went by its propulsion blast rocked the DC-3; then it pulled up sharply and disappeared.

• On October 1, 1948 Lt. George Gorman chased a UFO, which was lighted and maneuvering oddly, near Fargo, North Dakota. His report was confirmed by two airport-tower operators.

• On October 29, 1952 Lt. Burt Deane and Lt. Ralph Corbett were flying two F-94 jets at 2 A.M. over Hempstead, Long Island, each jet with a radar operator in the rear cockpit, when they suddenly saw a fast-moving object a few miles ahead. Corbett hooked on to Deane by radar while the latter tried to close in on the brightly lit object; but the UFO turned in a tight circle that would have caused a human to black out from the high acceleration. The chase went on for eight minutes, with Deane and Corbett never matching the UFO's performance. Then, at supersonic speed, the UFO disappeared. Lt. Deane believed the UFO's power and acceleration were superior to that of any American plane known to him.

• On November 16, 1952 at about 5 P.M. hundreds of people, including the air-traffic controller at the airport, had either seen or thought they had seen a huge, gleaming disc travelling across the sky near Florence, South Carolina. The controller, watching it through binoculars, saw the disc tilt sharply and climb out of sight. About six minutes later a *group* of glowing discs was sighted at nearby Landrum; and one observer, J. D. McLean, took 40 feet of film on an 8 mm camera using a telephoto lens. The details shown in the film were rather poor, though it was possible to discern five oval shapes.

• Early on the evening of January 9, 1953 Capt. George Madden was piloting a B-29 bomber, with Lt. Frank Briggs as his copilot, at 16,000 feet altitude over Santa Ana, California. The night was clear. Suddenly there was a flash of blue light, and looking out to the right, they saw a V-formation of blue lighted objects approaching at a fantastic speed. Madden swerved left. The lighted objects suddenly slowed, banked upward, and vanished. The total time the objects were seen: five seconds. Contacting Air Traffic Control by radio, he was informed there were no planes of any kind in the area.

Soon after the Mantell death, the Air Technical Intelligence Command established Project Sign to investigate the many UFO reports. After some investigation the Air Force claimed that at least three of the above accounts were explainable: Mantell had actually chased the planet Venus; Chiles and Whitted had seen a meteor; and Gorman had spotted a lighted weather balloon. Possibly these explanations, correct or not, would have quieted matters; but about this time Frank Scully wrote a book in which he described two flying discs from Venus that had crashed in the southwest.[3] According to Scully, the Air Force had found the bodies of several little men which it removed for examination. Although the Air Force denied the entire matter, many people chose to believe Scully, and his book became a best-seller. Many people who knew Scully testified that he was a very sincere person, one who would not conceivably pull a hoax. Still . . .

In 1949 the Air Force had declared "The saucers are misinterpretations of various conventional objects, mild hysteria, meteorological phenomena, aberrations, or hoaxes." But in 1952, the Air Force declared "These reports are coming from sincere people; they are not crackpots. They are seeing something." Yet, the Air Force still maintained that UFOs were just natural phenomena. The following table compiled from the later Condon report gives the number of UFO events classified by Project Blue Book for the years 1953–1965 inclusive:

1953—530	1960—557
1954—492	1961—591
1955—545	1962—474
1956—670	1963—386
1957—996	1964—563
1958—602	1965—845
1959—390	

It was clear that, despite all the Air Force statements, people were continuing to see UFOs.

THE CONDON INVESTIGATION

The Air Force recognized the need for an independent assessment of UFO sightings, and in 1966 a committee of scientists at the University of Colorado was given a grant of half a million dollars by the U.S. Air Force to make a scientific study of UFOs, completely independent of the Air Force. The committee was headed by Dr. Edward U. Condon, an outstanding physicist. In scientific work he had been a coauthor (with G. H. Shortley) of *The Theory of Atomic Spectra*, the first American textbook on the then new quantum theory. He had been the director of research for the Corning Glass Works, and also for the National Bureau of Standards. In administrative work he had been president of the American Association for the Advancement of Science (AAAS) and president of the American Physical Society. Yet, with all this, he was by no means an Establishment figure: he was cited by the House Un-American Activities Committee for attacking J. Robert Oppenheimer when the latter had named someone to the HUAC as a communist; and Richard M. Nixon had challenged Condon's security clearance. So, despite his preeminence in science, Dr. Condon was a bit of a maverick, and could by no means be attacked as a tool of the Air Force.

It was clear from the outset that no investigation could definitely establish that it was impossible for extraterrestrial visitors to come to Earth. Any investigation, because of the transient nature of the phenomena under investigation, could examine only *stories* about beings or objects, not the beings or objects themselves. The UFOs were gone by the time any investigator reached the scene, and all conclusions must be somewhat tentative. Suppose that, as a result of such an investigation, the following statement were made: "The UFO underwent an acceleration of 100g for 15 seconds during this sighting." The acceleration of gravity at the surface of the Earth is 1g. Since humans cannot survive a nonfree-fall acceleration of 100g for this length of time, can we therefore conclude that such a craft could not have been piloted by human beings or by other living beings? The statement, of course, does not exclude the possibility that the UFO was piloted by living beings, other than humans, who *could* withstand accelerations of 100g. (Surprisingly, it does not even exclude the possibility of human passengers. We float in water because the buoyancy of water annuls gravity; and passengers immersed in water would not feel the 100g the supposed craft was experiencing.)

Thus, the real purpose of such investigations would be to determine which UFOs were definitely explainable as natural phenomena of one sort or another; which could, either probably or possibly, be attributed to some well-understood causes; which were hoaxes; which could simply not be understood by conventional means; and which were actually known to be extraterrestrial—known to be, because we had miraculously captured and examined them and their passengers, and determined that they came from, say, Alpha Centauri.

Several things were learned soon after the Condon investigation began:

• The reports of UFO sightings did not center around military bases but, instead, showed a close correlation with the nonurban population density. (People in cities have little opportunity to see UFOs.)

• Flaps—the name given to bunchings, or clustering in time, of UFO reports— were probably due to the effect of news media. It was found that news reports stimulate sightings; which produce reports; which stimulate sightings; and so on.

• UFO reports were so numerous that it was not feasible, with the resources available, to investigate all of them. No effort was made, therefore, to contact all those in the vicinity of a UFO sighting who may have seen the UFO but had not reported it: there were more than enough reports already.

• Perhaps only one UFO sighting in every seven is reported to any official.

SOME EXPLANATIONS

One of the first things the Condon group did was to assign scientists to draw up a list of possible natural causes, aside from hoax and fraud, which could have produced UFO reports. This was done as an aid to the investigators who actually went to the scene of the reported UFO sightings. These natural causes were possible phenomena to check as an explanation of the sighting. The list of possibilities is very large; a Harvard astronomer, Dr. Donald H. Menzel, has listed some 111 in a separate study.[4] We will only enumerate a few. Some sound farfetched but they are listed anyway because, in one case or another investigated by the Condon committee, they actually were the suspected cause of a UFO sighting.

• There are two types of clouds, noctilucent and lenticular, which would be most likely to be erroneously identified as UFOs. A noctilucent cloud is produced by ice particles very, very high in the sky. It glows at dusk and dawn or in the brief summer night, when it is still quite dark at the surface of the earth, shining by the reflection of the sun's light—which is then present only in the upper atmosphere. A lenticular cloud, on the other hand, is shaped like a lens, or a disc, or a combination of such symmetrical shapes of various sizes. Many photos in the Condon report show clouds of this type, clouds which greatly resemble the image brought up in the mind by the term "flying saucer." Such clouds, of course, are not capable of acrobatic maneuvers.

• Sundogs, or mock suns, are glowing images of the sun produced to one side of the actual sun, sometimes with a halo. They are produced by the refraction of the sun's light in the ice crystals of which cirrus clouds are made. When the sun is near the horizon cirrus clouds appear white and filmy. They exist at elevations of 20,000–40,000 feet. Dr. Donald H. Menzel ascribed many early UFO sightings to this cause.[5] A mock image of the sun can never be caught up with— it races ahead with the speed of the pursuer.

• A subsun is an image of the sun which can be seen from planes or mountain tops above the clouds. It is a brilliant reflection of the sun in a mirrorlike layer of flat ice crystals in the clouds, the image lying as far below the horizon as the sun is above it. The image of the sun is often distorted, so that it looks elliptical, or like a parachute.

• St. Elmo's fire. This is the soft light, frequently shaped like a ball, given off by a corona electrical discharge in the atmosphere, generally near some sharp point. High-voltage transmission lines give off a similar light. During World War II many planes reported balls of fire accompanying their planes. They were called "foo fighters." The masts of sailing ships often show this phenomenon in storms.

• Ball lightning is a mysterious, spherical form of electrical discharge in the air. Its mechanism of production, its life history, and most of its other properties are barely understood.[6] Its unexplained occurrence is a crackling reminder to scientists that they still cannot work out all the consequences of their present knowledge.

• A meteor is a particle, passing through the Earth's atmosphere, which leaves a transient fiery streak in the sky. It is often called a shooting star. If it lands on the Earth, it is called a meteorite. Because meteors usually occur very high and far away—about 50 miles above the Earth's surface—they seem to move much more slowly than they actually do, as rapidly as 50 miles/second. Only several hundred years ago the existence of meteors and meteorites was treated as a myth by many scientists.

• The involuntary reentry into the air of man-made satellites, or of some of their parts, a reentry produced by atmospheric drag, often produces brilliant optical effects; and these are sometimes reported as UFOs.

• The planet Venus especially—very bright and low on the horizon—but other planets as well, have been suspected as UFOs. Venus will be observable only at dusk, when it is the evening star, or, at a different time of year, at dawn, when it becomes the morning star.

• Meteorological balloons, especially of the Skyhook variety, can be mistaken for UFOs. The Air Force now believes this to be the cause of Capt. Mantell's death in 1948, although its original belief was that the UFO was actually Venus.

• Aircraft, obviously, can be mistaken for UFOs. This is especially true of less common types of aircraft.

• Mirages, swamp fire (will-o'-the-wisp or jack-o'-lantern), are but a few of the additional natural causes that can be reported as UFOs. The list is a long one.

The Condon team then diligently investigated UFO case histories; interviewed witnesses, in some cases within a day of the sighting; carefully checked a promising number of photographs of UFOs; and assessed the evidence of radar observations.

It might seem that radar would offer an ideal, nonsubjective means of identifying UFOs: range, altitude, velocity, reflectivity, and (to some extent) size. But it turns out that there are many sources of possible error in the interpretation of the radar signals: lobes in the antenna pattern, ghosts (reflected waves), birds, ionization of the air, ducting of the beam. In many respects, therefore, radar is not superior to visible observation; it is, in fact, often inferior to it, and often leads to inconclusive results.

The committee's investigation of 14 sets of photographs of UFOs was both rewarding and frustrating. After close scrutiny six, possibly seven, pictures were clearly identified with natural phenomena: a flock of birds, Venus, the subsun, a man-made flare, a test explosion; and one or two photographs were suspected as fabrications. Certainly its diligence was rewarded with a reasonable physical explanation for some UFOs.

Nevertheless, the interpretation of several photographs was quite inconclusive; and one set of photographs presented a distinct dilemma. These photographs were of a metallic-looking, disc-shaped UFO sighted at 7:45 PST on a farm in Oregon on May 11, 1950 by a wife and husband. The study warranted the following statement, made after a diligent investigation that required eleven pages to summarize.

Conclusion:
This is one of the few UFO reports in which all factors investigated, geometric, psychological, and physical, appear to be consistent with the assertion that an extraordinary flying object, silvery, metallic, disc-shaped, tens of meters in diameter, flew within sight of two witnesses. It cannot be said that the evidence positively rules out a fabrication, although there are some physical factors, such as the accuracy of certain photometric measures of the original negatives which argue against a fabrication.[7]

If we accept the committee's assignment of natural phenomena to the previous six or seven photographic cases, must we conclude that the above statement assigns an unorthodox reality to this UFO? This puzzling sighting does not prove the origin of the UFO to be extraterrestrial; but the details of the case do tend to disprove a terrestrial origin whose explanation is within our present knowledge.

THE CONDON REPORT

In 1968 the committee headed by Dr. Condon published the results of its investigation under the title *Scientific Study of Unidentified Flying Objects;* it has, ever since, been universally referred to as the Condon report. The Condon report is an extraordinary document. It presents thorough studies of a wide range of possible explanations for UFO reports and, by reviewing a large number of actual case histories, illustrates the wealth of detailed knowledge that can be obtained about the objects sighted. Dr. Condon precedes the detailed studies with a summary which presents his conclusions about the UFO phenomena. In his summary Condon concentrated his attention on the large number of explainable UFO sightings. He concluded, essentially, that UFO sightings have a natural explanation within the realm of present-day science; and UFOs do not, reasonably, require an extraordinary origin. Dr. Condon did not draw any positive inference from the puzzling cases—those definite sightings uncovered by his own study and scattered throughout the report—which remained truly unexplained.

In order to forestall any charges of whitewash, the report of the Condon committee was examined, chapter by chapter, by a panel of eminent scientists chosen by the prestigious National Academy of Sciences. The following quotation is from the findings of this panel on its examination of the Condon report:

> We are unanimous in the opinion that this has been a very creditable effort to apply objectively the relevant techniques of science to the solution of the UFO problem. The report recognizes that there remain UFO sightings that are not easily explained. The report does suggest, however, so many reasonable and possible directions in which an explanation may eventually be found, that there seems to be no reason to attribute them to an extraterrestrial source without evidence that is much more convincing. The report also shows how difficult it is to apply scientific methods to the occasional transient sightings with any chance of success. While further study of any particular aspects of the topic (e.g., atmospheric phenomena) may be useful, a study of UFOs in general is not a promising way to expand scientific understanding of the phenomena. On the basis of present knowledge the least likely explanation of UFOs is the hypothesis of extraterrestrial visitations by intelligent beings.[8]

The findings were signed by 11 leading specialists in fields pertaining to the UFO problem—astronomy, meteorology, psychology, atmospheric physics.

Not all scientists, however, concurred with the Condon report's findings. Dr. James E. McDonald, Professor of Atmospheric Sciences at the University of Arizona, continued to maintain his position that UFOs were the biggest scientific puzzle of our time and that the extraterrestrial hypothesis was the most plausible explanation of UFOs. Dr. McDonald was subsequently involved in a brouhaha concerning a memo written (by Robert J. Low, a former assistant dean of the University of Colorado graduate school) to University of Colorado officials regarding the pros and cons of the then proposed Air Force proposal to them. The memo said, at one point, "The trick would be, I think, to describe the project so that, to the public it would appear a totally objective study but, to the scientific community, would present the image of a group of nonbelievers trying their best to be objective but having an almost zero expectation of finding a saucer."

Dr. McDonald and NICAP (one of the UFO societies) found the Low memo and passed it on to John G. Fuller, author of *Incident at Exeter* and *Interrupted Journey*—two books supporting the extraterrestrial theory. Fuller then wrote an article in *Look*, "Flying Saucer Fiasco—The Extraordinary Story of the Half-Million Dollar 'Trick' to Make Americans Believe the Condon Committee was Conducting an Objective Investigation." But *Science* magazine then quoted a statement by APRO (another UFO society) "... a strong attempt by NICAP to control the study. When they found they couldn't control it, they attempted to scuttle it." A few years ago Dr. McDonald was removed from the fracas in a most unfortunate manner: he became lost in the southern Arizona desert and was subsequently found dead.

About one third of the Condon committee report is devoted to a resumé of individual case histories. They are most interesting to read, to see the wealth of information obtained by questioning, the careful double-checking, the production and rejection of hypotheses. We would urge the interested reader to read a few of these case histories in their entirety, absorb their flavor, and look through the pictures of UFOs and unusual radar patterns. When read as a group, however, the section of case histories presented in the book is rather confusing. There is so much detail that one loses perspective.

We will restrict our further attention to a more detailed study of the *puzzling* UFO cases, which are far fewer in number than those which are explainable. But we will first summarize the general results found concerning UFO sightings, both by the Condon investigation and by other studies. Then we will be able to place the other, more interesting, UFO cases into a more general perspective.

THE FINDINGS

In addition to the initial, less detailed study of Project Blue Book and the later, exhaustive Condon investigation, a thorough scientific study of a medium-sized sample of UFO sightings was carried out by the Battelle Institute, a well-known private research laboratory. Table 10–1 summarizes the results.

TABLE 10–1
CATEGORIES OF UFO SIGHTINGS. The percentages have been
rounded off, hence they do not total 100 percent. The 59 cases
are those for which the Condon report gave summaries.

Category	Project Blue Book * 1953–1965		Battelle Study†		Condon Investigation	
	Number	Percent	Number	Percent	Number	Percent
Astronomical	2403	32	479	22	5	8
Aircraft	1367	18	474	22	5	8
Balloons	691	9	339	15	3	5
Others	1546	20	233	11	25	42
Insufficient Data	1313	17	240	11	12	20
UNKNOWN ORIGIN	253	3	434	20	9	15
Total	7573		2199		59	

* E. U. Condon and D. S. Gilmor, *Scientific Study of Unidentified Flying Objects* (New York: Dutton, 1969), sec. 4, chap. 2, p. 52.
† Summarized by Stanton T. Friedman, *Physics Today* (Jan. 1971), p. 97.

Since the Condon report often studied multiple sightings, a somewhat arbitrary assignment to natural categories was necessary. We were very conservative in assigning sightings to the UNKNOWN ORIGIN category; when in doubt concerning a particular conclusion by the Condon report on the origin of a sighting, we attributed that sighting either to some natural origin or to the Insufficient Data category. When reading the summary of several of the cases presented in the Condon report it becomes clear that the particular investigator often prefers to draw no conclusion whatever, rather than to conclude that the origin is unknown. In such cases the wording in the summaries becomes especially impenetrable, in sharp contrast to the clarity revealed when the investigator has nailed a sighting to a particular natural cause.

Differences in the studies are obvious at once. Despite the conclusions of the Condon report that the question of UFOs holds no new scientific content, fully 15 percent of its cases are of UNKNOWN ORIGIN; a total of 35 percent are unexplained (either UNKNOWN ORIGIN or Insufficient Data). These percentages are quite consistent with the Battelle study of a much larger sample. The Project Blue Book, with a minute staff studying a very large sample, classified 20 percent of its cases as unexplained, of which only 3 percent were of UNKNOWN ORIGIN. Both the Battelle study and the Condon investigation studied only a small section of all UFO reports; Project Blue Book, on the other hand, took whatever reports came in. This probably explains, in part, the low percentage in Project Blue Book in the UNKNOWN ORIGIN category. In view of the high percentage still found in this category for the much more detailed studies carried out by the Battelle and the Condon groups, however, a suspicion lingers that

Project Blue Book may have assigned natural explanations somewhat arbitrarily

Stanton Friedman has made an important point concerning UFO reports: the higher the quality of the sighting, the higher the probability that the sighting was ascribed to the UNKNOWN ORIGIN category.[9]

The overall finding of several studies of UFO sightings, therefore, is that a rather large segment are of UNKNOWN ORIGIN; between 16 and 20 percent for the two detailed studies outlined above. Logic would seem to dictate that these should be the cases studied further.

DR. HYNEK'S REBUTTAL

Another scientist who remained unconvinced by the Condon report was Dr. J. Allen Hynek, longtime chairman of the Department of Astronomy at Northwestern University. Dr. Hynek is also Director of the Center for UFO studies, an organization devoted to the scientific study of UFOs. Dr. Hynek had been a consultant to Project Blue Book for some 20 years. He believed the military had a built-in bias against not only the extraterrestrial hypothesis but even the reality of the UFO sightings. He thought the Condon committee should have investigated some cases in much greater detail—namely, those it could not explain—and he subsequently wrote a book outlining his arguments.[10]

Dr. Hynek strongly disagreed with the conclusions of the Condon report, feeling that the entire emphasis of the investigation had been in the wrong direction. He felt that it was first necessary to weed out the reports of natural origin, reports which would constitute the overwhelming preponderance of the UFO data. Whether these were due to readily explained natural phenomena, to error, or to hoax, it was on the remaining cases, those of unknown origin that could not be explained by experts, that he would concentrate. He felt that the Condon committee, like the Air Force, had prejudged the possibility that the UFO reports might be describing real objects; that because of this built-in bias it had refused to examine the individual cases objectively; and that it had concentrated its attention on the explainable reports, thereby building up a numerical margin against the unexplained reports. Even so, as we have seen, the margin is not overwhelming.

Hynek declares that most UFO reports are turned in by ordinary people. Rarely do UFO cultists turn in such reports; mental patients almost never do and, in fact, they cannot be made to have any interest in UFOs. Occasionally a scientifically trained person will turn in such a report, even though in fear of derision by peers. As an example, in 1965, the Gemini 4 astronaut, James McDivitt, reported a sighting during a space flight, when he vainly attempted to photograph the object.[11]

Most UFO reports contain very few facts; in some disagreement with the Condon study, Hynek feels it is necessary for an experienced investigator to uncover the facts by personally questioning the reporters. Hynek, himself, has photographed a UFO observed from a speeding jet airliner. (See Fig. 10–1.) We repro-

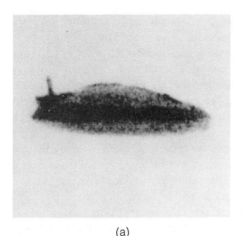
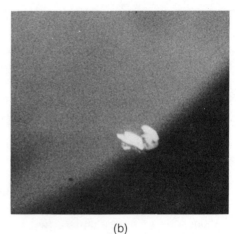

(a)   (b)

Fig. 10–1. Two UFO photos, one a hoax. (a) A picture taken in 1967 by two
brothers, aged 15 and 17, with a Polaroid camera near Selfridge Air Force Base,
not far from Detroit. The caption on the photoprint stated that Dr. J. Allen Hynek
had studied it. When we phoned Dr. Hynek in 1976 to verify the authenticity of
the photo, his secretary informed us that the two brothers had just revealed, the
week before (and nine years after the original claim), that the photo was a
childish hoax. (1967, Wide World Photos) (b) A picture taken by Dr. J. Allen Hynek
from a plane traveling at 600 miles/hour. Dr. Hynek had to reach under his
seat to open a suitcase and unpack his camera. The object remained in sight
during that entire time, thereby ruling out many natural explanations. (1976, Center
for UFO Studies, Northfield, Illinois)

duce here several direct quotes which exhibit the disingenuous quality that seems
to be typical of many of the remarks made to him in UFO investigations. These
led him to believe that those particular reporters were sincere, describing events
that were very real to them, as similarly attested to in the Condon case histories.

- By four boys: "There is no hoax implied since that is a serious offense at this
  school."
- By three boy scouts: "We give you our Scout's Honor."
- By a New Jersey reporter: "I didn't use any trick photography because I don't
  know how yet."
- By a child: "Please believe me."[12]

Dr. Hynek finds some definite patterns in the many UFO reports he has investigated. For one thing, there is a groping for words; this is to be expected
when people are trying to describe events of an uncommon nature. For another,
he finds the descriptions very limited in their imaginative qualities. There are no
flying submarines, no upside-down dinosaurs, no headless horsemen. The shapes,
the colors, the sounds (actually, the lack of such) are all more or less alike. What,
Dr. Hynek wonders, restricts the imagination of reporters, from all over the

world, if these reports are either phony or psychological phenomena? Despite this limited range of imagination, a trait which tends to make the reports believable, he thinks that most scientists nevertheless find it difficult to accept the reports as valid. Times apparently have not changed much in a hundred years. A century ago the famous scientist, Lord Rayleigh, made cutting remarks concerning the contempt earlier scientists had expressed when they refused to accept stories of rocks falling from the skies (meteorites), or to believe stories of ball lightning.

Experience has taught Dr. Hynek to be very wary of UFO reports made by one solitary observer, with no other witnesses. His case histories usually include a minimum of one witness in addition to the reporter. Incidentally, he says a trained questioner is quickly led to the actual events being described by UFO reporters. When, for example, fake UFOs are released for test purposes—hot air balloons, or a Chinese lantern tied to the leg of a crane which is released mid-air at night, or flares dropped from planes—the reports are accurate and lead the investigators very quickly to the actual events. There is, in such test cases, an almost complete absence of reports of occupants, of landing marks, or of interference with auto ignition systems.

Hynek classifies each UFO report he receives according both to its *reliability* and its *strangeness*. The strangeness, which ranges from 1 to 10, is a measure of the number of separate items in the report which require an explanation. The higher the strangeness value, the greater the odd-ball, unknown quality of the report. The more items in the report which violate present common sense, the greater this strangeness. A light in the night sky which moves in a manner unlike that of a balloon, artificial satellite, aircraft, or other known object has a strangeness, S, of 1. If the light hovers over an auto and the auto's ignition system fails, that adds an additional item, so S is now 2.

The reliability is Hynek's estimate, ranging between 1 and 10, of the probability that the report is as described. This rating is a highly subjective one, depending on corroboration, internal consistency, plausibility of reporters, and other items. No UFO report which has just one reporter (no witnesses) receives a reliability rating greater than 3.

It is clearly desirable that a UFO report have as high a reliability rating as possible, to engender believability. To make the case interesting in terms of new knowledge the report should have a high strangeness; but the larger the strangeness, the greater the reliability necessary to make the report acceptable to the open minded. Dr. Hynek believes that all cases that have a combination of strangeness greater than 3 and reliability greater than 5 constitute a challenge to our laws of science. Such cases should not be ignored, as probably fallacious, merely because they violate common sense.

The 60-odd UFO reports discussed in Hynek's book are segregated into six groups. The first three, Nocturnal Lights, Daylight Discs, and Radar-Visual, concern distant sightings; the last three, Close Encounter I, Close Encounter II, and Close Encounter III, concern sightings in which the distance between the UFO and the observer is less than 500 feet. These groupings, by the way, correspond fairly closely to those used by other investigators. Table 10–2 summarizes Hynek's listings in the various categories. In the next several sections we present cases illustrating his classifications and some of the most puzzling of the UFO sightings.

NOCTURNAL LIGHTS

The cases of distant lights in the night sky are the most frequently reported and the least strange. UFO reports of this type have a poor survival rate after investigation: they usually turn out to be meteors, aircraft landing lights, balloons, planets or stars, searchlights, advertisements on planes, refueling missions, or some such thing. However, cases of unexplained origin have been reported by airline pilots, air-control operators, and policemen and security officers—types of people from whom one would expect to receive sober, detailed accounts.

Here is a verbatim report pertaining to one representative case.

One night back in 1961 I was engaged in the noble American tradition of "parking" with a girl. . . . What caught my attention, and at that time it took an awful lot to distract me, was the way the thing [a bright Nocturnal Light] moved. . . . The object was noiseless and, not to sound corny, glowed. It was much brighter than any star in the sky. . . . So as it moved slowly northward,

TABLE 10–2
CHARACTERISTICS OF UFO SIGHTINGS OF UNKNOWN ORIGIN CLASSIFIED BY HYNEK. (In all cases, except for three cases of the category Close Encounter III, Dr. Hynek was personally involved in the investigation. Hynek uses the term Probability in place of Reliability.)

Type	Number of Cases	Average Strangeness	Average Reliability	Average Number of Observers	Duration
Nocturnal Lights	12	1.2	7.4	3.9	2 min.–1 hr.
Daylight Discs	14	1.9	6.8	3.7	30 sec.–45 min.
Radar-Visual	12	2.7	7.7	5.0	5 min.–5 hr.
Close Encounter I No Interaction	14	3.3	8.2	4.3	1 min.–1.5 hr.
Close Encounter II Physical Effects	23	3.4	6.1	4.4 *	1 min.–2.5 hr.
Close Encounter III Sentient Beings	5	5.0	5.6	3.7 †	5 min.–4 hr.

* Excluding the Tanarive, Madagascar sighting of 1954 (Close Encounter II-3) involving 2000 observers.

† Excluding the Boianai, New Guinea sighting of 1958 (Close Encounter III-3) involving 254 observers.

I figured it to be a weather balloon reflecting the sun's light. However, balloon's don't stand still, change direction, and have reverse gears, so to speak. . . . Well, I finally pointed it out to the girl to assure myself that it wasn't an illusion. She saw it with no trouble and got quite scared. We watched together as the thing went through its antics. . . . Finally, after some five minutes of fooling around, it took off for greener pastures. From far to the south it moved out of sight to the north in about five seconds. I timed it, I know it. I don't expect you to believe it, but it happened.[13]

An interesting footnote concerns an error frequently made by people estimating the apparent angular size of an object they are attempting to describe. An aspirin tablet held at arm's length has a solid angle, at the observer's eye, that is large enough to obliterate an image of the full moon. Yet many people will grossly exaggerate their estimate of an object's angular size by saying that a moon-sized object appeared as large as a half dollar held at arm's length.

Some typical attributes of a Nocturnal Light include a usually yellow-orange color, a fairly intense brightness, a finite size, an unnatural trajectory, the appearance of intelligent action, and no apparent attachment to any solid body.

DAYLIGHT DISCS

There are fewer daytime reports than nighttime reports; this is true both before and after weeding out the explainable cases. But a number of photographs of Daylight Discs exist, and ten photographs of them are presented in Hynek's *The UFO Experience*, on glossy paper to enhance the detail. In all cases, however, it would be extremely risky to state, for certain, just what it is that is being photographed. His Figs. 4 and 5, for example, are particularly clear; yet, are they photos of a large, far away spacecraft or of a small, nearby Frisbee? It's hard to say.

The following case is typical of the reports of this class of UFOs.

I have been an airlines pilot for nearly five years and have reasonable vision, and naturally I am used to observing things in the sky. This was not a fleeting glimpse. While I was watching, explanations occurred to me and were discarded on the spot. . . . Very briefly, what I saw was a small silvery white disc of unknown diameter, unknown altitude, but definite physical existence; it first appeared stationary, under visual observation, for about ten minutes. Then it moved across the sky, visually passing under the clouds and finally disappearing into the white clouds. No sound could be detected.

The white dot stood still too long and moved too silently to have been an aircraft; it appeared to travel in a direction distinctly inconsistent with the direction of the clouds so as to preclude . . . that it was a balloon.[14]

Practically all reports of Daylight Discs say they are noiseless and that they move away smoothly, often with fantastic acceleration. When moving they hug

the contours of the land, even when they are high enough to make this unneces-
sary. The color of the disc is usually described as white or silvery, either shining
by reflection or glowing. More than half the reporters of the cases cited by Dr.
Hynek are pilots, engineers, Air Force personnel, or technically trained in some
area.

Although there are many photos which are supposed to be of Daylight Discs,
Dr. Hynek follows some fairly stringent rules in determining which ones are valid
—hoaxers, too, understand that one picture is worth a thousand words. Dr.
Hynek insists that there be witnesses who saw the object at the time the photo
was made; that the original negative be available for study; that the camera be
examined also; and that the owner of the photo testify under oath as to the
legitimacy of the photo. Even so, he finds little in any photographs he has
examined so far that is of any real scientific worth.

RADAR-VISUAL REPORTS

This is the last of the three groups that deal with objects sighted at a distance
approximately 500 feet or more. Radar reports by themselves are not considered
reliable enough to form a separate group, so Dr. Hynek considers reports which
include both radar and visual sightings. A representative case is taken from a
letter:

> I have been an air-traffic controller for thirteen years, three actual years of
> control in the U. S. Air Force and ten with the FAA. What happened on May
> 4, 1966 is as follows: I was assigned the Charleston, W. Va., high-altitude
> radar sector on the midnight shift. . . . At approximately 04:30 a Braniff Flight
> 42 called me on a VHF frequency of 134.75 and asked if I had any traffic for
> his flight. . . . I looked at the radarscope and observed a target to the left of
> Braniff 42, who was heading eastbound on jet airway 6, about 5 miles off to
> his 11 o'clock position.
>
> I advised Braniff 42 that I had no known traffic in his vicinity but was
> painting a raw target off to his 10 o'clock position; however, it was not paint-
> ing a transponder and was probably at the low altitude sector (24,000 feet
> and below). Braniff 42 advised that the object could not be at a low altitude
> because it was above him and descending through his altitude, which was
> 33,000 feet. . . . I was completely at a loss for explanation for I advised him
> [that] at the time there were only two aircraft under my control—his flight
> and an American Airlines flight about 20 miles behind him. I asked Braniff
> 42 if he could give me a description of the object, thinking it might be an
> Air Force research aircraft or possibly a U-2 type vehicle. Braniff advised that
> whatever it was it was not an aircraft, that the object was giving off brilliant
> flaming light consisting of alternating white, green, and red colors and was at
> this time turning away from him. At the same time the American flight
> behind Braniff, who had been monitoring the same frequency, asked the
> Braniff if he had his landing lights on. . . . Which means to me that the

American saw the same brilliant object. When I asked the American if he could give me any further details, he politely clammed up. Most pilots know that if there is an official UFO sighting, they must (or are supposed to) file a complete report when getting on the ground. This report, I understand, is quite lengthy. . . . As I have stated, I think my previous experience speaks for itself, and I know what I saw; and I'm sure the pilot of Braniff 42 was not having hallucinations. The target I observed was doing approximately 1,000 miles an hour and made a complete 180-degree turn in the space of five miles, which no aircraft I have ever followed on radar could possibly do, and I have followed B-58s declaring they are going supersonic, all types of civilian aircraft going full out (in the jet stream), and even SR-71 aircraft, which normally operate at speeds in excess of 1,500 miles per hour.[15]

The incident referred to above occurred on May 4, 1966 at 4:30 A.M. and lasted for five minutes. Incidentally, for some unknown reason almost all the Radar-Visual cases listed take place at night.

Project Blue Book dismissed this case, explaining it as "landing lights," and took no depositions from any of the three principals involved.

It might be of interest to note that NORAD, the North American Radar Defense System, has a continuous radar monitoring system that works 24 hours per day, 365¼ days per year. *Any* foreign objects appearing in the sky would undoubtedly appear on their radar screens. Since UFOs do not follow ballistic trajectories, however, the computers associated with the radar screens would automatically reject any UFO painting on the radarscope as being of no further interest.

One of the most famous Radar-Visual cases occurred at ancient Lakenheath, England on August 13–14, 1956. It lasted from 10:30 P.M. to 3:30 A.M. and was noted by four independent observers: two separate ground-radar operators, a military pilot, and an air-control tower operator. It rates a strangeness of 3 from Hynek, with a reliability of 8. This case has been treated both by several scientists and by the Condon committee. James McDonald, an outstanding UFO proponent, wrote about this case in two reports.[16] and G. D. Thayer, of the British National Oceanic & Atmospheric Administration discussed it, with a wealth of detail, in another article.[17] The Condon report termed it

> the most puzzling and unusual case in the Radar-Visual files. The apparently rational, intelligent behavior of the UFO suggests a mechanical device of unknown origin as the most probable explanation of the sighting. . . . the probability that at least one genuine UFO was involved appears to be fairly high.[18]

CLOSE ENCOUNTERS

In a Close Encounter the distance between UFO and observer is less than 500 feet. Thus the UFO has an appreciable angular extension at the eye of the observer and misperceptions become less likely. The general category of sightings has three parts: Close Encounters of the First Kind, Second Kind, and Third Kind. In a Close Encounter of the First Kind no interaction occurs between the observer and the UFO. Reporters of these sightings represent a much broader segment of the population than those reporting distant sightings.

The typical UFO reported in this class is a luminous object whose brightness can be anywhere in a broad range—as bright as a welder's torch or as softly glowing as a neon tube. The shape is generally oval. Sometimes the light, sometimes the craft, sometimes both are described as rotating. Hovering is a common descriptive term, especially over small bodies of water. There are no wings reported, no wheels, no sound. Take-offs are extremely rapid, even when made at small angles with the vertical.

We will not go into the details of any of the cases of this type, for similar details occur in Close Encounters of the Second Kind, CEII. As a result of encounters of this type there is some sort of physical consequence or record. The physical effects reported include scorching or blighting of plants; temporary feelings of numbness or heat on the part of the observers; interference with electrical circuits of automobiles; causing auto engines to go dead; sometimes, even, a feeling of reduced gravitation. Surprisingly little harm is reported to people (with but a few isolated exceptions) in the reports of UFOs, including those of the Close Encounter categories.

One would think that here, at long last, would be an opportunity for a physicist to make some measurements and acquire some useful data. Strangely, it does not always work out that way. For example, a parched circle 40 feet in diameter was noticed and photographed after a brief UFO sighting in Van Horne, Iowa, on July 12, 1969 (Hynek CEII–12). Presumably the circle of destroyed crops was made by the heat issuing from a UFO hovering there; but the circle may have had another interpretation, and the evidence can only be accepted as suggestive. In any event, it is noteworthy that there are comparatively few cases of UFO reports of this type, CEII.

An extraordinary case of Close Encounter II (Hynek CEII–1) occurred on November 2, 1957, 11:00 P.M. at Levelland, Texas, with 12 observers in 10 separate groups, 2.5-hour duration. A patrolman, A. J. Fowler, received many phone calls, the first one coming from Pedro Sancedo who was driving four miles west of Levelland with a companion. A torpedo-shaped, brilliantly lighted object had rapidly approached their car, whereupon the truck headlights went out and the engine died. The object gave off considerable heat, and it had yellow and white colors. When the UFO moved away the lights came on, and Sancedo found he could start the car.

One hour later Officer Fowler got a call from a Mr. W., four miles east of Levelland. He had come upon a brilliantly lit egg-shaped object about 200 feet long sitting in the middle of the road. When Mr. W. approached it his engine failed and his lights went out. When Mr. W. got out of his car, the object rose and its lights went out when it was 200 feet above the ground. Then Mr. W. had no trouble starting the car.

Then came another phone call to Officer Fowler, this time from a man 11 miles north of Levelland. He'd come on a glowing object sitting on the road and his lights had gone out and his engine had stopped. When the object left, his lights went on and his engine could start.

A Texas Tech freshman later reported a similar encounter in the same vicinity at that time. In his case the object rose, almost straight up, in a split second. Another phone call to Officer Fowler, at 12:15 A.M., reported—you guessed it— an almost identical incident. So Fowler reported the stories to the local Sheriff and the latter sent out several investigators. Two of them reported seeing bright lights. Then, at 12:45 A.M., another witness; and at 1:15 A.M., still another. Both reported failure of engine and lights when the UFO was near. At 1:30 A.M., the Sheriff and a Deputy spotted the oval light. And others, too; a total of 15 phone calls were made to the police about the UFO, all of them very excited. It is difficult to explain away a case of this kind.

There are more than 300 cases of scorched, denuded circles or other landing marks connected with UFO landings. About 100 of these have two or more witnesses.

In a way, we wish that Dr. Hynek had stopped his categories at this point, for we think he has made a fairly good case for his point of view—based, in a sense, on circumstantial evidence only. In a murder mystery, of course, one really would want the body, itself, before presenting the solution to the murder. And in the last category, we are given a teasing glimpse of the body.

THE EXTRATERRESTRIALS?

In Close Encounters of the Third Kind, CE-III, we have several cases, each attested to by at least two witnesses, in which the observers report the presence of sentient beings in the UFOs. The beings may only be animated instead of animate; possibly robots. But they are aware: so-called humanoids. These cases, don't forget, are supposed to have survived the strict weeding-out process that Dr. Hynek employs: no publicity stunts, hoaxes, religious nuts, UFO cultists. Dr. Hynek recognized the possibility of disbelief in setting up the category; but he felt that he had to present the data as he knew it and let the chips fall where they may. In the interest of objectivity we must follow his lead.

So, boggle the imagination or not, here we go. Incidentally, one of the scientists in the field of UFO investigation, Jacques Vallee, has catalogued some 300 cases in which humanoids were reported;[19] while Hynek reports that there are now some 1500 reports of close encounter on record, with about half of them reporting craft occupants.[20]

Reports of close encounters with humanoids are widespread and do not seem to differ in essential respects from reports in the other groupings. Within the United States only two states of the mainland 48 have not reported any: Delaware and Vermont, and of these Delaware had one reported not far offshore.

One such case took place on April 24, 1964, at 5:45 P.M., in Socorro, New Mexico. It lasted 5–10 minutes and there were two unrelated observers. A policeman, Lonnie Zamora, saw a craft descending, emitting a flame and making explosive sounds. It landed, looking like an up-ended auto, and Zamora then saw two white-cloaked figures in its immediate neighborhood. When only 150 feet from the object he saw a strange insignia on the side of the craft. Some loud sounds from its interior caused him to run for shelter; glancing backward he saw it rise vertically, then take off horizontally.

The craft, but not the occupants, were seen by Sergeant Chavez, who came in response to Zamora's radio message. Several days later Dr. Hynek verified landing marks and charred plants at the site. He also learned of an unidentified witness who told a gas station attendant he had seen a strange landing craft that was apparently in trouble and trying to land.

This case is not very convincing to us as an example of this category. By the ground rule of two witnesses the case properly belongs in the CEII category; for though there were two witnesses to the craft, there was only one witness to the humanoids. The more bizarre the case, the more strictly should restraint and a conservative approach be applied.

Perhaps one of the classic cases of close encounter with humanoids occurred in the Kentucky back country on the evening of August 21, 1955, to a family named Sutton. The story begins, disarmingly enough, with the Suttons ridiculing a passerby who had just told them that a UFO had landed near their house. But about an hour later the Suttons' humor changed as they watched a "glowing" man with huge eyes approaching their house. Two Suttons reached for their guns and fired at the unwanted visitor from a distance of 20 feet. Somehow the visitor escaped; but soon another form appeared at a window. The Suttons fired again and, running outside to see the outcome, encountered two more of the beings. More shooting; but the bullets seemed to do no lasting damage; the beings floated down when hit and retreated. So terrified were the Suttons by now that all eleven of them jammed into two cars and raced the seven miles to town and the police. The police returned with the Suttons but, to the chagrin of the family, found nothing but their bullet holes. After a while the police left and the visitors reappeared.

The report is certainly nonsense; outlandish, even outrageous. But even though confronted by disbelief, adverse publicity, and harassment, and even though their own initial ridicule was returned in kind, "the Suttons stuck to their story. Stubbornly, angrily, they insisted they were telling the truth. Neither adults nor children so much as hinted at the possibility of a lie or a mistake—in public or to relatives; there was no trace of retraction."[21]

Honest scholars can only be dismayed. Certainly, the path to knowledge would be less jarring and less wearing on the nerves if people would only refrain from experiencing events that the scholars have not yet explained. Incidentally, if the reader should want to report a UFO, with or without humanoids, we would suggest he write the Center for UFO Studies, 2623 Ridge Ave., Evanston, Ill., 60201.

THE LADY OR THE TIGER?

The U.S. Air Force, after a study of 12,618 UFO sightings over a period of 22 years, came to the conclusion that further study would not be justified. Yet a *New York Times* story said that the APRO group, alone, was still getting in 1972, four years after the Condon study, 1,000 UFO reports each year.[22] The publicity about UFOs had died down markedly after the Condon report. The vast majority of scientists did not accept UFOs as extraterrestrial. Further, there was no direct evidence, whatever, nor had there ever been, for the claim that UFOs were spacecraft of another civilization visiting Earth. But the interest in UFOs was still there; the suspicion of visits by extraterrestrial beings was still there; the will to believe was still there, in many laymen—and the will not to believe was still there, in most scientists.

In simpler times, when our technology had developed sails but not yet rocket engines, numerous sightings of mermaids occurred throughout the world. Beautiful young girls, naked and voluptuous above the waist, but with the scales, fins, and tail of a fish below the waist, the mermaids were irresistible to sailors on their long, lonely, and often dangerous voyages; and many sailors were said to be led to an early grave by following them. No hard evidence for their existence has ever been found, and no scientific theory exists that makes their existence plausible. Similarly, in other places at other times, there have been sightings reported of the Loch Ness sea serpent in Scotland, and of the abominable snowman in the Himalayas.

It seems believable that the same phenomena that produced mermaids, sea serpents, and abominable snowmen would, in our technological age, produce UFOs. This is a logical thought, but not necessarily a true one. For the stories that included the mermaids and sea serpents also told of a mythical duck-billed platypus, of a storied gorilla, and of heavensent meteors—phantoms few knowledgeable persons would then accept.

It is possible that a UFO will eventually be captured, examined, and determined to be a vessel from Venus with little green, horned men inside. Frank Scully may yet be vindicated. It is possible. The considerations of the previous chapter make this most unlikely; but it is not impossible. The unresolved cases of the Condon report, however, and the considerations of Drs. McDonald and Hynek, make it believable that some UFO cases of high strangeness and high reliability occur continually, everywhere on Earth. Their truth may lie in an area we do not yet expect. These, the still unresolved cases, are the logical candidates for further serious scientific investigation.

The American Institute of Aeronautics and Astronautics (AIAA) seems to have come to a similar conclusion, for it not only published a report on UFOs which concluded that they were worthy of scientific study, but it also said they would publish news of selected cases from time to time in future issues of their magazine.[23]

What should be the view of the innocent bystander? Which shall we champion—The Lady or the Tiger? (Our apologies to Frank Stockton.) Should we wish for the logical, scientific explanation of all cases as natural phenomena, familiar to us? Should we hope for the discovery of extraterrestrial visitors? Or is there an in-between explanation? That, we think, depends on the individual—dogmatist, romantic, or realist.

In the meantime, for all individuals, of whatever persuasion, we refer the reader to the following commonsense formula offered by Bertrand Russell:

> The opinion of experts, when it is unanimous, must be accepted by nonexperts as more likely to be right than the opposite opinion. The skepticism that I advocate amounts only to this:
>
> **1** that when experts are agreed, the opposite opinion cannot be held to be certain;
>
> **2** that when they are not agreed, no opinion can be regarded as certain by a nonexpert;
>
> **3** that when they all hold that no sufficient grounds for a positive opinion exists, the ordinary man would do well to suspend his judgments.
>
> These propositions seem mild, yet, if accepted they would revolutionize human life.[24]

CHAPTER ELEVEN
THE MYSTERIOUS PAST

- *Immanuel Velikovsky* - *The Bible*
- *An Assessment* - *The Scablands Flood*
- *Erich von Däniken* - *Astronauts—The Ancient Gods*
- *Puzzles* - *Some Answers*
- *Mystery in the Far East* - *The Plains of Nazca*
- *Stonehenge* - *The Megalithic Sky Watchers*
- *The Great Pyramid* - *Scientists and Iconoclasts*

IMMANUEL VELIKOVSKY

Mystics, seers, and prophets peer into the crystal ball to envision the future. Dr. Immanuel Velikovsky is just the opposite: he figuratively gazes into the crystal ball to view the murky past. He sees there cataclysmic events that tormented entire continents and civilizations, here on Earth, thousands of years ago. Velikovsky's view of the world's ancient history belongs to a category of historical interpretations called "catastrophism"; it is the direct opposite of the theory that is generally espoused by most scientists that the Earth's history has been one of one slow, gradual change.

Velikovsky arrived at his interpretation of historic facts, as well as his estimate of the dates of various catastrophic occurrences, by comparing the folklore and legends of many ancient civilizations, including the Greeks, Hebrews, Egyptians, Polynesians, Incas, Japanese, and Eskimos. First published in 1950 in *Worlds in Collision*, his theories created quite a furor of interest among the general public. He attempted to show, among other things, that many events described in the Bible—for instance, the ten plagues preceding the Exodus of the Jews from Egypt—could be explained in connection with specific catastrophic occurrences.

The scientific community almost unanimously spurned his views and classed him as a pseudoscientist. He did not publish his views in scientific magazines where they would be subjected to examination and criticism. "Why not?" asked the scientists, "Does he consider his results revealed truth?" Further, he never seemed to have any doubts, since all his sources and references pointed in only one direction—his way. Velikovsky gives few references to contradictory evidence, making his conclusions less certain to unbiased readers. Nevertheless, many sprang to his defense.

Dr. Velikovsky has an M.D. degree. He has a fertile mind and an extremely varied, if unconventional, background, having studied natural science in Edinburg; history, law, and medicine in Moscow; biology in Berlin; the brain in Zurich; and psychoanalysis in Vienna. Born in Vitebsk, Russia, in 1895, Velikovsky has lived in the United States since 1939. He spent nine years in the library at Columbia University accumulating, by himself, the vast fund of knowledge that went into his books.

Scientists generally rankle when they are instructed by those outside their own field; and pioneers, even within their own fields, are resisted when they break sharply with tradition. Velikovsky sought, from outside, to foster ideas that would overthrow wide realms of beliefs in astronomy, archeology, history, and geology. To scientists, Velikovsky's ideas seemed obviously wild guesses; and many of his speculations appeared to be, most assuredly, incorrect. The scientific community rejected his ideas completely and, at times, almost brutally. He was attacked by scientists. He was denied the opportunity to answer his critics in reputable scientific journals. His best-selling book, *Worlds in Collision*, was boycotted by a segment of the scientific community, and its publisher was forced to assign the book to a competitor in order to protect sales of its other texts.

On the other side, in the popular press, he became the object of sympathy and defense of a wide variety of people having diverse reasons for their admiration: fundamentalists who saw justification for a literal interpretation of the Bible; humanists, envious of the prominence of science and not averse to the discomfiture of scientists proven wrong by an outsider; and literati attracted not only by his very readable style but also by an erudition that tied together ancient mysteries and myths with assorted solid facts. Throughout all this, Velikovsky maintained a dignified and gentlemanly attitude, replying to his critics where he could and working on several other books that he hoped would further propound his view of a cataclysmic past.

The most important idea proposed by Dr. Velikovsky is this: many times in the past, the Earth has been subjected to catastrophic upheavals of a global nature.[1] These events have altered the Earth's geography, changing seas to continents and continents to seas. Sometimes they almost completely wiped out all traces of life, human and otherwise. Earthquakes and volcanoes accompanied the formation of mountain ranges, new valleys, and long clefts at the bottom of the oceans. Huge rocks fell to the surface from the sky, accompanied by searing heat and fires. Velikovsky deciphered these events from fossils, rocks, and folk-lore—and then went further, asserting that these events were produced by near-collisions with other heavenly bodies.

The most recent of these cataclysms occurred within human memory. Twice, 50 years apart according to Velikovsky, about 1400 B.C., the Earth had a near-collision with Venus, which was then a comet only recently ejected by the planet Jupiter. About 800 B.C. Venus became a planet, Velikovsky maintained, when its orbit was again altered, this time by a near-hit with Mars. Thus propelled, Mars in turn assaulted Earth in another series of near-collisions. Velikovsky believed that these natural disasters were literally described in the myths and legends of all people; but hitherto the myths had been taken as flights of the imagination rather than as accurate descriptions of events.

THE BIBLE

According to Velikovsky, the first of the two disasters which took place near 1400 B.C. happened during the Exodus of the Hebrews from Egypt; the second happened during the time of Joshua, when the Hebrews were fighting the Canaanites. The Bible, he said, offered a description of many of these cataclysmic events. For example, Velikovsky considered the following from the third chapter of Habakkuk:

At his step the earth is shaken,
at his look nations are scattered,
the ancient hills are shattered,
mountains of old sink low . . .
the sun forgets to rise,
the moon to move . . .
Thou trampest earth in fury,
thou art threshing the people in thy anger.

Universally, of course, this had been regarded as poetic literature, not cold fact; but Velikovsky said, in effect, "No, they were describing events as they saw them. The sun did not rise. The moon did stand still." And that statement scientists find almost impossible to accept.

According to Velikovsky, the orbit of Venus was radically changed as a result of the close call with Earth. Nevertheless, it remained a comet. The subsequent encounter that occurred between Venus and Mars about 800 B.C. changed the greatly elliptical orbit of Venus, as a comet, to the nearly circular orbit it has today, as a planet. It is Velikovsky's belief that when Venus was still a comet it nearly collided with Mars several times. This occurred, he says, comparatively recently.

Since Velikovsky believed that Venus was formed by a violent disruption, (or fission) of an unstable Jupiter in a near-collision with Saturn,[2] he predicted that Venus was hotter than was then generally believed, and he said it was still cooling down. In 1959 the surface temperature of Venus was believed to be nearly the same as that of the Earth. Today we know, from satellite landings on it, that its surface temperature is about 900°F. Velikovsky did not state how hot Venus's surface would be—he merely said "hotter," though he now implies he meant "very much hotter."

Velikovsky believed that as a result of many such astronomical encounters the Earth's orbit and axis of rotation changed. This caused the North Pole and the South Pole to point to different parts of the sky, resulting in a melting of the polar ice and tremendous floods. It also caused a change of the length of day and a shift of old tropical regions into new polar regions. Velikovsky attributed reversals of the Earth's magnetic poles to electrical discharges between Earth and Venus when their atmospheres came into contact. He maintained that strong electromagnetic forces could act between planets. But the fact is that astronomers can calculate with exceptionally high accuracy the orbits of planets and artificial satellites using only gravitational forces and ignoring all electromagnetic forces. Velikovsky is vague about the nature of his electromagnetic forces, which presumably are appreciable only when the planets are very close; but then, he says, they are catastrophic.

Let us pursue some of the reasoning that led to Velikovsky's amazing assertions. Velikovsky quotes the Bible: "And he said in the sight of Israel, Sun, stand thou still upon Gideon; and thou, Moon, in the valley of Ajalon. . . . So the sun stood still in the midst of heaven, and hasted not to go down about a whole day." It is forgivable for Joshua never to have heard of the law of conservation of angular momentum, a law that demands that Earth keep spinning the same way, continually; but how does Velikovsky expect us to accept this statement as literal truth today? He finds his answer to this question, also, in the Bible: "As they fled from before Israel . . . the Lord cast down great stones from heaven upon them." [3]

Velikovsky claims that the stones were real—they were meteors and meteorites in the tail of a comet through which Earth was then passing, the errant Mars mentioned previously. And it was this comet that was responsible for altering the axis of Earth in such a way that the Sun appeared to stand still for a day. Velikovsky perceives in a prayer ascribed to Joshua a description of dreadful earthquakes and whirlwinds initiated by the awesome event.[4]

Velikovsky offered no mathematical equations to explain how a comet could exert such a strong torque (loosely, a twisting force) on a body so nearly symmetrical as the Earth, and the physical processes he suggests are quite vague; but this is not true of his anthropological arguments. He notes a legend from the Mexican *Annals of Cuauhtitlan* about a cosmic catastrophe of the remote past, when the night did not end for a long time—night in Mexico could be day in Canaan. He gives many other sources, at different places around the globe, where stories of a prolonged day, or night, arise at a time when the world is ablaze in a bombardment of stones. In fact, his erudition in such matters is most impressive.

Going back to the Bible, 52 years before Joshua, to a time when the Hebrews were about to start their wandering in the Sinai desert, Velikovsky said the accounts in the Bible are substantiated both by contemporary Egyptian documents and by the traditions of the Arabian peninsula. These tell of a series of disasters which befell the region, among the greatest catastrophes in the Earth's history.

One of the very first occurred when the Earth's surface became covered with a fine red dust, a dust which eventually made its way not only into the rivers and seas but also even into all vessels which contained water, and turned them all blood red. ". . . all the waters that were in the river were turned to blood" (Exodus 7, 20). "The river is blood" (Egyptian Papyrus Ipuiwer 2, 10).[5] The dust, by Velikovsky's interpretation, came from the tail of Venus, then a comet. Finnish, Mayan, Tartar, and Greek myths also mentioned such a tale; and if we assume they all refer to the same event, this is a cosmic, much more than a local, disturbance. The red dust, according to Velikovsky, is the plague of blood mentioned in the Bible, the first of the ten plagues visited upon the Egyptians by God for not allowing the Hebrews to leave Egypt.

The other plagues mentioned in the Bible were similarly explained. The second, third, and fourth—infestations of frogs, lice, and flies, respectively—were due to the great heat resulting from the proximity of Venus, a hot body. And these insects produced the fifth plague, a pestilence among all the horses, asses, camels, oxen, sheep, and other cattle.

Plague six was dust emitted by volcanoes activated by the near passage of the comet. Thunder and hail and a fire that ran on the ground formed the seventh plague. The thunder was, more likely than not, the noise of earthquakes and volcanoes that accompanied the vast disruption in the interior of the Earth; and the hail was not a hail of ice but of large rocks, also from the tail of the comet. Egyptian, Mexican, and Buddhist tales were mentioned in corroboration. The eighth plague, one of locusts, was accompanied by a strong east wind; and strong winds were to be expected when the atmosphere of Earth was mixed with that of Venus. In fact, they must have been of hurricane force; and there were many ancient tales, all over the world, of such strong winds.

The darkness that then enveloped the land for three days and nights was so deep that it could be felt. ". . . there was a thick darkness in all the land of Egypt" (Exodus 10, 22). "The land is not light" (Papyrus Ipuiwer, 9, 11). The feeling arose, according to Velikovsky, because the Earth had gone much farther into the comet's tail and had approached the body itself. The very rotation of the Earth was disturbed by this close approach to the body of the comet. The axis of the Earth's rotation was tilted, and this accentuated the darkness. Finns, Peruvians, Babylonians, Iranians, and Chinese all have legends about this great darkness.

The darkness was followed by an earthquake which shook the whole globe, not just one part of it near the Red Sea, if we read the accounts from these many other sources. This convulsion led to the tenth plague in the Bible, the decimation of the Egyptian first born. Compare ". . . the Lord smote all the first born in the Land of Egypt, from the first born of Pharoah that sat on his throne unto the first born of the captive that was in the dungeon" (Exodus 12, 29) with "He who places his brother in the ground is everywhere. . . . Forsooth, the children of princes are dashed against the walls" (Papyrus Ipuiwer, 2, 13; 5, 3; 5, 6). Velikovsky interpreted the tenth plague as a general decimation in which all suffered, but the Egyptians suffered more severely than did the Israelites.

Although this was the last of the ten plagues of the Bible the cosmic upheaval was not yet over, according to Dr. Velikovsky. There followed an enormous hurricane, of world-wide dimensions, produced not only by the gases from the comet but also by a viscous disturbance of the atmosphere that was due to the shifting of the Earth's axis of rotation. Then the gravitational attraction of the comet had a catastrophic effect on the oceans, producing unprecedented tides that flooded mountains in some areas and dried the ocean bottom in others. The Israelites were able to escape the Egyptians over the bottom of what had been, just a few days before, the Red Sea. Velikovsky believed that after the crossing by the Hebrews the Mediterranean Sea broke into the Red Sea in a great tidal wave.

Now Earth and the comet Venus started separating; and the eastern hemisphere was brought out of the darkness, caused by the comet's tail of dust, ashes, and meteorites, into a brilliant view of the main body of the incandescent comet. Violent lightning strokes filled the region between our atmosphere and the comet's tail. Velikovsky maintained that these brilliant events in the sky, viewed by all the peoples of the world, were regarded as a battle between an evil serpent and the god of light. They have entered the folklore motifs and religious beliefs of almost all peoples on Earth. He believes it was an electrical discharge between Earth and the atmosphere of Venus that caused the waters of the Red Sea, previously parted by the gravitational attraction of Venus, to fall back together again on the hapless Egyptians and drown them. Although only hinted at in the Bible, he thinks that, in actuality, a great number of the Israelites also perished in the multiple disasters of tide, fire, hurricane, cinders, plagues, rocks, and immense discharges from the sky.

Next, the interior of the Earth, boiling hot, erupted through the surface in lava from volcanoes, boiling the waters of the seas. Seven or eight weeks elapsed, according to the Bible, between the Exodus and the day of revelation on Mt. Sinai. Roaring noises and thunder came from the bowels of the Earth, as well as from the mountain, and this was taken to be the voice of God. Velikovsky claimed that this roaring thunder, which appears in the epic tales of all people, was interpreted by Moses at Mt. Sinai as the words of the Decalogue spoken at the presentation of the Ten Commandments to the Jews.

Velikovsky said that all the historical events accompanying these catastrophes could be found in the independent histories of other peoples throughout the world. He noted the ancient histories written in China about the time of the Emperor Yahow when vermin plagued the land, forests were ignited, the sun stood still for many days, and a huge flood engulfed the land for years.

AN ASSESSMENT

Although not all of Dr. Velikovsky's ideas are new, he has welded them into a unique framework. Velikovsky's ideas can be classified into two general theories plus a number of specific ones.[6] Both kinds are bolstered by his general supposition that myths carry important evidence of real occurrences. The two general theories of Velikovsky are (1) that global catastrophes have assaulted the entire Earth in the recorded past, and (2) that some planets in our Solar System have been born, and suffered near-collisions, in the recent past. His specific theories are many. They include a revised chronology of Egyptian history; the assignment of dates and locations of specific catastrophes to near-collisions with specific planets; and the inference of properties of Jupiter, Mars, and Venus.

The truth of one of Velikovsky's general theories does not necessarily impute truth to the other: catastrophism does not necessarily demand planetary collisions. Nor does the truth or error in his specific theories necessarily imply truth or error in his general theories. Velikovsky's impact is on many levels, each requiring separate, sometimes arduous, investigation. What would be a reasonable assessment of his ideas at present?

In several cases Velikovsky's predictions of the properties of the planets have proved surprisingly correct. In 1962 two scientists, Lloyd Motz of Columbia and V. Bargmann of Princeton, sent a letter to *Science* magazine stating in part:

> On 14 October, 1953, Immanuel Velikovsky, addressing the Forum of the Graduate College of Princeton University . . . concluded the lecture as follows: "The planet Jupiter is cold, yet its gases are in motion. It appears probable to me that it sends out radio noises. I suggest that this be investigated." . . . On 5 April, 1955, B. F. Burke and K. L. Franklin of the Carnegie Institution announced the chance detection of strong radio signals emanating from Jupiter. . . . This discovery came as something of a surprise because radio astronomers had never expected a body as cold as Jupiter to emit radio waves.

The letter also noted that Velikovsky had stated, in *World in Collision*, that the surface of Venus must be very hot even though the cloud cover of Venus was quite cold. It further pointed out that, subsequently, the high temperature discovered surprised scientists. The letter closed as follows:

> Although we disagree with Velikovsky's theories, we feel impelled to make this statement to establish Velikovsky's priority of prediction of these two points and to urge, in view of these prognostications, that his other conclusion be objectively re-examined.[7]

Another prediction that has proven true is that of an anomalous rotation of Venus. It is not always clear to an outside reader how Velikovsky's specific predictions follow from his general theories. He seems to have an amazing intuitive grasp of the implications of his theories.

Velikovsky's theories have had successes. What are the difficulties? We will concentrate only upon his planetary hypothesis. Some of his interpretations of Biblical events seem plausible; some are possible, if implausible; but there are two that scarcely seem possible within our present understanding. Velikovsky claims that many records of the ancients substantiate his belief that the axis and poles of the Earth have not only shifted many times in the past but have even completely reversed. Thus at some time in the past the Sun must have risen in the west and set in the east, or, as in Yahow's time, it did not set for days on end. There is scientific evidence for this, according to Velikovsky.

He pointed out that many rocks are magnetized, and the direction in which they are magnetized is something which can be measured. In the case of igneous rocks—for instance, rock formed upon the solidification of molten lava produced by a volcano—we may assume that the direction of magnetization is that of the Earth's magnetic field that prevailed at the time and place of the formation of the rock. In many cases the direction of magnetization of igneous rocks does differ markedly from the direction of the Earth's magnetic field that now exists there. Assuming that the magnetization of the rocks has been unchanged since solidification of the magma, one is forced to the conclusion that the direction of the Earth's magnetic field today is different from that which existed in antiquity; that this direction has shifted many times in the distant past; and that this direction has often reversed itself.[8]

So far, so good—no one can argue with this. It is the next logical step that causes the difficulty. Must we conclude that a reversal of the direction of magnetization of the Earth's magnetic field is intimately connected with the axis of rotation of the Earth? The origin of the Earth's magnetic field is uncertain, but scientists see no reasonable way in which the Earth's *rotational* axis could have changed as many times as the magnetic field. Even Velikovsky's theory proposes no more than three recent changes in rotational axis. It does not explain the very many ancient magnetic reversals, if these magnetic reversals are also taken to represent reversal in the direction of rotation. This throws the assumption that magnetic reversals represent rotational reversals into serious doubt.

Why do scientists hesitate to accept shifts in the Earth's rotation? To change the direction of rotation of a body requires an external torque such as one employs for twirling a baton. Neither scientists nor Velikovsky have found a reasonable way by which Venus could develop the necessary torque on the Earth in the relatively short period of a close encounter. The Earth travels nearly 19 miles a second in its orbit around the Sun, moving over eight times its diameter in one hour. In a close encounter its separation from Venus cannot have remained small—less than several Earth diameters—for more than one hour if we are to take any reasonable orbit of Venus.

The second unresolved problem lies in the actual orbit that Venus followed after its supposed disruption from Jupiter; and in the orbit which Mars travelled after its projection by Venus. Investigators have calculated a set of possible orbits that Jupiter, Venus, Earth, and Mars may have traversed in agreement with Velikovsky's scenario and still allow for proper celestial mechanics to operate.[9] These orbits maintain conservation of angular momentum but require substantial energy loss. The major difficulty faced by Velikovsky's planetary hypothesis is this loss of energy at each successive stage. This lost energy presumably reappears as internal energy in the planets Venus, Earth, and Mars. We have calculated this energy loss and it corresponds to half the Earth's present orbital energy. Appearing as heat within these planets, this energy would increase their temperatures (if they remained solid) all the way to 30,000K. This is five times as hot as the Sun's surface. The planet's surface would vaporize!

This objection is basic, and it does not depend on precise orbits. In going from an orbit near Jupiter to one near Mars, Venus *must* lose energy. Only a small fraction could be picked up by the much smaller Mars and have it end up with an orbit smaller than Jupiter's orbit. There just is no reasonable way to get rid of this energy and yet scale the catastrophe down to a size small enough to leave a solid Earth.

Other difficulties occur with Dr. Velikovsky's planetary scheme. For example, the energy required to free Venus from Jupiter, whether by fission or eruption, is more than the energy radiated by the Sun in a half year.[10] Again, the astronomer Carl Sagan noted that the surface of Venus is heavily cratered, suggesting an age in the *billions* of years, not in the thousands of years suggested by Velikovsky.[11] Still other objections exist; in discussing Stonehenge, later in this chapter, we shall discuss one of these.

The objections to Velikovsky's planetary theory are quite real. Velikovsky's followers seek to blunt some of these objections by appealing to effects usually neglected in planetary calculations, including electromagnetic effects. The final decision, though, on Velikovsky's schema is far away. For even if his planetary hypothesis is disproved, his hypothesis of global catastrophes may still stand the test of time; and his general ideas may well affect our thought in ways we still do not see. Within the last few years we have begun to see a new approach taken toward Velikovsky's ideas. Scientists and Velikovsky's adherents have finally begun to talk with each other. Calculations have narrowed the area of disagreement, and we can begin to see crucial points on which further research is needed.

We have praised Velikovsky's attitude and actions in his long fight with organized science. There was none of the denigration, on his part, that seemed to characterize the remarks of many of his opponents. It is necessary to add some notes that balance the picture somewhat. Velikovsky's frame of reference is elitist. He obviously considers himself above the common herd of scientists: not subject to their rules, their scrutiny, their impudence. Let lesser mortals have doubts—Velikovsky, like General de Gaulle, had none. And his idea of truth is one that is foreign to science; he is the leader, the truth teller to the host of the ignorant. Further, Dr. Velikovsky is obviously well versed in the art of publicity. Velikovsky conspicuously invokes the name of his onetime neighbor, Dr. Albert Einstein, implying, with little real evidence to back him up, that Dr. Einstein approved his ideas. We believe that, given his attitudes, Velikovsky is himself responsible for a part of the opposition to his ideas.

Velikovsky's theories are interwoven in a webbing of catastrophic events. Let us now take a look at one catastrophe not linked to his name. It is not really an occult event. This one happened, and here we do know how. We mention it because it was cataclysmic, and as such it fits snugly into the general ideas of "catastrophism."

THE SCABLANDS FLOOD

A lonely tribal hunter, long ago, stopped wearily halfway up a long mountain in the Bitterroot Mountain range in what is now Idaho. He lay down under the warm sun and, in a short time, the first familiar hypnogogic images of incipient sleep crossed his mind. But then unfamiliar rumbling sounds mushroomed slowly in his twilight consciousness. He felt his body trembling in reply to the mounting ferocity of the sound. He awoke, glanced slowly down the hill, and urgently sprang to his feet. A huge flood of water filled the valley below. The water's flanks were mounting rapidly up the hillside, making terrifying sounds. The scurrying hunter suddenly felt the deep panic of the hunted.

We can only imagine such panic scenes some 18,000 years ago as the huge Lake Missoula cracked its ice dam and dumped all its contents, half as much as the waters of Lake Michigan, onto the tilted Scablands basin below it. Cataclysmic quantities of water poured at a rate ten times that of *all* the rivers of the world combined. In two days the ancient Lake Missoula, filled at some points to a depth of 2,000 feet, was completely drained in the awesome deluge. This deluge scarred the land that now extends from western Montana, through Idaho, to eastern Washington. The ancient water marks of the lake scribed lines that are still visible, high above the surrounding flatlands.

The stupendous inundation spread across the Scablands basin in several enormous rivers, forming temporary lakes here and there, tearing deep channels across the earth, and sculpting cataract ledges and cascade buttes onto its face. Rocks, boulders, gravel of all kinds were swept along by the torrential waters. Giant ripple marks and immense gravel bars show up clearly when viewed from the far-off perspective of a space satellite. Five hundred cubic miles of water surged down the grade of the Scablands basin, in one giant gush with huge walls, draining toward the southwest to the Columbia River and thus, finally, to the sea.

J. Harlen Bretz of the University of Chicago proposed, in the 1920s, this origin for the unusual features of the Washington state area called Scablands. Recent satellite photographs have supported this interpretation. This huge flood, often termed the Spokane Flood, was one result of the glacial ice age that placed an ice dam across the Clark Fork River and gave birth to the ancient Lake Missoula. The waters rose slowly, finally reached the top of the dam, twice as deep as Lake Superior, and eventually spilled over. The flowing water quickly eroded the ice damming the lake. Then a giant fissure in the dam spilled the contents of the lake onto the Scablands below.

In a strange twist, satellite photographs of five Martian valleys—Kasei, Ares, Tiu, Sinud, and Mangala—also show features that strongly resemble the Scablands feature photographed by satellites about the Earth.

ERICH VON DÄNIKEN

Erich von Däniken is a self-taught man with no pretensions of scholarship. Nevertheless, with a wide-ranging curiosity about things that happened in the past (events normally the province of archaeologists, paleontologists, geologists, and astronomers) he has written several provocative books that challenge some widely accepted scholarly beliefs. Alluding to a number of exotic and puzzling facts—but with little in the way of hard, supporting evidence—he raises a startling, dramatic, and apocalyptic hypothesis that makes Velikovsky's proposals seem tame by comparison. He replaces the slow, dull process of Darwin's evolution by a stunning idea—that the human being on Earth has roots in other stars.

Von Däniken was born in Zofingen, Switzerland in 1935. Early on, he had some trying experiences with the Swiss law. His first book, *Chariots of the Gods?*—provocative, but without the scholarship, grace, or style that is Velikovsky's—has sold nearly 5 million copies and has been made into a very successful movie. People want to believe the things von Däniken says.

Any minority tries desperately to establish an identity for itself by investigating its past, and *Homo sapiens*—not a minority, not a majority, but the entire genus—is most anxious to do the same: it is very, very curious about its roots. Where do we come from? Who are our ancestors? How old are we? Von Däniken, in answering these questions, considers many separate incidents in our remote history and weaves them, sometimes uncertainly, into his theory that brings the gods down from heaven.

ASTRONAUTS—THE ANCIENT GODS

Von Däniken claims that at some time in the distant past the Earth was not only visited by extraterrestrial beings but was also settled by them. The new settlers found the natives to be dull brutes, immeasurably inferior both in culture and in technology. The local inhabitants, dazzled, considered the visitors as gods. The "gods" mated with the brutes, thereby producing intelligent *Homo sapiens;* then they departed. Thousands of years later the gods returned and found a few isolated examples of *Homo sapiens* and many unsuccessful hybrids, definitely neither *homo* nor *sapiens*. To keep the intelligent breed pure they destroyed these inferior specimens and then they left again. Thus, in von Däniken's words, the modern human being is both the child of Earth and the child of the gods.

When considering von Däniken's works one should bear in mind that he does not so much supply answers as raise questions. Thus, like the queries of a persistent child, his curiosity is intriguing rather than obtuse and a consideration of the problems he raises becomes fun. His puzzles are treated in a rather disjointed manner, both by him and by us; and some of them are completely unrelated to each other.

PUZZLES

• The Piri Reis Maps. In the early eighteenth century a number of ancient maps that had belonged to an officer in the Turkish navy, Admiral Piri Reis, were found in the Topkapi Palace, in Istanbul; two related maps were also found in the Berlin State Library. These maps and atlases (which were not originals but copies of copies) contained detailed reproductions of the area around the Mediterranean Sea and, in particular, of the Dead Sea region; but they also had reproductions of areas lying far away from these. These maps, according to von Däniken, were extremely accurate. This was very surprising, for the people who drew the originals could scarcely have been familiar with some of the regions. Antarctica, for example, had certainly not been explored yet the maps of it were accurate.

In 1957, von Däniken goes on to say, the accuracy of the maps was checked by a Jesuit priest, Father Joseph Lineham, who was a cartographer for the U.S. Navy. Further studies by Professor Charles H. Hapgood and a mathematician, Richard W. Strachan, then showed, he claims, that the maps could only have been made from aerial photographs taken from a great height. Yet our ancient ancestors, having no airplanes or spacecraft, had no means of taking photographs from great heights. Von Däniken, in explaining the maps, considers it most logical to assume that the photographs were taken by ancient astronauts from an advanced civilization who then passed them on to our brutish ancestors. How else can these fantastically accurate maps be explained?

• The Bay of Pisco. Overlooking the Bay of Pisco on the coast of Peru there stands an ancient gigantic statue, 820 feet high, shaped like a trident. Who built it? For what purpose? When? Nobody knows. Von Däniken wonders if it could not have been built as a guide, visible from great distances for either sea ships or space ships.

• Tiahuanaco. At Tiahuanaco, a city built at an altitude of 13,000 feet near Cuzco, Peru, there are huge blocks of sandstone, some weighing as much as 100 tons, with very smooth surfaces and edges that have been chamfered very accurately. To what purpose? Nobody seems to know. Von Däniken suggests that an old, local legend may provide a clue. The legend tells of a golden spaceship which came from the stars. A woman from the craft, Oryana, who had four webbed fingers, gave birth to 70 Earth children over a period of time and then departed.

At Tiahuanaco, incidentally, there is one huge stone ten feet high and sixteen feet wide, weighing ten tons, from which has been carved a Gate of the Sun. Various figures have been carved on this monolithic gate, one of which is a figure of a flying god.

• The Block of Sacsahuaman. At Sacsahuaman, Peru, there are some extremely massive blocks of stone lying about, not very far from the ancient Inca defense works near Cuzco. *One* of these blocks, von Däniken says, weighs 20,000 tons. It has steps, holes, spirals, ramps. Why was it built? Nearby, there are some pieces of vitrified rock similar to the stone that became vitrified in the Nevada desert when the atom bomb was exploded. Such vitrification has also been found, he says, in the Gobi desert of China and at ancient sites in Iraq.

• The Origin of the Sumerians. Where did the ancient Sumerians come from? They suddenly arose, he says, about 40,000 years ago, among a group of semi-barbaric tribes, with an advanced culture and a knowledge of mathematics and astronomy. All their symbols of gods were connected with the stars in one way or another. And cuneiform tablets from their city, Ur, tell of gods who came from the stars with terrible weapons, gods who eventually returned to the stars.

• Ancient Technology. In the Baghdad Museum there is on display an ancient artifact which, according to von Däniken, has definitely been established as part of an electric dry battery. Similarly, in Helwan, Egypt, there is on display an ancient fabric so fine that we, ourselves, von Däniken maintains, can only produce it in special factories. An ancient iron column in Delhi, India, von Däniken claims, is made of an unknown alloy and does not rust. Where did our half-savage ancestors acquire such skills?

• The Bible. Genesis 6:1: "And it came to pass . . . that the sons of God saw the daughters of men that they were fair. . . ." And in Genesis 6:4: "There were giants in the earth in those days . . ." Also, in Ezekiel: ". . . the heavens were opened . . . and behold a whirlwind came out of the north, a great cloud, and a fire infolding itself, and a brightness was about it. . . . I heard also . . . a noise of a great rushing." Can these not be taken as references to astronauts and their space ships? Further, in Genesis 19:24–26: ". . . and the Lord rained upon Sodom and Gomorrah brimstone and fire from the Lord out of heaven. And he destroyed these cities and all the country about and his (Lot's) wife looking behind her was turned into a statue of salt."

Did these astronauts destroy Sodom and Gomorrah, von Däniken wonders, with an atom bomb? Was Lot's wife, turning to witness the holocaust, the first radiation victim?

• Ancient Legends. Many ancient legends and myths refer to gods from the skies. The religion of the pre-Incas held, in fact, that the gods came from a definite place in the sky, the Pleiades. The Ramayana of India refer to machines, navigated at great heights by great winds and quicksilver, that could move up and down. Twelve clay tablets written in Akkadian were found about 1900. They had belonged to an Assyrian king, Ashurbanipal, and they told the epic of the hero, Gilgamesh, who was two-thirds god and one-third man. They tell how the heavens roared and a sun god came in a cloud of dust and seized Enkidu. While being taken away, the weight of his body seemed like the weight of a boulder. "How could the writer know the weighting effect of a high acceleration?" asks von Däniken. The Mahabarata refers to a single projectile that gave off light 1000 times brighter than the sun. An H-bomb?

• Pyramids. How were the pyramids of Egypt built? They were erected a thousand years before the horse and cart were introduced into Egypt, about 1600 B.C. There were no trees to supply wood for rollers to move the huge stones. Is it mere coincidence that when the height of the Great Pyramid of Cheops is multiplied by one billion one obtains a distance which is approximately equal to the distance from the Earth to the Sun? Is it only a coincidence that the meridian through this pyramid divides the continents and oceans into two exactly equal halves? Is it only coincidence that the center of gravity of the continents lies at the pyramids? How did the 2,600,000 blocks in the Great Pyramid get fitted to each other, within a tolerance of 1/1000 of an inch?

• The Statues of Easter Island. On Easter Island, 2,350 miles west of Chile, there are hundreds of statues, some as high as 66 feet and weighing 50 tons. (See Fig. 11–1.) There are only 200 inhabitants there today; at most there could be 2,000, far too few to make the statues in any reasonable time. The statues are hewn from nearby lava quarries and, von Däniken states, their material is too hard to fashion by crude tools. Who made these huge statues? How were they erected? The ancient myths of Easter Island call the island the Land of Bird Men. Were the statues transported by these Bird Men to Easter Island?

• Prehistoric Painting. Prehistoric paintings are found in various parts of the world. The stone age paintings found in 1940 in the Lascaux caves in the south of France present a problem. No soot appears on the ceilings over the paintings, so fires could not have been used to light the caves, von Däniken notes. How, then, were the caves illuminated? Why, in fact, were the walls decorated?

SOME ANSWERS

If the eye looks, there are real mysteries to be found—today. Some lurk in hidden crannies while others lie open for all to see. Von Däniken's writings have brought some of these mysteries to the focus of popular attention. We will look at three of these in the following sections, but some of von Däniken's questions can be answered immediately, and we will see that many of his questions pose no mystery.

Fig. 11–1. Statues on Easter Island. Several of the Moai stare mutely into the distance. Their buried portion equals in height the part seen here. When excavated, these giant statues may tower 60 feet or more. (Wide World Photos)

The human mind has been imaginative for a *very* long time; and ancient peoples had resources and capabilities that we can only vaguely see. Imaginative drawings and sculptures, as well as prodigious works of organization and skill, fit the human pattern then, in the dim past, as much as they do now. If one believes in the continuity of our artistic and technological ability, back to our ancient ancestors, few of the puzzling questions that von Däniken asks point beyond humanity to the stars in the heavens. We here comment on the questions asked in the previous section that have a straightforward answer.

• Piri Reis Maps. Piri Reis had consulted 20 earlier maps in fashioning his own maps and he used this knowledge. However, the maps, although remarkable, are not "fantastically accurate." The Amazon River is shown twice on one of his maps.[12] The South American coast has nearly one thousand miles missing. A nonexistent land bridge is shown between Chile and Antarctica.

• Ancient Technology. The Baghdad artifact and the Egyptian fabric are unusual. The iron column in Delhi is not. It is not an unknown alloy, and it does rust.[13]

• The Bible. An alternative to the atomic destruction of Sodom and Gomorrah was proposed by Clifford Wilson.[14] He noted that Mount Jebel Usdum (Arabic for Mt. Sodom), situated near the southern part of the Dead Sea, lies atop an area which has large deposits of oil, sulphur, and salt and is replete with geological cracks. There is evidence of an intense eruption which, Wilson proposes, may have occurred when an earthquake ignited escaping gases. He notes that the word usually translated as "brimstone" in the Bible actually means "bituminous material."

• The Pyramids. We will discuss the Great Pyramid in detail later in this chapter. Suffice it to say here that this pyramid does not coincide with the center of gravity of the continents, nor does it divide the continents and oceans exactly in two.

• The Statues of Easter Island. Thor Heyerdahl, of Kon-Tiki fame, also wondered at those statues and, pragmatically, asked the present inhabitants if they could make a new statue, or reerect a fallen one and move it across the island. They replied that they could; and photographs in Heyerdahl's book show the results.[15] Time and patience are all that are needed. A six-man crew took but three days to chisel the contours of a statue out of the rock wall, using stone picks abandoned in the quarry, although a year's time was estimated as necessary to complete the statue. A group of 180 natives, hauling away gleefully at a thick rope attached to the neck of a fallen statue in a huge game of tug-of-war moved it across the land "as quickly as if they each were hauling an empty soap box."[16]

MYSTERY IN THE FAR EAST

Collision craters dot the surfaces of the Moon, Mercury, and Mars. Here on Earth weathering rapidly smooths out crater features but, still, impact craters do exist. Thus, an ancient and awesome impact feature still etches the face of Gosses Bluff in Australia. Three miles in diameter, the feature has been estimated as nearly 130 million years old. The ancestral impact released an energy equivalent to 24,000 million tons—24,000 megatons—of TNT,[17] dwarfing the largest H-bomb explosion. A catastrophic collision with a comet, over one-third of a mile in diameter, would be required to form the immense Gosses Bluff crater of Australia. Extremely impressive.

Consider, now, another very impressive event. At 7:17 A.M. on July 30, 1908 a huge fireball was seen falling in the Tunguska area of Siberia. The thunderous noise carried more than 600 miles away and the seismograph in Irkutsk, 550 miles distant, vibrated for almost an hour. Had a huge comet collided with the Earth?

In Siberia it was not until 1921 that some eyewitness accounts of the fireball were collected by Professor Kulik. When the professor finally reached Tunguska, in 1927, he found *no* crater whatsoever, though there was still visible damage to the trees as far as 37 miles away and considerable evidence of a devastating conflagration.

Though holes were dug over 100 feet down, no metal or stone remnants could be found. Expeditions made in 1961 and 1963, sponsored by the Soviet

Academy of Sciences, led to the conclusion that a nuclear explosion had occurred there. They found that trees eleven miles away had been set on fire. Knowing the heat needed to set a growing tree on fire they calculated a total radiant energy equivalent to a several-megaton atomic bomb.

Other propositions have been advanced to explain this mysterious event. One is that a bit of antimatter from outer space collided with ordinary matter in Siberia, both matter and antimatter disappearing in a burst of radiation. It now appears that the Siberian fireball could not have been due to a comet or a meteor. The latest suggestion is that an errant, tiny black hole entered our Solar System and went right through the Earth, leaving the fireball in its wake. Black holes (which we discuss briefly in the last chapter) have, theoretically, many highly unusual properties. They have not yet been found experimentally. Von Däniken has his own theory to explain the fireball. He thinks that the nuclear pile of an extraterrestrial spaceship exploded in 1908 over Siberia, but he offers no substantiating evidence. Perhaps we will never learn the true answer.

THE PLAINS OF NAZCA

Almost no rain falls upon the tropical, desert plains situated on a high plateau near Nazca, an ancient city in Peru. What rain does fall evaporates almost immediately. Any new footprints made today on the flat, featureless, moonscape-like surface remain unchanged for years. Huge drawings, scraped upon the hard surface, have survived for two thousand years. They display their artistry to the skies, but they remain quite hidden from any one who walks across their rocky canvas; for one needs the perspective of height in order to see that the drawings are there. They stand out vividly and starkly if viewed or photographed from an airplane.

The plains of Nazca hold a gigantic series of straight lines, geometric figures, and animal drawings. Some lines run parallel to each other, some cross. Single lines run for miles, perfectly straight, only to end up on a slight rise. A huge rectangle, 70 yards across, runs straight—just like a huge landing field a half mile long. Rocks have been scraped up, lifted, then dumped at the edges, there to stay quietly for 20 centuries. Pottery fragments, an estimated 200,000 items, were originally strewn over the entire area. Mounds of rocks, 3 feet high and 90 feet long, stand in a geometrical array, but there is nobody buried beneath them. Figures of a giant spider, a lizard, a monkey glare at the sky. A lonely penguin seems lost here, far from its antarctic home. A condor spreads its wings in endless flight.

The figures are so large that an individual standing in them cannot notice them. The Spanish conquerors of this land made no mention of these figures in their detailed records, for they did not know they existed. The figures were first revealed to our modern eyes by Paul Kosok of Long Island University; and they were first popularized by Erich von Däniken, to his credit.

Large and unusual as these figures are, their construction did not require excessive labor, certainly nothing like that which went into the building of a pyramid. Hawkins estimates that a line five miles long and six inches wide might take two men less than a week to scrape into the base material of the plateau.[18] By dating the pottery strewn about, apparently near the time of construction, he places the age of the lines at about 2,000 years, predating a later Inca conquest.

The pictures, all drawn in one continuous line, raise fascinating questions. What was their purpose? How did the tropical Nazcans know about the penguin, native to the antarctic? The huge spider scraped upon the plains (Fig. 11–2) is, apparently, an image of the tiny, quarter-inch long tropical spider, *Ricinulei*. The blind *Ricinulei* is an extremely rare species having an unconventional mating organ. The third of its eight legs can be somewhat extended and, under a microscope, the organ used for copulation can be seen at the tip of this extended third leg. The Nazcan enlargement shows the extended third leg and has a copulatory tip! How did the Nazcans know about this rare *Ricinulei* spider? And how, without microscopes, did they learn about the secrets of its sex life?

The lines are not roads; they lead nowhere. Hawkins tested their star alignments thoroughly using a computer and found they pointed at no particular objects in the heavens. Von Däniken suggested that the giant rectangle was an ancient landing strip for extraterrestrial craft of the gods from outer space. But only terrestrial fragments have been found there. Nothing of an extraterrestrial nature has ever been discovered there to support such a theory. Were the lines and drawings just giant doodles? Were they drawings meant only to be seen and enjoyed by the real gods?

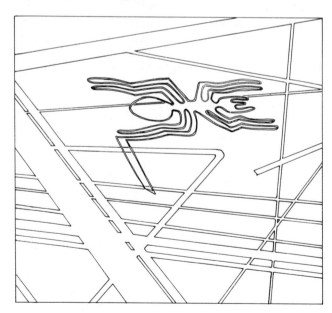

Fig. 11–2. The spider at Nazca. A line drawing from an aerial photograph. The quarter-inch spider extends itself over 100 feet in length on the Nazcan plane, enmeshed in a chaotic, man-made web.

STONEHENGE

One of the authors visited Stonehenge recently. Talking to a government guard late in the afternoon—after the other tourists had gone and using subdued voices —against the background of the stark plains and the massive stones—was an extraordinary experience. Although the guide had been there a quarter century, his interest in Stonehenge was still obviously keen and his speech was animated. "Sometimes," he said, "when I'm here alone, after everyone has gone home and the shadows are lengthening, I can feel the presence of other things here. And I know, for a fact, that I am not alone. I get frightened, then. This is an evil place."

The evil place the guard was talking about is situated in southwest England, not far from Bristol and just south of Wales. It is the remains of the most famous prehistoric temple in all of Europe, and is still shrouded in mystery. It has been established that Stonehenge was actually built and rebuilt several times. Stonehenge I was erected about 2500 B.C., during the new stone age or Neolithic period. A large circular ditch and a bank just inside it stem from this age. There were only three or so stones erected then, and all but one of them were removed in the next stage, Stonehenge II, some 500 years later. A circle of holes in the ground was also made during Stonehenge I. They were never used for stones or posts, but many of them served as places to bury the bones of humans who had been burned on funeral pyres. In the center? Nobody knows the frightening ceremonies that Stonehenge harbored.

Stonehenge was a temple, but we do not know to whom. There are no written records. It has been suggested that it was used for sun worship, since the entrance to the circle points toward sunrise on the longest day of the year at the summer solstice. We will return to this point in the next section. It is widely believed that Stonehenge was built by the Druids, but this is not so. The Druids were priests in Britain and France during the several hundred years before the time of Christ and, by then, Stonehenge was already millenia old and probably in ruins.

The second period of building, Stonehenge II, took place sometime around 2,000 B.C. The land was then inhabited by the Beakers, a people who had come from across the North Sea 100 or 200 years before. They dismantled the few stones and a timber archway from Stonehenge I, built a large avenue to Stonehenge from the nearby River Avon, and brought one of the two kinds of stones used in Stonehenge, the bluestones from Wales, mostly over water along Bristol Channel.

Some 80 bluestones, with a total weight of well over 100 tons, were transported in this fashion for close to 250 miles. About ten percent of the journey had to be made on land. Here, undoubtedly, wooden rollers were used under sleds holding the stones. Something of the order of 100 men was needed to pull the heavier, four- to five-ton bluestones, when the going was uphill. After half the bluestones had been arranged in two circles, about six feet apart, the builders changed their minds and, for some unknown reason, took them down.

Stonehenge III started about 1600 B.C. and lasted intermittently for 300 years. This was the period of the early bronze age, and the profits made by the early English in trading Irish bronze tools and weapons to the Saxons and French on the Continent possibly paid for the cost of completing Stonehenge. The big sarsen stones, the second of the two kinds of stones used in Stonehenge, were brought in at this time. These were made of a natural limestone found in large boulders on the Marlborough Downs only 20 miles away. Lifting these stones into position was not easy, but archaeologists know how it could be done by the use of only the simplest instruments. Our ancestors at that time may have been rude, crude, and uncultured, but they were definitely not stupid. And by all the indications here, in some areas they were extraordinarily advanced.

Figure 11–3 is an artist's conception of the appearance of Stonehenge after its final rebuilding, about 1300 B.C. There were originally 30 large impressive stones —the sarsens, weighing some 25 tons each and standing 14 feet high—arranged in a circle. On the top of these was pinned, 30 centuries ago, a complete ring of

Fig. 11–3. Stonehenge past. The stones as they may have appeared at dusk 3300 years ago—1200 years after the stones were first put in place. (British Crown copyright reproduced with permission of the Controller of Her Britannic Majesty's Stationery Office.)

flat lintels forming a broad, smooth circle, but of these most are now missing. Within this complete ring was another collection of sarsens, arranged in the shape of a horseshoe. These were in five groups of three, two uprights supporting a flat member on top. All the sarsens were very carefully shaped to fit together exactly: tongue and groove joints, knobs of one fitting into holes of another, and so forth. And there was a ring and a horseshoe of the small bluestones.

Outside the circles of bluestones and sarsens there were three circles of holes, now mostly filled up and only recognizable as slight hollows, and outside them all a large ditch. A part of the ditch and many of the holes contain cremated human bones. Near the center of all the circles is one stone called the altar stone. There is an entrance gap in the great circular ditch and bank that surround the circles of stones and holes, and just outside it is the heelstone. This stone, viewed from the center, points precisely toward the sunrise on midsummer day, the longest day of the year. Because of this many investigators now believe that this temple was devoted to astronomical observations. But the cremated bones lend credence to the popular belief, including that of at least one guard at the present remains of the ancient temple, that it was also a place for the sacrifice of human beings.

THE MEGALITHIC SKY WATCHERS

Stonehenge was not an isolated occurrence in the British Isles. The pre-Druid culture that conceived Stonehenge had started the emplacement of various stone circles perhaps as early as 2800 B.C. These early builders continued the construction of monolithic circles, flattened circles, and ellipses throughout the entire British Isles for at least another 13 centuries. The ancients in other parts of the world knew about Stonehenge. The historian Diordorus Siculus, using the lost work of Hecataeus from the fourth century B.C., refers to ancient spherical temples upon an island beyond the land of the Celts, apparently meaning Stonehenge.

A long list of investigators, beginning with Dr. John Smith in 1771 and continuing to the present, have developed the thesis that the megalithic circles, and Stonehenge in particular, served as astronomical observatories as well as ritual temples. There are, in the British Isles, nearly 50 known megalithic circles which are over 100 feet in diameter; and there are nearly a hundred which are less than 100 feet in diameter.[19]

Detailed investigation of alignments looking through members of the circles indicates that the various circles were used as polar, lunar, and possibly stellar observatories.[20] When viewed through archway 30–1 at Stonehenge, sunrise just above the distant heelstone marked the midsummer solstice there, preparing the ancients for the summer's waning. What a list of astronomical data these circles produced! The winter and summer solstices; the equinoxes, marking the beginning of spring and fall; the witching days Beltane, Lammas, Martinmas (near Halloween), and Candlemas; the lunar risings and settings; possibly the rising of the stars Capella, Deneb, Vega, and Arcturus; and perhaps even the solar eclipses. The megalithic circles may have whispered, magically, all of this to their priestly masters.

This fascination with the regularities of the heavens, based perhaps on need, seems more widespread than we recently would have guessed. It has been proposed that as early as 13,000 B.C. people used counting notations on bone tools and animal images as a record of lunar phases.[21] Patrick points out the impressive megalithic art in the Newgrange burial mound in County Meath, Ireland.[22] He further notes that a solitary one-meter-long gap in the thick walls of the cave entrance allows the sun's light to enter just after sunrise on the winter solstice, and only within a few days of the solstice; and it has done so ever since its construction, 5000 years ago. Further ancient astronomical alignments have been noted in the Great Temple of Amon-Ra.[23] More recent alignments have been found in Uaxactun in Guatemala; in the "American Woodhenge" of Illinois; and in the Big Horn Medicine Wheel of Wyoming.[24]

An interesting observation on the first sections of this chapter can be made here. Should Stonehenge or any related megalithic structure prove, indeed, to be a device designed to mark the heavenly cycles of the sun, moon, or stars (in addition to their religious functions), then Velikovsky's theory of the Earth's near-collision with a comet that shifted the Earth's axis will be in grave difficulty. The alignments of these structures could not serve this astronomical function if the Earth's axis was but a few degrees different when the structures were first put in place. This argues against any such shift of axis.

In viewing the plains of Nazca, the circle of Stonehenge and its sister circles and mounds, the temple of Amon-Ra, and the pyramids, we cannot help but be impressed by the observational and technical prowess of our ancient ancestors. Vast technical accomplishments have apparently sprouted and flourished many times within our history, only to perish, leaving but enigmatic traces for us to contemplate.

THE GREAT PYRAMID

About ten miles west of Cairo, Egypt, there stands a group of nine stone pyramids known, after the region, as the Giza Complex. These are not the only pyramids in Egypt for, stretched out on the west bank of the Nile River for a distance of about 70 miles southward toward the Sudan, there can be found about 100 other pyramids. But the Giza Complex is by far the most famous of all the pyramids. In this complex there are six rather diminutive pyramids and three large ones. The latter are named, today, after three ancient Pharoahs who ruled, in succession, about 4,500 years ago and are presumed to be somehow connected with their construction. Actually, the builders left no written records and there are no writings on the subject by their successors. So we do not even know how the three larger pyramids were referred to when they were built, nor who built them, nor why.

Today the largest of these three pyramids is sometimes called the Pyramid of Cheops, Cheops being the Greek name for the Pharoah Khufu, who is thought to have built it. Khufu's successor was the Pharaoh Kephren; and the second largest of the three is, accordingly, called the Kephren Pyramid. The third largest is the Mykerinos Pyramid, after the successor to Kephren. But the largest pyramid is the only one we will be concerned with here. It is so outstanding that it is usually referred to, simply, as the Great Pyramid. Figure 11–4 shows what it looks like.

The Great Pyramid was one of the ancient Seven Wonders of the World. It is, in fact, the only one of those wonders surviving today. Its name and reputation were well justified. The reasons for its construction remain hidden to us, and we can only make educated guesses. Experts are divided. Some, and popular opinion agrees with them, think that the pyramids were primarily built as tombs for Pharaohs; others think they were just monuments; still another suggestion is that the pyramids were constructed as a huge public-works project!

We, here, will limit ourselves to some of the features associated with the Great Pyramid's design and construction. Consider the following:

• The Great Pyramid contains 2,300,000 blocks of limestone or granite, each weighing somewhere between two tons and seventy tons. There is more stone in this one pyramid than in all the chapels, churches, and cathedrals erected since

Fig. 11–4. The Great Pyramid of Cheops. The pyramid is 481 feet high. The camels are dwarfed by comparison. (Wide World Photos)

the time of Christ in all of Europe. The volume of blocks is sufficient to build a wall 10 feet high and 3⅓ feet thick around all of modern France, including the coasts on the Mediterranean Sea and the Atlantic Ocean.

• The base of the Great Pyramid is a square, the average length being 755.79 feet. The deviation of each of these four sides from the average length is so small that the average magnitude of the deviation is only 0.18 foot, or less than 1/40 of 1 percent.

• Two sides of the base are directed almost due north and south, while the other two point almost due east and west. The average angular deviation from the exact N-S and E-W directions is only 3.1 minutes of arc. This angle is approximately the same as that subtended at the eye by a penny held 70 feet away.

Two geophysicists argue that the slight discrepancy from the true north-south direction was not a builders' error but was caused by slight movements over the centuries.[25] According to the present theory of continental drift, the movement would not be large enough to account for this, but since other explanations of the wandering of the pole produce even smaller figures, the authors believe that continental drift is the most likely explanation of the discrepancy. Think of the accuracy this imputes to those ancient, crude stone haulers.

• The base of the Great Pyramid, covering an area of 13 acres, is level to within one-half an inch.

• The outer stones of the Great Pyramid, which are now visible, were once within the interior under polished limestone casing stones. Two of these original casing stones have been found in their original place at the base. These are 12 feet long, 8 feet wide at the bottom, and 5 feet high. One vertical side rises perpendicular to the base, while the other makes an angle of 51°51′ with the base. Why 51°51′? Why not the symmetrical 60°, which would make each of the four triangular sides perfect equilateral triangles?

The total perimeter of the square base divided by twice the height of the pyramid is 3.143. The number $\pi \approx 3.142$ represents the ratio of the circumference of a circle to twice its radius. Were the builders of the Great Pyramid incorporating a mathematical fact into the structure? If this is so, it agrees to three significant figures with the value of π which we know today.

But there is one peculiarity about this fact: the value of π was not known to the Egyptians of 4,500 years ago. At least, the earliest Egyptian record indicating the value of π is the Rhind papyrus, which is dated about 1700 B.C., some 800 years later. Very odd.

• The main chamber found within the interior of the Great Pyramid had—within its walls, floor, and ceiling—dimensions which made the Greek mathematician, Pythagoras, famous some 2,000 years later. These dimensions were related to each other in the ratio 3:4:5; the same ratio as the sides of one particular right triangle. Pythagoras showed, two millenia later, that $5^2 = 3^2 + 4^2$ for such a triangle.

Is it plausible to regard these agreements as accidental? Coincidence? For what other purpose than revelation of these mathematical truths was the main chamber hollowed out? The common assumption that the Great Pyramid was a Pharoah's tomb built to memorialize him cannot be completely true, for nobody was ever found in this pyramid. However, it is true that a treasure-laden burial vault was, once, found in the main chamber.

• The latitude of the Great Pyramid is 29°58'51". Why the 1'9" difference from an exact 30°? A people so precise could be expected to choose the round number. Various explanations have been offered. A onetime Astronomer Royal of Scotland, C. Piazzi Smyth (one of the many people who devoted years, decades, or even their entire lives to the study of the pyramids) suggested that the discrepancy accounted for atmospheric refraction. Another theory attributes the difference to an attempt to allow for the fact that the Earth is not exactly spheroidal but bulges slightly near the equator. And a third explanation is more pragmatic: the Great Pyramid now rests on the solid rock of the Giza plateau, while just a few miles north it would have had to be built on the sand of the Nile valley.

Pyramidologists and talmudic students have one thing in common: give them one grain of sand and they will build on it a mighty stone pyramid. Often resting on its apex.

• C. Piazzi Smyth, who has been referred to as a pyramidiot, is the source of knowledge of still another widely quoted fact. If one takes the height of the Great Pyramid, from base to apex, as 5819 inches and converts this distance to miles one obtains a height of 0.09184 miles. Interestingly enough, this distance multiplied by one billion is 91,840,000 miles, which is roughly equal to the mean radius of the Earth's orbit about the Sun. Were the ancient Egyptian builders of the Great Pyramid aware of this? Is it sheer coincidence? Or is it just an example of the nonsense patterns to be found in any data?

• The Great Pyramid acts as a huge sundial whose shadow on the flat ground around the base serves to mark the equinoxes within an error of less than one day and the solstices within an error of less than two days. In the six winter months a shadow is cast on squares laid on the north side of the pyramid. There is no shadow in the other six months, but then a reflected triangle of sunlight is cast on the ground at the south side. As a result, the ancient priests were able to establish the length of a year to within less than a quarter of a day.

There are dozens of other facts and speculations about the Great Pyramid which have been suggested in the last 200 years, but it would serve no useful purpose to mention them all. Instead, perhaps we will be able to fathom the immensity of the task of construction if we give a few estimates that various experts have made.

Most of the blocks of limestone came from quarries directly across the Nile, though some of the large, 70-ton blocks that were used around the main chamber came from the region where the Aswan Dam now stands, 500 miles south.

To cut these blocks at the quarries some presently unknown method for tempering bronze must have been employed.

Herodotus was told that the Great Pyramid was built in 20 years and that it took 100,000 men to transport the blocks. Studies indeed have concluded that large numbers of men, working in unison, could haul the 60-ton block up greased inclined ramps and so build the Pyramids. The ramps may have required more "rock" than the Great Pyramid itself, while an auxiliary force of helpers and a standing army of soldiers, each larger than 100,000 workers, may have been needed to keep the project moving.

The logistics of the whole operation is simply overwhelming. Who paid for it? Just to put the 2,300,000 blocks in place in the 7,300 days of 20 years required that 315 blocks be mounted and joined (with their very close tolerance) each day. What was done with the waste chips? The stones for the ramp? How many men were necessary just to clean up? How did they illuminate the interior? Or get air there? Was the supervision done by a society, a group, or just one driven genius? Who drew up the plans?

Research on the pyramids is still going on. In 1974 a Nobel Prize-winning physicist, Dr. Luis W. Alvarez, ended an eight-year test of the interior of the smaller Kephren Pyramid, seeking for hidden chambers or passageways by using the cosmic rays from the sky.[26] If a cavity had existed it would have shown up as a bright spot for the detectors in some particular direction. No chamber was found. The Stanford Research Institute announced that it was going to continue the arrangement Dr. Alvarez had with Egyptian authorities to explore the Kephren Pyramid, but using radar instead of cosmic rays. To date, however, nothing has been discovered.

Nobody really knows for certain why the Great Pyramid was built. The famous aphorism made by Winston Churchill, in a completely different context, is certainly applicable here: "It is a riddle wrapped in a mystery inside an enigma."

SCIENTISTS AND ICONOCLASTS

In this chapter we have presented some of the unorthodox ideas of Velikovsky, von Däniken, and the investigators of Stonehenge. Science, of course, must respond to the ideas of imaginative outsiders and of iconoclasts. The ideal response is to evaluate all ideas objectively, with no prejudice to their origin— but practicality often betrays this ideal. A nonprofessional scientist who attempts to solve difficult problems with broad generalizations is likely to be dismissed out of hand as a pseudoscientist. This attitude is exemplified by Dr. Donald Menzel:

> For every Velikovsky . . . who manages to reach the general public, there are thousands of would-be scientists who send their pitiful papers to universities or scientific journals, pleading for recognition. Few of them write as well as Velikovsky, but their ideas are no more scientific. Do we scientists reject them,

along with Velikovsky ... simply because they are "overpoweringly unorthodox" or because they are not "members of the club?" No. We reject them because their ideas are vague, speculative, distorted. They ignore the simplest of established scientific principles. The chances are vanishingly small that the unsubstantiated doctrine we reject represent genius in disguise.[27]

Difficult as it is for anyone outside science to obtain a fair appraisal, the path is often little easier for those within science who propose the unorthodox. An entrenched dogma resists revision no matter how true the proposed change may be. Charles Darwin met scientific resistance when he proposed his theory of evolution. Darwin and Velikovsky have this much in common: the work of each is built around a central idea, with the supporting evidence accumulated, over a long period of time, from the most varied sources. But Darwin was cautious, he almost lost priority rights because of his hesitation in publishing evidence that he did not consider totally conclusive. Velikovsky was, indeed, intellectually persecuted; but so was Darwin. Not only scientists but organized religion, politicians, and many others were outraged by Darwin's theories. In the state of Tennessee it was a crime, not very long ago, to teach his theory of evolution.

Just how should professional scientists who spend their working lives attempting a rational explanation of the world around us deal with amateurs? Not too long ago the ideas of the nonscientists, the unorthodox, the uninformed, the misinformed, the occultists, the pseudo-scientists, and the antiscience establishment were simply dismissed by the professionals; and that was that. Today this is becoming increasingly difficult to do. Science is losing its prestige. A large gap exists between scientists and lay people, and the lay people will no longer automatically accept the conclusions of science. If science continues to consider with disdain, rather than compassion, the beliefs and interests that stem from outside its disciplines, then the gap will widen. Science flourishes only when it is receptive to ideas from all segments of society.

Even if it learns to handle its involvement with society more skillfully, science still stands between the horns of a dilemma in attempting to handle the unorthodox. The first cardinal error, one it cannot ever afford to make, is to accept that which is known to be incorrect. But suppose we don't really know what is correct. Do we accept all views then? Should the unorthodox view of ancient Stonehenge prevail then Velikovsky's collision theory will be invalidated. If the walls of Jericho tumbled in an earthquake, as Velikovsky proclaimed, they could not have fallen, as believed by von Däniken, at the sound of unearthly trumpets. The "purity" of science can, indeed, be preserved by rejecting all unorthodoxy. But this will, inevitably, lead to the second cardinal error—to reject that which is right. Without important new truth, which can *only* come from the unorthodox, science will stagnate. It will slowly decay under a mantle of confining dogma. So, in treating the unorthodox, iconoclasts, revolutionaries, it should behoove the science establishment to proceed very, very cautiously. One must go forward. But one must be careful. Like a porcupine making love.

CHAPTER TWELVE
WRITTEN IN THE STARS

THE ANCIENTS AND THE HEAVENS

The foundations of astrology were formed during the awakening of the human intelligence many, many millenia ago. As early peoples groped to make sense of the physical world about them, they naturally questioned the skies. What were those pinpoints of light glittering in familiar patterns in the night sky? What did they mean? How could one read their meaning? The patterns seemed to be connected with the cyclic events that were of the utmost importance to human survival—the times of the annual floods, the spring planting, and the onset of winter. Perhaps by studying the motions of the Sun and the Moon, the stars and the planets, people could learn how to understand, maybe even to control, the strange ways of nature.

Regularities in the motions must have been recognized by many individuals, unknown to each other—only to have the knowledge die with them. But eventually the knowledge was shared with others and then was passed on from generation to generation. At first this must have occurred by word of mouth, but subsequently knowledge became tradition; then tradition was ritualized and a vested few learned to make and keep records on wood, stone, and papyrus. Many of these recordings have been lost to us forever. This early astrology, the forerunner of our present astronomy, must represent but a very small portion of the many records that were made, only to be buried or destroyed by any one of countless causes. The few records that have survived give but intriguing glimpses of the early search for an understanding of the patterns. Table 12–1 gives a brief reconstruction of some of the more memorable dates in this search.

TABLE 12–1

CHRONOLOGY. (Partially adapted from M. Gauquelin, *The Cosmic Clocks*)

28,000 B.C. —	Stone notches believed to record the phases of the moon.
6000 B.C. —	Sumerians begin to observe the sky.
4241 B.C. —	Egyptian calendar stone.
2800 B.C. —	Stonehenge constructions begin in the British Isles.
2767 B.C. —	Egyptian "horoscope of eternity." *
2073 B.C. —	A sacrifice to the planets by Emperor Chounn of China.
1375 B.C. —	Hymn to the Sun by Pharaoh Iknaton.
650 B.C. —	Restoration of Chaldean observatories begun.
409 B.C. —	The oldest known Chaldean horoscope.
63 B.C. —	Theogenes casts the horoscope of Emperor Augustus.
140 A.D. —	"Tetrabiblos" written by Ptolemy.
1543 A.D. —	Copernicus fixes the sun at the center of the solar system.

* Cyril Fagan, Astrological Origins (St. Paul: Llewellyn, 1971), chap. 8.

ASTROLOGY

Beyond any doubt, the occult subject which has received the most interest from the general public is astrology. *Subject Guide to Books in Print, 1975* lists some 350 titles under this topic! According to Webster's *New International Dictionary*, astrology is defined as "the pseudoscience which treats of the influence of the stars upon human affairs, and of foretelling terrestrial events by either positions or aspects." It is an interpretive art based on a set of factual and scientific elements—the location and orientation of the planets, the sun and the moon with respect to each other and certain "fixed" stars.

There are different branches of astrology, depending on the use to which the interpretation is placed. The most common one is natal astrology, the study of individual birth charts; mundane astrology is concerned with national affairs, and assumes to foretell future trends; medical astrology seeks to answer problems of health; natural astrology attempts to predict events in inanimate nature. We will only deal with natal astrology.

The arrangements of the planets and stars at the time of birth constitutes a horoscope, a view of the hour. Casting a horoscope involves the use of tables of planetary positions and of the zodiac signs at the instant of birth. This part of astrology is an exact science.

The second part of astrology, the interpretation of the horoscope, is not a science—it is an art. Two highly skilled and competent astrologers could easily arrive at contradictory conclusions concerning the significance of a horoscope, provided that the interpretations were made for subjects whose identities were unknown; for many of the attributes assigned to different factors in the horoscope are not mutually exclusive, do not have a unique hierarchy of weights, and are often vague. In a sense, the possibility of multiple interpretations reminds one of a similar characteristic of the ancient Chinese art of divination, the *I Ching*.

The basic elements that determine a horoscope are the planets, the signs of the zodiac, and the houses. Once these are determined, at the time and place of birth, a horoscope can be cast. The relation of these basic elements to the angles between the planets, called the aspects, governs the interpretation of the horoscope. We will concern ourselves exclusively with these factors as they are found in present Western astrological practice.

THE PLANETS

In scientific usage, the planets are large bodies which are satellites of the sun and revolve about it. Ranging outward in order from the Sun, they are Mercury, Venus, Earth, Mars, Jupiter, Saturn, Uranus, Neptune, and Pluto. An asteroid belt exists between Mars and Jupiter, and is commonly presumed to be the remnants of an unformed planet. There is unconfirmed evidence of an additional planet, Planet X, beyond Pluto.[1] Astrological usage, however, includes both the Sun and Moon among the planets but excludes the Earth.

Astrologically, the planets are considered from an Earthcentered viewpoint, although they actually revolve around the Sun. It is typical of much of modern astrology that it places emphasis on things as they seem, not on things as they are. It is highly pragmatic.

Astrologers attribute specific influences to each planet. Among the ancients, Jupiter and Venus were considered especially favorable planets (benefics); Saturn and Mars were unfavorable (malefics). Modern astrological practice does not ascribe such good or bad influences directly to a planet; rather, it considers the influences as presenting problems or characteristics that must be dealt with. Thus, an afflicting Saturn, if properly met, may strengthen rather than weaken a character. This, of course, leaves much latitude in interpretation. Table 12–2

TABLE 12–2
THE PLANETS

Name	Symbol	Influence	Sphere of Influence
Sun	☉	Life, Vitality	Self, Purpose
Moon	☽	Emotions, Feelings	Subjective feeling
Mercury	☿	Reason, Intelligence	Mentality
Venus	♀	Love, Artistry	Acquisitiveness
Mars	♂	Drive, Energy	Initiative
Jupiter	♃	Idealism, Expansiveness	Enthusiasm
Saturn	♄	Restraint, Limitation	Sensitiveness
Uranus	♅	Sudden Change, Altruism	Independence
Neptune	♆	Intuition, Uncertainty	Obligation
Pluto	♇	Regeneration, Slow change	Obsession

lists the planets, their symbols, and the astrological influences associated with them. The attributes stem from ancient Babylonian mythology as modified through the ages, especially by the Greeks.

SIGNS OF THE ZODIAC

Looking at the sky on a clear night far from any city lights, when there is no Moon, one can count about 3,000 stars with the unaided eye. Some of the stars are brighter, some dimmer. Looking for several hours a night, one soon recognizes that the stars all sweep across the sky from east to west, just as the Sun does during the day. Looking for several months, at about the same time each night, one eventually recognizes that the stars all sweep past the Sun also, again from east to west. At the end of one year the Sun is back in the part of the sky where it started. Nevertheless the stars keep their same positions relative to one another.

The brighter stars were long ago imagined to be formed into groups called constellations—the Big Dipper, for example. The constellations all silently wheel across the sky in synchronism, changing their positions gradually from east to west in the course of a day, then setting beyond the western horizon. New ones continually arise from below the eastern horizon. Not *all* the stars do this, however. Over 2,500 years ago the ancient Babylonians counted five which moved through the constellations, each at its own rate—sometimes faster, sometimes slower, and sometimes in the reverse direction. These five were the planets visible with the naked eye: Mercury, Venus, Mars, Jupiter, and Saturn. Together with the Sun and the Moon, which also moved relative to the constellations, the ancients counted seven planets. (Today's science counts neither the Sun nor the Moon as a planet but does count the Earth.) After the invention of the telescope three more planets were discovered, Uranus, Neptune, and Pluto. So astrologers today deal with ten astrological planets.

To the naked eye, all the stars seem equally far away; they are merely pinpoints of light against the dark velvet curtain of the sky. It is easy to imagine this curtain in the form of a sphere with the Earth as its center point. The curtain is called the celestial sphere, and all the stars and constellations appear imbedded in it. To a person at the center of the sphere, the Earth, each star scribes a yearly circle about the axis, travelling clockwise from east to west.

The bright constellations of the stars are embedded on all parts of the celestial sphere. But the Babylonians learned 2,500 years ago that the planets, wandering about on the surface of the celestial sphere, were all restricted in their motion, staying within an equatorial belt, a total of 16 degrees wide, about the middle circle traced by the Sun in the course of a year. This middle circle, called the ecliptic, is analogous to the equator on Earth. The constellations of fixed stars that lie in this narrow belt took on special importance for the ancients. In astrology only these constellations are assumed to affect us strongly, and brighter constellations lying outside this belt are, therefore, ignored. This belt of constellations astride the ecliptic is called the zodiac and is shown in Fig. 12–1. It was divided, for convenience, into 12 equal parts called the signs of the zodiac.

The position of the Sun against the fixed stars can be easily determined each day of the year. The Sun tracks through the 12 constellations, or signs, familiar to the ancient star gazers: Aries, the Ram; Taurus, the Bull; Gemini, the Twins; Cancer, the Crab; Leo, the Lion; Virgo, the Virgin; Libra, the Balance; Scorpio, the Scorpion; Sagittarius, the Archer; Capricorn, the Goat; Aquarius, the Water Bearer; and Pisces, the Fish; returning, once again, to cross Aries as a new yearly cycle begins. The Sun will lie in a given sign at roughly the same period each year, as seen from Earth. The dates shown in Fig. 12–1 are only approximately accurate.

In its apparent annual motion relative to the celestial sphere along the ecliptic the Sun seems to move slowly counterclockwise, from west to east. On the other hand, the Sun's fast daily revolution along the equator of the celestial sphere is clockwise—that is, from east to west.

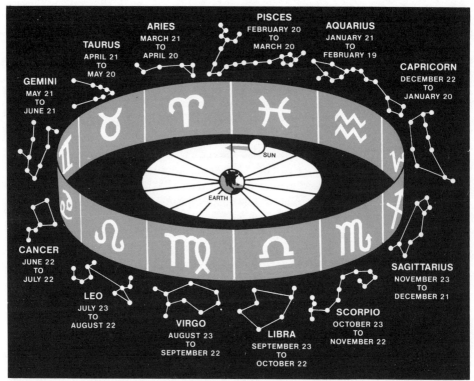

Fig. 12–1. The zodiac. This is the belt of constellations straddling the ecliptic, the Sun's apparent path on the celestial sphere.

CONTENDING ZODIACS

An interesting point arises in connection with the signs of the zodiac and the constellations with which they were originally associated. There is a very slow astronomical effect known as precession: the axis through the Earth's poles does not stay pointed along the same direction toward the stars but, instead, executes a slow circular motion, completing one revolution in 26,000 years. The poles of the celestial sphere precess relative to the Earth, just as the axis of a spinning top precesses about the vertical. In 2,200 years this corresponds to about 30 degrees—the width of one sign of the zodiac. Thus, the constellation Aries now coincides mostly with the sign of the zodiac Taurus. In the time of Christ the constellation Aries coincided mostly, but not exactly, with the sign Aries.

The Sun is in the sign of Aries in the early spring. This is the time of the spring equinox, when the length of the day equals that of the night. The junction of the signs of Pisces and Aries is known as Point Gamma. Today this point of the zodiac actually lies in the constellation of Pisces. In Ptolemy's day it was in the constellation of Aries, about to enter Pisces in a few hundred years and set the stage for the Piscean age. About 600 years from now Point Gamma will enter the constellation of Aquarius. For this reason we are said, a bit prematurely, to be entering the age of Aquarius.

A basic question arises: If our fate is written in the stars, which stars should be considered—those of the actual constellations or those of the zodiac? The two do not coincide. A few astrologers take the first choice and cast a sidereal horoscope by the actual constellations near the Sun and planets at the time of birth. But most astrologers use the signs of the zodiac defined by the time of the year and cast a so-called tropical horoscope. This is another example of the pragmatic rule in much of modern astrology: the important thing is the surface appearance, here and now, without paying too much attention to underlying processes or to what might have been. Thus, the actual position of the constellations, which had certain attributes assigned to them, is not important; what does matter is the sign of the zodiac and the time of the year. The attributes now belong to the zodiac, not to the constellations. It is then not really correct to say "It is written in the stars"; it should be "It is written in the signs."

According to astrology the sign of the zodiac when a person is born (that part of the ecliptic through which the Sun is then passing), plays a fundamental role in that individual's personality. In Table 12–3 we also list some of the qualities associated with the various signs. The historical reasons for these associations are complex and stem largely from the polytheistic beliefs of the Babylonians and Greeks, especially the latter.

The actual beginning of each sign may vary slightly by about a day from year to year. When the Sun, or some given planet, appears within a particular sign of the zodiac in a horoscope, the qualities of the sign are assumed to interact with the spheres of influence of the planet to produce definite traits and influences. The simplest example of this is found in the Sun sign, determined solely by the position of the Sun in a particular sign of the zodiac at the time of birth. Astrologically, someone born on August 17 is a Leo; their self, or individuality, is signified by the Sun to follow the traits attributed to Leo: outgoing, energetic, courageous, proud, but sometimes arrogant and conceited. The popular, single-minded use of Sun signs in newspaper horoscopes, for example, to describe the influence of the planets on a person's personality is a horrible oversimplification for professional astrologers.

Ptolemy (ca. 100–170 A.D.), a Greek born in Egypt with a Roman name, wrote the book *Tetrabiblos*, the astrologers' Bible. He attributed a ruling planet to each sign in a somewhat arbitrary fashion, a fact which irks many present-day astrologers. The comparatively recent discovery of the planets Uranus, Neptune, and Pluto thus required that these be added, to form dual rulership, in three signs, Aquarius, Pisces, and Scorpio. The concept of rulership is therefore followed with great misgiving (if followed at all) by many astrologers.

Ingenuity could surely find a way of delineating a finite number of personality traits and then assigning exactly the right portion of a given trait among the various signs. This would correct some of the uncertainty that otherwise exists in the interpretations; for, with a given natal chart, different astrologers very often now come to quite different conclusions. This situation is made much

TABLE 12–3
THE SIGNS

Sign	Symbol	Quality Represented	Bodily Influence	Ruler
Aries— the Ram	♈	Creation, Self-assertiveness	Head, Brain	Mars
Taurus— the Bull	♉	Perpetuation, Determination	Neck, Throat	Venus
Gemini— the Twins	♊	Versatility, Correlation	Shoulders, Upper arms, Lungs	Mercury
Cancer— the Crab	♋	Personal attachment, Assimilation	Chest, Elbows, Breasts, Stomach	Moon
Leo— the Lion	♌	Creativity, Individualization	Upper back, Forearms, Wrists, Spine, Heart	Sun
Virgo— the Virgin	♍	Service, Discrimination	Abdomen, Hands	Mercury
Libra— the Balance	♎	Cooperation, Harmony	Lower Back, Kidneys	Venus
Scorpio— the Scorpion	♏	Emotional power, Elimination	Pelvis, Reproductive organs	Mars, Pluto
Sagittarius— the Archer	♐	Aspiration, Spirituality	Hips, Thighs, Sacral region	Jupiter
Capricorn— the Goat	♑	Perfection, Materialism	Knees, Bones	Saturn
Aquarius— the Water bearer	♒	Altruism, Dissemination	Lower legs, Ankles, Blood circulation	Saturn, Uranus
Pisces— the Fishes	♓	Intuition, Self-sacrifice	Feet, Liver, Lymphatics	Neptune, Jupiter

worse when the other planets, and their aspects, enter. Once having the different personality traits, and the portion of each assigned to Aries, Taurus, and the other signs, it then becomes simply a matter for the computer. Computer studies and computerized horoscopes have proliferated widely. This is really attempting to turn astrology into a science and this, indeed, is the goal of a number of astrologers.

THE HOUSES

The basic complexity of astrological computations stems from the fact that there are two, quite different, rotational cycles involved in the motion of the Earth—motions which occur about different axes. The first cycle is the annual revolution of the Earth about the Sun; or, what is the same thing, the apparent revolution of the celestial sphere, in the reverse sense about its center, the Earth, in one year. This leads to the ecliptic in astronomy; and, in astrology, to the signs of the zodiac, which we have already considered. The second cycle is the diurnal, or daily, revolution of the Earth about its own axis through the poles. This cycle is 365¼ times as fast as the previous one and leads to one apparent revolution of the celestial sphere in each day, again about its center, the Earth, but this time about the diurnal axis, inclined 23° relative to the annual axis.

Just as astrologers divided the sky into 12 regions (the signs of the zodiac) for the annual revolution of the stars, so they divided the sky into 12 zones, called houses, for the daily revolution. The Sun and the planets wander slowly through the signs of the zodiac, but they race through the various houses. The houses supply astrology with the ability to impart the required diversity into the psychological traits of people born almost simultaneously, but at different places.

Figure 12–2 illustrates the houses. The houses are not given names but are simply designated by numbers. The first house is defined uniquely for each person: it has an edge, or cusp, on the eastern horizon at the time of birth and extends 30° westward.

A person born at sunrise has the Sun at the cusp of the first house. Someone born at noon has the Sun at the cusp of the tenth house; at sunset the Sun is at the cusp of the seventh house; and at midnight the Sun is at the cusp of the fourth house.

To each house here is assigned a sphere of action, and this applies to the person's mode of behavior as determined by his planets and signs. Table 12–4 lists these spheres of action.

At any moment the Sun illuminates half the Earth while the other hemisphere

TABLE 12–4
THE HOUSES

House	Influence
1	Personality, Body shape
2	Money, Possessions
3	Relatives, Neighbors, Communications
4	Home, Parents
5	Love, Pleasures
6	Obligations, Health, Service
7	Marriage, Partners
8	Death, Inheritance, Sex
9	Religion, In-laws
10	Career, Honors
11	Friends, Hopes
12	Misfortune, Enemies

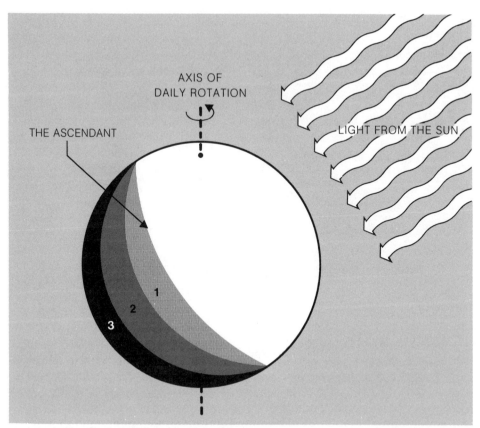

Fig. 12–2. The Sun's house at time of birth. This shows the house in which the Sun appears for people born at several locations on Earth. Thus a baby girl born somewhat before sunrise, where night's darkness still lingers, has the Sun in her first house. The houses 1 through 6 are the nighttime houses; the houses 7 through 12 are the daytime houses.

is in darkness. The line of demarcation between the two is termed the horizon in astrology; and the horizon at the instant of a person's birth has two points of great significance, called the Ascendant and the Descendant. The Ascendant, or cusp of the first house, is the point at which the ecliptic is about to start rising above the horizon into daylight; the Descendant is the point where the ecliptic is about to start setting below the horizon.

In Western astrology the sign of the zodiac in which the Ascendant appears has an importance equal to that given the signs in which the Sun and other planets appear. Astrologically, the Ascendant points in the direction toward which a person is heading: the person's true nature, if his or her potential is fulfilled. Thus, Sun in Aries, Ascendant in Cancer means aggressive, impulsive, plus home-loving.

THE HOROSCOPE

The locations of the planets, signs, and houses at the time of a person's birth constitute the natal horoscope of that person. But horoscopes can be cast for the birth of any event, not just a person's birth; for example, the start of a new business may be examined by a horoscope.

We present in Fig. 12–3 the horoscope of the pioneer movie comic, Charlie Chaplin. The arrangement of the elements in the horoscope is indicated in a variety of ways, depending on the taste of the one casting the horoscope. Generally, the houses are segmented as in Fig. 12–3, with the cusp of the first house at the left (9 o'clock). The houses then increase, numerically, counter-clockwise. The location of the house cusps, in angular degrees, within each sign is shown on the outside rim of the horoscope. There, for example, the cusp of the first house, Charles Chaplin's Ascendant, is 8° in Scorpio. The locations of the planets are given inside each house. Although the houses are equally divided on paper, in the horoscope of Fig. 12–3 they are *not* equally spread through the zodiac signs of a horoscope. This may result in more than one sign being included in any given house. This complicating feature emerges because the signs constitute 12 divisions along the ecliptic, while the houses constitute 12 divisions along the equator. The ecliptic and the equator are two completely different circles, inclined to each other by 23°. One of the odd results of this fact is that it is not possible to cast a reasonable horoscope for a person born within either the Arctic or Antarctic circles, where it is possible for weeks to pass when the Sun lies below the horizon.

ASPECTS

The interpretation of the horoscope is governed by the location of the planets in the signs and houses; by the position of the signs with respect to the houses; and by certain angles, or aspects, involving the planets and the Ascendant. The angles between any two planets, as well as between a planet and the Ascendant, are used to determine the various aspects.

In Fig. 12–4 the Earth is at the center of the celestial sphere, while the circle represents the ecliptic—that slice of the sphere traversed by the planets. A number of planets are shown on the sphere in order to illustrate the principal aspects. Here the angle between the line from Earth to Sun and the line from Earth to Mercury, is 0°: the two lines coincide and the Sun and Mercury are said to be in conjunction. Several aspects are illustrated for the actual angles of the planets about the Earth.

Trines and sextiles, which split the circle into threes or sixes, respectively, are soft, or harmonious aspects in astrology. On the other hand, the square and opposition are taken as hard, or inharmonious, aspects. Conjunctions fall in between these two: they take their influence from the context; that is, two planets in conjunction are assumed to mingle their influences. If the planets are beneficial—say, Venus and Jupiter—then a conjunction of these two planets

Name *CHARLES CHAPLIN*   NATAL CHART   Birthplace *LONDON, ENGLAND*

Birthdate *16 APRIL 1889*   Birthtime *8:00 P.M., G.M.T.*

51°N. 32'
0° W. 05'

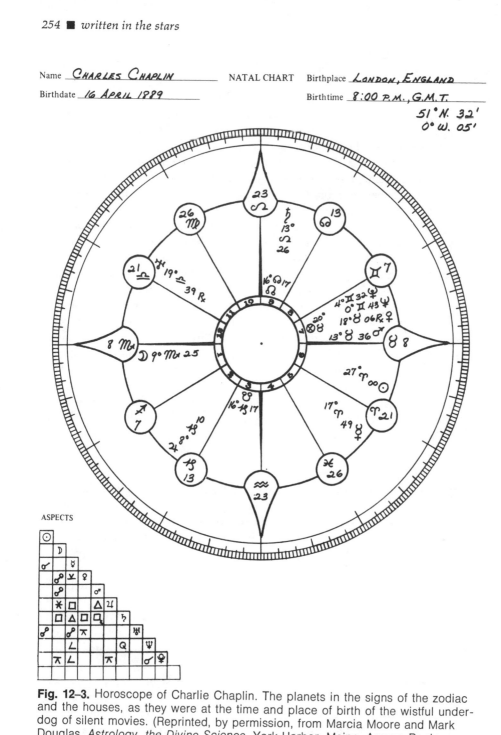

Fig. 12–3. Horoscope of Charlie Chaplin. The planets in the signs of the zodiac and the houses, as they were at the time and place of birth of the wistful underdog of silent movies. (Reprinted, by permission, from Marcia Moore and Mark Douglas, *Astrology, the Divine Science,* York Harbor, Maine, Arcane Books, 1971, p. 654.)

Name of Aspect	Symbol	Degrees	Orb	Astrological Significance
Conjunction	♂	0	8°	Blended Power
Sextile	⚹	60	4°	Creativity
Square	□	90	8°	Stress
Trine	△	120	8°	Ease
Opposition	☍	180	8°	Awareness

Thus, in the above diagram the Sun has the following aspects with the other planets shown:

⊙ ♂ ☿   ⊙ ⚹ ♂   ⊙ □ ♄   ⊙ △ ♆   ⊙ ☍ ♃

Fig. 12–4. The aspects. These are the angles, as seen on Earth, between pairs of planets, or between the Ascendant and a planet.

is favorable; if, like Saturn and Mars, the conjunction is between harsh planets, then the conjunction is unfavorable.

The aspects express an ancient astrological principle of relativity: influences are controlled by the relative angular positions of the planets and Earth. Relative position might seem to be a reasonable element in assessing the effects of the planets on Earth. But neither the mass of a planet nor its actual distance from the Earth is accorded any importance, whatsoever, in astrology. This is a distinctly unphysical feature, in view of the great importance of mass and distance in governing the known physical properties of the Solar System.

From Charlie Chaplin's horoscope, Fig 12-3, an astrologer might pinpoint several features of Chaplin's personality. The Ascendant and the Moon are both in Scorpio, at $8°$ and $9°25'$ respectively. This confers, astrologically, a sultry, erotic side to his character. A qualistic feeling. The Sun is $29° 0$ in Aries, thereby implying a strong, supreme drive for creativity. Aggressive Mars is $13°38'$ within conservative Taurus, the sign of perpetuation, determination, and prodigious labor. This suggests a basic conflict between risk and conservativeness, to be overcome by hard work. The Moon in Scorpio opposes Mars and is square to a restraining Saturn at $13°26'$ of individualistic Leo. This leads to a major problem in his life: the control of erotic instincts. Ignoring Pluto, three planets—Mars, Venus, and Neptune—all fall in the seventh house, the house of marriage and partners. Its cusp is in procreative Taurus at $8°$. Chaplin's prodigious artistry, his rich love life, his four marriages and numerous offspring would scarcely surprise an astrologer.

EXPERIMENTAL INFLUENCES OF THE PLANETS

Astrology gives a detailed, systematic method—actually based on scientific observations—for casting a horoscope. But the reading of a horoscope is subject to a wide latitude of personal interpretation, even though the general outline for such a delineation is reasonably clearcut. The freedom of personal interpretation may, however, be no greater in astrology than in many of the psychological and social sciences which also deal with the behavior of people. The important question then is: what experimental basis is there for astrology? What are the real, observed influences of the planets on the personalities and potentials of people? Indeed, are there any?

One source for answers to this question of the validity of astrology lies in the personal experience of practicing astrologers. Conscientious astrologers who practice their art assiduously over many years and constantly compare the results of their work with observation of the actual facts, obtain a great storehouse of empirical information. Their appraisal of this information, however, runs into more difficulty than the appraisals of scientists reviewing their own work. For the scientist's experiments are checked, independently, by other scientists before the results are generally accepted; while the knowledge gained by an astrologer is personal and is not easily subject to general scrutiny. By general exchange of information among astrologers, however, a common consensus makes its way into the main stream of astrological lore. We may suppose that this lore contains some nucleus of empirical fact. The important question, of course, concerns the actual size of this nucleus. Is it the majority of the lore? Is it some, but not all, of the commonly assumed interpretations? Or is the lore, essentially, almost all invalid? Scientists, who are outside the field of astrology, need to maintain an open mind, but one combined with an arms-length approach, concerning the body of astrological lore. Most of the nucleus of fact in astrology *can* be determined: the predictions of astrology must be tested. Tested against fact. Barring either the will to believe or the will not to believe, this is simply common sense.

Our present developments in data gathering, computer processing, and statistical analysis now make the task of testing astrology practical. Psychological barriers in the various sciences may have to be overcome to mount this task; but such testing, applied to the general public, should clearly establish either the truth or the error of astrology.

A small number of previous pioneering attempts have already been made to determine how well astrology reflects the facts of nature. A French scientist, Michel Gauquelin, reviewed those attempts and concluded that the earlier experimental efforts by the astrologers Paul Choisnard and Karl Ernest Kraft to verify astrology suffered from a number of fundamental errors and were not successful.[2] Farnsworth attempted to find a correlation between artistic predisposition and either the Ascendant or the Sun in the sign of Libra, representing artistic talent. He did this by examining the births of 2,000 famous painters and musicians, and he found no correlation with their birth dates. The famous American Astronomer, Bart J. Bok, likewise could find no evidence that the professions of people listed in *American Men of Science* had any connection with the zodiac birth sign.

In his initial studies, Gauquelin examined the births of 25,000 famous people. He found that there was no correlation between either their temperament or their profession, on the one hand, and the sign of the zodiac at their birth, on the other hand, for either the Sun, the Moon, or the Ascendant. He found that chance, not the planets, related the forces tested.

Astrologers remained unconvinced by statistical studies which showed that as many future soldiers are born under the tranquil sign of Libra as under the aggressive one of Aries. But those astrologers who did allow Gauquelin to test them could not distinguish between the horoscope of convicted murderers and those of famous artists, scientists, or politicians. Gauquelin was, therefore, driven to a definite conclusion: *there is no basis in fact for the usual claims of astrology.*

All this and more is documented by Gauquelin in his widespread initial statistical studies. These all show the lack of any correlation between actual fact and the usual predictions of astrology. He is not hesitant in stating that while astrology is a belief held by many sincere people, these people are misguided. Their belief, he says, is unjustified in fact.

We can but imagine Gauquelin's surprise at the result of a subsequent statistical study that he conducted himself which showed that *a definite correlation existed between the position of certain planets at birth and the future occupation of people.*

In one of Gauquelin's continuing investigations, involving a group of 576 medical academecians in France, he noted an unexpectedly high correlation between the moment of birth and the position of a particular planet. This planet could be either Mars or Saturn; and its position on the celestral sphere could be either just beyond the Ascendant or just beyond the Zenith—i.e., either just in the 12th house, or just in the 9th house. This coincidence was much too high, statistically, to be considered a chance effect, averaging at least 17 percent above the chance expectation. What his study seemed to show was that certain people, who were to become eminent doctors later in life, were likely to have been born at a moment when Mars or Saturn had either just risen or was half way across the overhead sky. Examining a sample of ordinary births, taken from a random sample of people, he found no such effect: the coincidence was only true for senior doctors.

Disbelieving his data, Gauquelin checked another group of 508 ordinary doctors and found the same correlation. Then he examined a total of 25,000 births of German, Italian, Belgian, and Dutch celebrities—just to make sure this was not an effect peculiar to France. The results were the same. In fact, he also found other correlations between different professions and various planets. The man who had so laboriously accumulated statistical evidence contradicting the claims of conventional astrology was finding that there were other effects of planets on human beings! It was not conventional astrology, perhaps, but it was not very far removed from it. It is certainly far removed from conventional science. Still, it is nothing more than the statistical analysis of data—hard facts. The planets at birth seemed to correlate with a person's choice of his or her future profession.

PLANETARY INHERITANCE

Gauquelin then had to face the same commonsense questions that plague all astrologers: How does a planet cast its spell suddenly, altering the effects of heredity? Why does the effect begin only at birth—why not at conception? In what way does the effect of one planet differ from that of another? Why don't the actual masses or the distances of the planets affect their efficacy? Gauquelin was scientifically trained, so rather than simply ignoring these questions, he invented an hypothesis and tested it. Instead of assuming that the planets altered an infant's organism at birth by some mysterious rays, he assumed that the foetus had a predisposition to be born when certain planetary positions conformed to its biological constitution. This is astrology with a reverse twist. It isn't that the stars determine the child's nature; the child is merely waiting for the right moment to be born.

Of course, the question then becomes: How does the foetus know the planetary positions? It would seem that such an effect, if it exists, must be hereditary. This idea turned out to have an advantage—a simple test could be made to check its validity. If this hypothesis were true, then a child awaits his or her time of birth according to some hereditary mechanism; and this hereditary mechanism should then have existed in the parents too. Thus the father also must have awaited the same conditions before his own birth. Gauquelin spent the next five years examining the birth registers of 15,000 parents and all their children. On the basis of this study he came to the conclusion that there was a definite cor-relation, averaging about six to ten percent, between the birth sky of parents and the birth sky of their children. The correlation he obtained was so high, for this large number of cases, that Gauquelin gave the odds against it being a chance effect at 500,000 to 1.[3] Gauquelin claims a further confirmation of the hypothesis in the results of his examination of induced, Caesarian, births. In such cases he should not find the high correlation with the birth skies of the parents; and indeed, he found none.

Gauquelin believes that this planetary heredity effect applies, at the very least, to the professions of scientists, doctors, athletes, actors, soldiers, ministers, play-wrights, politicians, and journalists; that the effect applies to mothers as well as to fathers; to daughters as well as to sons; and that the effect follows definite, well known, genetic laws.

He further has found effects for Venus, Mars, Jupiter, Saturn, and the Moon— the nearest or the largest of the planets. He has found no evidence that Mercury (which is very small) or Uranus, Neptune, or Pluto (which are very far away) exert an influence.

Gauquelin states explicitly that he does not consider his results definitive until other investigators obtain similar results with completely different groups of people. In this attitude he places himself squarely on the side of a commonsense, rational approach. He admits it is an improbable fact that people destined for success in a given profession tend to be born at a particular time. But there is no "planet of the professions" for him; the planets are simply clocks which mark out certain definite time intervals connected, in a still unknown manner, with the Earth's rotation.

Of course, until other investigators independently study such seeming correla-tions between the planetary positions at birth and the later occupations of indi-viduals it is reasonable to assume that there is merely some artifact involved. There are at least two recent, independent investigations which do indicate that planetary influences upon occupation may, indeed, be more than an artifact.

One study, by Joe Cooper and Alan Smithers of Bradford University, analyzed the birth dates of 16,000 officers in the British Army.[4] Of these, 12,000 were culled from the (British) Army List of 1909 and another 4,000 from the 1968 List of Retired Officers. The results of the study showed that as many as 15 percent more officers than expected were born in midsummer and midautumn. The authors concluded that either there had been some situational or environ-mental influence, or that it was a manifestation of an annual endogenous rhythm. Either one of these could conceivably affect personality characteristics.

Another study, by D. A. Windsor in the prestigious British magazine *Nature*, considered the birthdays of two different kinds of biologists—taxonomists and molecular biologists.[5] The birthdays were found for biologists as listed in the Discipline Index of *American Men and Women of Science* (12th Edition). The author found that births of the general population varied only slightly (between a high of 8.8 percent in September and a low of 7.9 percent in December) for all births in the United States in 1934. But among the molecular biologists the range was from a high of 12.3 percent in Aries to lows of 6.8 percent in Taurus and 6.8 percent in Leo. The maximum in birth signs is 80 percent higher than the minima. Yet again, among taxonomists Windsor found a high of 11.1 percent in Cancer and a low of 5.3 percent in Scorpio. The ratio of high to low here is greater than two to one. The total number of taxonomists studied was 342; the number of molecular biologists was 470. None of the peaks in sign of birth for the biologists, of either kind, coincide with the much smaller peaks for the general population.

An analysis of these figures employing standard statistical methods gives the following results if the slight variation of births in the general population is ignored.

Category	Births in sun sign	Number of standard deviations from ex-pected mean value	Odds against this result occurring by pure chance
Taxonomists	Maximum	1.8	32:1
	Minimum	2.0	50:1
Molecular Biologists	Maximum	3.1	1200:1
	Minimum	1.2	9.2:1

In the ultraconservative field of psychic investigation little significance would be attached to odds of 50:1 or less; and there even the odds of 1200:1 against chance would be given only fair, less than good, significance. Still, isn't it an odd fact?

We shall now examine some other odd effects (if that's what they are) of the planets.

SHORT-WAVE COMMUNICATIONS

John H. Nelson worked for many years as a short-wave propagation analyst for RCA Communications. This was in the days before there were artificial satellites, high in the sky and rotating at the same rate as Earth, to act as relay stations for messages back and forth from different parts of the Earth's surface. In those days transatlantic communication was accomplished by bouncing short-wave radio beams off ionized particles high in the air, in the so-called Heaviside layer; and this is still the way such messages are transmitted to and from ships at sea (though this is already changing).

Every so often the short-wave transmission would deteriorate to such an extent that there was no communication. It was well known that *sunspots*, as well as other solar activities, were connected with the emission of high-energy protons which streaked out into space and altered the ionization levels of the Heaviside layer drastically. This alteration made short-wave communication virtually impossible during solar activity. Nelson found an unexpected correlation: the *aspects* of the planets affected the degree of communicability of various short-wave channels.[6] He developed a technique, based on the aspects of various planets, but with respect to the Sun rather than the Earth, for predicting with high accuracy the exact times when various channels would be disrupted by sunspot activity. The empirical rules he developed used multiples of three angles: 15°, 18°, and 22.5°. These are, respectively, a sixth, a fifth, and a quarter of 90°. In a conversation with us he said he had no theory to explain these rules, but he obtains an accuracy of more than 90 percent in his predictions of radio blackouts.

Nelson is merely trying to draw some conclusions from a lifetime of professional communications work. Astrologers woo him avidly, for his results tend to lend some degree of scientific credibility to the beliefs of the ancient Babylonians and Greeks. But John Nelson maintains a definite reserve toward conventional astrology: nothing in his professional work leads him to believe in the validity of horoscopes. To us Nelson may be a pioneer, one who has shown that the gravitational effects of the planets on the Sun *do* produce important physical effects here on Earth. There must be other phenomena, not just the interference of short-wave communication, which are attributable to the effects of the planets on the Sun. (Indeed, in the last section of this chapter we will discuss another one that has recently been reported.) Possibly a new field of science will someday be born, its central theme being the importance of the planetary aspects relative to the Sun. Perhaps what astrology needs is a step from the Ptolemaic view of the Earth as the center of importance to the Copernican view of the Sun as the center.

A GOVERNING MOON

The Moon is responsible for a number of effects on life here on Earth. The biologist H. Casper found that a certain mosquito, *chironomis clunio marinus*, living in the North Sea always went from the larva to the mosquito stage either just after the full moon or just after the new moon.[7] He took the larvae to an aquarium in Bulgaria and tried to modify the time of transformation by making artificial tides at different times, or by lighting the room brightly at different times. But the larvae kept changing to mosquitoes only at the new moon and full moon. How did the larvae know the Moon's rhythm?

The American biologist F. A. Brown studied the change of color of the fiddler crab.[8] This change was in synchronism with the Moon's cycle, even if the crab was in a completely enclosed dark room. Then he studied oysters, whose life rhythm (the frequency of the opening and closing of their valves) was geared to the tides of their normal home in the Long Island Sound and thus to the Moon's cycle there. He then shipped the oysters in sealed containers to Illinois. At first they kept their original rhythm, but within a month or so they had adjusted to the Moon's cycle in Illinois. This rhythm corresponded to what would have been the cycle of sea tides in Illinois if there had been a sea there.

Stories of the Moon's intrigue with lunacy and death are ancient. Arnold Lieber and Carolyn Sherin at the University of Miami School of Medicine tested some of these stories. They reviewed data on all homicides committed both in Dade County, Florida, from 1956 to 1970 and in Cuyahoga County, Ohio, from 1958 to 1970.[9] The results showed that homicides in Dade County were highest at the full and new Moons. (The data from Cuyahoga County, however, showed a smaller lunar influence.) Lieber and Sherin suggest that the Moon's cyclic tidal influence on the body may trigger these effects.

In all three cases it would seem that there must be some mechanism by which some Earth creatures can sense the Moon cycle. The effect, if it exists, must surely be a delicate one. The original scientific work in this area is now a quarter century old, but the lore is ageless. The gestation period for new ideas which have mystical overtones would seem to be a rather long one.

JOURNEY THROUGH SPACE

There is a small extraterrestrial effect that is possibly attributable not to the planets but to the motion of the entire Solar System within our Galaxy! While Earth revolves about the Sun at 18 miles per second, the Sun is moving at 12 miles per second toward the constellation of Hercules, in a direction inclined somewhat to the plane of the Earth's nearly circular trajectory. (The speed of a point on the Earth's surface about the Earth's axis is small—less than 0.3 miles per second.) Since the Sun carries the solar system along with it, the Earth is thus executing a wavering, rather than a simple circular, path in our Galaxy. Professor Giorgio Piccardi, Director of the Institute of Inorganic Chemistry at the University of Florence, Italy, calculated that in March of each year the Earth's motion through the galaxy, axial plus ecliptic, is in the plane of the Earth's equator and its speed has a maximum value—29 miles per second; while in the month of September the motion is more or less perpendicular to this plane, and the speed has a minimum value—14 miles per second.[10]

This motion intrigued Professor Piccardi since, for over ten years, he had studied an effect involving the rate at which an inorganic colloid, oxychloral bismuth, dissolved in water. He had found that the solubility rate was not a constant but, instead, varied from day to day. This solubility rate was affected by solar eruptions, sunspots, and bursts of cosmic rays; the rate varied with the 11-year cycle of the sunspots; and, most significant for him, the solubility rates speeded up each March and, to a lesser extent, each September. He had taken great pains to eliminate all extraneous effects including temperature, pressure, humidity.

Piccardi's hypothesis was, therefore, that cosmic forces from outside our solar system somehow affect the solubility rate of this inorganic colloid in water. But, if this is true of inorganic colloids, why not of organic colloids also? The human body is 80 percent water and it contains many organic colloids; therefore, people should be subjected to these cosmic forces also. Are these forces real?

Again, only independent verification by other experimenters can answer this question. The problem itself is now over a quarter century old, and newer information is just beginning to emerge. Pioneer 8 is now on a journey that will carry it on an ageless trek among the planets. Micrometeorite detectors aboard the spacecraft have begun to detect minute interstellar particles, racing through our Solar System at about 60 miles per second, which come from that direction of Hercules toward which the Sun and its planets hurtle in their motion through the Galaxy.[11]

THE SUN'S INFLUENCE

The direct influence of the Sun on the Earth is both great and obvious. Its gravity holds the Earth in its great orbit. The unending cycle of day and night, summer and winter, both continue as the Sun's radiation bathes a rotating and spinning Earth. The Sun raises ocean and land tides on Earth which are added to the greater Moon tides.

In addition to these obvious effects, however, a wide number of more subtle effects are spawned by the 11-year cycle of solar sunspot activity. Abrupt explosions, hurling gas millions of miles into space, are observed in periods of high sunspot activities. These eruptions strengthen, many times, the continual solar wind that sweeps toward the planets. This strengthened solar wind, still unbelievably tenuous but laced with extremely high energy particles, bombards the Earth's upper atmosphere, thereby producing numerous subtle effects at the Earth's surface. These phenomena are obscure ones, just edging their way into the accepted body of scientific fact.

A summary of reported planetary effects, adapted from Gauquelin, is given in Table 12–5.

TABLE 12–5

A LIST OF PLANETARY INFLUENCES ON THE EARTH. (Partially adapted from M. Gauquelin, *The Scientific Bases of Astrology* [New York: Stein and Day, 1970]. Used with permission.)

A. *Caused by the Sun*

1. The seasons; day and night; the solar tides (smaller than those caused by the Moon).

2. Sensing of the seasons by isolated grains in a controlled atmosphere; of the time of day by shielded hamsters and by chick embryos.

3. Effects correlated with sunspot activity. This activity shows strong, sudden changes and long (11-year and possibly 80–90 year) cycles.

   a) Weather effects—tree rings, fur trapping; vintage wines; locusts; icebergs; the water level of Lake Victoria; tree potentials; mud deposits (back to 2 billion years ago); droughts—22-year cycle (maximum drought conditions now, 1976, approaching).

   b) Diseases—myocardial infarction; cardiovascular diseases; blood-clot for-

TABLE 12–5 (*cont.*)

mation; tuberculosis and respiratory ailments; eclampsia; blood flocculation index; blood components; admissions to mental hospitals; pulmonary hemorrhage.

    c) Economic activity—cycles of stock market activity; of business production; of financial indices; of commodity prices. These suggest periods of 3.5, 9, 18, and 54 years—partially correlating with subperiods of the overall sunspot activity.

    d) Miscellaneous effects—microseismic Earth tremors; the death of sturgeon; migratory pattern of locusts.

4. Seros—the eclipse cycle of the Sun and the Moon, every 18.64 years, correlates with the water level of the Nile River for the past several thousand years.

B. *Caused by the Moon*

  1. Twice-daily effects.

    a) The tides. Peak tides occur twice monthly, when the Moon and the Sun are in conjunction or opposition.

    b) Tidal rhythms of diatoms and crabs.

  2. Bimonthly effects.

    a) Thunderstorms; excess precipitation; atmospheric-pressure blockages; tree potentials; the Earth's magnetic field.

    b) Homicides; antisocial behavior; head-chest potential difference in mental patients.

    c) Tuberculosis; postoperative bleeding; pneumonia; the pH content of the blood.

    d) Egg-laying of sea plants and sea animals; development of insects; coral striping; fireworm swarms; motion of *planaria* and mollusks.

    e) Slight changes in the length of day; lunar earthquakes.

  3. Daily influence.

    a) The Earth's magnetic field.

    b) The activity of potatoes, carrots, algae, salamanders, earthworms, rats, oysters, and hamsters when tested in a completely controlled, isolated environment.

C. *Caused by the planets*

  1. Correlation of the occupations of professional people with planetary positions at the time of birth.

  2. Short-wave radio propagation on Earth; radio waves received by Earth.

  3. Climatic and glacial epochs.

  4. The production of the Sun's 11-year sunspot cycle. (See the next section.)

  5. Variations in the solar wind. This wind of energetic charged particles vastly affects the ionization of our upper atmosphere, and this must greatly affect the lower atmosphere and the Earth's surface; but the latter effects are incompletely known. (See the next section.)

THE REIGNING PLANETS

We have just seen how the Sun extends its influences over earthly events by its sunspot eruptions. A recent scientific investigation has given an unexpected astrological twist to this solar influence upon the Earth. It had previously been thought that sunspots were produced by unknown events deep in the million-mile bowels of the interior of the Sun. Instead, it was recently suggested that they were correlated with the tides raised, by *planetary* gravitation, on the surface of the Sun. It is the planets that seem to control the sunspot activity. If this is true, then the planets may rule the Earth.

Tides arise from the gravitational attraction of one planetary body on another. The tidal force is large for massive bodies that are close, and it is weak for light bodies far away. The mass of the nearby Moon exerts a strong tidal influence on the Earth's surface directly underneath the Moon and, also, an equal tidal influence on the side of the Earth opposite the Moon. The tidal influence acts both on the solid body of the Earth and on the oceans. But the fluid oceans respond more easily to the Moon's influence, raising the two tides that sweep daily across the Earth's face as the Earth revolves under the Moon.

The Sun also exerts a tidal pull on the Earth. Its enormous mass partly counterbalances its remoteness; the solar tidal force is fully 45 percent as strong as the lunar tidal force. While the Moon slowly works its way around the Earth once each month, the lunar tides and the solar tides alternately merge and separate. At the new moon phase (as seen from the Earth), the Moon is in opposition to the Sun. The tides of the Moon and Sun merge, producing two high "spring tides" sweeping across the Earth beneath them. This is true when the Moon and Sun are in conjunction. But at the Moon's first and last quarter the Sun lies at 90°—square—to the Moon. The lunar and solar tides then separate and pull at right angles to each other, leaving only weak "neap tides" on the Earth.

Just as the Sun raises tides on the Earth, so the Earth and all the planets raise tides on the Sun, thereby stressing the Sun's entire mass by their pull. A planet's tidal stress on the Sun depends both on the planet's mass and on its distance from the Sun. Massive Jupiter exerts the strongest tidal pull on the Sun. It is followed closely by Venus, then Mercury, and then the Earth. No other planet exerts a tidal force as large as two percent of the Earth's pull. Mercury's effect had earlier been found in the sunspot data. Recently K. D. Wood at the University of Colorado succeeded in correlating the *sunspot activity* directly to the *planetary tides* on the Sun raised by Jupiter, Venus, and the Earth.[12] The effect of Mercury was neglected because Wood was primarily interested in the long, eleven-year period which came out cf the data while Mercury had only a short, three-month period.

Wood considered the height of the tide on the Sun directly under the planet Jupiter; that is, he chose that spot, P, on the Sun's surface that lay on the line from the Sun's center to Jupiter. The height of the tide at that point would be affected appreciably by any conjunction or opposition of the Earth-Venus axis at that time. If the Earth and Venus were either in conjunction or in opposition relative to the Sun, and if their axis lay along the Sun-Jupiter direction, then the tide at P would be high, like a spring tide. If the Earth-Venus axis was perpendicular to the Sun-Jupiter direction then the tide at P would be much lower, like a neap tide. What Wood considered was the difference in height between one such spring tide at P and the very next neap tide.

Figure 12–5 gives two graphs. The first shows the difference between these two tide heights at P as a function of time from the year 1900 to the year 2000 A.D. Those points between the present time and 2000 are, of course, a forecast; those preceding the present are, however, also based on Wood's equations, not on observation.

The other graph in Fig. 12–5 presents the number of sunspots on the Sun during the twentieth century. Before 1973 this curve is based on observation; from 1973 on it is a forecast. There is a remarkable similarity between these two graphs. A second figure in Wood's article shows a similar correspondence between the two factors (the tide height difference at P and the number of sunspots) for the eighteenth century. One would certainly have to consider a cause-and-effect relationship between these factors as a strong possibility.

Not all investigators are ready to accept Wood's graphs and analysis at face value, however. In a review of *The Jupiter Effect* by J. R. Gribbin and S. L. Plagemann, the following remark on Wood's work is made by the reviewer, William M. Kaula of the Department of Planetary and Space Science at UCLA: "A good example of how a significant correlation can be found if the data are arranged in a sufficiently arcane way."[13] One reason for this verdict is the fact that a direct comparison of *actual* tide height with sunspot number, rather than a *difference* of tide heights, would *not* show the marked similarity of the graphs of Wood. So some further work in this field is necessary.

But Gribbin and Plagemann themselves[14] have no doubts about the planetary influences. In *The Jupiter Effect* they link the planetary tides on the Sun to the sunspots; the sunspots to the Earth's weather; the Earth's weather with the Earth's rotation; and, finally, the Earth's rotation with earthquakes. It turns out that a 179-year cycle exists: once every 179 years the major planets are *all* in one straight line relative to the Sun. The next "grand alignment" will be in 1982. The book asserts that this planetary alignment will set off a chain of events that will, finally, trigger a huge earthquake along the San Andreas fault in California. In that year, the authors state "When the Moon is in the Seventh house, and Jupiter is aligned with Mars and with the other seven planets of the Solar System, Los Angeles will be destroyed."[15]

Criticism of the Jupiter effect, so called because Jupiter makes the largest contribution to the tides on the Sun, centers on a number of areas. First, the tidal influence on the Sun of the other planets—those besides Mercury, Earth, Venus, and Jupiter—is negligible. Mars is too small, Saturn, Uranus, and Neptune are too far away; and Pluto is both. So the "grand alignment" has a tidal effect which is not much larger than other, more common, alignments.

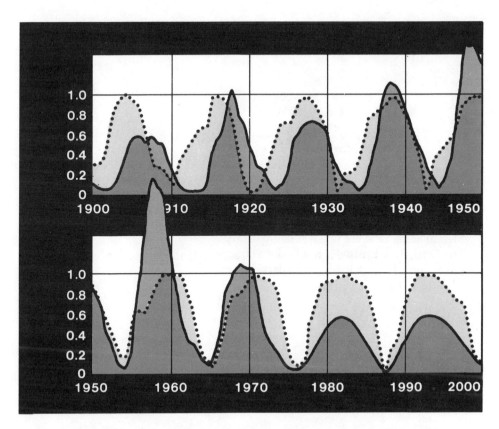

Fig. 12–5. Planetary tides on the Sun and the number of sunspots. This solid curve gives the observed sunspot activity from 1900 to date, plus Wood's estimate to the year 2000. The dotted curve gives the difference in the height of a spring tide and the next neap tide at a point on the Sun's surface directly under Jupiter. The positions of the peaks and valleys agree well, but the discrepancy in heights argues for other effects besides those mentioned by Woods. (Figure adapted, by permission, from K. D. Woods, "Sunspots and Planets," *Nature*, November 10, 1972, p. 91.)

Second, the linkage of the sunspot activity first to the Earth's rotation and then to major earthquakes is very nebulous. There does happen to be a correlation with small earth tremors—microseismic tremors.

Finally, and this is a very telling argument, the last "grand alignment" occured in 1803. No evidence of any increased seismic activity on Earth in 1803 can be found. Why not, unless the Jupiter effect is rather insignificant?

The last word on these subjects has, obviously, not been written. But such arguments are both common and healthy, though they prompt conflicting thoughts concerning the stars and our destiny. The immortal William Shakespeare expressed his own confusion:

From *King Lear:*
Act 4
Scene 3

It is the stars, the stars above us govern our conditions.

From *Julius Caesar:*
Act 1
Scene 2

Men at some time are masters of their fates.
The fault, dear Brutus, is not in our stars,
But in ourselves, that we are underlings.

CHAPTER THIRTEEN
WONDERLAND

- Mae West's Aphorism
- P.A.M. Dirac's Unseen Sea
- Albert Einstein and Time Dilation ▪ Einstein's Twins
- Isaac Newton and Action at a Distance
- Heisenberg's Uncertainty ▪ de Broglie's Waves
- Schrödinger's Cat ▪ Niels Bohr's Complementarity
- Everett's Many Worlds ▪ Schwarzschild's Holes
- Our End

MAE WEST'S APHORISM

In this, our final chapter, we discuss several scientific ideas which are very far removed from common sense. These ideas are universally accepted as valid by the scientific community. But, judged by the standards of the average person, they really sound crazy. Physicists, however, have long recognized that common sense is a very poor guide in the uncommon areas of knowledge they treat. What is needed there is uncommon sense.

The average person has never heard of the way-out ideas we will treat here. We think some may find them as hard to accept as many of the topics we have discussed earlier, in our other chapters. That is one of our reasons for discussing these strange scientific topics. But we have another reason in mind, also. We hope there will be some scientists, engineers, and mathematicians who will read this book, trained technical people who will completely understand the topics we deal with here. When such a person reads this chapter we hope he or she will perceive how shockingly absurd these ideas will probably seem to a layman. If such a trained professional can appreciate how bizarre, how implausible, how ridiculous such ideas must seem to an outsider, dare we hope that he or she may, possibly, draw an analogy and pause before applying the same adjectives to all of the phenomena we have discussed earlier in this book?

Our thoughts are captured by a small aphorism which we have adapted from a most unlikely, but very commonsense, source: Mae West. Her comment: "When I'm good I'm very, very good. But when I'm bad, I'm better."

P.A.M. DIRAC'S UNSEEN SEA

For our first example of a long-standing, yet completely wild scientific idea we consider the theory that underlies the positron. The positron is the antiparticle, or mate, of the electron. Whereas the electron has a negative electric charge, the positron has the same amount of positive electric charge. Both the electron and the positron have the same amount of mass. (The positron is not to be confused with the proton, which is 1840 times as massive; although it, too, has the same amount of electric charge.)

Now, electrons and protons have been known for a long time. Together with a third kind of particle, the neutron, they are the building blocks of which all atoms are made. So molecules, and thus, all matter we know, is constructed of electrons, protons, and neutrons. Some questions arise: Where are the positrons hiding? Why weren't positrons discovered until Carl Anderson found them in 1932, long after the discovery of the electron? Do we ever see traces of these elusive positrons?

Electrons and positrons are fiery mates, for should an electron meet a positron then the two would annihilate each other, and both would disappear completely. They leave, in their wake, only bits of electromagnetic energy, called photons, which travel off as waves. On the other hand, sometimes electromagnetic energy becomes converted into two particles going off in opposite directions—one electron and one positron. Neither the electron nor its positron mate had existed previous to the conversion. These two bits of matter were created out of pure energy. This process is called pair production. Electrons and positrons would survive indefinitely, but only so long as one did not encounter the other. If they should do so, the electron and the positron would annihilate each other and a burst of energy, photons, would mark their demise.

We turn to P.A.M. Dirac, an English theoretical physicist who may very well be the outstanding physicist living today. In 1928 Dirac proposed a weird theory designed to explain the electron.[1] His theory seemed to suggest that all matter is immersed in—is permeated with, completely surrounded by—a sea of uncharged, but negative energy, particles. This sea of particles was given no name, for *these particles were assumed to be unobservable.* Unseeable, untouchable, unmeasurable. Like a fish is unaware of water, like a baby is unaware of air, so are we completely unaware of this sea of negative energy particles that, according to Dirac, fills all of "empty" space and all of occupied space, too.

Sometimes a photon of light can, in a collision, impart its electromagnetic energy to one such unobservable particle. That electrically neutral particle, with a negative energy, then gobbles the photon up and acquires the photon's energy. It becomes a particle—one with negative charge but positive energy, an *electron*. The photon disappears. The place in the sea of unobservable neutral particles that was previously occupied has now become unoccupied. A bubble has been produced in the sea. And Dirac suggested that this hole was an observable particle, the *positron*. This particle, the paired twin of the electron, has a positive charge—zero minus a negative equals a positive. Four years after Dirac proposed his theory the positron was found, experimentally. The creation of mass from energy was explained, here, as the liberation of matter from an unknowable state to two recognizable states.

Positron annihilation is similarly explained. The positron is, as we say, a hole in the otherwise unobservable sea of uncharged particles. If an electron, a particle with negative charge but positive energy, comes along near such a hole then the electron simply flops down into the hole. The positive energy particle becomes a negative energy particle, the difference in energy going off as photons. The electron disappears in a flash of energy. The hole in the sea of unobservable particles, the bubble, is filled. The positively charged positron is annihilated.

This Dirac theory of the positron is now quite ancient. There are, of course, many details which we have omitted. Suffice it to say that the theory has passed the test of time. It has become part of the accepted body of knowledge called physics. To accept it, all one has to believe is that we, all of us, all the time, everywhere, are completely immersed in a sea of undetectable particles that fills empty space to the brim. This sea must remain, forever, completely foreign to all our senses and instruments. Our only awareness of its existence is limited to those rare, occasional bubbles of emptiness which make the surrounding sea perceptible.

Now, if one can accept that, is it so much more difficult to accept the mere possibility of the power of a witch to cast a spell? Of course, we await the Dirac and Anderson of witchcraft. But can we, already, rule out the possibility of its existence?

ALBERT EINSTEIN AND TIME DILATION

Our earlier chapter on UFOs mentioned an effect which has long held great appeal for those interested in interstellar travel. According to this effect, part and parcel of the theory of special relativity which sprang from the fertile brain of Albert Einstein in 1905, time does not run at the same rate for all observers.[2] For every year spent on a spacecraft streaking toward some distant star there is more than a year that elapses for the people left back on Earth. Just how much more than a year goes by on Earth depends on how fast the spacecraft is going. The effect is negligibly small except if the spacecraft speed is close to the speed of light in vacuum—almost 670 million miles per hour.

To see why this effect is not noticed in our everyday life we note that even if the spacecraft were going at 10 percent of the speed of light, an incredible 67 million miles per hour, then one year on the spacecraft would correspond to 1.005 years on Earth. If the speed were 90 percent that of light, or 600 million miles per hour, then the spacecraft year would correspond to 2.3 years on Earth. But for 99 percent the speed of light, 7 years would elapse on Earth for each year on the spaceship. And if the speed were even higher, and closer yet to the speed of light, then any count of years on Earth would pass during one year in flight.

Of course, this effect is only fool's gold for interstellar travel. For the energies required to attain such high speeds are simply too large to be realistic, at least for vehicular-sized masses. But that is not the point we wish to stress here. The point is: *time does not run at the same rate for all persons.* That is a fantastically noncommonsense idea, one foreign to all our experience. We are speaking about biological, not psychologically perceived, time: the rate at which cells are born, live, and die, for example; or the rate at which the hands of a clock revolve. Time dilation, as the effect is known, is an occult idea which was eventually proven to be true experimentally, using subatomic particles as the test objects.

Incidentally, if any reader has been led to think that time always runs more slowly on the moving vehicle, it should be pointed out that the effect is also true in the reverse sense. The spacecraft is quite justified in saying the Earth is moving away from it at a constant speed. If that speed is thus 67 million miles per hour, then one year on Earth would correspond to 1.005 years on the spacecraft. In other words, as long as the spacecraft keeps going away with a constant speed and does not reverse its direction to return, then, on the one hand, one year on the spacecraft corresponds to more than one year on Earth; but, on the other hand, one year on Earth corresponds to more than one year on the spacecraft.

That seems contradictory, does it not? Yet, as long as the distance between Earth and the spacecraft keeps increasing at a uniform rate, a check can only be made by communication. And it would be found that both viewpoints are correct. The effect is a relative one, seemingly more illusory than real. But there are circumstances when the illusion changes to a stark reality. This enigmatic, believe-it-or-not phenomenon is known as Einstein's twin paradox.

EINSTEIN'S TWINS

Suppose that, in the previous example of time dilation the spaceship stops its outward journey, turns about, and heads back for home. When the spaceship finally returns, the crew could greet their friends and families, long left on Earth, scan their faces, compare the ship's calendar with that on Earth and learn for certain how their time rates compared. How will the calendars and faces compare?

In this case the journeys are not symmetrical; only the spacecraft turns about in space. On landing, a strange meeting unfolds. Suppose, for example, that we originally had a pair of twins on Earth, and that a spaceship departed with one twin on their 20th birthday.[3] If the ship went at a constant velocity of 96 percent of the speed of light toward Alpha Centauri until the ship twin's 25th birthday, then turned around and headed back toward Earth at the same speed, it is clear the ship twin would arrive home on his 30th birthday. Strangely enough, the day the spaceship docked would be well past the Earth twin's 55th birthday. There would no longer be a symmetrical effect. *The two siblings, formerly twins, are no longer twins.*[4]

This justly famous "paradox of the twins" is quite distinct from time dilation, though related to it. How can people accept with equanimity such an outrageous result as the statement that two siblings, born twins, can yet grow to differ in age?

The paradox of the twins can be couched in other terms which bear still a different strange message. Let a record be made of the spaceship's journey on a so-called space-time diagram. The record will consist of two straight lines, one giving an account of the outward trip, and the other an account of the inward trip. The start of the first line would be the take-off event; the end of the second line would be the home-coming event. One could go along these two lines to determine the separation between the start and finish. This would not be called a distance because in this diagram it does not depend on length alone, but also on time. Here the separation between any two events is called the interval between them; and the interval is very closely related to the time that it took to traverse the path of the two lines, the time as measured by the spacecraft.

Thus, the two lines on the space-time diagram would yield the proper time of the spaceship's journey, as measured by the spaceship. Suppose, then, we now drew a third line on the space-time diagram between start and finish—a straight line, completing the triangle. That gives a record of the Earth from start to finish of the spaceship's journey. We can now find the separation between the start and finish along *that* straight line; and, from that, the proper time of the Earth for the trip's duration, as measured on Earth.

What do we find? The interval along the straight line corresponds to an Earth proper time of 35.7 years; so the twin remaining on Earth is 55.7 years old. But the interval along the other two lines corresponds to a spaceship-proper time of 10 years, so the space twin is 30 years old. In fact, for any triangle on a space-time diagram *the interval along any side of a triangle is greater than that along the other two sides.* A straight line on such a diagram is *not* the shortest distance between two points; a straight line is the *largest* interval between those two points. On such a diagram a straight line gives the *longest* proper time between two events.

The human mind boggles at accepting such statements. Most people do so only because we trust the people who make them. Should we not extend the same trust to experimenters who, having tested psychics under rigorous conditions, say psychics have strange abilities to reproduce unseen drawings?

ISAAC NEWTON AND ACTION AT A DISTANCE

Isaac Newton is probably the outstanding physicist of all time. He invented the calculus; showed that white light consists of components of all the colors of the rainbow; discovered the optical effect now known as Newton's rings; formulated the three laws which serve as the basis for classical mechanics; first proposed the now very widely used Newtonian telescope; and made numerous other discoveries of a scientific nature. The one we are concerned with here is his universal law of gravitation.

Newton intended this law to explain the motion of the planets of the Solar System. Using it, we are able to predict planetary motion with an accuracy that is phenomenal. And yet, as an intrinsic part of this law Newton proposed something that was absolutely unprecedented, completely nonunderstandable. He proposed that any mass exerted a force on any other mass, no matter how separated they were and regardless of whether there was any intervening medium. And this force was to be considered as acting instantaneously.

Up until then the nature of a force was clearly connected with a physical juxtaposition of two objects. The force exerted by a horse's hooves on the ground only came into action when there was intimate contact between a hoof and the ground. When they were separated the force could not be exerted. To pull a tree stump out of the ground an individual had to exert a force on it by physically pulling on it. Force was connected with contact.

What Newton proposed was that *a force could act* at a distance, *with no contact between any bodies.* How? Newton proposed no method, because he knew of none. It defied common sense but it worked. Newton's terrific prestige carried the day, and his theory became so accepted that schoolboys who learn about action at a distance today do not even realize what a nonsensical idea it really is. It is truly preposterous.

Newton's idea of action at a distance has been displaced, today, by James C. Maxwell's idea of a field, emanating from a body, that pervades all space—even a vacuum. It is a field, be it electric, magnetic, gravitational, or nuclear, that is then assumed to exert the force on another body when that one is introduced near the first one. Iron filings, hanging from a magnet, can map this magnetic field right before our eyes. But: how does the gravitational field act? It is as big a mystery as Newton's theory. Scientists think there may be particles, called gravitons, emanating from any mass and spreading out as a wave to form the field. Gravitational attraction would then be due to the interchange of gravitons between masses, and scientists are now looking for gravitational waves. Action at a distance or gravitational waves: strange ideas at the dark edge of knowledge.

HEISENBERG'S UNCERTAINTY

One of the two really big developments in twentieth-century physics is *quantum mechanics;* the other is *relativity,* in both the *special* version of 1905 and the *general* variety which is only just now becoming important. While relativity was the work of one man, quantum mechanics was developed, in the late 1920s, by a host of men of whom Werner Heisenberg was an outstanding member. And it was he who first lay down a principle which is an integral part of quantum mechanics, one which is variously called the uncertainty principle or the indeterminancy principle.[5]

According to this principle of modern physics, *not everything in nature is knowable;* there are limits to the preciseness with which one can determine certain quantities. One can determine a particle's energy to any degree of preciseness that one wishes; but the more exact our knowledge of its energy becomes then the less exact becomes our knowledge of the time when the particle has that energy. Energy and time are complementary factors, and we only obtain preciseness in the knowledge of one at the expense of knowledge of the other. Thus, light is a vibration in "empty" space and its color gives it energy. The better known its energy, the more pure its color. However, if we try to grab a ray of red light within one cycle of vibration (in order to time it precisely), the red color (its energy) will spread out and turn to white. The better we time it, the fuzzier the color becomes. The position and the momentum of a particle constitutes another such pair of complementary factors.

In accepting such a premise one has to surrender, in part, the connection of cause to effect. It is impossible to predict precisely the future trajectory of a particle after a collision if we cannot know its position and momentum accurately. And so Einstein, for example, never accepted quantum mechanics as complete. It was too occult for him. The idea that there were unknowable things in nature was foreign to his way of thought.

Surely the uncertainty principle is a very radical idea; no amount of money, insight, or effort suffices to penetrate a veil that nature has hung over her private, most intimate affairs. And this in such a materialistic age, in such a rational science.

de BROGLIE'S WAVES

One of the shibboleths of our commonsense understanding of nature is that no more than one body can occupy a given space at a given time. Quantum mechanics is in violent disagreement with this.

According to quantum mechanics any bit of matter is described by a wave. The electron is a wave in Dirac's unseen sea. The smaller bits of matter, such as atoms or nuclei, are dominated by these waves; they spread throughout a broad space. So, if there are two electrons present in an atom, there are waves for each electron spread throughout the atom. The two individual electrons may interfere markedly with each other in such a manner that one is forced to conclude that the *two bodies do occupy the same space at the same time.*

How do we reconcile this violent affront to our common sense with our everyday observation to the contrary? It turns out that our classical, everyday understanding of nature is but a limiting case, an extreme condition, of the broad reach of nature whose furthest edge is far beyond our sight. Associated with the wave is a wave function, termed psi, that gives the probability of finding a bit of matter at a given time and place. When bodies are of atomic size and mass then their waves are spread out over regions of space that are not localized close to the bodies; but when the bodies are of ordinary size the waves become sharply localized near the bodies. One can then speak of distinct bodies and say, "Two bodies cannot occupy the same space at the same time."

Louis de Broglie first proposed that electrons can sometimes behave as waves— matter waves similar to light waves.[6] Just below we give an example where this is brought out sharply. Electrons and light waves thus form a symmetrical pair of concepts; for Max Planck and Albert Einstein showed that light waves sometimes possessed particle properties. They called such light particles photons—the photons we have already met—while scientists commonly refer to the lightest charged matter waves as electrons.

Let us consider a beam of electrons which is directed at an opaque screen having one small hole in it. Any electrons going through the hole then proceed to a distant photographic plate, where they leave a record of their distribution on the screen. It is found that the electrons do not form a sharply delineated image of the hole; the image is not only bright in the center, with a sharp edge and a dark shadow outside. Just as with careful experiments with light, the image is found to form a diffraction pattern. The image is very widely spread out—the smaller the hole, the wider the spreading. The image on the screen is brightest in the center, dims to extinction at some distance from the center; then brightens a bit again further out; and so forth.

We accept this as showing that electrons, which we normally think of as particles, can behave as waves. The two concepts—waves and particles—are totally complementary; for particles are normally considered to be localized in space, while waves have to be considered as spread out through regions which cannot be sharply delineated. Here we see that electrons can sometimes be particles, sometimes waves—an occult idea if there ever was one. But the paradox can be made much stronger.

Let us close the hole we had in the otherwise opaque screen above and instead open another, similar, hole close by. Then, not surprisingly, the image on the photographic plate will be similar to the first one, only shifted a bit.

Now suppose we open both holes to the beam of electrons. Is the image of the electrons on the distant screen the sum of the two separate, individual images— that from the first hole plus that from the second hole? It is not. A series of wiggles makes itself apparent on the pattern. The new variations in the density of developed silver in the photographic screen give a typical interference pattern, shown also by light waves. Paradoxically, the silver atoms which are developed on the plate do so as *specks*, showing that they were hit by small *particles*; but the overall pattern with fine *shading* is typical of what it should be if the electrons were large *waves*.

Just to make the situation even stranger, let the intensity of the incoming electron beam be reduced by a very large factor—such a large factor that on the average only one electron per hour comes to the opaque screen with the two small holes. Then, of course, we will have to perform the experiment for a much longer time to develop a noticeable blackening on the photographic plate. One electron will reach the plate somewhere and cause a silver atom of that plate to reveal itself as darkened when the plate is finally developed. But it will be, on the average, another hour before a second electron comes along to darken another silver atom somewhere. Do we expect any interaction between these two electrons? Any correlation in their effects? Common sense tells us we do not. One effect is long over and done with before the second one occurs.

What do we find experimentally? We find the same interference pattern on the photographic plate that would occur if millions of electrons each second poured through the two holes. How can electrons interfere if they are an hour apart? How can two waves interfere if one wave is gone by the time the other arrives? We must conclude that *the single electron particle*, small enough to be trapped by minute silver atoms, *has interfered with itself as a wave*, wide enough to cover both holes. The paradox of matter small enough to fit an atom yet wide enough to fill all space still puzzles science deeply. And the paradox does not stop here.

SCHRÖDINGER'S CAT

The wave function of quantum mechanics is connected, as we mentioned in the previous section, with the probability of finding a particle at a given place at some time. Very roughly, the greater the wave function at a point the greater the probability of finding the particle there in any measurement. Erwin Schrödinger first found an equation the wave must satisfy, and this is the starting point of most treatments of quantum problems. If we know the wave at any one time then the solution of Schrödinger's equation gives us exact knowledge of the wave at each later instant. The equation gives us a continuous, deterministic change of state, with time, of the system under consideration.

Now, nature allows only certain waves or states to fit Schrödinger's equation. These unique states are, technically, called the eigenstates. If we start with a system that is definitely known to be in one eigenstate, then the Schrödinger equation tells us that at the end of a certain time the system will be in a predictable mixture of such states.

Schrödinger's equation takes us continuously from a wave for one specific state (at the start), to a wave that is a mixture of states (at the end). Any quantity, such as the energy, has a unique value in each state; and nature may allow for an atom only certain energies: $E_1, E_2, E_3, \ldots$. Let us start with an atom initially of energy, E_1; and let the wave develop its mixture according to Schrödinger and his equation. As long as no attempt at measurement of the final energy is made, the energy does not have any *one* of these values, uniquely. Rather, as long as no attempt is made to measure the energy then it is a sum, each term of the sum being one of its possible values multiplied by the probability, p, that the wave will be in a state corresponding to that value of the energy: $p_1E_1 + p_2E_2 + p_3E_3 + \ldots$

What happens should one attempt to verify this experimentally? According to the standard, so-called Copenhagen, interpretation, as soon as any attempt is made—no matter how subtle, sneaky, or sophisticated—to measure the energy, then a very peculiar occult phenomenon occurs. An immediate, discontinuous change is brought about in the wave state of the system, reducing the wave from its mixture of states to just one of the states. A probable value can be calculated for which state will turn up as victor; but, in a single test, sometimes one state survives and sometimes another.

Schrödinger, who was responsible for the equation that lay at the basis of this so-called reduction of the wave function, was most unhappy with this interpretation. He invented an example to show that the reduction of the wave function was a *reductio ad absurdum*.[7] Consider, he said, a cat in a box. See Fig. 13–1. Let there also be a glass flask filled with a deadly poison, prussic acid, in the box. And over the flask let there be a hammer, poised to strike and break the flask upon receipt of a suitable trigger. Such a trigger would be provided by a Geiger counter, activated by a nearby speck of radioactive material.

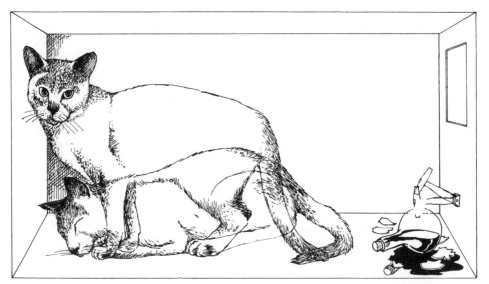

Fig. 13–1. The ghostly quantum cat. An hour has passed, and the hammer, triggered by radioactivity, now has a fifty-fifty chance that it has struck the flask of prussic acid. Schrodinger taunts the cat, and us, by pointing out that conventional quantum physics now deems the cat to be half dead and half alive. But the slightest peek through the window instantaneously ends this schizophrenia: half the time in the cat's favor, half the time in favor of his ghost. (Figure adapted, by permission, from Bryce S. DeWitt, "Quantum Mechanics and Reality," *Physics Today*, September 1970, p. 32. © American Institute of Physics.)

Arrange things such that the speck of radioactive material has a 50–50 chance of emitting one gamma ray in one hour. Starting with one live cat, then, we will have one live cat at the end of the hour if the gamma ray was not emitted by the radioactive material; while, if it did emit the gamma ray, we will have one very dead cat at the end of the hour.

How does the conventional Copenhagen interpretation of quantum mechanics describe this case? We start with a wave function corresponding to a live cat. There are two states for the wave function at the end of the hour: one state for a live cat and one state for a dead one. The probability for each state is ½. The wave function describing the cat at the end of the hour, but *before* any attempt at *observation* has been made, puts the cat into a schizoid state which is *half alive and half dead*. That is the Copenhagen interpretation, associated with the home of that most esteemed developer of quantum mechanics, Niels Bohr.

We're not done yet, however, with Schrödinger's half-dead cat. What happens if we attempt to learn if the cat is really dead or really alive? *As soon as* we open the door, or even if we merely *look* through the glass in the door, *the wave function magically* (and instantaneously) *collapses:* from half dead-half alive to either all dead or to all alive. If a test were made on 1,000 stray cats—we are describing the theory, not advocating the practice—then we would know that the test would leave us almost 500 live cats, the remainder joining their ancestors.

Well, that's the story. Any working quantum physicist uses this Copenhagen viewpoint. It leads to right answers. The reader can muse, with the physicist, the sense it makes as we explore ways out of the paradoxes posed by quantum mechanics. It looks very much like a mixed state: half sense-half nonsense.

NIELS BOHR'S COMPLEMENTARITY

The Copenhagen interpretation of quantum mechanics is based on the strange idea that a particle is not only a particle;[8] sometimes it acts like a wave. Further, a wave is not only a wave: sometimes a wave acts like a particle. There is no rhyme or reason which explains, in advance, which of these two radically different views to adopt for a given type of experiment. One has to try both of these two complementary aspects and see which one fits the particular experimental facts better. The one that fits is then the right one. This view of two coexisting, but opposite, sides of nature is called complementarity.

Consider the following imagined experiment. Suppose a lone light source is established on a planet of a distant star. Matters are so arranged that the source emits a single pulse of a light wave and this wave is emitted equally in all directions. We know the source emits a wave, not particles, because previous interference experiments have shown this to be so. Further, let the energy of the light wave that the source shakes off in its pulse be very, very small—so small that it corresponds to the energy of only one photon.

This emitted light pulse now spreads out uniformly, as a spherical wave, at the enormous speed of light in vacuum. At the end of one year the wave will have reached a distance of nearly 6 trillion miles from the source. And the minute energy of one photon, which was originally concentrated at the source, will then have become spread out uniformly over the surface of a sphere with the huge radius of one light-year. In any small region on this sphere the energy of the light pulse will be incredibly small. Certainly it would be too small to trigger off a light detector which required the energy of one photon to activate it.

Suppose, nevertheless, we have arranged a fantastically huge number of individual light detectors side by side along the surface of the sphere completely covering it. All the detectors are at a distance of 6 trillion miles from the source and, since they are equally spaced in all directions, some of them are twice that distance from each other. Let each detector require an energy of at least one photon to activate it. What happens when the emitted light wave hits the line-up of anticipatory detectors?

A strange thing happens, according to the view of complementarity. The energy in the wave front collapses, instantaneously, from everywhere on this huge surface, into one whole photon at one particular detector, and there triggers it off. The wave has suddenly collapsed to a particle, triggering only one counter. All the others, of the huge multitude of detectors, stay unactivated. Of the myriad of photon counters only one is picked out. Which one? No one can say in advance—it is all a matter of chance. With one wave some particular detector is selected. With each successive pulse some other detector is chosen (though it could be, most unlikely, the same one). For a large number of pulses the distribution of the triggered counters would tend to be spread out uniformly on all parts of the sphere.

The light wave travels out uniformly in all directions, yet only one counter is triggered. By one photon. Was the photon everywhere? Or did it exist only along one trajectory? One point? According to complementarity the answer is that the light was both a wave and a particle, first one, then the other. But this poses a serious dilemma. Since the collapse of the wavefront was instantaneous, the energy must have been collected with infinite speed. Certainly the speed must have been greater than that of light. How is this reconciled with relativity? Could strange faster-than-light particles, tachyons, rush out at infinite speed from the one activated counter to signal the other counters instantaneously—as far as two light-years away—not to turn on? Nobody knows.

Light photons are not the only entities which exhibit this paradoxical behavior of being, at the same time, both in one place and everywhere. All other particles behave this way also—electrons, protons, neutrons, their antiparticles, and so forth. But is not this behavior reminiscent of the diffuse, yet precise, property of Psi which we discussed in connection with psychic phenomena? Recall that Hubert Pearce was quite capable of guessing one precise target card that was surrounded by all sorts of other printed materials in the Duke University Library —other cards, books, magazines. Are we, then, to accept paradoxical behavior for familiar "particles," but not accept it for the unfamiliar entities of Psi?

EVERETT'S MANY WORLDS

In an attempt to eliminate the paradoxes inherent in the Copenhagen viewpoint of the way nature works, a number of different suggestions have been made. A Nobel prize winner, Eugene P. Wigner, has proposed that the Schrödinger wave function is strictly deterministic in its behavior at *all* times.[9] It varies in a smooth, continuous fashion—always satisfying Schrödinger's linear equation. When, however, any attempt at measurement is made—whether by a direct observation, or by the reading of an instrument pointer, or by a subsequent deciphering of a record on tape—then a discontinuous change occurs, one that is due to the interaction between the *consciousness* of the observer and the system being monitored. If, for example, the measurement had been recorded on tape then everything would change smoothly, even during the recording process, *until a person* started to read the tape. Then, and only then, does a discontinuous process occur—the wave function describing the experiment suddenly collapses to exactly one of its possible values.

We wish to emphasize that this interpretation was proposed by a sane physicist. Wigner thinks that the consciousness exerts some kind of effect on nature, as described by the Schrödinger equation, making nature respond to the consciousness. He has proposed that a search be made to determine the effects of consciousness on matter. Could he have sensed this very book you are now reading before it was written?

Wigner's view is not too unusual for a theoretical physicist; it actually seems conservative in comparison to the attempt made by another physicist to eliminate the dilemmas in the Copenhagen interpretation of the measurement process. This more radical proposal was first made by a student, Hugh Everett, III, writing his Ph.D. thesis under the supervision of the famous physicist John A. Wheeler. Everett not only passed his tests on his dissertation, and thus obtained his degree, but he also attracted so much attention for his views that a book has appeared containing a number of papers, by himself and other physicists, investigating his thesis.[10]

Everett assumed that *our universe was not unique*. There exist a vast number of complete worlds, all existing simultaneously, all unknown to each other. When a measurement is made in our world it leads, without collapse, to just one result. But in another world it leads, with no wave collapse in that universe, to a different unique result. And so forth, in each world. There are as many worlds as there are states mixed together to make up the wave function. This mixture of states does not apply to our world but to all the simultaneous worlds. In our world only one state exists in the wave function. The wave function, obeying Schrödinger's mathematics, describes not our world but a vast world of *multiple universes*.

Everett's ideas are completely self-consistent. It is entirely possible that Everett's apparently outrageous idea could become the generally accepted version of the way nature works. Nevertheless, this basically simple idea is as weird, as crazy, as way-out, as bizarre as anything we have discussed earlier in this book. Physicists are very broad-minded—about physics.

Everett's approach was the opposite to Wigner's. The observer was to play no active role, whatever, in any measuring process. Whatever happened was quite independent of whether anyone was watching. There is a wave function that describes a system, and it *always* obeys Schrödinger's equation. So it always varies continuously, and in a deterministic manner. Probability just does not enter the picture here—not yet. There are no discontinuous changes in this wave function, ever. There is no collapse of any wave function—either from a sphere, a light year in size, to one photon counter; or from a phantom cat, half dead and half alive, to one all dead or all alive.

The basic problem to be solved is that of the sudden collapse of the wave function from a mixture of all possible choices to just one particular one. Bohr's Copenhagen viewpoint is that it is all essentially a philosophical matter; that we can't really understand it, but that that's not so important. What is important is that it works. Perhaps. But then this is not so much a philosophical view as an engineering one. Wigner's viewpoint differs from this. To him the sudden collapse of the wave function is a problem in psychology. Or, more likely, parapsychology. But to Everett (and also to Wheeler, DeWitt, Cooper, and others) the problem of the collapse is a problem in pure physics, and one which has an elegant solution: there is no collapse of the wave function.

Suppose we give an example of Everett's many worlds. Let us return to the myriad photon counters spaced on a sphere of radius one light-year. In our universe just one counter would trigger. According to Everett the wave function in our universe for that experiment would not be a mixture of states but would only consist of one state, that of our world, corresponding to the photon arriving at the one counter in our world which it turns on. In our world there would be no collapse because there would be nothing to collapse: the wave function only has one state, that of the particular counter that was triggered in our world.

But, and this is a very big but, in another world sitting right on top of ours at the very same time, but completely unknown to us, it was the next counter to the left that was triggered—not the one that triggered in our case. And in still another universe still a different photon counter was triggered—uniquely and deterministically. And so forth. We could think of the mixture of terms in the wave function (for all the worlds) sorting out just one term for our world in this particular measurement; a different term for another world; and so forth.

This splitting of the universal wave function takes place at each and every measurement. So the number of worlds, each an almost duplicate of another, keeps growing continuously as other worlds keep branching off with each new measurement. In practicality a measurement may be taken to be an occurrence, any occurrence. So the number of independent worlds is unbelievably large; there are googles and googles of them. And they are, all of them, completely unaware of each others' existence.

Now, of course, this last viewpoint has to supply a different meaning for a probabilistic basis in the standard version of quantum mechanics. That probability was not an integral part of the Schrödinger equation but was an additional assumption needed to yield agreement with nature. In some manner the wave function of Schrödinger's mathematics *knows* the behavior of all the multiple universes. When an event happens in our world the process proceeds in a deterministic fashion to its end and there will be no discontinuous collapse of any wave function in our world. The probability yielded by the wave function is then only a measure of the different numbers of worlds on which a specific result —a live cat, say—is obtained. It is all explained in a logical, self-consistent manner. In our world probability does not play any crucial role; everything is deterministic. It is only if we wish to compare our results with those obtained in the collection of all possible worlds that it becomes necessary to introduce the concept of probability; and of an all-knowing wave that determines that probability.

The many-worlds theory explains everything that the Copenhagen interpretation explains, as well as some other things. Suppose, for example, we have observer A carrying out a test on Schrödinger's cat and initiating a collapse of his wave function when he looks in and sees the cat dead. Now suppose observer B is carrying out a test that checks A, as A performs his experiment. Then for B everything is continuous until B actually looks at the results; even though A says that something discontinuous happened when *he* checked the cat and found the cat dead. Which one is right? And if B should introduce the discontinuity by looking at A's results, so that they now both have a discontinuity, can they be sure this is valid? Maybe an observer C is watching them, and she will only make the collapse of the wave function valid when *she* chooses to examine the results. All of this is a serious problem in the Copenhagen interpretation but not in the many-worlds interpretation of quantum theory.

To sum up. Dirac's positron theory had us all immersed in one invisible sea of undetectable particles; but Everett has us submerged in a vast number, a fantastic number, of *undetectable worlds*. In some world you have already finished this chapter and set the book down; while in still another you have not taken it up to start the first chapter. And that is just 2 out of 10^{100+} worlds; and the number keeps growing.

Now, if we can entertain such an idea, should we not be open to the suggestion that there might be some lonely, gifted people—psychics—who can somehow bridge the gap between two such separate worlds, using the same aspect of nature that allows an all-knowing wave function to bridge the gaps between these googles of worlds? Perhaps other "nearby" worlds are not absolutely and completely unknowable to all of us. Should their present lie close to our future, then precognition is no longer such a shocking idea. Is a prophetic dream more a glimpse of the present in a "close by" universe? Then the mother in Chapter 4, who moves her child to avoid its harm from the falling chandelier seen in her dream, does not really change the future—it has not yet occurred. Unfortunately, in this view, she does not alter another's tragic present in the separate multiple world seen through her dream. So if we can contemplate multiple universes calmly, precognition hardly seems worth a stir.

SCHWARZSCHILD'S HOLES

What is space? Until 1916 a typical answer might have been that space was what was left, in a box attached to a vacuum pump, after the pump had removed all the matter in the box; space was the vacuum that was left when there was no matter.

The idea of an electromagnetic wave with its vibrating electrical and magnetic fields propagating through a vacuum—a region devoid not only of matter, but also of properties—made the late-nineteenth-century scientific world feel uneasy about the nature of space. It took Albert Einstein, with his view that *empty space possessed distinct geometric properties,* to change, forever, our concept of space. In 1916 in his theory of *general* relativity Einstein formulated equations that described how the presence of matter warped the nature of the "empty" space in its vicinity. It was this warping of space, he said, that affected the trajectories of other nearby masses. It was not necessary to postulate supposed forces of gravitation in order to account for the orbits.

That very same year, when Einstein's equations first appeared, one solution to them was quickly found by Karl Schwarzschild. The Schwarzschild metric has since been studied extensively and, merely on the basis of these theoretical studies, it is widely believed that there are scattered throughout the vast space of the skies numerous *holes in space.* There are two kinds of such holes—worm holes and black holes. So great is the confidence of physicists today in the validity of general relativity that the experimental hunt for one of these kinds of holes in space, the black holes, is going on all over the world. This is true even though black holes cannot, in fact, be seen. The search for the worm hole is not yet in as advanced a stage; but its time will surely come.

Black Holes

Any mass warps the space near it, according to Einstein. Yes, the *empty space gets twisted.* That, in itself, is a fact of the strangest kind. But we will take it for granted. A star has so great a mass that it deforms its space a great deal and any object passing nearby seems to be attracted to the star. If such an object— be it a rock, or a spaceship, or a comet—passed too close to the star it would fall into the star.

Further, if we could stand a space station on the surface of a star and if we tried to blast a rocket up, away from the surface, then the rocket would be pulled back toward the surface—just as on Earth. Only if the initial speed is great enough to exceed the escape velocity can the rocket escape the gravitational attraction of the star and fly free into space. And if a ray of light were emitted at the surface of the star radially outward then the ray too would be affected by the star's mass, but in a somewhat different manner. The photons of light would lose energy as they rose, and they would get redder. The greater the mass of a given size star, the greater the loss of energy by the light as it moves outward. When the star's mass is great enough so that the escape velocity is greater than the velocity of light, even light cannot leave its surface.

Suppose our blazing Sun, with a diameter of 860,000 miles, were somehow to shrink in size to a diameter of four miles, or smaller, while keeping its original mass. Then the warping of space near its new surface would be tremendously magnified. The warping would be so great that any object which came within one mile of this surface would be inexorably sucked into the surface. This would be true no matter how much energy the object had and whatever its direction or speed. It would be true, in fact, even for a ray of light. If we tried to see our shrunken Sun by its own blazing light we could not do so. The brilliant light on its surface would not escape the massive warping of space at the surface. If we wanted to find our lost Sun by shining our light on it and examining the reflected

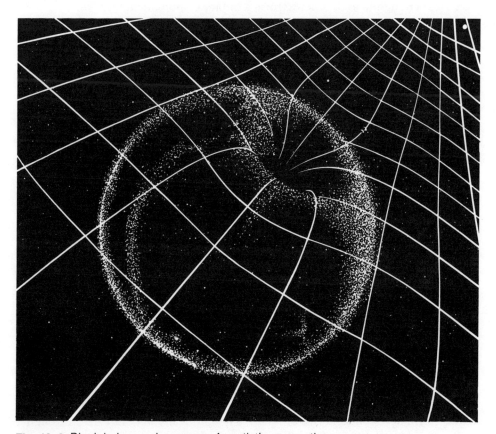

Fig. 13–2. Black hole warping space. An artist's conception.

rays we would be unable to do so, since there would be no reflected light. Our blazing Sun would be absolutely dark.

The stellar counterparts of our shrunken Sun neither reflect, transmit, nor emit light. They are black. Anything that gets too close to one can only fall in; it can never come out. Hence, a black hole.[11] An artist's conception of a black hole is shown in Fig. 13–2.

In the case of a black hole with a mass equal to that of our Sun and a diameter of four miles the gravitational force at its surface would be 40 billion times as great as that at the surface of the Sun. Astronomers think that many stars end up as black holes in the normal course of their life cycle—at the end, when they die. That being so, there should be many of them all around us in outer space. The total mass of such black holes might be great enough to affect the nature of the expansion of the universe; it would greatly affect the future which astrophysicists see for the universe. So the search for black holes is important. One way that a black hole can be detected is by the slight wiggle the black hole would put into the motion of some normal, companion visible star if the two were close enough to each other to form a binary combination.

There is a fascinating speculation about black holes: it is supposed that there may be nothing to stop them from shrinking indefinitely. If that is so then it may be that in the end, when the black hole's diameter has shrunk to zero and it is a true point, the black hole vanishes. Question—Is it possible that its mass then reappears in some other universe?

Worm Holes

The second kind of hole in space, also arising from K. Schwarzschild's analysis of Einstein's equations, is the worm hole.[12] To picture what this warp in space looks like, think of a powdered doughnut lying between two sheets of stiff paper. Take the top piece of paper off the doughnut and cut a hole in it where it just lays on the doughnut (along the ring of powder); and now center it over the top of the doughnut. Do the same with another piece of paper at the bottom of the doughnut. Remove most of the dough of the doughnut, leaving only the part near the hole; and make a smooth connection between the two sheets along this remaining inside surface of the doughnut. The resulting surface would be a simplified, two-dimensional view of a worm hole.

A worm on a flat portion of the top sheet could go to another flat portion of the top sheet some distance away in a normal manner. But by going through the worm hole the worm could leave a flat portion of the top sheet altogether, and wind up on a flat portion of the bottom sheet. Remembering that these two-dimensional sheets actually represent three-dimensional space, we are saying that the worm hole is a hole in space, from one ordinary region of space to another such region—far, far away. Perhaps in a different world?

The worm hole connects two different, asymptotically flat, universes through a region of space that is far from flat. If the two flat regions are connected to each other in some very distant region then the worm has an interesting choice. It can get from one flat region, not too far from the top of the worm hole, to another flat region, not too far from the bottom of the worm hole, by either one of two paths. One path would stick, always, to a flat region of space. That would be a long journey. The other path would head for the short cut through the worm hole—short, but perilous.

Could either a photon or a massive particle actually traverse a path such as this second one? Disappearing like magic from one ordinary region of space only to reappear, quickly, in another? It appears that the answer is "No." The particle or photon would be crushed out of existence. So there is no active hunt for such worm holes in space, and the topic remains one of academic interest only. Meanwhile, for further nontechnical details see Lewis Carroll's "Alice's Adventures in Wonderland"; or his "Through the Looking Glass."

Where is there anything as absurd as holes in empty space?

OUR END

Our own universe rushes madly outward. Born perhaps 17 billion years ago in an enormous explosion, observations show that the remnants of this explosion rush more rapidly the closer they lie to the edge of the universe. Near this edge huge collections of stars and protostars cluster together in galaxy-like fashion and hurl outward. These collections, quasars, seem bent upon testing light's own speed limit as they rush outward at velocities of one-quarter, one-half, three-quarters that of light. Will this mad rush continue forever?

The mass of the whole universe tugs it back from this brink. Scientists count and recount, as best they can, the mass within the confines of the universe: stars, the dust between them, the galaxies, the debris between them, energy in its mass equivalent, pulsars, black holes, and quasars. At present the mass appears to be not enough ever to hold the universe together; the far reaches of the universe seem to be rocketing apart at velocities well beyond their escape velocity. To hold the universe together perhaps ten times more mass is needed. But there are hints that suggest there is hidden mass, laying undiscovered, in sufficient quantities to bind our universe together and stop the outrush. Should this hidden mass actually exist, what is the consequence to our universe?

If enough mass does exist the gravitational pull upon our expanding universe must eventually slow down the expansion. In time, perhaps 35 billion years from its start, the expansion will stop; and then gravity will take over. Inexorably, gravity will pull back the stars and galaxies—inward. Slowly at first, but then more and more rapidly, a collapse will take place. Nothing we presently know will stop the collapse until the time, perhaps 70 billion years after the initial explosion, the universe collapses into one tiny, seething point in space. As one immense black hole our entire universe—dust, planets, stars, galaxies, and black holes—will all funnel into one agonized point of space. In the black depths of this one, ultimate black hole the old universe itself may be refashioned into a new one, destined to emerge, phoenix like, when time again has meaning. And a new cycle of an expanding universe will begin.

If there are multiple universes, do these all collapse in one final, multiple catastrophe? Each universe might be pulled through its own annointed point in space, only to reemerge as a completely new universe. The sacred "constants" of science—electrical charge, the speed of light, the gravitational constant—may emerge with different values in each new multiple universe different from each other and different from that before the collapse. Would collapsing multiple universes reprocess themselves into a new family of other multiple universes, in which no offspring universe knew its own parents?

We have talked of many strange, occult things: of witches and magic; of psychics and Psi; of ghosts and reincarnation; of prophecy; of the unknown depths of the mind; of ancient mysteries, other civilizations, other intelligences. They are not as strange as some of the things we have seen in this chapter, in science itself: twins aging differently; instantaneously collapsing wave functions; unknowability; waves and particles here but everywhere; holes in empty space; multiple universes; unseeable seas; the universe as a point, writhing to be reborn.

How can these things be? Perhaps John Wheeler gave the answer: "We are talking about things that are absolutely crazy. Can anything that is less crazy be right?"[13]

REFERENCES

CHAPTER 1

1. W. Crookes, *Journal of the Society of Psychical Research* 6 (1894): 341.

2. H. Houdini, *A Magician Among the Spirits* (New York: Harper, 1924), p. 49.

CHAPTER 2

1. Theodore Roszak, *Science* 178 (1972): 960.

2. Patrick Wall, *New Scientist* 64 (1974): 31.

3. Walter Kilner, *The Human Aura* (New Hyde Park, N.Y.: University Books, 1965).

4. Jack Schwartz, *Esquire,* December 1972, p. 209.

5. Marvin Karlins and Lewis M. Andrews, *Biofeedback* (Philadelphia: Lippincott, 1972), chap. 2.

6. Michael S. Cazzaniga, *American Scientist* 60 (1972): 311.

7. Partially published in *International Journal of Parapsychology,* (Winter 1968). Pop-

ular reports appear in *Winter Wildlife* (February 1969) and *Psychic* (December 1972).

8. H. Burr, *Blueprint for Immortality* (London: Spearman Ltd., 1972).

9. *Time* (19 June 1972), p. 68. Reprinted by permission from *Time,* the Weekly Newsmagazine; Copyright Time Inc.

CHAPTER 3

1. *Encyclopedia Britannica,* s.v. "witchcraft, Vol. 23 (1970).

2. Sybil Leek, *Diary of a Witch* (Englewood Cliffs, N.J.: Prentice-Hall, 1970), p. 3.

3. Paul Huson, *Mastering Witchcraft* (New York: Putnam, 1971), foreword.

4. Kurt Seligman, *Magic, Supernaturalism, and Religion* (New York: Grosset & Dunlap, 1968), p. 70.

5. Ibid., p. 70.

6. Anton LaVey, *The Satanic Bible* (New York: Avon, 1959), pp. 30, 33, 34, 40. Reprinted with permission.

7. Pennethorne Hughes, *Witchcraft* (Baltimore: Penguin, 1965), chap. 6.

CHAPTER 4

1. J. B. Rhine, *New World of the Mind* (New York: Sloane, 1953), p. 4.

2. Louisa E. Rhine, *Mind over Matter* (New York: Macmillan, 1970), p. 343.

3. Ibid., p. 332.

4. George R. Price, Letter to the Editor in *Science* 175 (1972): 359.

5. Louisa E. Rhine, *Mind over Matter,* p. 140.

6. Pierre Duval and Evelyn Montredon, *Progress in Parapsychology,* ed. J. B. Rhine (College Station, N.C.: The Parapsychology Press, 1971), p. 17.

7. J. B. Rhine, *New Frontiers of the Mind* (New York: Farrar & Rinehart, 1937), p. 222.

8. Helmut Schmidt, *Progress in Parapyschology,* ed. J. B. Rhine (College Station, N.C.: The Parapsychology Press, 1971), p. 28.

9. M. Ullman, S. Krippner, and A. Vaughan, *Dream Telepathy* (New York: Macmillan, 1973), p. 148. Copyright © 1973 by Montague Ullman, Stanley Krippner, and Alan Vaughan.

10. G. A. Sergeyev, *Proceedings of Symposium of Psychotronics* (Prague, 1970), p. 47.

11. Benson Herbert, *Parapsychology Review* 4 (1973): 5.

12. Edgar Mitchell, *Psychic Exploration,* ed. John White (New York: Putnam, 1974), appendix.

13. Russell Targ and Harold Puthoff, *Nature* 251 (1974): 602.

14. J. Hanlon, *New Scientist* 64 (1974): 170; and The Amazing Randi, *The Magic of Uri Geller* (New York, Ballantine Books, 1973).

15. G. R. Schmeidler and R. A. McConnell, *ESP and Personality Patterns* (New Haven:

Yale University Press, 1958); and J. Palmer, *Journal of the American Society for Psychical Research* 66 (1972): 1.

16. C. Honorton and S. Krippner, *Journal of the American Society for Psychical Research* 63 (1969): 214. R. L. Van de Castle, *American Journal of Clinical Hypnosis* 12: 1 (1969), p. 37.

17. E. Douglas Dean, *Psychic Exploration*, ed. Edgar Mitchell and John White (New York: Putnam, 1974), p. 153.

18. One solution to these equations for massless, free particles is the so-called trivial solution: it states that the psi function is independent of both time and distance!

CHAPTER 5

1. Charles T. Tart, *Science* 176 (1972): 1203.

2. D. H. Rawcliffe, *Occult and Supernatural Phenomena* (New York: Dover, 1952), chap. 17.

3. J. D. Green and A. A. Ardinni, *Journal of Neurophysiology* 17 (1954): 532. E. Gratsyan, K. Lissak, J. Madarasz, H. Donhoffer, *Electroencephalography, Clinical Neurophysiology* 11 (1959): 409.

4. R. Laverne and C. Johnson, *American Scientist* 61 (1973): 326.

5. Kilton Stewart, *Altered States of Consciousness*, ed. Charles T. Tart (New York: Wiley, 1969), p. 159.

6. William C. Hunter, "Bits of Old China," (1885), p. 170, quoted in *Ceremonial Chemistry*, Thomas Szasz (Garden City, N.Y.: Anchor Press, 1974), p. 141.

7. *New York Times*, 6 September 1973, p. 21.

8. *New York Times*, 31 January 1974, p. 35.

9. *Newark Star-Ledger*, 26 January 1974, p. 1.

10. *New York Times*, 18 April 1974, p. 14.

11. Thomas H. Maugh II, *Science* 185 (1974): 683 and 185 (1974): 775.

12. UPI release, Los Angeles, as printed in certain New Jersey editions of *New York Times*, 26 January 1974, p. 35.

13. *New York Times*, 19 November 1974, p. 17.

14. John Kaplan, *Science* 179 (1973): 167. Copyright 1973 by the American Association for the Advancement of Science.

15. *New York Times*, 4 December 1972, pp. 1, 34.

16. Ernest Jones, *The Life and Work of Sigmund Freud*, vol. 1. (London: Hogarth Press, 1961), p. 81.

17. Thomas DeQuincey, *Confessions of an English Opium Eater* (New York: Illustrated Editions Co., 1932), p. 205.

18. From *The Varieties of Psychedelic Experience* by R. E. L. Masters and Jean Houston. Copyright © 1966 by R. E. L. Masters and J. Houston. Reprinted by permission of Holt, Rinehart, and Winston, Publishers.

19. Thomas H. Maugh II, *Science* 179 (1973): 1221.

CHAPTER 6

1. J. M. Cohen, trans., *The Life of Saint Teresa* (Baltimore: Penguin, 1957), p. 142.

2. R. Fischer, *Science* 179 (1973): 982.

3. R. K. Wallace and H. Benson, *Scientific American*, February 1972, p. 84.

4. Jane Hamilton-Merritt, "A Land of Saffron Robes," *New York Times* (14 October 1972), op-ed page.

5. Peter Hyun, "Zen, American Style," *New York Times* (18 May 1972), op-ed page. © 1972 by The New York Times Company. Reprinted by permission.

6. Ernest R. Hilgard, *American Scientist* 59 (1971): 567.

7. F. L. Marcuse, *Hypnosis—Fact and Fiction* (Baltimore: Penguin, 1959), p. 74. Reprinted by permission.

CHAPTER 7

1. St. Augustine *Confessions* bk. 7, chap. 6.

2. Sigmund Freud, *The Standard Edition of the Complete Psychological Works of Sigmund Freud*, ed. James Strachey (London: The Hogarth Press and The Institute of Psycho-Analysis, 1961), vol. 19 (1923–1925), p. 136.

3. Robert D. Nelson, *Psychic* (Mar./Apr. 1970): 27.

4. *National Enquirer*, 13 January 1973 and 14 January 1974.

5. Jess Stearn, *Edgar Cayce, The Sleeping Prophet* (Garden City, N.Y.: Doubleday, 1967), p. 220.

6. E. Z. Vogt and Ray Hyman, *Water Witching U.S.A.* (Chicago: University of Chicago Press, 1959), pp. 55, 56. (See also pp. 71–79.)

7. R. Cavendish, ed., *Man, Myth and Magic*, vol. 5, part 24 (New York: Marshall Cavendish, 1970), p. 685.

8. M. Faraday, "Experimental Investigation of Table Turning," *Athaeneum* (July 1853): 801–803.

9. Alfred Douglas, *How to Consult the I Ching, the Oracle of Change* (New York: Putnam, 1971), p. 41. Reprinted by permission of Harold Ober Associates Incorporated. Copyright © 1971 by Alfred Douglas.

CHAPTER 8

1. Slater Brown, *The Heyday of Spiritualism* (New York: Pocket Books, 1970), p. 133.

2. Hereward Carrington, *The World of Psychic Research* (New York: Barnes, 1973), p. 43.

3. Hereward Carrington, *The World of Psychic Research* (New York: Barnes, 1973), p. 33. Reprinted by permission.

4. Ian Stevenson, *Journal of American Society for Psychical Research* 66 (1972): 375–400.

5. *Denver Post*, September 12, 19, 26, (1954).

6. Ian Stevenson, *Proceeding of the American Society for Psychical Research* 26 (1966): 1–362; *Journal of American Society for Psychical Research* 66 (1972): 288–309; 67 (1973): 244–266 and 361–380; 68 (1974): 58–90.

7. R. C. Morton, *Proceeding of the Society for Psychical Research* 8 (1892): 311.

8. G. Schmeidler, *Journal of American Society for Psychical Research* 60 (1966): 137–149; and R. Moss and G. Schmeidler, *Journal of American Society for Psychical Research* 62 (1968): 399–410.

9. Robert Morris, *Theta* 33–34 (1972). Published by the Psychical Research Foundation, Inc., Duke Station, Durham, N.C. 27706.

10. John Palmer, *Journal of American Society for Psychical Research* 68 (1974): 1–33.

11. D. Scott Rogo, *Psychic*, April 1973, p. 51.

12. Russell Noyes, *Newsweek*, 6 May 1974: 62.

CHAPTER 9

1. Harlow Shapley, paper published in 1962 by the National University of Tucuman, Argentina. See Walter Sullivan, *We Are Not Alone* (Baltimore: Penquin, 1976), p. 83.

2. Sebastian von Hoerner, "The General Limits of Space Travel," *Science* 137 (1962): 18. See also his chapter in *Interstellar Communications*, ed. A. G. W. Cameron (New York: W. A. Benjamin, 1963).

3. Freeman J. Dyson, "Gravitational Machines," in *Interstellar Communications*, ed. A. G. W. Cameron (New York: W. A. Benjamin, 1963), p. 115.

4. Freeman J. Dyson, "Search for Artificial Stellar Sources of Infrared Radiation," *Science* 131 (1959): 1667. (Also included in *Interstellar Communications* Ref. 2.) *Science* 132 (1960): 250, has three letters objecting to the practicality of the scheme.

5. I. S. Shklovskii, "Is Communication Possible with Intelligent Beings on Other Planets?" in *Insterstellar Communications*, ed. A. G. W. Cameron (New York: W. A. Benjamin, 1963), p. 5.

6. Peter L. Auer, *Science* 184 (1974): 293.

7. G. L. Verschuur, *Icarus* 19 (1973): 329.

8. A. G. W. Cameron, *Physics Today* 27 (1974): 49.

CHAPTER 10

1. Air Force Regulation 80–17, issued Washington, D.C., 19 September 1966.

2. These cases were taken from some of the many books on the subject by Maj. Keyhoe. We should warn the reader that such books all, more or less, present the same information; they are written in a breathless journalese style, where incident upon incident is ever more astounding than all the previous ones. Although the interpretation of the sightings is conjectural, these cases are discussed in the Condon report.

3. Frank Scully, *Behind the Flying Saucers* (New York: Holt, 1950).

4. Donald H. Menzel, *Flying Saucers* (Cambridge: Harvard University Press, 1953).

5. Carl Sagan and Thornton Page, eds., *UFOs—A Scientific Debate* (Ithaca, N.Y.: Cornell University Press, 1972), p. 177.

6. S. Singer, *The Nature of Ball Lightning* (New York: Plenum Press, 1971).

7. E. U. Condon and D. S. Gillmor, *Scientific Study of Unidentified Flying Objects*, sec. 4, chap 3 (New York: Dutton, 1969), p. 396–407, case 46.

8. Walter Sullivan, "Scientific Study of Unidentified Flying Objects," *New York Times* (20 October 1965). © 1975 by The New York Times Company. Reprinted by permission.

9. Stanton Friedman, *Physics Today* 24 (1971): 27.

10. J. Allen Hynek, *The UFO Experience, A Scientific Inquiry* (Chicago: Henry Regnery, 1972).

11. James McDivitt, taped interview on Channel 4, New York City, 10 P.M., 15 December 1974.

12. Hynek, *The UFO Experience*, p. 14. Reprinted by permission.

13. Ibid., p. 39. Reprinted by permission.

14. Ibid., p. 53. Reprinted by permission.

15. Ibid., p. 73. Reprinted by permission.

16. James McDonald, *The Flying Saucer Review*, vol. 16, no. 2 (Mar./Apr. 1970), pp. 9–17 and Project Blue Book Special Report No. 14, UFO Research Institute, Pittsburgh.

17. G. D. Thayer, *Astronautics & Aeronautics*, vol. 9, no. 9 (September 1971), p. 60.

18. Condon and Gillmor, *Study of Unidentified Flying Objects*, p. 164 and 256.

19. Jacques Vallee, *Passport to Magonia* (Chicago: Henry Regnery, 1969).

20. Sagan and Page, *UFOs—A Scientific Debate*, p. 47.

21. Hynek, *The UFO Experience*, p. 155.

22. Michael Waldron, "After 25 Years Flying Saucers are Still Reported," *New York Times*, 25 June 1972, p. 36N.

23. "UFO: Appraisal of the Problem," *Astronautics & Aeronautics*, vol. 8, no. 11 (November 1970), p. 49.

24. Bertrand Russell, *Skeptical Essays* (London: George Allen & Unwin Ltd., 1928), p. 61. U.S.A. rights (New York: Barnes & Noble). Reprinted by permission.

CHAPTER 11

1. Immanuel Velikovsky, *Worlds in Collision* (New York: Macmillan, 1950).

2. Immanuel Velikovsky, *Yale Scientific* XLI (April 1967): 14.

3. Joshua, 10:11.

4. Velikovsky, *Worlds in Collision*, p. 59.

5. Our quotes from the Egyptian Papyrus are from A. Gardiner, *Admonitions of an Egyptian Sage from a Hieratic Papyrus in Leiden* (1909) as quoted in Ref. 1, and from *Pensee* 4 (Winter 1973–1974): 39ff.

6. Evan W. Mackie, *Pensee* 3 (Winter 1973): 6.

7. V. Bargmann and L. Motz, *Science* 138 (1962): 1350. Copyright © 1962 by the American Association for the Advancement of Science.

8. N. D. Watkins and H. G. Goodell, *Science* 156 (1967): 1083.

9. L. Rose and R. Vaughan, *Pensee* 2 (May 1972): 42 and C. J. Ransom and L. H. Hoffee, *Pensee* 3 (Winter 1973): 22.

10. Lloyd Motz, *Yale Scientific* XLI (April 1967): 12 as corrected by Velikovsky, Ref. 2.

11. C. Sagan, *Science News* 105 (1974): 132 and *Science* 183 (1974): 1061.

12. Clifford Wilson, *Crash Go the Chariots* (New York: Lancer, 1972), p. 76ff.

13. Erich von Däniken, *Playboy*, August 1974, p. 51.

14. Wilson, *Crash Go the Chariots*, chap. 5.

15. Thor Heyerdahl, *Aku-Aku—The Secret of Easter Island* (London: George Allen and Unwin, 1958): 192–193.

16. Ibid., p. 150.

17. D. J. Milton, et al., *Science* 175 (1972): 1199.

18. Gerald S. Hawkins, *Beyond Stonehenge* (New York: Harper & Row, 1972), p. 104.

19. Aubrey Burl, *American Scientist* 61 (1973): 167.

20. A Thom, *Megalithic Sites in Britain* (Oxford: Clarendon Press, 1967); also *Megalithic Lunar Observations* (Oxford: Clarendon Press, 1971); G. S. Hawkins and J. B. White, *Stonehenge Decoded* (New York: Dell, 1965); G. Evelyn Hutchinson, *American Scientist* 60 (1972): 210.

21. A. Marshack, *Science* 178 (1972): 817.

22. J. Patrick, *Nature* 249 (June 7, 1974): 517.

23. Hawkins, *Beyond Stonehenge*, chap. 11, see especially Fig. 34.

24. John A. Eddy, *Science* 184 (1974): 1035.

25. G. S. Pawley and V. Abrahamsen, *Science* 179 (1973): 892.

26. *New York Times*, 23 April 1974, p. 8.

27. Donald Menzel, *Harper's*, December 1963, p. 83. Copyright © 1963 by Harper's Magazine. Reprinted from the December 1963 issue by special permission.

CHAPTER 12

1. J. L. Brady, E. M. Carpenter, and F. M. McMahon, *Publications of the Astronomical Society of the Pacific* (Apr. 1972).

2. M. Gauquelin, *The Scientific Bases of Astrology* (New York: Stein and Day, 1970), chap. 10. M. Gauquelin, *The Cosmic Clocks* (Chicago: Regnery, 1967), p. 87.

3. M. Gauquelin, "Die Planetare Hereditat," *Zeitschrift fur Parapsychologie und Grenzgebiete der Psychologie*, Band V, No. 2/3 (1962): 168–193.

4. Reported in the English newspaper, *The Guardian* (5 April 1973): 13 and attributed to that week's *New Society* magazine.

5. D. A. Windsor, *Nature* 248 (1974): 788.

6. J. H. Nelson, *R.C.A. Review* 12 (1951): 26.
7. Gauquelin, *Scientific Bases of Astrology*, p. 191, 192.
8. F. A. Brown, *Science* 130 (1959): 1535.
9. A. L. Lieber and C. R. Sherin, *American Journal of Psychiatry* 129:1 (1972): 101.
10. Gauguelin, *Scientific Bases of Astrology*, p. 218.
11. *Science News* 102 (1972): 247.
12. K. D. Wood, *Nature* 240 (1972): 91.
13. W. M. Kaula, *Science* 186 (1974): 729.
14. J. R. Gribbin and S. H. Plagemann, *The Jupiter Effect* (New York: Walker, 1972).
15. Ibid., p. 116.

CHAPTER 13

1. Max Born, *Atomic Physics*, 4th ed., (New York: Hafner, 1935), p. 182.
2. A. Shadowitz, *Special Relativity* (Philadelphia: W. B. Saunders, 1968), p. 28.
3. Ibid., p. 43.
4. Experimental verification of the twin effect has been obtained both in round trips of muons circling in a magnetic field which have lived 12 times longer than their stationary twins (See J. Bailey et al, Phys. Lett. 28B (1968): 287; F. J. M. Farley, J. Bailey, and E. Picasso, *Nature* 217 (1968): 17; J. Bailey, E. Picasso in *Progress in Nuclear Physics* 12 (New York: Pergamon, 1970), p. 62; and in flight circumnavigation of the Earth in which small but verifiable time differences occur. (See J. C. Hafele and Richard E. Kealing, *Science* 177 (1972): 166, 168.
5. W. Heisenberg, *The Physical Principles of the Quantum Theory* (Chicago: University of Chicago Press, 1930), chap. 2.
6. Stephen Gasiorowicz, *Quantum Physics* (New York: Wiley, 1974), pp. 13, 20, 34.
7. Bryce DeWitt, *Physics Today* 23 (1970): 155.
8. N. Bohr, *Atomic Theory and the Description of Nature* (London: Cambridge University Press, 1934).
9. E. P. Wigner, *Symmetries and Reflections* (Bloomington: Indiana University Press, 1967).
10. Bryce S. DeWitt and Neill Graham, eds., *The Many-Worlds Interpretation of Quantum Mechanics* (Princeton, N.J.: Princeton University Press, 1973).
11. D. Goldsmith and D. Levy, *From the Black Hole to the Infinite Universe* (San Francisco: Holden-Day, 1974); John G. Taylor, *Black Holes: The End of the Universe?* (New York: Random House, 1973).
12. C. W. Misner, K. S. Thorne, and J. A. Wheeler, *Gravitation* (San Francisco: W. H. Freeman Co., 1973) (See, especially, chap 44.)
13. John Wheeler, "Beyond the End of Time," address at the New York Academy of Science, 10 March 1972, New York.

INDEX